What's Left of Marxism

The Politics of Historical Thinking

Edited by
Brigitta Bernet, Lutz Raphael, and Benjamin Zachariah

Volume 2

What's Left of Marxism

Historiography and the Possibilities of Thinking with Marxian Themes and Concepts

Edited by
Benjamin Zachariah, Lutz Raphael & Brigitta Bernet

DE GRUYTER
OLDENBOURG

ISBN 978-3-11-099259-5
e-ISBN (PDF) 978-3-11-067774-4
e-ISBN (EPUB) 978-3-11-067779-9
ISSN 2625-0055

Library of Congress Control Number: 2020939086

Bibliographic Information published by the Deutsche Nationalbibliothek
The Deutsche Nationalbibliothek lists this publication in the Deutsche Nationalbibliografie; detailed bibliographic data are available on the Internet at http://dnb.dnb.de.

This volume is text- and page-identical with the hardback published in 2020.
Cover image: Debojit Thakur (based on an anonymous portrait of Karl Marx by an unknown artist).
Printing and binding: CPI books GmbH, Leck

www.degruyter.com

The Politics of Historical Thinking

Historical thinking has a politics that shapes its ends. While at least two generations of scholars have been guided into their working lives with this axiom as central to their profession, it is somewhat of a paradox that historiography is so often nowadays seen as a matter of intellectual choices operating outside the imperatives of quotidian politics, even if the higher realms of ideological inclinations or historiographical traditions can be seen to have played a role. The politics of historical thinking, if acknowledged at all, is seen to belong to the realms of nonprofessional ways of the instrumentalisation of the past.

This series seeks to centre the politics inherent in historical thinking, professional and non-professional, promoted by states, political organisations, 'nationalities' or interest groups, and to explore the links between political (re-)education, historiography and mobilisation or (sectarian?) identity formation. We hope to bring into focus the politics inherent in historical thinking, professional, public or amateur, across the world today.

https://doi.org/10.1515/9783110677744-001

Preface

On the occasion of the two hundredth birth anniversary of Karl Marx, a group of historians gathered at Marx's place of birth in Trier, Germany, to discuss the ways in which Marxian ideas have been relevant or influential in the writing and interpretation of history, and to what extent they could continue to be relevant (or not). Anniversaries mean nothing, we might say, but they make us feel more at home and somehow more entitled to speak on a subject or person whose anniversary we are celebrating; in 2018, also the hundred and seventieth anniversary of the publication of the *Communist Manifesto*, and in a city that had become a site of strange pilgrimages for a variety of people who to a greater or lesser extent related to the thinking of Marx, to that of his friend and collaborator Friedrich Engels, and to the variety of conflicted and conflicting thinkers and thought-processes referred to now as 'Marxist' or 'Marxian', this gathering acquired a relevance of time and place that it perhaps should not have needed. It would not, however, be wrong to say that Marx is now sticking his head out of what Marxists might polemically have called the dustbin of history to peer at us in many of our current predicaments.

Over the years, Marxist frameworks of analysis have retreated to the shrinking circles of vestigial communist parties, been muted by its practitioners in the interests of avoiding old Cold War polemics, or found their way at first or second remove into fields such as cultural studies, women's studies or postcolonial studies, where they are often disavowed. This volume asks the question: what are the productive possibilities of thinking with Marxism today? To answer this question, it is also necessary to have a clear picture of what Marxism has discussed and achieved in the field of historiography, and how much of this must be remembered and analysed in order to recover insights from earlier debates that have in the process of disavowal been forgotten.

We were not centrally interested in arguments with(in) the official Marxisms of really existing socialist states, nor of recovering counterfactually the possibilities of older movements that might have gone in different directions. We were, however, interested in frameworks of analysis that might be productive of a (re)new(ed) set of debates in the study of economic and social history; and in the traces and afterlives of Marxist thinkers and Marxist debates in other fields and discussions, where in many cases their Marxism has in the last few decades been underplayed or even erased. Interconnectedly, what can be gained by an analysis conducted through the frameworks of earlier debates? What are the Marxist legacies that are now re-emerging in present-day histories?

https://doi.org/10.1515/9783110677744-002

The volume that is now before you has its origins, as alluded to above, in a workshop organised by the (DFG-Leibniz) Research Group on 'The contemporary history of historiography' situated at Trier University, on the occasion of an international conference on Marxism at this University in the bicentenary year of Karl Marx's birth in May 2018. The workshop was concerned with the relevance of Marxian concepts and approaches for the discipline of history today, which in part was also an attempt at relearning what the discipline of history once knew – insofar as there is such a thing as a 'discipline' of history, to be a part of it once meant to engage closely with Marxian ideas about the course of human history, whether one considered oneself a Marxist, a non-Marxist, or an anti-Marxist. This is an attempt to think with a historical and philosophical tradition that, to our minds, is still productive of much creative thinking.

We should like to thank Niklas Penth for standardising and double-checking the references, Kate Tranter and Bernard Heise for their translations from the German original texts, Anwesha Roy for her careful copy-editing and for bringing all the texts written in our contemporary lingua franca into readable English, and Debojit Thakur for the cover illustration, which had its origins in his design for the conference poster.

Table of Contents

Benjamin Zachariah, Lutz Raphael, Brigitta Bernet

Introduction

Revisiting Marxian thinking today is beset with a striking contradiction. It was long expected of Karl Marx by Marxists, especially those of a party-political persuasion, that he be a transhistorical prophet. At the same time, Marxian thinking has made much use of history, situating itself firmly in what it understood as historical context. Historians' engagement with Marxian thinking is by now inseparable from the discipline of history itself, because arguments with and within Marxism were intimately connected with historical thinking since the mid-nineteenth century, and perhaps more so as a consequence of the Cold War, when Marxist, non-Marxist and anti-Marxist accounts of history all had a tendency to be mutually dependent caricatures of themselves and of one other. After the Cold War, the quick retreat of Marxian thinking in academic systems led to a curious scenario: history survived as a discipline with many of its debates disavowing their origins and intellectual underpinnings. Later readers had to contend with the equivalent of eavesdropping on one side of a telephone conversation and having to guess what was being said on the other side.

A Return to Marx, or the Rediscovery of Lost Debates and Forgotten Answers

Two 1950s science fiction accounts come to mind in connection with this. The first is the *Foundation* Trilogy by Isaac Asimov, a Russian-Jewish immigrant in the United States, whose account of 'psychohistory', with its laws of prediction of history, made him suspicious to the House Committee on Un-American Activities in the United States (psychohistory, in Asimov's account, is a Jewish conspiracy of Freudian-Marxist prediction). Asimov's implied critique of mechanistic notions of predictable historical trajectories could easily be overlooked: the Mule, a figure intended to invoke the Third Reich and Adolf Hitler, clearly interrupts the progress of psychohistory that its founder, Hari Seldon, had envisaged.[1] The second account, *A Canticle for Leibowitz*, by Walter Miller Jr, is one in which, after the inevitable nuclear holocaust, all of human knowledge had to be reconstructed painstakingly from the shopping list of a man called Leibo-

1 Isaac Asimov, *Foundation* (New York: Gnome Press, 1951); *Foundation and Empire* (New York: Gnome Press, 1952); *Second Foundation* (New York: Gnome Press, 1953).

https://doi.org/10.1515/9783110677744-003

witz.[2] The first can be taken as a metonymy for the promises and failings of Marxian thinking in history; the second, as a metaphor for the loss of knowledge and its slow recovery, and although we are not quite in this unfortunate latter position, it needs to be said that what the historical profession once knew of Marxism is not the common knowledge it once was; nor can historians rely on working with a background in Marxian thinking, which they can choose to deploy in novel and unpredictable ways (or, indeed, in mechanistic or Stalinist ways). The task of this volume has been, in many ways, to revisit former frameworks as part of a collective relearning process, as well as to revisit those frameworks from the perspective of new research and a new set of problems, to ask the question: what's left of Marxism that can be still considered useful to the historical profession?

We can leave aside the larger question of whether there is still *one* historical profession or a set of at best similar professions pretending to be part of a scholarly unit today, or whether we have ceased to speak to one another, for one of the premises of a volume such as this is that we can make that attempt to speak to one another. In accordance with this principle, we have made no attempt to coordinate approaches, to set the parameters of what contributors ought to address, or to attempt anything like completeness of thematic or geographical coverage. Nor have we picked fights among ourselves or with others, despite the undeniably entertaining side of the Marxian heritage of polemics. What we are concerned with is to open out a period of fruitful and renewed communication, and the distance kept here from strong disagreement is in the interest of future disagreement on substantive issues.

Even a cursory glance at the contents of this volume, however, indicates a few important points. *Firstly,* the claim that Marxism is inherently 'Eurocentric' (a claim, it must be added, made mostly by those with little acquaintance with Marx's own writings, or with those of Marxian thinkers more generally) has been historically, and is today, a load of old cobblers. We use the term 'Marxian' here by way of contrast with 'Marxist', the first indicating a softer tendency to draw on ideas from Marx or a Marxist tradition, the second a harder (and more organised, sometimes party-political) tendency, though the dividing line between the two is hardly a hard one. Marxian ways of thinking about history have been, and continue to be, influential in studying historical change in disparate parts of the world, across chronological periods and geographies, and it is possible to maintain a comparative framework precisely because Marxian ways of thinking comprise not merely evaluative terms but also explicit criteria for what they eval-

2 Walter M. Miller Jr., *A Canticle for Leibowitz* (Philadelphia: JB Lippincott, 1959).

uate (thereby giving one the opportunity to dissent or re-evaluate). Non-Europeans, notoriously, refused to accept the (European?) judgement on the Eurocentrism of Marxism or Marxian thinking, and continued to try and develop it.

Secondly, if one is not invested in a literal-minded reading of Marxian received wisdom, and historical stages do not need to follow one another in exactly the same way across the world, there is much to be gained from trying to understand the dynamic of changes in modes of production and relations of production and from changing relationships of people to work. Breaking up the linearity of a conventional 'Western' Marxism (which is a curious polemic, given that within European debates, 'Western' Marxism and 'Eastern' or 'Soviet' Marxism are distinct entities), or not subscribing to 'Eurocentric' ideas of steps or stages of social formation, are desirable goals, but the entities that we claim to be breaking up turn out mostly to be straw figures, if we look more closely at them.

Thirdly, following from that, we are not restricted to, or by, the recovery and rereading of earlier debates in order to recapture their subtleties and contexts, but if we are willing to accept that analogy and historical parallel, when not used as blunt instruments, can yield insights into other contexts, the recoveries are not merely pedantic and academic. And *fourthly*, there has been a habit of conflating the programmatic texts of Marxism with Marxian historical texts and Marxist-influenced historical studies, to the detriment of them all, thereby missing Marx's point that his provisional judgements were, in his own assessment, to be rewritten in the light of detailed historical study.

A productive rediscovery of Marxian thinking as a critical resource for the present depends on re-historicising and thus simultaneously re-politicising it. At the beginning of the 1960s, Jean Paul-Sartre described Marxism, then still very much a part of mainstream social and political thinking, as the impassable horizon of thought of his time: as part of an overall process of social questioning and self-reflection. At the same time he pointed out that all thinking, including and especially philosophical thinking, is historically "situated".[3] *Situations* was not selected as a term by chance. Sartre also chose this title for his collections of essays on literature, politics and philosophy, which were published from 1947 and had swollen to ten volumes by 1976.[4] Sartre's interventions disrupted the tendency of the orthodox Marxism of his time to close itself off to theoretical interventions from outside, or to absorb them by assimilating them to its own fa-

3 Jean-Paul Sartre, *Critique de la raison dialectique*, Vol. 1 (Paris: Gallimard, 1960), 148.
4 Jean-Paul Sartre, *Situations*, 10 vol. (Paris: Gallimard, 1947–1976).

miliar schematic frameworks, but they simultaneously demonstrated the essential place in the history of thinking that Marx and Marxism had come to occupy.

The subsequent erasure of Marxian thinking from much of public debate after the Cold War was a paradoxical success of the "really existing socialist" states that survived their real existence. It was their success in their attempt to appropriate Marxism to themselves and to what might be called "orthodox Marxism" that led to these states being identified closely with the fate of Marxism as a whole; and consequently led to the Western Bloc being able to claim the end of the Soviet Union and the Soviet Bloc as a defeat for Marxism and a demonstration of its inability to achieve its alleged telos as a possible better future for mankind.[5] As a consequence, the canards thrown indiscriminately for nearly three decades thereafter at 'Marxists', 'socialists' and 'communists' for being economically determinist, culturally blind, market insensitive, or incapable of understanding 'human nature', in a period of the rise and fulfilment of a market-driven neoliberalism, did not meet a sufficiently robust counterwind – which, admittedly, was difficult to provide given the amorphous and ill-defined nature of what amounted less to an informed critique of Marxism and more to a set of received shibboleths of the post-Cold War era, none of which could be pinned down to a set of texts, or to specific political or academic debates. Thus, ground was not so much conceded as never claimed.

The Hidden Traditions of Marxism as a Creative Political and Historical Culture

Before too long, an emphasis on "culture" in history and the social sciences was being claimed as a replacement for the alleged "economic determinism" of "Marxism". The use of "culture" as an exercise in anti-Marxism sets up a false dichotomy between "economics" and "culture" that does not appear to be informed by any actually existing Marxist debates or practices – and since much of the enforced forgetting of Marxian thinking has been in the name of "culture", it is worth lingering on this point. It is usually said of Marx's and Engels' writing that they viewed cultural developments as a movement of superstructure dependent on changes in the economic base. What they called materialism was a critical answer to the dominant idealism or even spiritualism of the

5 See, symptomatically, Francis Fukuyama, *The End of History and the Last Man* (New York: Free Press, 1992).

early nineteenth century intellectuals, left or right;[6] but Marxists were not all prone to seeing culture as non-material; and indeed, Marxists sought to be part of an everyday cultural reality whose potential for creating meaning could extend to several areas of life. That which we refer to as "Western Marxism", for instance – and the same could be said for many entities informed by Marxian thinking – was also always a "Weltanschauung", implying a far broader set of concerns that might be gleaned from a casual reading of Nikolai Bukharin and Yevgeni Preobrazhensky's *ABC of Communism.*[7]

And there were important differences internally within such an entity as "Western Marxism", named and thereby constructed as a unity, these differences amounting to what might be described, even at the risk of sounding ironic, as different national communist cultures. In contrast to France, where the communist party was reluctant to risk diluting its purity by moving too freely in the waters of the cultural mainstream, the communist party in Italy tried to become a formative force in all areas of national life – potentially opening itself to the criticism that an internationalist movement was moving too strongly in national contexts.[8] Almost everything that Italy contributed to post-war culture, also internationally, came from this Marxist culture, which was a counter-world in its country of origin. The iconic image of this world was the opening sequence of Bernardo Bertolucci's film "Novecento": a front of workers and peasants marching into the future, to the accompaniment of music by the nineteenth century Italian romantic composer Giuseppe Verdi. To this world belonged a scientific culture directed against the old Catholic power elites, where the entire tradition of the country was re-examined and surveyed with the enormous large-scale projects of the Einaudi publishing house on Italian history, art history, literary history. But it also included the summer "Feste dell' Unità", where people ate, drank, sang and danced on long benches in the open air, and where any writer, actor or director came to the podium to discuss the situation. Neorealism in film and literature,

---

6 Gareth Stedman Jones, *Karl Marx. Greatness and Illusion* (Cambridge, MA: The Belknap Press of Harvard University Press, 2016), 68–167.

7 Nikolai Bukharin and Yevgeni Preobrazhensky (trans. Eden and Cedar Paul), *The ABC of Communism: A Popular Explanation of the Program of the Communist Party of Russia* (n.p.: Communist Party of Great Britain, 1922) [1919]. Written in the context of the Civil War, and even at its moment of writing not representing a consensus among Bolsheviks, this book nevertheless had a long afterlife and several reprints, including one with an introduction by EH Carr (Harmondsworth: Penguin, 1969), and has often been used as an introduction to Soviet Marxism and to a concern with communism. See Sheila Fitzpatrick, "The ABC of Communism Revisited," *Studies in East European Thought* 60 (2018): 167–179.

8 Silvio Pons, "Stalin, Togliatti, and the Origins of the Cold War in Europe," *Journal of Cold War Studies* 3, no. 2 (2001): 3–17, 15.

the tragic black and white cinema of Roberto Rossellini or Vittorio De Sica, the peasant narrative art of Pavese, the Franciscan poetry of Pier Paolo Pasolini, the turning to the dialect and the local language traditions – all this would not have come about without the Marxist background of ideas.[9]

The idea of creating a specific proletarian counter-culture in response to bourgeois culture already found supporters at the end of the nineteenth century. On the eve of the October Revolution, the cultural-revolutionary movement *Proletkult* emerged, which aimed to develop an independent proletarian culture (without bourgeois influence) as a necessary condition for revolution.[10] However, it soon came into conflict with Vladimir Lenin. For Lenin, cultural revolution was a process *after* the actual revolution, and not part of the revolution itself. Furthermore, his cultural-political concern was to convey the progressive heritage of bourgeois culture to the popular masses rather than postulate or invent a proletarian culture that would replace or surpass bourgeois culture, whose achievements had to be built upon rather than disavowed or bypassed.[11] The dispute over how and whether bourgeois culture could be overcome, transformed, or built upon, remained central to Marxist cultural debate. It is also open to the question, raised by Perry Anderson, Martin Jay and others, as to what extent the Marxist preoccupation with cultural struggle and ideology that began in the West in the 1920s and 1930s was a reaction to the defeats and setbacks of that period.[12] The turn to culture would in such a reading thus be above all a symptom of the extreme difficulties and, to a certain extent, the powerlessness with which revolutionaries were confronted. Of course, this question is particularly explosive for Antonio Gramsci, who began to discuss cultural hegemony in a fascist prison,[13] but also with regard to the Communist Party of Italy (PCI), whose shift from class struggle to cultural struggle cannot be sufficiently ex-

---

9 Stephen Gundle, *Between Hollywood and Moscow. The Italian Communists and the Challenge of Mass Culture, 1943–1991* (Durham: Duke University Press, 2000).

10 Lynn Mally, *Culture of the Future. The Proletkult Movement in Revolutionary Russia* (Berkeley: University of California Press, 1990).

11 Zenovia A. Sochor, *Revolution and Culture. The Bogdanov-Lenin Controversy* (Ithaca: Cornell University Press, 1988).

12 See Enzo Traverso, *Left-Wing Melancholia: Marxism, History, and Memory* (New York: Columbia University Press, 2017).

13 Antonio Gramsci, *Quaderni del carcere. Edizione critica dell'Istituto Gramsci*, 4 vol. (Turin: Giulio Einaudi, 1973–1975) in particular: Quaderni 12 (1511–1552), 16 (1835–1904), 21 (2105–2136), 22 (2137–2182), 26 (2295–2308), 27 (2309–2318).

plained without the historical context of the immediate post-war period and the PCI's renunciation of any revolutionary action.[14]

Nonetheless, the idea of a Marxian concern with "culture" being the product of a retreat from revolutionary action into defensive defeat is extremely reductive. Questions of cultural characteristics and characterisations form a recurrent theme in Marxian thinking, whether it was on the "woman question" and the failure of the Russian Revolution to automatically pave the way for a changing view of women's social roles and sexual rights due to the changes in relations of production (Kollontai),[15] the dangers of the reification of and support for a non-progressive nationalism in the course of detaching the colonies from their imperial overlords (Luxemburg, Lenin or Roy),[16] or on the search for, and work with, 'progressive writers' and 'people's theatre' during the Popular Front years – the examples could be multiplied.[17] It needs to be said clearly that in organisations inspired by Marxism, from socialist or communist parties to progressive artists' associations and various other fellow travellers, the need to understand, engage in and shape cultural context, as part of historical and political context, was a necessary way of being able to act, operate, and mobilise. Marxism as a "Weltanschauung" among activists of the left had to operate on the basis of the cultural formations that it encountered in the historial contexts it found itself in; and a preconception of the nature and bounds of what the word "culture" meant outside of a given context could only be counterproductive. Marxisms' historiographical equivalents could also hardly afford to be culturally blind.

Marxian thinking also travelled in cultural forms; and the culture that travelled with Marxian thinking brought distant spaces and apparently disparate "cultures" together in an internationalism that was tangible, in a sensory way. Perhaps also audibly: with a song written by Jerome Kern with lyrics by Oscar

14 Albertina Vittoria, *Togliatti e gli intellettuali. La politica culturale dei comunisti italiani (1944–1964)* (Roma: Carocci, 2014).

15 Alexandra Kollontai, *Sexual Relations and the Class Struggle; Love and the New Morality* (transl. Alix Holt) (Bristol: Falling Wall Press, 1972) [1919]; Alexandra Kollontai, *Die Situation der Frau in der gesellschaftliche Entwicklung* (Frankfurt a.M.: Verlag Neue Kritik, 1977) [1921].

16 Rosa Luxemburg, *The National Question* (1909), online at https://www.marxists.org/archive/luxemburg/1909/national-question/index.htm, accessed April 21, 2020; Vladimir I. Lenin, *The Right of Nations to Self-Determination* (1914), online at http://www.marxists.org/archive/lenin/works/1914/self-det/index.htm, accessed April 21, 2020; MN Roy, "Supplementary Theses on the Colonial Question" at the Second Comintern Congress (July-August 1920), online at https://www.marxists.org/history/international/comintern/2nd-congress/ch04.htm accessed April 21, 2020.

17 On India, for instance, see Sudhi Pradhan (ed), *Marxist Cultural Movement in India: Chronicles and Documents* (3 vols, Calcutta: Navana, 1979–1985).

Hammerstein II and adapted by Paul Robeson[18] making its way to India, to Bengal via a translation by an Assamese singer, Bhupen Hazarika,[19] and with the imperatives of coordinating Muslim and Hindu peasants in a sharecropper's movement giving birth, in the music of Salil Choudhury, to the use of harmony and counterpoint in Indian music,[20] or in the worldwide search for folk traditions "progressive" enough to be adaptable or amenable to Marxist creative appropriation (which led to "folk" compositions by Pete Seeger for the Weavers or by Woody Guthrie or Leadbelly).[21] Does an "organic intellectual", to borrow a phrase from Antonio Gramsci, get to license himself or herself to write in a "folk" idiom, as a logical step forward from attempting to recover the folk songs, of, for instance, the 1857 Revolt in India?[22] Is this a version of "authenticity" that leads to a form of populism? How does Marxism attempt to achieve cultural hegemony? However one attempts the answers to these questions, it is clear that Marxian thinking has engaged closely with these questions, as historical, historiographical and political ones.

We have returned to the catchwords of re-contextualisation and re-politicisation. The insight that man is situated in a concrete history, a concrete milieu, a concrete problem field, is central to Marxian thinking. It always starts from history from which it draws its problems and returns to history by turning to the same problems again, but now on the basis of a critical analysis. To be situated also means to be engaged in a lifeworld that inscribes itself into thinking as horizon and perspective. If Marxism is reduced to a collection of dogmas, theories, strategies and ideas, if the "classical" texts and their interpretation become more important than the reconstruction of the social realities with which they corresponded, the analysis becomes flat and poor.

---

18 Todd Decker, *Who Should Sing 'Ol' Man River'? The Lives of an American Song* (New York: Oxford University Press, 2015); see in particular the chapter "Robeson's Revisions": 28–50.

19 Benjamin Zachariah, "What I Learned From My Grandparents, and Other Stories: Fragments of Biography, Autobiography and a History of Calcutta," in: TRAFO – Blog for Transregional Research, 31.03.2020, https://trafo.hypotheses.org/23490, accessed April 21, 2020.

20 See Sumangala Damodaran, 'Music and Resistance: The tradition of the Indian People's Theatre Association in the 1940s and 1950s', *Nehru Memorial Museum and Library Occasional Paper*, New Series, no. 56 (2014): 24, 29.

21 The best-recorded example is the United States: see for instance Dick Weissman, *Which Side Are You On? An Inside History of the Folk Music Revival in America* (New York: Continuum, 2006), esp. 36–71; and on the question of the authenticity of folk music, Robert Cantwell, "Smith's Memory Theater: *The Folkways Anthology of American Folk Music*," *New England Review* 13 (1991): 364–397.

22 PC Joshi, ed., *1857 in Folk Songs* (Delhi: People's Publishing House, 1994).

Themes and Contributions

The stakes of history, for the engaged intellectual, are never merely historical; on the other hand, historians do not always see themselves as engaged intellectuals. And yet, an engagement with politics aside, there are disciplinary reasons to expect Marxian thinking to reappear on historians' agenda. The rise of the tendency towards writing 'global history' has (or ought to have) placed a renewed engagement with the histories of capitalism and of critiques and critics of capitalism back on the agenda of historical research. This brings back to the centre of historical thinking a critical engagement with earlier Marxian debates. An understanding of the immediacy of Marxist perspectives for the analysis of the entangled structures of world history might be said to have returned as a result – or at least, an impending return might be said to be foreshadowed or accompanied by this volume, and other similar volumes that have accompanied the anniversary. But such an update of Marxisms can only survive the anniversary year when it is accompanied by a certain historical vigilance and succeeds in historicising its own rich Marxist inheritance and the many connected research debates. This volume attempts to do that, in several chapters that attempt a critical history of Marxian approaches and their use in history and the social sciences.

The book, like ancient Gaul according to René Goscinny and Albert Uderzo, is divided into four parts, entitled "Marxism and the Intellectual Production of History"; "Marxism and the Pre-Modern Worlds of the Near East"; "Marxism and the Beginnings of Western Capitalism"; and "Marxism and the Study of the Contemporary World" respectively. The first part contains a general survey of the (re)new(ed) uses of and engagements with Marxisms (Jakob Tanner); the emergence of microhistory from a Marxist (and Gramscian) milieu in Italy (Brigitta Bernet); the adaptations of Antonio Gramsci to the study of Indian history and politics (Benjamin Zachariah); and the critical possibilities of a Marxian history of science and technology, drawing on Friedrich Engels, recontextualising his text in terms of what was understood as science in his own times, and following the trend of Marxist-inflected histories of science to more contemporary times (Kavita Philip). The second part contains a study of the histories of the 'cradle of civilisation' and the critical role played by Marxist historiography in that research (Mohammad Maraqten); and a historiographical school of Marxist historians founded by the Egyptian scholar Mahmud Isma'il that studied the medieval Islamic world (Amar Baadj). The third part contains a chapter on the historiography of the 'great divergence' read through a Marxist lens (Nasser Mohajer and Kaveh Yazdani); and one on Marxist debates on Brazilian slavery (Jorge Grespan). The fourth, dealing with contemporary and near-contemporary times, has a chapter on thinking about labour and work in present-day western Europe beyond a traditional Marxist understanding of a working class (Lutz Raphael); one on global histories and Marx (Matthias Middell); and a global reserve army of labour (Preben Kaarsholm).

Jakob Tanner opens the volume with a contribution that subjects the diverse uses of Marx to a critical assessment, in parallel to and in conjunction with other critical but non-Marxist or anti-Marxist readings of capitalism. He takes us through the proliferation of reinterpretations of Marx and Marxist theory, as a result of which "the concept of capitalism has become increasingly complex"; and he reminds us of the wider historiographical and social-scientific contexts within which these debates took place. He also elucidates Marx's thoughts on liberty, and takes us through a continuing tradition of Marxist anthropology, which to his mind contains a kern of historicity. In a sense, this is a chapter that provides a context for the rest of the book, a chapter in which the author also attempts a historicisation of his own participation in Marxist-influenced debates over the time-span of his own career, and makes an appeal to think beyond static Marxist categories such as 'fictitious capital' when studying the effects of financial markets.

Brigitta Bernet traces the winding way that led communist and left-socialist intellectuals and scholars in Italy from orthodox Marxism to *microstoria*. She notes the paradox that critics of microhistory saw its emergence as the first step on the slippery slope to culturalism and depoliticisation, whereas its protagonists saw themselves as part of a lineage from Marx to Gramsci and beyond, and most often saw themselves as part of the Marxist left – though Bernet notes that Italian Marxism's (and Gramsci's own) closeness to the 'idealist' tradition of Benedetto Croce made it vulnerable to the charge that it remained "committed to the primacy of the political" – a remark that connects later in the volume with Benjamin Zachariah's reflections on the relative paucity of political-economy analyses in both Gramsci and in Indian uses of Gramsci. Bernet traces the roots and concerns of Italian *microstoria* to an engagement with Gramsci, and to Carlo Levi's autobiographical novel *Christ Stopped at Eboli* (1950), a reference to the (unhegemonised) peasants in Levi's southern Italian exile in 1935 who did not think of themselves as Catholics or Fascists. This was part of the origins of attempts to study 'progressive folklore' mobilised by Ernesto de Martino from 1949; it emerged from the same 'southern question' that had concerned Gramsci and Levi, and was to be read later by the future historian of witchcraft and popular religion, Carlo Ginzburg, for instance.

Benjamin Zachariah's contribution addresses the migration of Antonio Gramsci to India, where his initial reception among orthodox and heterodox Marxists was discussed in terms of the concepts of 'passive revolution', the nature of 'subaltern' autonomy, hegemony, the search for the 'national-popular' and the role of intellectuals. In the aftermath of the failure or stalling of a world revolutionary moment that had been premised on the success of agrarian revolution from China through India to Vietnam, and with many of the protagonists of the Indian debate reflecting on the defeat of the student revolts of the late 1960s that drew upon a perceived Maoism to attempt to link up with peasant revolution in India in the Naxalbari Movement, Gramsci's writing, appearing in (truncated) English translation in 1971, seemed to provide an opportune set of theoretical and historicising tools to reflect on this moment and on the nature of the Indian political order. Yet Gramsci's impact on India within a Marxist framework was short, appearing at a window in time that closed with the fall of the Soviet Bloc and the retreat from Marxism of many academics and formerly radical intellectuals; and soon seemed to open the way to thinking about an Indian exceptionalism. The reception of Gramsci appears to have focused mostly on a somewhat mythologised 'subaltern', and even as some selected aspects of Gramsci's reflections were taken seriously in isolation from one another, the larger context for Gramsci's writing, that of the fascist danger, appears not to have been taken seriously in Indian writings that drew on him. Zachariah makes a case for looking again at Gramsci in the light of the current (neo)fascist threats, in India and elsewhere; but that question remains an open one until such research is actually attempted. Gramsci is part of a Marxian moment of world-historical retreat or defeat, and it is at these moments, Zachariah argues, that Marxian thinking has been, and has to be, at its most creative and rigorous.

Kavita Philip addresses a greatly neglected theme in present-day Marxian debates: the perspective of developing a materialist theory of science and of scientific research, one that has so far been seen as owing its origins mainly to Friedrich Engels, but now, according to Philip, attributable to both Marx's and Engels' continuing concern with the scientific claims of their times. This has been a subject of some embarrassment to Marxists, given that they have appeared to require an ahistorical version of science, at times in order to justify a Marxist project as a whole as 'scientific'. Philip asks questions about the historical contexts and chronologically specific nature of the original interventions, but also recovers this for a critical research agenda for science and technology for the present times. It is this part of Marxism that, perhaps because of the larger developments of the twentieth century, after its canonising in the Soviet Union's dialectical materialism and the science politics of Cold War confrontations, has largely been lost. Philip suggests that the importance of a rereading of Marxist traditions of understanding science helps us to "historicise systems of rationality in relation to systems of production and labour relations", which is essential, because "there is no field that exemplifies the production of power and inequality more vividly than technoscience in the twenty-first century."

In the second part of the volume, the centrality of the Marxian category 'mode of production' is made clear in the chapter by Mohammed Maraqten, who stresses the enduring influence of orthodox Marxist research questions for the study of economic and social structures of the early high culture of the Fertile Crescent and the Arabian Peninsula. The specifics of early state-formation, the developments in agrarian production and related property relations are still current themes of interdisciplinary research on the region, and were sustained through empirical research (primarily through cooperative archaeological digs during the Cold War period) and explanatory models that depended on Marxist intellectuals from the (former) Soviet Union or the German Democratic Republic, but also from France and Italy. The inheritance of these Marxist explanatory models is still very influential in the field, even if they are no longer explicitly referred to; they endure in the studies of material cultures, state-formation and economic organisation of the ancient history of the region.

Amar Baadj's chapter on the *oeuvre* of the Marxist historian of Egyptian origin, Mahmud Isma'il, indicates the richness and centrality of a Marxian historical research agenda in the Arabic-speaking world, which might, for some readers trained in the somewhat dismissive Anglo-American and Edward Saidian anti-Marxist tradition, come as something of a surprise. In the social and cultural history of the 'classical' epochs of Islam, from the sixth to the sixteenth centuries, the inheritance of Marxist approaches is alive and well. Isma'il, research-active in Egypt, and later in Morocco and Kuwait, together with several of his students, had an enormous impact on the writing of the social and economic history of this time-frame. Isma'il's concept that Islamic civilisation swung between two central modes of production, a 'bourgeois' and a 'feudal' one, was a break with an orthodox Marxist idea of the correct order and steps taken by succeeding historical modes of production, which tended to be somewhat linear. Isma'il saw state-building, religion and culture as related to a more city-led trading-bourgeois developmental phase and a feudal-landowning reactionary phase, with connected religious and social conflicts being an outcome of this switching of phases of dominance (thus, a Marxian understanding of modes of production without a Marxist linear-developmental path). One of the key problems is the significance of the institution of the *iqta*, fiefdoms granted by dynasties to warriors and noblemen, whose character, Baadj points out, has been regionally and epochally quite differently interpreted by Isma'il and his school. This case study of the trajectories of Marxian historical research on Egypt and the Maghreb is also a glimpse into the vastly divergent possibilities and effects of the use of

Marxian categories during the heyday of Marx-influenced historical and social sciences research between 1945 and 1990.

The third part, on transitions to capitalism, is opened by Nasser Mohajer and Kaveh Yazdani, who show that the concept of 'original accumulation' (their preferred translation of 'ursprüngliche Akkumulation') can prove its usefulness in the debate on the 'great divergence' of European and Asian paths of development from the late eighteenth century to the end of the twentieth century. They emphasise the fruitfulness of Marxist analyses and observations for a more precise recording of obstacles to development and contrary trends that in India – more concretely, in the regions of Gujarat and Mysore, which Yazdani has studied in comparison[23] – stood in the way of an enforcing of a capitalist mode of production and a consequent dynamisation of economic and social development, in contrast to what happened in Great Britain at about the same time. In the critical reconstruction of central arguments of current economic history debates, a resort to Marx's categories is especially useful when it comes to developing a differentiated model of an endogamous developmental dynamic in Western Europe. The authors are thereby able to grant an important role, alongside the state as central actor in the service of or against capitalist accumulation, to geographical or geo-strategic factors.

Jorge Grespan shows, in his chapter on the research on slavery in Brazil, that Marxist analyses stressed the structural integration of Brazilian plantation slavery into the mercantile capitalism and thereafter the industrial capitalism dominated system of the Atlantic and western Europe, before the debates of the 1940s to the 1960s brought the transitional character of the slave economy to the foreground, and simultaneously led into a debate on the contemporary options for socialist politics in Brazil. At the end of the twentieth century, Brazilian research on slavery took up the impulse provided worldwide by the work of the British Marxist E.P. Thompson, and concerned itself with forms of resistance and class conflicts between slaves and their masters. This led to a particular emphasis on the cultural and ideological contexts of plantation slavery. The debates showed that the Atlantic plantation economy and the slave trade had a central significance for current debates about the overestimation of 'free wage labour' as a factor in the unfolding of industrial capitalism in its British version; and secondly that the racism that was inseparable from Atlantic slavery played a central role as a key analytic for historical research, following on from Marx's critique.

---

23 Kaveh Yazdani, *India, Modernity and the Great Divergence. Mysore and Gujarat (17th to 19th C.)* (Leiden, Boston: Brill 2017).

Racism, according to Grespan, was a central and continuing element in a Brazilian mode of production.

The fourth part addresses the possibilities of Marxian analysis suitably modified for the contemporary world. Lutz Raphael makes a case in his chapter for an analysis of the social structures of a developed capitalism in Western Europe that abandons the established schema of Marxist class analysis, in favour of a political-economy framework of analysis and a detailed social-historical analysis of diverse concepts of class, which need to be used so that the usual economistic shorthand can be avoided and worked around. Historical analysis can thereby avoid using the categories of political mobilisation, which then lead to both practical and theoretical dead ends.

Matthias Middell reflects on the possibilities and limits of a return to Marx in the context of present-day attempts to write 'global history' and 'world history', two trends which Middell finds useful to treat together, despite the more Marxian concerns of the latter. Marx's world-encompassing curiosity in relation to the first wave of capitalist globalisation in the nineteenth century is definitely a starting advantage which makes him greatly interesting to us today as an eyewitness to those times. Middell follows Marx's concern with the transition to capitalism, and traces it through several of the central debates that were conducted among historians, not least on the Great Divergence of Europe and Asia, a non-Marxian phrasing of a phenomenon that calls out for a Marxian analysis (*à la* Yazdani and Mohajer, for instance), and subsequently into debates on globalisation(s), the plural being his own preferred characterisation. Middell flags Marx's concept and expectation of revolution, borrowed mostly from the French Revolution, that appears today to serve, in connection with and in contradistinction to a liberal-evolutionary mainstream ideology of Anglo-American practitioners of global history, as a fruitful provocation and source of inspiration.

Preben Kaarsholm points to the continued importance of Marxism in theories of history, of development, and of globalisation, and in particular to the necessity of Marxist frames in writing histories of globalisation. In particular, he suggests that Marx underestimated the continuing processes of 'original' (or 'primitive') accumulation, which even in the current phase of globalisation since 1989 is important, through the worldwide freeing-up of a workforce of free wage labour, the creation of a global market for labour (despite bottlenecks), in which a whole new global reserve army of exploitable labour became available for use.

One of the key categories emerging from this volume is the continuing analytical usefulness of the Marxist idea of a 'mode of production'. This concept is as ambiguous as it is heuristically fruitful, because it serves as an abstract universal concept to order and compare, and to discuss the differences among, chronologically, geographically and structurally different economic forms, property orders and the related social structures that were shaped by them. At the same time, 'mode of production' also serves as a description for local or regional variations of an overarching social formation, so that this Marxian concept serves the interests of historians to get close enough to developing an empirically grounded model with an adequate feel for historical sources. As the diverse contributions to this volume suggest, Marxist researchers who have concerned themselves with earlier epochs and different regions of the world outside of Western Europe have long left behind the stageist lessons of orthodox Marxism-Leninism (slavery-feudalism-capitalism-socialism), and have found very different uses for the concept of a 'mode of production'. This leads us to the second significant point of focus that this volume has thrown up, alongside the need for a historicisation of Marxian research traditions: there is a need for a Marxian approach to global and world histories, just as there needs to be a global historical dimension to Marxian approaches and concepts. The chapters gathered in this volume confirm the trend of using Marx as a counterweight to more or less badly theorised metaphors of networks, notions of transnational cultural transfers, or quantification and analysis of big data. And if Marxism has appeared to lose itself in a somewhat conservative and self-referential world, a circle of self-delusion, in the recent past, this is an opportunity to look to the left of what was once Marxism, and to find a left of Marxism again.

Part One: **Marxism and the Intellectual Production of History**

Jakob Tanner

Smoke from the Volcanoes of Marxism?

Multifarious Theoretical and Political Debates

In the 1984 introduction to his *Theory of Social Systems*, the sociologist Niklas Luhmann painted an evocative picture of flying at a high level of abstraction over a "rather thick cloud cover" which offered occasional "glimpses of a land below", including "a larger stretch of landscape with the extinct volcanoes of Marxism".[1] It was, however, premature to draw the conclusion that the magma of these Marxist volcanoes had petrified. For sure there have been no major eruptions for some time. But anyone testing with the probes of conceptual history or the history of knowledge can soon see that beneath the sedimentary layers the Marxist lava has never been settled. The question remains whether these volcanoes will soon erupt again.

Marx is out – Marx is in. Looking back, it is noticeable how often theoretical and political debate turned away from Karl Marx and pronounced him 'defunct', only to turn back to him with surprising intensity and often in unexpected contexts.[2] This is an ambivalent finding. On one hand, in spite of its being shaken to the core by the end of the Cold War and the implosion of the Eastern Bloc, the 'Marxist–Leninist' ideology has proven capable of remarkable continuity in some places, especially in the People's Republic of China. This kind of power-saturated state Marxism is theoretically frozen and further intellectual eruptions are not to be expected.

On the other hand, the task of 're-reading' *Capital* – Karl Marx's main work from 1867 – has become more attractive.[3] Capitalism's vulnerability to crisis, persistent exploitation within global hierarchies and the worsening environmental crisis are all factors that have bolstered theoretical approaches that draw on is-

---

1 Niklas Luhmann, *Theorie sozialer Systeme* (Frankfurt am Main: Suhrkamp, 1984), 12–13.

2 For the most recent study of the debates around Karl Marx see: Jeff Diamanti, Andrew Pendakis and Imre Szeman, eds., *The Bloomsbury Companion to Marx* (London: Bloomsbury Academic, 2019).

3 Karl Marx, *Capital: A Critique of Political Economy. Volume I: The Process of Capitalist Production* (New York : The Modern library) (first published Hamburg: Meissner, 1867). An inventive new reading can be found in: Wolfgang Fritz Haug, *Das "Kapital" lesen – aber wie?: Materialien zur Philosophie und Epistemologie der marxschen Kapitalismuskritik* (Hamburg: Argument Hamburg, 2013). See also the review by Mario Wimmer, "Marx neu lessen," *Werkstatt Geschichte* 77 (2017): 111–116.

https://doi.org/10.1515/9783110677744-004

sues discussed by Marx. Close links are seen between social inequality and the exploitation of the natural world. Historians such as Timothy Mitchell and Andreas Malm have created models which demonstrate the connection between fossil fuels, industrial economic growth and capitalist regime of exploitation, not only from an economic perspective but also from a political point of view.[4] The philosopher Kohei Saito assumes that Marx not only casually addressed the capitalist overexploitation and degradation of natural resources, but also placed them at the very centre of his theory of accumulation. In fact, Marx drew an analogy between the exploitation of nature and the exploitation of labour. Towards the end of his life, he tried to prove that capital accumulation had natural limits.[5]

These and further considerations mean that approaches to Marxist theory have become more differentiated and that the notion of capital and the concept of capitalism has become increasingly complex.[6] It is not easy to keep track of all the different strands, but then Marxism has never been famous for being easy. Any attempts to use Marx as the basis for a theoretically integrated global *total history* or even to develop any coherent analytical perspective have repeatedly failed for the simple reason that Marx intended his work to be polarising and broadly based rather than consensual and one-dimensional. It begins with the fact that Marx himself never wanted to be a 'Marxist'.[7] Within the Marxist community, both in internal debates and when countering critics of Marx, there is an enormously wide range of interpretations.

---

4 Timothy Mitchell, *Carbon Democracy: Political Power in the Age of Oil* (London: Verso, 2013); Andreas Malm, *Fossil Capital: The Rise of Steam-power and the Roots of Global Warming* (London: Verso, 2016); *The Progress of This Storm: Nature and Society in a Warming World* (London: Verso, 2018).

5 Marx' environmental criticism is addressed in: Kohei Saito, *Karl Marx's Ecosocialism: Capitalism, Nature, and the Unfinished Critique of Political Economy* (New York: Monthly Review Press, 2017). For a critique of this position, see the book review by Naeem Inayatullah auf adacemia.edu. See also: John Bellamy Foster and Paul Burkett, *Marx and the Earth: An Anti-critique* (Leiden: Brill, 2016) and Elmar Altvater and Birgit Mahnkopf, *Grenzen der Globalisierung: Ökonomie, Ökologie und Politik in der Weltgesellschaft* (Münster: Westfälisches Dampfboot, 2007).

6 Nancy Fraser, "Behind Marx's Hidden Abode: For an Expanded Conception of Capitalism," *New Left Review*, 86 (2014): 55–72. Friedrich Lenger, "Die neue Kapitalismusgeschichte: Ein Forschungsbericht als Einleitung, " *Archiv für Sozialgeschichte*, 56 (2016), 1–36. See the "Varieties of Capitalism" debate: Peter A. Hall and David Soskice, *Varieties of Capitalism: The Institutional Foundations of Comparative Advantage* (Oxford: Oxford University Press, 2001).

7 'The only thing I know is that I'm not a Marxist'. Recorded twice as oral statements by Karl Marx in letters from Friedrich Engels: Engels to Conrad Schmidt on August 5 1890; Engels to Paul Lafarque on August 27 1890; *MEW* Vol. 37 (Berlin: Karl Dietz Verlag, 1967), 436.

Looking back, historically various reception strands can be identified. The first, emerging in the 1890s, is social democracy with its mobilising self-assurance by means of a 'historical materialism' suitable for the masses. After 1917, this was both rivalled by and co-existed with Marxism–Leninism, which became state official and was followed by Stalinism and Maoism. Although the various critical politico-economic analyses of capitalism and imperialism still interact with these ideologies, they provided new and distinct lines of reasoning. The works of Rudolf Hilferding, *Finance Capital*[8], and Rosa Luxemburg, *The Accumulation of Capital*[9], acted as important catalysts here. At the same time came the development of 'Western Marxism'[10], represented since the 1920s by the 'critical theory' of the University of Frankfurt Institute for Social Research. In the post-war period, its epicentre shifted to France where at the beginning of the 1960s an esoteric theoretical language served to advance a comprehensive synthesis of structuralism, psychoanalysis and Marxism. More down-to-earth critics such as Edward P. Thompson rejected these attempts, calling them an 'orrery of errors' and later the 'poverty of theory'.[11]

In the early 1960s, Marxism was at its epistemological zenith. For all its many facets and inner rivalries, the theory of Marxism in all its shapes and forms was part of an overall process of questioning and self-reflection within society. In 1960, Jean-Paul Sartre in his *Critique of Dialectical Reason* claimed that Marxism was the untransgressable horizon of all thought. For him, this was not tantamount to certainty of knowledge. He rather was stretching the metaphor of a common boat sailing on the high seas of ignorance.[12] In emphasising this, he turned himself against the determinists among the Marxists, convinced that liberty was no more than the realisation of necessity, purported to be in possession of a scientific compass which would guide them to the far shores of Communism. Sartre, however, had broken with the French Communist Party in 1956 and insisted that liberty itself should be put on the rowing bench. By 1965, Marxism seemed to have aligned itself to structuralism. The stage on which the renewal

8 Rudolf Hilferding, *Finance Capital. A Study of the Latest Phase of Capitalist Development*, ed. Tom Bottomore (London: Routledge & Kegan Paul 1981) (first published Vienna, Wiener Volksbuchhandlung, 1910).

9 Rosa Luxemburg, *The Accumulation of Capital*, ed. Dr. W. Stark (London: Routledge and Kegan Paul 1951 (first published Berlin: Buchhandlung Vorwärts Paul Singer 1913).

10 Perry Anderson, *Über den westlichen Marxismus* (Frankfurt am Main: Syndikat, 1978).

11 Edward P. Thompson, "The Poverty of Theory or an Orrery of Errors" (1978), in *The Poverty of Theory and Other Essays*, ed. Edward P. Thompson (New York and London: Monthly Review Press, 1979) https://www.marxists.org/archive/thompson-ep/1978/pot/essay.htm accessed April 21, 2020.

12 Jean-Paul Sartre, *Critique de la raison dialectique* (Paris: Gallimard, 1960).

of Marxism was being played out was dominated by Louis Althusser's *For Marx* and the anthology *Reading Capital* (with Etienne Balibar, Jaques Rancière and others).[13] Writing about this period in his *History of Structuralism*, François Dosse noted: "Marx became the interface of all research, a veritable common denominator in the social sciences."[14]

However, after the *annus mirabilis 1966*[15] Marxism was plunged into a crisis. Sartre's unattainable horizon was shattered. Dialectics, based on the interaction of antagonistic forces, was pushed onto the back foot by a mode of thought oriented towards the never-ending play of differences. Criticism of the Hegel–Marx continuum was itself varied and reached from the structuralism of Claude Lévi-Strauss and Roland Barthes through structural–functional approaches and the interpretive analytics of Michel Foucault to the post-modern perspective of François Lyotard. Nevertheless, this did not spell the end of engagement with Marxism. On the contrary, both with and alongside this anti-dialectic challenge, a broad spectrum of Marxisms prospered. Besides the revival of a dull 'state- monopoly capitalism' there was also a renaissance of more sophisticated Marxist theories. Significant examples are the crisis theories of 'late capitalism'[16], the new gender history studies of the rise of housework in capitalism,[17] and the diagnosis of a 'crisis of state planning' and of the transition to a 'crisis of the state' and to 'empire'.[18]

In 1976, as one of a team of authors, I also published in the 'critical tradition' of the theory of capital accumulation and crisis.[19] The book dealt with the eco-

---

13 Louis Althusser, Étienne Balibar, Rober Establet, Jacques Rancière, Pierre Macherey, *Reading Capital: The Complete Edition* (London: Verso, 2015). This re-reading of Marx was initiated by Althusser in the mid 1960s: Louis Althusser, *Lire le Capital* (Paris: Maspero, 1965); Louis Althusser, *Pour Marx* (Paris: Maspero, 1966).

14 François Dosse, *Geschichte des Strukturalismus, Vol. 1: Das Feld des Zeichens, 1945–1966*, (Hamburg: Junius, 1996), 447.

15 Dosse, *Strukturalismus*, 456 (chapter heading).

16 Jürgen Habermas, *Legitimationsprobleme im Spätkapitalismus* (Frankfurt am Main: Suhrkamp 1973); Claus Offe, *Strukturprobleme des kapitalistischen Staates: Aufsätze zur politischen Soziologie* (Frankfurt a. M.: Suhrkamp, 1972).

17 Gisela Bock and Barbara Duden, "Zur Entstehung der Hausarbeit im Kapitalismus," in *Dokumentation der Berliner Sommeruniversitäten: Frauen und Wissenschaft. Beiträge zur Berliner Sommeruniversität für Frauen*, Juli 1976 (Berlin 1977), 118–199.

18 Michael Hardt and Antonio Negri, *Empire* (Cambridge/Mass.: HUP, 2000); see also: Antonio Negri and Timothy S. Murphy, *Modernity and the Multitude* (Cambridge/Mass.: Polity Press, 2012).

19 Autorenkollektiv (Felix Müller, Hans Schäppi and Jakob Tanner), *Krise– Zufall oder Folge des Kapitalismus? Die Schweiz und die aktuelle Wirtschaftskrise: Eine Einführung aus marxistischer Sicht* (Zürich: Limmat Verlag, 1976), citation 9.

nomic crisis of 1974–1975 and was entitled *Crisis – Accident or a Consequence of Capitalism?*. In it we tried to use 'a Marxist perspective' to explain the prosperity of the *trente glorieuses* ('glorious thirties') between 1945 and 1973 and the subsequent economic setback. It was intended as an introduction, particularly for use in political education offered by trade unions. At the same time, its aim was similar to that of many other authors of the time[20], namely, to find a mathematical expression for Marx's law of the tendency of the rate of profit to fall and to prove it empirically. From the point of view of its foundation on the labour theory of value, this endeavour can barely withstand retrospective evaluation. By contrast, its critique of capitalism and its analysis of the dynamics of crisis within capitalist economic and social systems seem more compelling than ever.

Up to the mid-1970s, Marx was everywhere. Anyone who went to university to study humanities or social sciences in a western European country at the beginning of the 1970s was immediately introduced to fields of theory which were unmistakably shaped by Marxist theories. Looking at the whole spectrum of historical research from the Annales historians, social history and 'world-systems analysis', the history of everyday life, cultural history and microhistory, right through to gender history, historical anthropology and postcolonial studies, the history of knowledge and important perspectives in environmental history, it can be seen that the most important theoretical innovations in the study of history and cultural theory can only be explained in the context of Marx – whether for or against him – even if Marx himself is sometimes conspicuous by his absence.[21]

Images of Marx and the 'Marx Effect'

However, Marx is generally not absent but ever-present, even if only as a stereotyped reference. As such he is reduced to several specific roles. The sociologist

20 Still the most impressive in terms of its mathematical grounding and nuanced conclusions: Hans-Werner Sinn, "Das Marxsche Gesetz des tendenziellen Falls der Profitrate," *Zeitschrift für die gesamte Staatswissenschaft* 131 (1975): 646–696. http://www.hanswernersinn.de/dcs/1975_ZGS131_Marxsches_Gesetz_Profitrate.pdf. Accessed April 21, 2020.

21 For the influential Marxist traditions in Cultural Studies see: https://oxfordre.com/communication/view/10.1093/acrefore/9780190228613.001.0001/acrefore-9780190228613-e-911 Accessed April 21, 2020. Overviews tend to waver between acceptance and disassociation. The complexity of the relations and the interaction in all these cases is shown by the example of the 'Annales' by: Peter Schöttler, *Die "Annales"-Historiker und die deutsche Geschichtswissenschaft* (Tübingen: Mohr-Siebeck, 2015), chapter 11, 203–220.

Wolfgang Essbach recently identified four stereotyped images of Marx: the "radical journalist" around 1850, the "intellectual socialist and leader of the international labour movement" around 1870, the "founder of historical materialism" around 1900 and "the theorist of the revolution" in the mid-1920s.[22] Essbach points out that these four figures prevent the recourse to an authentic Marx. The search for what he really meant by what he wrote only engenders a mystification of origins. All those who battle their way through Marx's writings today are reading through the kaleidoscope of previous interpretations. However hard they try, neither language nor theory can wholly avoid being influenced by this kind of cross-fading of images.

Considering the appropriation of Marx in the years around 1968, Essbach argues convincingly that the 1968 protest movements did not create a genuinely new image of Marx. On the contrary, in their first "hippy phase", he argues, they combined the first and last images (celebrating the radical journalist as the theorist of the revolution), whereas later, in the "'communist-group (*K-Gruppen*) phase", they concentrated on the second and third images, that is on the leader of the First International and the intellectual founder of historical and dialectical materialism. Further, he wonders whether a fifth Marx image has been created since the end of the Cold War, that of the "classic" Marx. Could it be that Marx has now become "a great figure in our discipline, a social scientist of historical standing"[23], who has to hold his own with Émile Durkheim, Max Weber, Maurice Halbwachs, Hannah Arendt, Norbert Elias and others? If this were the case he would be relieved of his unique position as the ultimate reference for a critical theory of capitalist society. He would be neutralised as one of many players in the market of ideas.

In fact Marx has already been relativised and historicised. Nowadays 'Marx' always means 'after Marx' in both senses of the phrase.[24] Three different contexts were (and are) particularly important for my own exploration of Marx. The *first* is Arendt's Marx critique. In the 1950s she depicted Marx as both sympathiser and opponent of Friedrich Nietzsche. Arendt describes the partisans' logic which was evident in thinkers like Nietzsche and Søren Kierkegaard. It was particularly distinct in the case of Marx, because he defined politics as class struggle

---

22 Wolfgang Essbach, *Marxbilder 1848 bis 1968: SWR 3 Tele-Akademie, Sendung vom 21.10. 2018*, see: https://swrmediathek.de/player.htm?show=276a0fc0-d1dd-11e8-9a07-005056a12b4c Accessed April 21, 2020.

23 See e.g. Heinz D. Kurz, "Hin zu Marx und über ihn hinaus," *Perspektiven der Wirtschaftspolitik*, 19,3 (2018), 246–265, 263.

24 Rahel Jaeggi and Daniel Loick, eds., *Nach Marx: Philosophie, Kritik, Praxis* (Berlin: Suhrkamp, 2013).

and thus identified any theoretical alignment as a positioning in the system of political coordinates. The result was: pro-Marx = progressive, anti-Marx = reactionary.[25] Arendt rejected this antagonism and instead emphasised what Marx and Nietzsche had in common. Both had brought about a radical reversal. In her view, Marx had turned Hegel 'upside down' and seen dialectics not as an intellectual transformation but as a material process, while Nietzsche turned Platonism around and demanded the 'revaluation of all values'.[26] Arendt found both of these reversals equally daring and 'extraordinarily significant', but suggested that neither of them transgressed the basic problem but reified it on a different level. This interpretation invalidates the idea that Marx had made a quantum leap forward in thinking.

The *second* context in the discussion involves the French philosopher Paul Ricoeur, who anchored Marx in a specific historical tradition. In his 1965 study *Freud and Philosophy: An Essay on Interpretation*, he describes the theoretician of capital, together with Friedrich Nietzsche and Sigmund Freud, as 'masters of suspicion'.[27] These three, he says, were striving to expose what was socially evident as the effect of a hidden essence (Marx: 'all history is the history of class struggle'). Consequently, the ruling consciousness for Marx is necessarily a wrong one. From this point of view, the impenetrable is the non-existent.[28] Any socially produced 'appearance' is ideology because it supports the illusion that consciousness is the source of all meaning, whereas in fact, meaning is determined by other completely different factors (for Marx, by the commodity mode of value; for Nietzsche, the form of discourse; for Freud, the structure of the psyche). This classification, according to Ricoeur, means that Marx represents an intellectual stance whose systematic premise is that the role of social 'appearance' is to obscure deeper insights into social, cultural and psychological connections. For Ricoeur, Marx is a theoretician who denounces any form of trust in existing

25 Hannah Arendt, "Karl Marx and the Tradition of Political Thought," in *The Modern Challenge to Tradition: Fragmente eines Buchs (= Kritische Gesamtausgabe Vol. 6)* (Göttingen: Wallstein, 2018), 245–255, 245.

26 Hannah Arendt, "Von Hegel zu Marx," in *The Modern Challenge to Tradition: Fragmente eines Buchs (= Kritische Gesamtausgabe Vol. 6)* (Göttingen: Wallstein, 2018), 89.

27 Paul Ricoeur, *Freud and Philosophy: An Essay on Interpretation* (New Haven, CT: YUP, 1970), 33 and 35.

28 Emil Angehrn, "Vom Sinn des Sinnlosen: Die Herausforderung der Psychoanalyse für die Philosophie," in *Freuds Aktualität (Freiburger literaturpsychologische Gespräche. Jahrbuch für Literatur und Psychoanalyse, Vol. 26)*, eds. Wolfram Mauser and Joachim Pfeifferd, (Würzburg: Königshausen und Neumann, 2006), 85–96. http://www.jp.philo.at/texte/AngehrnE1.pdf; Accessed April 21, 2020.

circumstances as naïve and assumes that the only way to penetrate this social context of delusion is by means of suspicion based on dispassionate distrust.[29]

Third there is Jacques Derrida, who in 1993, thirty years after Ricoeur, coined this necessity for suspicion 'Hauntology' (an amalgamation of haunting and ontology). In his book *Spectres of Marx*, Derrida adopts an approach of 'unfaithful fidelity' (*une fidélité infidèle*) towards Marx, whose impetus for international criticism of society he says, can only be maintained if the theoretical premises of his work are subjected to fundamental questioning.[30] The spectre metaphor used by Derrida takes up a motif from the Communist Manifesto of 1848 and helps resist the temptation to idealise Marx as a timeless revelation of the communist future through the medium of class struggle and to endow him with a higher, even religious aura. Derrida's account helps us to understand why Marx triggered a tremendous theory effect rather than being an outstanding hero of the intellectual world. Derrida's deconstruction apparatus manages to undermine Hegel's hubris in seeing himself as the embodiment of the absolute and the voice of the 'Weltgeist' (world spirit), who found knowledge of himself through his phenomenological work. It also undermines the image of 'progress' around which the eschatology of political Marxism crystallised. Marx has no salvation to offer, insists Derrida, but if one is prepared to put in the effort, he can be useful as a productive theoretical force.

Together these three relativising contexts show the theoretical productivity and the epistemological limitations of Marx. They deflate exaggerated expectations and demonstrate the wide variety of ways his work can be appropriated. This seems to me to be essential to make it possible for continuing to engage with Marxist approaches and defending them against alternative theories.

Democracy and Liberty

One of the most firmly-held convictions of the twentieth century was that socialism came at the expense of liberty while capitalism came at the expense

29 Alison Scott-Bauman, *Ricoeur and the Hermeneutics of Suspicion* (London: Continuum, 2009); Andrew Dole, *Reframing the Masters of Suspicion: Marx, Nietzsche, and Freud* (London: Bloomsbury, 2019).

30 Jacques Derrida, *Marx Gespenster. Der Staat der Schuld, die Trauerarbeit und die neue Internationale* (Berlin: Suhrkamp, 2004). Derrida uses this term "fidélité infidèle" for his own work. Entretiens avec Jean Birnbaum, "Je suis en guerre contre moi-même," *Le Devoir*, September 4, 2004, https://www.ledevoir.com/lire/62927/entretien-avec-jacques-derrida-je-suis-en-guerre-contre-moi-meme. Accessed April 21, 2020.

of equality. The trade-off between these two basic principles began in the French Revolution and soon became an undisputed absolute. Historians and social scientists, however, would do well not to consider the demand for liberty – or freedom or liberation, as it was referred to in the socialist tradition – to be in competition with the theory of equality.

The concept of liberty developed by Marx is highly compatible with a democratic society. He rarely mentioned communism as an aim. When he did, (such as in his 1875 critique of German social democracy and its Gotha programme),[31] he made it clear that individual freedom and 'rich individuality' took precedence over schematic equality or abstract justice. This striking preference for liberty or freedom has often been overlooked. The main reason is that the tensions between anarchists and Marxists, which first surfaced in the early 1870s in the International Labour Association, seemed to express a sharp antithesis between federalism and centralism. On one side were the bottom-up anarchists surrounding wild Mikhail Bakunin and on the other the top-down communists under the thumb of Marx. This juxtaposition is misleading, because the split was about something completely different. Marx criticised Bakunin's tendency towards authoritarian violence, 'barracks communism' and a 'levelling out of classes and individuals'.[32] Marxs' objection to Bakunin was the same as his objection to capitalism – both prevented the individual from finding self-fulfilment.[33] Marx, on the contrary, wants the liberated individual. He is a philosopher of freedom.[34]

However, this does not mean that Marx's writings offer concrete insights into the theory of democracy. This becomes particularly clear by comparing Marx's *Capital* and Thomas Piketty's *Capital in the Twenty-First Century.*[35] Both works advance the theory that capitalism and democracy are incompatible or in a strong contrast. But their approaches are strikingly different. Marx's *Capital* contains powerful descriptions of the capitalist labour process, whereby "the pro-

---

31 Karl Marx, *Kritik des Gothaer Programms*, 1875, published posthumously (1891) by Friedrich Engels, in *Karl Marx, Friedrich Engels Werke (MEW)*, Vol. 19 (Berlin: Dietz, 1973), 13–32.

32 Urs Marti, *Die Freiheit des Karl Marx: Ein Aufklärer im bürgerlichen Zeitalter* (Reinbek b. Hamburg: Rowohlt, 2018), 236–246, 238, 241.

33 This is not to dispute the importance of the role individuality plays in anarchism and the collectivist, violence-prone tendencies in party-Marxist strands; these statements refer precisely to the writings of Bakunin that Marx studied and criticised.

34 Michael R. Krätke, *Karl Marx und die Kritik des Gothaer Programms*, unpublished paper, Lancaster University, https://lancaster.academia.edu/MichaelKr%C3%A4tke. Accessed April 21, 2020.

35 Karl Marx, *Das Kapital: Kritik der politischen Ökonomie*, Vol. I, in *MEW* Vol. 23 (Berlin: Karl Dietz Verlag, 1972); Thomas Piketty, *Capital in the Twenty-First Century* (Cambridge/Mass.: Belknap, 2014) (first published 2013).

ductive activity of the human organism" expresses itself as "abstract human labour".[36] Democracy as a social institution and legal construction is hardly mentioned. In fact, Marx ignores the intrinsic value of institutionalised democratic structures. He understands political violence as 'economic power' and vice versa. If capitalists are not willing to relinquish control voluntarily when the bell tolls for private property at the moment of revolution, he writes, the "class dictatorship of the proletariat" will appear "as the necessary transit point to the abolition of class distinctions generally".[37] In this context, categories such as the rule of law, checks and balances and formal processes are of little use.

At the same time Marx sublimates the principle of democracy. In his early works he draws enigmatic parallels between democracy and communism. In the same way as democracy is "the riddle of all constitutions solved", he says communism is "the riddle of history solved" and knows it.[38] This inconsistency has frequently been alluded to. Although Marx is a political writer through and through, he never developed a systematic political theory that would have satisfied his own analytical standards in his study of capitalism. What Marx did was to react to political movements and class struggles in particular situations but at no stage in his life was he willing or capable of providing a stable theoretical basis for the concept of the political and the idea of democratic socialisation.[39]

Piketty adopts a completely contrasting approach. He does not base the capitalist accumulation mechanism on a labour theory of value and although his descriptions are often lengthy, the labour process remains completely underexposed.[40] Workers are treated by him as citizens and, in respect of their purchasing power, as consumers (whereby the gender aspect is generally disregarded). Piketty's central question is whether and how "democracy can regain control over capitalism" someday.[41] As distinct from "the human disasters caused by Soviet-style centralized planning",[42] he consistently argues for "so-

---

36 Marx, *Das Kapital*, 61, 510.

37 Karl Marx, *Die Klassenkämpfe in Frankreich* (1850), in *MEW*, Vol. 7 (Berlin: Karl Dietz, 1973), 89.

38 Karl Marx, "Zur Kritik der Hegelschen Rechtsphilosophie 18343/44," in *MEW*, Vol. 1 (Berlin: Karl Dietz, 1976), 231; Karl Marx, *Ökonomisch-philosophische Manuskripte* (1844)," in *MEW*, Ergänzungsband, 1. (Berlin: Karl Dietz, 1968), 536.

39 Bruno Bosteels, "Political Theory," in *The Bloomsbury Companion to Marx*, eds. Jeff Diamanti, Andrew Pendakis and Imre Szeman (London: Bloomsbury Academic, 2019), 585–596. On 585, Etienne Balibar is cited.

40 Piketty tends to use 'assets', 'wealth' and 'capital' more or less synonymously.

41 Piketty, *Capital*, 570.

42 Piketty, *Capital*, 532.

cial-democratic avenues". Piketty is not interested in providing a manual for class struggle but in "contributing, however modestly, to the debate about the best way to organise society and the most appropriate institutions and policies to achieve a just social order ... under the rule of law, which should apply equally to all and derive from universally understood statutes subject to democratic debate."[43]

Politics and democracy are key categories for Piketty, whereas in Marx's work they only appear as derivatives of class struggle. For Arendt, this militant over-politicisation has turned down into institutional depoliticisation. She considers Marx dreadfully 'unpolitical' because he was not prepared to take politics seriously as a space where a society can reach an understanding on the institutional and material conditions under which it operates. The significance of Marx's work lies neither in his economic theories nor in its revolutionary content, but in the stubbornness with which he clung to these two chief new perplexities, was her harsh verdict.[44] It is indeed the case that Marx places too much faith in his concept of freedom and that this results in his being a weak theorist of democracy. This is a serious deficiency, and it helps explain why a hostile takeover of Marxism by authoritarian and dictatorial movements has been possible. It is also a further reason why the problem of politics and the necessary conditions for a democratic society must be placed at the core of Marxist-based theoretical models.

Marxist Anthropology and Value Analysis

Most Marxist debates in the German-speaking world have focussed on the philosophy of history, political economy and commodity aesthetics. Debates in the Anglosphere and France, on the other hand, particularly within social and cultural anthropology, have for a long time concentrated on the question of Marxist anthropology. Marx's many ethnographic writings do not constitute a discrete level of observation but record the manifestations of capitalist exploitation across all social scales, from global imperialism and the world market through the analysis of individual regions and countries to micro-worlds of the capitalist factory where exploitation practices are concentrated. This suggests re-reading of *Capital*, in which Marx portrays social power relations as material violence and social coercion and provides a vivid description of how labour is in

---

43 Piketty, *Capital*, 31
44 Hannah Arendt, "Karl Marx and the Tradition of Polical Thought," 248.

fact subsumed under capital and how this is inscribed in the human body. Marx vividly evokes the "incessant sacrificial feast of the working-class" in which that "monstrosity, an industrial reserve army, kept in misery in order to be always at the disposal of capital" coexists with the "absolute disposability of humans for the changing requirements of labour".[45]

Ideas such as these became highly relevant in the late 1970s, when neoliberalism advanced to become the ruling ideology of political activity in many economically advanced countries, especially in the United States and Britain. Efforts to bring Marxism up-to-date intensified, not only on the left, but also within scientific research. However, the new methodological approaches that were nominally based on Marx were diametrically opposed to each other. In 1980, the so-called Analytical Marxism (AM) project was launched. Its major impetus came from Gerald A. Cohen's *Marx's Theory of History: A Defence* [46] and its main protagonists were Jon Elster, David Miller and John Roemer. This approach was like trying to combine fire and water. AM wanted to apply paradigms of rational choice theory and methodological individualism to Marx's critique of capitalism in a way that was in accordance with analytical philosophy. Its goal was to rationalise Marx by operationalising the terminology. It aimed to clear the ideological fog that surrounded the Marxism of class struggle and seemed to be blurring scientific analysis. Cohen called this 'Non-Bullshit Marxism' which was to bridge the gap between the social sciences and contemporary philosophy. It was an ambitious project that was guided by a rigid but theoretically stringent model of rationality. In the 1990s, however, it lost its impetus and mutated into a politically undefined "new Marxist research on an analytical basis".[47]

In the same period there was an upsurge in approaches of cultural anthropology towards 'the social' and social anthropology of 'the cultural'. Two seminal works here were Eric Wolf's *Europe and the People Without History* and Sidney Mintz' history of sugar, *Sweetness and Power.*[48] They both aspired to a global history of capitalism, adding substance to an approach whose potential is still by no means exhausted. This is evident in Frederick Cooper und Ann Laura Stoler's

---

45 Marx, *Das Kapital*, 511.

46 Gerald A. Cohen, *Karl Marx's Theory of History: A Defence* (Oxford: Clarendon Press, 1978).

47 Marco Iorio, "Analytischer Marxismus," in *Marx–Handbuch. Leben – Werke – Wirken*, eds. Michael Quante and David P. Schweikard (Stuttgart: Metzler, 2016), 351.

48 Eric Wolf, *Europe and the People Without History* (Berkeley/ Los Angeles: University of California Press) 1982; Sidney Wilfred Mintz, *Sweetness and Power: The Place of Sugar in Modern History* (New York, New York: Viking 1985).

Tensions of Empire[49] and Thomas Carl Patterson's *Karl Marx, Anthropologist.*[50] In their introduction to *Capitalism and Global Anthropology: Marxism resurgent* Patrick Neveling and Luisa Steur quite rightly refer to "fundamental inspirations for 21st century anthropology".[51]

Further theoretical impulses for Marxist anthropology emerged from its confrontation and cooperation with related approaches. The French ethnologist Marcel Mauss was particularly qualified for a dialogue with Marx. Although he was not a Marxist himself, he shared Marx's criticism of capitalism. He saw the Soviet system as nothing but a travesty of the capitalist market system. In his major work of 1923/4, *Essai sur le don* (English: *The Gift* 1925), Mauss summarily dismissed the utilitarian optimisation paradigms of the neoclassical economy.[52] Mauss was a reform socialist with revolutionary aspirations and the fact that every kind of human interaction was forced into market price categories was to him European capitalist prejudice.[53] His idea of a 'gift economy' which is neither structured by optimising self-interest nor by calculated reciprocity enabled him to make a cultural comparison of various forms of gift exchange. The more the principle of wastefulness of the gift contrasts with the accumulation dynamic of capital, the clearer various parallels between Mauss and Marx become. An example would be the attempt to understand economic transaction models as a 'total social phenomenon' and relate them to emotional dispositions, or the analysis of 'alienation' and 'objectification' evident in so many different, even opposing forms of socialisation.[54] Such reference, however, assume an eclectic self-conception, present in the *Mouvement Anti-Utilitariste dans les Sciences So-*

---

49 Frederick Cooper and Ann Laura Stoler, *Tensions of empire: Colonial cultures in a bourgeois world* (Berkeley: UCP, 1997); vgl. auch Ann Laura Stoler, *Duress: Imperial Durabilities in our Times* (Durham: DUP, 2016).

50 Thomas Carl Patterson, *Karl Marx: Anthropologist* (Oxford: Berg, 2009).

51 Patrick Neveling and Luisa Steur, "Introduction," *Focaal*, 82, Special Issue: Capitalism and Global Anthropology: Marxism resurgent (Dec 1, 2018): 1–15, 3. This introduction gives many clues to the variety of reception and further development of Marx' anthropology in France. https://www.focaalblog.com/2018/10/11/focaal-volume-2018-issue-82-capitalism-and-global-anthropology-marxism-resurgent/ Accessed April 21, 2020.

52 Marcel Mauss, *Essai sur le don: forme et raison de l'échange dans les sociétés archaïques. Vorwort Florence Weber* (Paris: Presses Universitaires, 2008). For the reception of this work in the anthropology of the 21st century see: David Graeber, *Toward An Anthropological Theory of Value: The False Coin of Our Own Dreams* (Basingstoke: Palgrave, 2002).

53 For a critical discussion of Marcel Mauss see: Don Kalb, "Trotsky over Mauss: Anthropological Theory and the October 1917 Commemoration," in *Dialectical Anthropology* 42, no. 3 (2018): 327–343.

54 David Graeber, "Give it away. On Marcel Mauss," in *Free Words* http://www.freewords.org/graeber.html; Accessed April 21, 2020.

ciales (M.A.U.S.S.). This movement began in 1980 – at exactly the same time as 'Analytical Marxism'– and caused a furore with its 1997 *30 Theses for the New Left.*[55]

Those approaches to Marxist anthropology and capital analysis that are historically oriented avoid presentist short-circuits as well as a relativist historicism and suggest a model of multiple temporalities.[56] Here simultaneity generally proves to be the 'simultaneity of the non-simultaneous'. Seen from this angle, the idea of a homogeneous global 'capitalist mode of production' is not plausible. It would make more sense to study various different combinations of capital accumulation, market types, gift economies, everyday routines and lifeworld habits. Then a Marx-inspired approach is able to relate the transformation of societies to concepts such as commodification, exploitation, globalisation, social inequality, fictitious capital and financial capital accumulation regimes.[57]

Critique of Capitalism beyond the Labour Theory of Value

In terms of the analysis of the production of added value and the increasingly organic composition of capital, Marx is situated in the context of factory capitalism and working world of the nineteenth century. There are still a number of authors today who consider labour value theory to be fundamentally valid and updateable; in my view, it makes far more sense to examine the rise of financial market capitalism as the emergence of a new regime of capital accumulation that requires a new value theory. Over recent decades, 'fictitious capital', referred to by Marx in the context of stock exchanges and the creation of credit, has gained overwhelming dominance.[58] The term 'financialisation' has made it possible to conceptualise the process by which the managing class has seized a growing share of aggregate value added.[59] It also shows how the shareholder

---

55 Christian Papilloud, "MAUSS: Mouvement Anti-Utilitariste dans les Sciences Sociales," in *Kultur: Theorien der Gegenwart*, eds. Stephan Moebius and Dirk Quadflieg (Wiesbaden: VS Verlag für Sozialwissenschaften, 2011), 394–408.

56 Wimmer, *Das Kapital.*

57 Michael Brie and Claus Thomasberger, "Die neue grosse Transformation," *Blätter für deutsche und internationale Politik*, 3 (2019): 119–123.

58 Jens Beckert, *Imagined Futures: Fictional Expectations and Capitalist Dynamics* (Cambridge/Mass: HUP, 2016).

59 Greta R Krippner, "The Financialization of the American Economy," in *Socio-economic Review* 3 (2005): 173–208.

value maxim has reversed the labour theory of value, because appreciation in value and the capitalisation of the stock exchanges is interpreted exclusively as a consequence of investor activity.[60] This assumption can be considered as a productive fiction, causing real effects and being one of the major causes of increasing inequality of distribution of income and wealth in most countries.

Luc Boltanski and Eve Chiapello have described this 'new spirit of capitalism' in detail. In another study entitled *Enrichissement* ('Enrichment'), Boltanski and Arnau Esquerre advance the thesis that in recent decades the accumulation of capital has been reconfigured, with far-reaching consequences.[61] The theory is that it is no longer mass production and a correspondingly 'throw-away'-society that produce the dynamic of economic growth but an appreciation in the value of the past, which then becomes a scarcity factor and is instrumentalised as a resource for increasing value all over the place. Anything seen as 'heritage', 'vintage' or 'historical' is integrated in a value-creating narrative and appreciates in esteem and consequently in monetary worthiness across the whole spectrum of commodified objects, from rare specimens, connoisseur antiques, and cult works of art at record-breaking prices to 'historical' city quarters and buildings. The combination of tradition, security and exclusivity deepens class divisions and represents the transition from an imagined future (as the driver of added value production) to a valourised past (as the trigger of increasing value). Boltanski and Esquerre point out the 'statistical indeterminacy' of this process; they assume that the 'national accounts' (or 'national accounting') that was developed in the course of the twentieth century is not up to adequately measuring these new value-added chains that are intimately interwoven with stories and rituals. There is a parallel to be drawn here with Marx's unwillingness to provide his theorems with a statistical basis (identified by Piketty). Just as it would have been helpful if Marx had paid more attention to quantification, it is important today for historians writing from an interdisciplinary angle to combine cultural approaches about new forms of wealth production with purposeful empirical and statistical research strategies.

The accumulation regime described by Boltanski and Esquerre certainly does not represent the main vector of contemporary societal evolution. Rather it comes in stark contrast to the huge increases in factory capitalism and proletarianisation currently observed in many regions of the world. For several de-

60 Jakob Tanner, "Wirtschaften, Wertlogik und die 'Religion des Kapitals'," in *Wirtschaften. Kulturwissenschaftliche Perspektiven*, eds. Karl Braun et. al. (Marburg: MAKUFEE, 2019), 91–108.
61 Luc Boltanski, Ève Chiapello, *The new spirit of capitalism* (London: Verso 2007); Luc Boltanski and Arnaud Esquerre, *Enrichissement: Une critique de la marchandise* (Paris: Gallimard, 2017).

cades, diverse political factions have promoted industrialisation processes which can be analysed using Marx's tools.[62] Similarly, applying a broader concept of 'labour' inspired by Marx could be a promising way of cataloguing the growing importance of reproductive and care work, as well as the seemingly limitless reserves of informal employment, jobs in the shadow economy and other types of invisible work.[63] It can also be applied to the rise of 'human capital' and the proliferation of micro-businesses around the world and the analysis of persistent forms of slavery and many types of bonded labour.[64] Any attempt to write a global history of labour and work is doomed to fail unless it includes these worldwide and widely ramified power structures and inequalities, (neo)colonial domination techniques and international capital markets, while remaining aware of the relational concept of capitalism.[65] In the context of global warming, the concept of a 'capitalocene' is also gaining explanatory power because, in contrast to the popular catchword 'anthropocene', which represents the causation complex of climate change in terms of general human activity, it embraces the power structures of a resource-intensive economic growth that externalises both hazardous work processes and pollutants, thereby creating 'toxic commons'.[66]

Such an attempt to assemble a toolbox of different approaches to 'Marx beyond Marx' and to use them in innovative ways will no longer cling to Marx as its principal authority.[67] The 'theoretical practice' of the past 150 years which was inspired by Marx has produced many ideas that he as the 'spiritus rector' of Marxism had not thought of or had not thought through. Thompson, the British

---

62 As far as such processes are still regarded as achievements of a "Marxism-Leninism", such theories must not be treated as explanans, but as explanandum.

63 Brigitta Bernet and Jakob Tanner, eds., *Ausser Betrieb: Metamorphosen der Arbeit in der Schweiz* (Zürich: Limmat-Verlag, 2015).

64 See also: The Global Slavery Index: http://www.globalslaveryindex.org/ and the Report "The Global Slavery Index 2014": http://d1p5uxokz2c0lz.cloudfront.net/wp-content/uploads/2014/11/Global_Slavery_Index_2014_final_lowres.pdf. Accessed April 21, 2020. For new approaches see: Alessandro Stanziani, *Bondage: Labor and Rights in Eurasia from the Sixteenth to the Early Twentieth Centuries* (New York: Berghahn, 2014).

65 The leading journal in the field is called "International Labor and Working-Class History". Marcel van der Linden, "The Promise and Challenges of Global Labor History," *International Labor and Working-Class History*, 82 (2012): 57–76.

66 Jason W. Moore, *Anthropocene or Capitalocene? Nature, History, and the Crisis of Capitalism* (Oakland: PM Press, 2016); Erik Loomis, *Out of Sight. The Long and Disturbing Story of Corporations Outsourcing Catastrophe* (New York: The New Press, 2015).

67 Marcel van der Linden and Karl Heinz Roth, eds., *Über Marx hinaus: Arbeitsgeschichte und Arbeitsbegriff in der Konfrontation mit den globalen Arbeitsverhältnissen des 21. Jahrhunderts* (Berlin: Assoziation A, 2009); Antonio Negri, *Marx Beyond Marx. Lessons on the Grundrisse* (New York: Autonomedia, 1991).

Marxist who aspired to a cultural history of the social, expressed this by saying "Marx is on our side; we are not on the side of Marx."[68] This partisan statement has an epistemological flipside. The reason why Marx has remained relevant is not because he paved a way from the nineteenth century to the present, but because in his infallible sense for exploitation and the global scope of the problems he addressed, his ideas have remained productive for the kind of theoretical state of the art research carried out nowadays on this planet under the terms set by digital capitalism. This explains why once again more smoke is rising over the volcanic cataracts of Marxism. And Marx is still standing out there in front with a smoking gun.

---

68 Quoted from: Stephen Henry Rigby, *Marxism and History: A Critical Introduction* (Manchester: MUP, 1987), 12.

Brigitta Bernet

The Postwar Marxist Milieu of Microhistory

Heterodoxy, Activism and the Formation of a Critical Historiographical Perspective

It always annoyed Carlo Ginzburg when his 1976 microhistory classic *The Cheese and the Worms* was referred to as a catalyst for the historiographical 'cultural turn' toward postmodern arbitrariness.[1] It was Eric Hobsbawm, of all people, who judged that it marked the demise of Marxist historical culture, which had still been vibrant in the early 1970s. In his autobiography, Hobsbawm singled out microhistory as a particularly clear expression of the cultural turn, which he maintained had caused historiography to abandon one of its main principles, namely to distinguish between the important and the trivial.[2] Even now, the cultural turn is often still associated with a depoliticisation of history. This view sees the focus on the value of common human subjects with their acts of agency and interpretation closely linked to the decline of criticism and of politics. In the rather sharp assessment of Wolfgang Reinhard, microhistory is a science that legitimises a post-modern individualistic society in which people focus only on their 'narrow private happiness' and adapt to the anonymous processes of power.[3]

Such assessments conflict sharply with how the pioneers of microhistory understood their work. Ginzburg wanted *The Cheese and the Worms* to be explicitly

---

1 Carlo Ginzburg, "Following the Tracks of Israel Bertuccio," in *Threads and Traces: True False Fictive*, ed. Carlo Ginzburg (Berkeley: University of California Press, 2012), 126–136; Carlo Ginzburg, "Microhistory: Two or Three Things I Know about it," *Critical Inquiry* 20, no. 1 (Autumn, 1993): 10–35, 31. Regarding this assessment, see also Richard J. Evans, *In Defense of History* (New York, London: Norton, 1999), 162; Franklin R. Ankersmit, "Historiography and Postmodernism," *History and Theory* 28 (1989): 137–153, 143 and 149; Matti Peltonen, "How Marginal are the Margins Today? On the Historiographical Place of Microhistory," in *Microhistory and the Picaresque Novel: A First Exploration into Commensurable Practices*, ed. Binne de Haan and Konstantin Mierau (Newcastle upon Tyne: Cambridge Scholar Publishing, 2014), 29–46, 37.
2 Eric Hobsbawm, *Interesting Times: A Twentieth-century Life* (London: Allen Lane, 2002), 294.
3 Wolfgang Reinhard, *Lebensformen Europas: Eine historische Kulturanthropologie* (Munich: Beck C. H., 2004), 31. See also Thomas Kroll, "Die Anfänge der Microstoria: Methodenwechsel, Erfahrungswandel und transnationale Rezeption in der europäischen Historiographie der 1970er und 1980er Jahre," in *Perspektiven durch Retrospektiven: Wirtschaftsgeschichtliche Beiträge*, ed. Jeanette Granda and Jürgen Schreiber (Cologne: Böhlau, 2013), 267–287. Similarly also Kalle Pihlainen, "The End of Oppositional History?," *Rethinking History: The Journal of Theory and Practice* 15, no. 4 (2011): 463–488.

https://doi.org/10.1515/9783110677744-005

understood in terms of a "concept of class structure" in the tradition of Marx and Gramsci.[4] The political undertones of his work did not remain hidden from contemporary reviewers either. The American early-modern historian Anne Jacobson Schutte, for example, did not conceal her surprise at her Italian colleague's air of leftist provocation. For non-Italians, the way Ginzburg at times laid his political cards on the table was 'disturbing,' she noted in a 1976 review.[5] The Turin group around Giovanni Levi also illustrates the fact that this outsider perception fully matched the insider view of actors at the time. As pointed out by Levi's long-term colleague Maurizio Gribaudi, in the 1970s microhistory was less of an academic project and more of a political intervention in the debates of the Marxist Left.[6] In various interviews Levi himself similarly emphasised that he always understood his work to be primarily political and only secondarily as academic historiography.[7]

My chapter takes this paradoxical assessment with respect to the politically critical content of microhistory as an occasion to elucidate some of the contexts and constellations in which the approach took shape and also intervened.[8] In contrast to today's often-hasty equation of cultural history with depoliticisation, in the following section I portray the approach as part of the Italian Left's debates on Marxist self-understanding during the 1950s and 1960s and thus also focus on the leftist milieu in which microhistory developed. Apart from a few general remarks, I refrain from outlining the specifics of the approach itself, since numerous rigorous and concise accounts already exist.[9] Instead, I seek

---

4 Carlo Ginzburg, *The Cheese and the Worms: The Cosmos of a Sixteenth-Century Miller*, trans. John Tedeschi and Anne Tedeschi (Baltimore: John Hopkins University Press, 1992), xxiv.

5 Anne Jacobson Schutte, "Carlo Ginzburg," *The Journal of Modern History* 48 (1976): 296–315, 299 and 307.

6 Maurizio Gribaudi, "La lunga marcia della microstoria," in *Microstoria: A venticinque anni da "L'eredità immateriale,"* ed. Paola Lanaro (Milano: Franco Angeli, 2011), 10; Giovanni Levi, "Il piccolo, il grande, il piccolo," *Meridiana* 10 (1990): 211–234, 225.

7 Giovanni Levi, "On Microhistory," in *New Perspectives on Historical Writing*, ed. Peter Burke (Cambridge: Polity Press, 2001), 97–119, 97; Consejo de Redacción, "Entrevista con Giovanni Levi," *Salud mental y cultura* 71 (1999): 483–499, 488.

8 The intellectual history of microhistory has not yet been written. For interesting hints in this direction see Carlos Antonio Aguirre Rojas, *Microhistoria italiana: Modo de empleo* (Rosario: Prohistoria Ediciones, 2017); Alessandro Casellato, "L'orecchio e l'occhio: Storia orale e microstoria," *Italia contemporaneo* 275 (2014): 255–292; Francesca Trivellato, "Microstoria/ Microhistoire/ Microhistory," *French Politics, Culture & Society* 33 (2015): 122–134; Gribaudi, "La lunga Marcia"; Kroll, "Die Anfänge."

9 Good introductions are available from Henrique Espada Lima, *A micro-história italiana: Escalas, indícios e singularidades* (Rio de Janeiro: Civilização Brasileira, 2006); Sigurdur Gylfi Mag-

to foreground the political strategies, social contexts and intellectual conflicts that shaped the historical initiatives of the Left and played an important role in the formation of the microhistorical perspective.

First I investigate Marxist historical culture in postwar Italy as fostered within the context of the two left-wing parties – the Italian Communist Party (PCI) and Italian Socialist Party (PSI) – which were united in the Popular Democratic Front until 1956. As I show next, the interpretations and understanding of history were largely under the influence of Antonio Gramsci, whose deliberations on culture and hegemony motivated various revisions of Italian history. Third, using the example of the so-called folklore debate of the 1950s, I show how the critiques leveled by unorthodox Marxists at the PCI's elitist and nationalist views of politics translated into new conceptions of history and its practice. Turning to Ernesto de Martino, I focus on a protagonist of this debate, whose historical-anthropological approaches came to be adopted by microhistory. Fourth, looking at the Turin group around Giovanni Levi and at Carlo Ginzburg, I show how experiences in the political sphere contributed to changes of historiographical perspectives. In general, I seek to recall the connections to Marxism that played a constitutive role in the rise of microhistory and thereby contribute to the historicisation and repoliticisation of the cultural turn.[10]

Marxist Historical Culture of the Popular Front

New historiographical perspectives neither arise from an accumulation of knowledge nor do they appear out of thin air. Rather, they too are socially situated and their function – related to the respective social contexts of their deployment – can always change. As an important medium for the self-description and self-reassurance of groups, historiography is subject to more than merely internal rules of scholarship. Its acceptance also substantially depends on the plausibility of the meaning it provides for those collectives to which historiography – in its

---

nússon and István M. Szijártó, ed., *What is Microhistory? Theory and Practice* (London,New York: Routledge, 2013).

10 This article is part of an ongoing research project. In terms of source material, the article is based on major microhistorical works, biographical texts, and interviews with/from Simona Cerutti, Maurizio Gribaudi, Carlo Ginzburg, Giovanni Levi and other persons associated with the development of microhistory.

broadest sense as historical culture – invariably refers.[11] Particularly in the labour movement and other left-wing social movements, the reference to history is crucial. A 'historicist prism' already became ensconced in the political culture of the Left at an early stage. "Much of what is spoken within the Left is spoken in history," notes David Mayer aptly in this regard. Whether for the formation of its own collectives or the legitimation of its actions, within the Left history is one of the main currencies for negotiating ideas, fundamental hopes and internal differences.[12]

Although left-wing historical culture is not fully defined by Marxist-inspired historiography, Karl Marx in any case serves as an influential reference point. His understanding of history, first invoked by social and political movements and parties and later by Communist regimes, consists of various elements. One crystallisation point for Marxist historical debates of the twentieth century was surely the question (long since central elsewhere as well) of the tension between individuals and society. Marx had this tension in mind when stating in *The Eighteenth Brumaire of Louis Bonaparte* that "men make their own history, but they do not make it just as they please; they do not make it under circumstances chosen by themselves, but under circumstances directly encountered, given and transmitted from the past."[13] Thus, proceeding from Marx, either of these aspects can take center stage: the concrete historical practices of people and their opportunities for action, appropriation, resistance, struggle and intervention; or the structures, social constraints and supraindividual determinants and mechanisms that precondition the actions of individuals. Viewed from the first 'subjective' observation point, analysis begins with the actions of individuals and their experiences. However, from the second 'objective' position, these individual actions and experiences appear as the product of social structures, technological-material artifacts and sociocultural norms, which are consequently where the analysis must begin.[14]

---

11 Still fundamentally relevant: Maurice Halbwachs, *Les cadres sociaux de la mémoire* (Paris: Presses Universitaires de France, 1952); Peter Burke, "History as Social Memory," in *Varieties of Cultural History*, ed. Peter Burke (Ithaca, NY: Cornell University Press, 1997), 43–59.

12 David Mayer, "Contrahistorias – historische Deutungen und geschichtspolitische Strategien der Linken im Wandel," in *Vielstimmige Vergangenheiten: Geschichtspolitik in Lateinamerika*, ed. Bertold Molden and David Mayer (Vienna: LIT-Verlag, 2009), 125–148, 132.

13 Karl Marx, "The Eighteenth Brumaire of Louis Bonaparte," in Karl Marx and Frederick Engels, *Collected Works*, vol. XI (New York: International Publishers, 1979), 103–198, 103.

14 Lutz Raphael, *Geschichtswissenschaft im Zeitalter der Extreme: Theorien, Methoden, Tendenzen von 1900 bis zur Gegenwart* (Munich: Beck C.H., 2010), 117–137.

The second position dominated orthodox Marxist historiography from the 1920s and into the 1960s, epitomised by the historical materialism of the Communist Party of the Soviet Union (CPSU), where history appeared as a teleological sequence of progressive epochs determined by material factors and was analysed using concepts such as relations of production and productive forces as well as base and superstructure.[15] Similar priorities, however, were also fostered by structuralist and systemic interpretations within the framework of Western Marxism, flourishing, for example, in the postwar academic milieu of France.[16] In the 1920s, Marxist approaches increased their influence in Italian historiography as well. Yet a special feature of Italian Marxism (from Antonio Labriola to Antonio Gramsci) is that it developed in the context of the predominant idealist tradition of Benedetto Croce and remained committed to the primacy of the political – even in its historiography.[17]

The 'Italian Road to Socialism' and the Rewriting of History

To better understand the historiographical breakthroughs of the 1950s and 1960s and thus the origins of microhistory – meaning here its ties to the political (historical) culture of the Left – it is helpful to look at the configuration of powers after 1943, since it engendered many of the visions of history that shaped leftist political culture into the 1960s. So let us look back to 1943 as the antifascist forces (from communists to liberals) united as the National Liberation Committee and took up armed resistance against German troops and Italian fascists. A substantial number of communists and socialists, who comprised the majority in the struggle for liberation, associated the Italian resistance movement (*Resistenza)* with the goal of socialist revolution. The transition to socialism seemed palpably near.[18] However, when Palmiro Togliatti – the general secretary of the

15 Helmut Fleischer, *Marxism and History*, trans. Eric Mosbacher (New York: Harper, 1974); David Mayer, "Lokomotive Zwei Neun Drei – Marxismus, Historiographie und Fortschrittsparadigma," *Österreichische Zeitschrift für Geschichtswissenschaften* 20 (2009): 13–41, 17.

16 Perry Anderson, *Considerations on Western Marxism* (London: New Left Books, 1976).

17 Daniela Coli, "Idealismo e marxismo nella storiografia italiana degli anni '50 e '60," in *La storiografia contemporanea: Indirizzi e problemi*, ed. Pietro Rossi (Milan: Il Saggatore, 1987), 39–58; Paolo Favilli, *Marxismo e storia: Saggio sull'innovazione storiografica in Italia (1945–1970)* (Milan: Franco Angeli, 2006).

18 Paul Ginsborg, *A History of Contemporary Italy: Society and Politics 1943–1988* (London: Penguin Books, 1990), 39–71.

Italian Communist Party, banned under Benito Mussolini – returned from Russian exile in March 1944, he did not produce any plans for revolution. Given the emerging world order of the Cold War, in which Italy fell within the Western zone of influence, Moscow failed to provide any support for revolutionary activities. As in neighbouring Greece, the danger of a return to monarchy existed in Italy as well. Togliatti clearly understood that the objective preconditions for seizing power according to the model of the October Revolution did not obtain.[19] In light of this situation, he found himself compelled to perform a political about-face, the so-called Salerno turn (*svolta di Salerno*). Against substantial resistance from its own ranks, the PCI committed itself, alongside all of the antifascist parties, to joining a national unity government, disarming the *Resistenza*, and working out a democratic constitution. Togliatti subsequently propagated an 'Italian Road to Socialism,' which was supposed to bring about a new and better type of democracy (*democrazia progressiva*) that would enable the working class to become the leading political force. In taking this road, the PCI pursued a dual strategy (*doppiezza*), working on the one hand to create bourgeois-democratic conditions, rebuild the economy, and modernise society, and on the other hand holding fast to the project of a longer-term socialist transformation.[20]

The influence of the Cold War increased the country's social divide, on one side a deeply rooted Catholic tradition with the presence of the Vatican and a strong Christian-democratic party, and on the other the simultaneous existence of the largest communist party of the West, which was shut out of government after the Christian Democratic Party (DC) waged its 1948 election campaign as an anticommunist crusade. Within this divide, the PCI developed into a mass party that soon dominated the opposition. In this constellation, politics was also always politics of history. For communists and socialists, the rewriting and revision of Italian history formed a central political imperative.[21] This became manifest not only in the PCI's Cultural Commission founded in 1948,

---

19 Joseph V. Femia, "Gramsci, the 'Via Italiana,' and the Classical Marxist-Leninist Approach to Revolution," *Government and Opposition* 14 (1979): 65–95; Luca Baldissara, "Tra governo e opposizione: Il ruolo del PCI nella costituzione della democrazia in Italia," in *Il PCI nell'Italia repubblicana 1943–1991*, ed. Roberto Gualtieri (Rome: Carocci, 2001), 141–180.

20 Critical of this strategy: Pietro Di Loreto, *Togliatti e la "doppiezza": Il PCI tra democrazia e insurrezione (1944–49)* (Bologna: Il Mulino, 1991): Philip Cooke, *The Legacy of the Italian Resistance* (Basingstoke: Palgrave Macmillan, 2011), 17.

21 Gilda Zazzara, *La storia a sinistra: Ricerca e impegno politico dopo il fascismo* (Roma-Bari: Laterza, 2011). For the broader context see: Andrea Mariuzzo, *Communism and Anti-Communism in Early Cold War Italy: Language, Symbols, and Myths* (Manchester: Manchester University Press, 2018), 74–130.

which in the person of Emilio Sereni was directed by a historian who declared historiography along with cinematography as the commission's most important mainstay.[22] Emphatically demanded as a necessity by communists and socialists, the project to retell and restudy the history of Italy from the perspective of the working class and its struggles was supported by various journals and institutions – for example: the journal *Movimento operaio*, established in 1949 and exclusively dedicated to the history of the workers' movement; *Movimento operaio e socialista*, a journal founded in 1955; and the journals *Rivista storica del socialismo* and *Problemi del socialismo*, both founded in 1957. Committed to the same objective was the Biblioteca Giangiacomo Feltrinelli, created in 1949 and renamed Istituto Giangiacomo Feltrinelli in 1956, which collected material on the history of the workers' movement and encouraged research activity. So too was the Istituto Gramsci, founded in 1951 in Rome by the PCI as a party research institute, which in 1959 began publishing *Studi storici*, a prestigious specialised journal for Italian historical scholarship.[23] History was also prominent within the bountiful journalistic landscape of the left-wing intelligentsia, which viewed itself as part of the country's cultural renewal. The journal *Società* – the intellectual flagship of the PCI founded in 1945 and likewise directed by a historian in the person of Gastone Manacorda – regularly weighed in on disputes over historiographical interpretations.[24] Being fostered within this broader context – even by the Einaudi publishing house, which re-envisioned and surveyed the country's traditions in large-scale publication projects on Italian history, art history, and literary history – was a new Marxist historical culture directed against the old Catholic power elites and the dominance of bourgeois middle-class intellectuals.[25]

The Marxist historiography promoted in the postwar period distinguished itself from the then dominant historical approach of the liberal-conservative Benedetto Croce. Nonetheless, the latter's 'ethical-political' understanding of history also remained operative in Marxist historiography, as documented, for example, by the great importance attached to the organised workers' movement – its po-

---

22 Albertina Vittoria, "La commissione culturale del PCI dal 1948 al 1956," *Studi storici* 31 (1990): 135–170. Ernesto Galli della Loggia and Raffaele Romanelli, "Età contemporanea: Storia del capitalismo o storiografia 'volgare'?," *Quaderni storici* 22 (1973): 20–49, 42.

23 Zazzara, *La storia a sinistra*. See also: Bruno Groppo, "Die Kommunistische Partei Italiens und ihre Historiographien," *Jahrbuch für Historische Kommunismusforschung* (2013): 191–210.

24 Luisa Mangoni, "'Società': Storia e storiografia nel secondo dopoguerra," *Italia contemporanea* 33 (1981): 39–58.

25 Luisa Mangoni, *Pensare i libri: La casa editrice Einaudi dagli anni Trenta agli anni Sessanta* (Turin: Bollati Boringhieri, 1999).

litical institutions, parties, and leaders.[26] This understanding was also expressed in the myth of the *Resistenza*, which was elevated to the master narrative that legitimised the parliamentary democratic republic.[27] The Communists were assigned a major role in this interpretation, in which Mussolini alone was guilty for the war and the national struggle for liberation was borne by the antifascist masses. Opposing critics within its own ranks who in the wake of the 1946 amnesty laws decreed by Justice Minister Togliatti spoke about a "betrayed resistance", even the PCI was anxious about maintaining the official account of antifascist unity. This account essentially described the resistance as a popular movement led by the Communists, who in a guerilla war effectively liberated Italy from the *nazifascisti*. What's more, Palmiro Togliatti even spoke in the same breath of the *Resistenza* as a second *Risorgimento* – a genuine national popular movement that now under communist leadership could finally realise the project of Italian unification, which had been started in the nineteenth century but betrayed by the bourgeoisie.[28]

Gramsci and Marxist Historical Culture

The most important reference for the postwar Italian Left's understanding of culture and history was surely Antonio Gramsci, the co-founder and general secretary of the Italian Communist Party, who died in 1937. Until 1948, Gramsci was largely unknown to many left-wing intellectuals. In that same year when Togliatti began working with the Einaudi publishing house to bring out the *Prison Notebooks* written by Gramsci while imprisoned by the fascist regime, the latter's idealistic and voluntaristic interpretations of Marxism were widely received. Setting up a contrast to the mechanistic determinism of the Second International, while in Mussolini's prisons Gramsci had tried to explain why the October Revolution had been possible in the East, whereas in the West, despite political and eco-

---

26 Coli, "Idealismo e marxismo," 41; Groppo, "Die Kommunistische Partei Italiens," 195.

27 Filippo Focardi, *La guerra della memoria: La Resistenza nel dibattito politico italiano dal 1945 a oggi* (Rome: GLF editori Laterza, 2005).

28 Alexander Höbel, "Storia d'Italia e PCI nell'elaborazione di Palmiro Togliatti," in *Il Risorgimento: Un'epopea? Per una ricostruzione storico-critica*, ed. Cristina Carpinelli and Vittorio Gioiello (Milan: Zambon editore, 2012), 185–205; Eva Müller, "Mythen und Gegenmythen: Zur öffentlichen Wahrnehmung der Rolle der italienischen Kommunisten in Antifaschismus und Resistenza," in *Wissen im Mythos? Die Mythisierung von Personen, Institutionen und Ereignissen sowie deren Wahrnehmung im wissenschaftlichen Diskurs*, ed. Christina Böker et al. (Munich: Akademische Verlagsgesellschaft, 2018), 159–188, 165.

nomic crises, capitalism reestablished its power, albeit it as a totalitarian fascist variant. Key Gramscian concepts for resolving this question were "cultural hegemony" and "passive revolution." His deliberations on the function of culture could be suitably deployed to provide a solid theoretical foundation for the already adopted 'Italian Road to Socialism.' Gramsci also introduced a cultural dimension to Marxist analysis that effectively anticipated the so-called cultural turn, opening up ideas and critical perspectives that even today are gainfully used as a basis for engaged cultural research.[29]

Cultural Hegemony and the Interpretation of the *Risorgimento*

After losing the election in 1948, the Left could draw faith from Gramsci that a society such as Italy, which was backward according to Marxist criteria, could be revolutionised starting from the superstructure. With a view to the differences between developments in the East and West, in the 1920s and 1930s Gramsci developed the concept of 'cultural hegemony'. He uses it to describe the institutions and strategies, apart from pure manipulation, that ruling powers use to gain the support (or at least the acceptance) of the ruled. Gramsci viewed the central role played by the Catholic Church in the hegemony of the dominant classes as a special feature of Italy. For this reason it seemed that the seizure of power by the proletariat required more than simply the occupation of key political and military positions and the take-over of economic capital; this needed to be preceded by the capture of political and ideological hegemony in the society by the revolutionary forces.[30]

The effort to gain cultural hegemony also included working on history. In the first prison notebooks Gramsci had dismantled Italy's foundational myth and portrayed the *Risorgimento* (literally: the Resurgence – the nineteenth-cen-

29 Paul Piccone, "Gramsci's Marxism: Beyond Lenin and Togliatti," *Theory and Society* 3 (1976): 485–512; Perry Anderson, *The Antinomies of Antonio Gramsci* (London: Verso, 2017); Peter Thomas, *The Gramscian Moment: Philosophy, Hegemony and Marxism* (Leiden: Brill, 2009); George Hoare and Nathan Sperber, *An Introduction to Antonio Gramsci: His Life, Thought and Legacy* (London: Bloomsbury, 2015).

30 See for example: Antonio Gramsci, "The State," in *Antonio Gramsci: Selections from the Prison Notebooks*, ed. and trans. Quintin Hoare and Geoffrey Nowell Smith (New York: International Publishers, 1971) 257–264, 258; Antonio Gramsci, "The Formation of the Intellectuals," in *Antonio Gramsci: Selections from the Prison Notebooks*, 5–14.

tury movement for Italian unification) as a "passive revolution."[31] According to this view, the new Italy was established in 1861 through revolutions imposed by the elite from above, even though the preceding uprisings came from below. With the Expedition of the Thousand, Garibaldi admittedly liberated southern Italy from Spanish Bourbon rule, but he failed to convert the demands of the popular masses – particularly the southern Italian peasants – into a program for government. Italy therefore remained a constitutional monarchy in the hands of a 'historical bloc' consisting of industrialists and large landowners. The industrialised North advanced its development at the expense of the agrarian South and the old elites retained their privileges. In order to secure these privileges against the demands of the workers' movement, the elite then handed political power to the fascists in 1922. All told, according to Gramsci, the revolutions of 1861 did not – as claimed – unify Italy but rather divided it into two classes.[32] The explicit objective of the *Risorgimento* – Italian unification – was therefore unrealised. Its realisation depended on overcoming class antagonism through an "active" socialist revolution. Togliatti's PCI took up this idea when it called the party the legitimate heir to the *Risorgimento* and its goal of national unity.[33] In doing so the PCI inscribed itself symbolically into the republican postwar order and reiterated its commitment to parliamentarianism. But this self-portrayal also resulted in an ever more nation-centric Marxist historiography that searched the past for continuities with the *Risorgimento* to demonstrate the historically evolved role of the PCI as the party of national unity. In the process, other aspects relevant to labour history were winnowed out. These included the history of conflicts within the Communist International; various currents of the workers' movement such as anarchists, proto-socialists and syndicalists; the deeply anti-statist tradition of the working class and its internationalism;

---

31 Antonio Gramsci, "The Concept of Passive Revolution," in *Antonio Gramsci: Selections from the Prison Notebooks*, 106–114.

32 Antonio Gramsci, "The Problem of Political Leadership in the Formation and Development of the Nation and the Modern State in Italy," in *Antonio Gramsci: Selections from the Prison Notebooks*, 55–90; Jane Schneider, "The Dynamics of Neo-orientalism in Italy (1848–1995)," in *Italy's Southern Question: Orientalism in One Country*, ed. Jane Schneider (Oxford: Berg, 1998), 1–26; Giuseppe Galasso, *Il mezzogiorno: Da "questione meridionale" a "problema" aperta* (Manduria: Piero Lacaita, 2005); Gabriella Gribaudi, "Images of the South: The Mezzogiorno as Seen by Insiders and Outsiders," in *The New History of the Italian South*, ed. Robert Lumley and Jonathan Morris (Exeter: University of Exeter Press, 1997), 83–114

33 John A. Davies, "Rethinking the Risorgimento?," in *Risorgimento in Modern Italian Culture: Revisiting the Nineteenth-Century Past in History, Narrative, and Cinema*, ed. Norma Bouchard (Madison: Fairleigh Dickinson University Press, 2005), 27–56.

and the co-founder of the PCI, Amadeo Bordiga, who was expelled from the party in 1930.[34]

The New Historiographical Survey of the 'Southern Question'

The ambition to become a genuine national force was crucial to Togliatti's strategy for the PCI. Against this backdrop, the unfinished business of the 'Southern Question' was vital to the communists' reading of Italian history. As early as the 1920s, Gramsci had described the split between North and South as the biggest problem confronting the working class in devising its strategy to seize power in Italy.[35] Since the establishment of the central Italian state in 1861, the *questione meridionale* – the enormous economic and cultural differences between the industrial North and agrarian South – posed a problem of national significance. While northern Italy had expanded economically since unification, the southern part of the country remained stagnant as preindustrial and quasi-feudal structures remained in place. Under fascism the problem was disavowed, and if it was raised anyway then one ascribed the poverty and distress of southern Italy's rural population to its ostensible biological or moral inferiority.[36] A similar view was also put forward by liberal bourgeois scholars like Benedetto Croce. He classified the inhabitants of the South as "people without history," as "primitive people" who could be objects of anthropological study, but, unlike "civilised people," not subjects of history. And these second-class "living beings who are only zoologically and not historically human beings" needed to be tamed "like

34 Groppo, "Die Kommunistische Partei Italiens," 196; Gianpasquale Santomassimo, "Togliatti e la storia d'Italia," *Studi Storici* 26 (1985): 493–506, 502.

35 Antonio Gramsci, "Some Aspects of the Southern Question," in *Antonio Gramsci: Selections from Political Writings (1921–1929)*, trans. and ed. Quintin Hoare (New York: International Publishers, 1978), 441–462.

36 Nelson J. Moe, "Questione Meridionale," in *Encyclopedia of Italian Literary Studies*, ed. Gaetana Marrone, Paolo Puppa, and Luca Somigli (New York: Routledge, 2007), 1531–1535; David Forgacs, *Italy's Margins: Social Exclusion and Nation Formation since 1861* (Cambridge: Cambridge University Press, 2014), 139–196; Ian Chambers, "The 'Southern Question' ... again," in *The Routledge Handbook of Contemporary Italy: History, Politics, Society*, ed. Andrea Mammone et al. (New York: Routledge, 2015), 13–22.

animals," trained through political stimulation and punishment, or allowed to die out.[37]

These assumptions became unsustainable in the course of the peasant insurrections and battles for land that began in 1943. In the Po Valley, the backbone of modern Italian agriculture, rural workers demanded the abolition of large land ownership and the social distribution of production, while landless peasants in the South regularly occupied land to fight for the redistribution and self-administration of the fields of large land owners (*latifondisti*).[38] Interventions by police or soldiers often resulted in bloody revolts. As we shall see, the Left evaluated these revolts in different ways, but the consensus nonetheless prevailed that it was crucially important for the left-wing parties of the North to link up with these mobilisations (which were unprecedented in the history of the Mezzogiorno) and to establish roots in the South. For decades an alliance between the southern Italian rural proletariat and the industrial workers of northern Italy had been a central requirement of the PCI's party program.[39] This alliance also included incorporating the long history of rural protests and uprisings into the history of class struggle. Communist historians like Emilio Sereni, for whom the Southern Question clearly constituted a class issue rooted in the capitalist system, put historiographical revisions of the established picture of the South forward. Sereni's economic-historical studies about post-unification peasant society elucidated the connection between the capitalist transformation of rural areas and the formation of a mass peasant proletariat. His analytical perspective conjoined with political perspectives on the solution of the Southern Question that envisaged both extensive land and structural reforms and the channeling of the peasant movement in the direction of revolutionary democracy.[40]

There was also little doubt (at least among the PCI's top leadership) that the peasants and rural workers could develop a socialist consciousness only through persistent cultural education within the framework of a Marxist-Leninist cadre

---

37 Benedetto Croce, "L'umanità e la natura," in *Benedetto Croce: Filosofia e storiografia*, ed. Stefano Maschietti (Naples: Bibliopolis, 2005), 234 – 236. On Croce see: Domenico Conte, *Weltgeschichte und Pathologie des Geistes: Benedetto Croce zwischen historischem Denken und Krise der Moderne*, trans. Charlotte Voermanek (Leipzig: Leipziger Universitätsverlag, 2007).

38 Ginsborg, *A History of Contemporary Italy*, 122 – 124.

39 Antonello Matteone, "Partito communista e contadini nel mezzogiorno," *Studi storici* 14 (1973): 940 – 952; David Forgacs, "People, Nation and Culture," in *Antonio Gramsci: Selections from Cultural Writings*, ed. David Forgacs and Geoffrey Nowell-Smith (London: Lawrence & Wishart, 1985), 196 – 198.

40 See R. Burr Litchfield, "Introduction to the English Translation," in *History of the Italian Agricultural Landscape*, Emilio Sereni, trans. R. Burr Litchfield (Princeton: Princeton University Press, 1997), xxii – xliv.

party. As has been pointed out by Paul Ginsborg, the leadership of the PCI always remained skeptical about grassroots initiatives in the South. None of the support from communists and socialists at the local level could conceal the fact that headquarters in Rome ultimately viewed self-government as a threat to the intended alliance with the DC. The peasants and rural workers of the South were paternalistically addressed as passive recipients and not as independent producers of culture. Their traditional forms of life, values and beliefs were considered reservoirs of backward, irrational and primitive forms of thought and ways of life that needed to be modernised and overcome.[41]

Before and after Eboli: Carlo Levi, Ernesto de Martino and the *civiltà contadina*

The 1950s witnessed the development of a new dissenting interest in the traditions and ways of life of the subaltern world, which critically distanced itself from the orthodox Marxism of the PCI by refusing to view the South primarily as a problem of cultural or economic backwardness. Published as early as 1945, Carlo Levi's novelistic ethnographic memoir *Christ Stopped at Eboli* (*Cristo si è fermato a Eboli*) played an especially important role in this regard.[42] On the surface, Levi's book records his encounter with the peasant world of Basilicata in southern Italy during his year-long banishment by the fascist regime, describing how he was shipped there in 1935 due to his co-founding role in the antifascist movement "Justice and Freedom" (*Giustizia e Libertà*). But at a deeper level it documents the hopes and fears for post-fascist Italy that he felt as a member of the Action Party (*Partito d'Azione*), which brought together social-liberals and socialists for the collective struggle against fascism.

The memoir draws much of its energy from the contrast between the two irreconcilable experiential worlds: on one side the self-serving and envious local bourgeoisie (*signori*) of the villages, who were all members of the Fascist Party and saw themselves as historical actors; on the other the peasants (*contadini*), who were neither fascists nor even Catholics, because for them both of these belonged to a different world – the world of power and the state. Levi portrayed the mountain villages of the South as places where the peasants had lived in poverty

41 Ginsborg, *A History of Contemporary Italy*, 63.

42 Carlo Levi, *Christ Stopped at Eboli*, trans. Frances Frenayc (New York: Farrar, Straus and Company, 1947); Angiolina Arru, "Anthropologische Neuorientierung in Italien," *Historische Anthropologie* 3 (1995): 168–177.

and resignation for centuries, without expecting the slightest thing from politics or taking note of official history. They distrusted any type of authority because they had only ever experienced it as oppression. Levi described his encounter with these people as a journey to another world: a world of misery and superstition where numerous heathen and magical practices continued to live alongside Christian beliefs. However, Levi nonetheless viewed this mythical-archaic culture in a positive light. In the peasant civilisation (*civiltà contadina)* he saw the positive antidote to the Italian central state.

Published just after the war, Levi's book was an attack on an ideology that, while manifest most extremely as fascism, characterised modernity as a whole and divided the world into people of greater and lesser value – masters and slaves – and excluded the latter from history. His critique did not apply merely to the southern policy of the fascists. He knew that similar prejudices were also widespread among left-wing comrades, because their vision of history, saturated by Croce and Marx, kept them from seeing the Southern Question as anything but a developmental problem. In the book's conclusion he then also formulated numerous arguments as to why the Southern Question could not be solved from above – that is, through central government – but needed to be approached from below, namely, by strengthening the autonomy, self-administration, and collective values of the *contadini* at the local level. Unless this occurred, prophesied Levi, the slide of peasant's world into deeper resignation would continue, interrupted only sporadically by despondent uprisings, revolts and brigandage.[43]

Levi's memoir quickly became an international bestseller and reference point for political debates about the Southern Question. The book inspired a popular literary genre, which also included the works of Rocco Scotellaro, Pier Paolo Pasolini, Cesare Pavese and Italo Calvino.[44] Moreover, it marked the beginning of a debate that in the 1950s would turn on the question about the role that traditional popular culture should play in the transition to socialism. Though sparked by the subject of popular literature, the debate was by no means limited solely to literary questions but also concerned issues of political organisation and autonomy, and thus ultimately included the differences looming in the unity of action of the left-wing parties.

43 Carlo Levi, *Christ Stopped at Eboli*, 248–254.

44 Michael Caesar, "Writing and the Real World: Italian Narrative in the Period of Reconstruction," in *The Culture of Reconstruction: European Literature, Thought and Film, 1945–50*, ed. Nicholas Hewitt (New York: Palgrave Macmillan, 1989), 37–50.

Breaking into History: Ernesto de Martino

Forming an important link in the reference chain of this debate were the radical theses on 'progressive folklore' of Ernesto de Martino, an ethnologist and historian of religion from Naples, who came into contact with the experiential world of the peasantry via the *Resistenza.*[45] The realisation that substantial numbers of peasants had supported the guerilla war against the fascists and joined the partisans compelled the left-wing intelligentsia to revise its image of the rural world as backward and reactionary. It now seemed to them that popular peasant culture contained dormant progressive and oppositional energies, which increasingly interested Ernesto de Martino.[46] After joining the resistance and the Action Party in 1943, he served as a member and secretary of the PSI in Bari after the war, where he organised the land battles of the Apulian peasants and rural workers. In 1949 he joined the Communist Party. With his book *The World of Magic (Il mondo magico)* published in 1948, de Martino laid the foundation for Italian anthropology, which became a source of inspiration for a heterodox Marxist historical culture that also included microhistory.[47] This connection becomes especially clear in the early research on witchcraft by Carlo Ginzburg. He traced his interest in peasant culture back to discussions about populism and literary criticism in Pier Paolo Pasolini's journal *Officina* and to de Martino's book, which greatly impressed him as an eighteen-year-old. Ginzburg long remained fascinated by de Martino's radical critique of historicism and Eurocentrism in the writing of history.[48]

Indeed, de Martino called for the radical historicisation of the categories previously used to think about problems such as the Southern Question. He sharply criticised the conventional division of humanity into 'civilised' and 'primitive'

---

45 On Ernesto de Martino see: Dorothy Louise Zinn, "An Introduction to Ernesto de Martino's Relevance for the Study of Folklore," *The Journal of American Folklore* 128 (2015): 3–13; George R. Saunders, "'Critical Ethnocentrism' and the Ethnology of Ernesto De Martino," *American Anthropologist* 95.4 (1993): 875–893.

46 Fabrizio M. Ferrari, *Ernesto De Martino on Religion: The Crisis and the Presence* (New York: Routledge, 2012), 7–27.

47 Ernesto de Martino, *Il mondo magico: Prolegomeni a una storia del magismo* (Torino: Einaudi, 1948); English translation: Ernesto de Martino, *The World of Magic*, trans. Paul Saye White (New York: Pyramid Communications, 1972).

48 Carlo Ginzburg, "Preface to the Italian Edition," in *Clues, Myths, and Historical Method*, ed. Carlo Ginzburg, trans. John and Anne C. Tedeschi (Baltimore: Johns Hopkins University Press, 2013), xv–xx; Carlo Ginzburg, "Qué he aprendido de los antropólogos," *Alteridades* 38 (2009): 131–139, 131–132.

peoples, which recognised culture and history only for the former and with respect to 'primitives' was interested only in seeing their archaism, immobility and irrationality. In his opinion, the supposedly primitive, barbaric and wild – previously falling within the purview of anthropology – needed to be integrated into historical analysis. Influenced by not only Gramsci and Marxism but also his experiences in southern Italy, de Martino did not describe the magico-religious world of the poor peasants as irrational or backward portraying the archaic cults and magical rituals, instead as historically evolved and hence comprehensible elements of an oppressed counterculture: in helpless situations that could not be managed with real-world methods, they offered compensatory options for creating agency.[49] Thus within the resilience of these cultural forms, he detected not only backwardness but also resistance. As de Martino further showed in his study on Lucanian funerary cults, one could not speak of any genuine dominance of the official Catholic religion in the peasant culture of the South.[50] Beneath the culture of church and state imposed from above he found a much older and deeper layer of vibrant popular belief and oral tradition that managed to exist more or less independently from hegemonic high culture. At certain times, however, the subalterns rebelled against the conditions of their own subalternity.

Progressive Folklore

In 1949 when de Martino contributed to the journal *Società* with a call for the renewal of historiography, he felt certain that the present was witnessing such a rebellion and that the fire of the Russian revolution was now flaring up in the then so-called Third World. In the struggles of the peasants in the Mezzogiorno (viewed by many Italians as part of the Third World) and in the anticolonial wars of liberation on other continents, he saw what he believed to be the subaltern masses fighting worldwide for their "entry into history" and to overthrow

---

49 De Martino, *Il Mondo magico*, 193.

50 Ernesto de Martino, *Morte e pianto rituale nel mondo antico: Dal lamento funebre antico al pianto di Maria* (Turin: Einaudi, 1958). The study forms the first part of de Martinos trilogy on the religious history of the South. The other two parts are Ernesto de Martino, *Sud e magia* (Milan: Feltrinelli, 1959) and Ernesto de Martino, *La terra del rimorso: Contributo a una storia religiosa del Sud* (Milan: Il Saggiatore, 1961). Dorothy Louise Zinn has translated the latter two works into English – Ernesto de Martino, *Magic: A Theory from the South*, trans. Dorothy Louise Zinn (Chicago: Hau Books, 2015) and Ernesto de Martino, *The Land of Remorse: A Study of Southern Italian Tarantism*, trans. Dorothy Louise Zinn (London: Free Association Books, 2005).

the order that rendered them subaltern.[51] According to de Martino, since ruling-class hegemony was also secured by historiography, the struggle of subalterns needed to be waged on this field as well, namely, by reincluding and reevaluating as history those elements previously rejected from history as folklore. De Martino advocated a radically new historiography as a political empowerment initiative. But this was not conceived as a one-sided process of adapting popular culture to bourgeois historical culture. Rather, while former objects of folklore were in the process of becoming subjects of history, bourgeois high culture (even Marxism) had to be 'barbarised' – albeit only up to a certain point and just temporarily.[52] In the 1950s under the slogan 'progressive folklore,' de Martino forcefully argued that peasant culture contained potential not only for conservative stabilisation but also for revolutionary progress. Precisely because the masses could learn to understand their cultural forms and history in this vein, folklore held a potential for agency that could guide them to resistance.[53] Another point of contact for this project was Gramsci. In his "Observations on Folklore" (and quite in contrast to statements made elsewhere) Gramsci argued for reading folkloric insights quasi against the grain, that is, differently than intended from above, and using them as 'indirect' sources for an emancipatory historiography.[54] Accordingly, the historical researcher's task was to uncover and document this 'progressive folklore' – the concealed and suppressed popular cultures of resistance and utopias, which accrued not only in magical cults but also in songs, jokes, and rituals – and to use it as a resource for progressive cultural transformation in the present.[55]

---

51 Ernesto de Martino, "Intorno a una storia del mondo popolare subalterno," *Società* 5, no. 3 (1949): 411–35, included in *Il dibattito sul folkore in Italia*, ed. Pietro Clemente, Maria Luisa Meoni, and Massimo Squillacciotti (Milan: Edizioni di cultura popolare, 1976), 63–81.

52 De Martino, "Intorno a una storia del mondo subalterno," 68.

53 Ernesto de Martino, "Il folklore progressive: Note lucane," *Unità* (June 28, 1951): 3; also in *Il dibattito sul folklore in Italia*, ed. Pietro Clemente, Maria Luisa Meoni, and Massimo Squillacciotti (Milan: Edizioni di cultura popolare, 1976), 123–124.

54 Antonio Gramsci, "Observations on folklore," in *The Antonio Gramsci Reader: Selected Writings 1916–1935*, ed. David Forgacs (New York: New York University Press, 2000), 360–362; Antonio Gramsci, "History of the Subaltern Classes: Methodological Criteria," in *Antonio Gramsci: Selections from the Prison Notebooks*, ed. and trans. Quintin Hoare and Geoffrey Nowell Smith (New York: International Publishers, 1971), 52–55. See also: Marcus Green, "Gramsci Cannot Speak: Presentations and Interpretations of Gramsci's Concept of the Subaltern," *Rethinking Marxism* 14, no. 3 (2002): 1–24, 3.

55 Ernesto de Martino, "Gramsci e il folklore nella cultura italiana," *Il Calendario del popolo* 7 (1952): 1109; also in *Il dibattito sul folklore in Italia*, ed. Pietro Clemente, Maria Luisa Meoni, and Massimo Squillacciotti (Milan: Edizioni di cultura popolare, 1976), 123–124.

De Martino's views undoubtedly were at odds with the understanding of the PCI, where folklore was considered a symptom and instrument of servitude and popular beliefs could only be seen as false consciousness. His theses triggered a fierce debate, which in the 1950s became a focal point for the smoldering political differences between the PCI and PSI.[56] The position of the PCI was clear. Cultural Director Mario Alicata was wholly uninterested in any renewal of Marxist culture from below, not to mention its barbarisation. Like other key figures in the Communist Party's cultural policy, such as Ambrogio Donini and Cesare Luporini, he accused de Martino of being an apologist for dangerous "irrational populism." Alicata felt that conceding a rudimentary form of self-consciousness to the peasants was not only wrong but risky because it jeopardised the modernisation of the South.[57] Raniero Panzieri, the cultural secretary of the PSI, viewed this very differently. Replying to Alicata, he criticised the "unbroken paternalism" of the PCI toward subaltern popular culture, which had always defined the North's relationship to the South. In contrast, he elevated the notions of autonomy, authenticity and freedom to inviolable concepts of socialist cultural policy. Instead of being imposed from above, these were supposed to start from the concrete experiences of peasants and workers and proceed from there to reveal prospects for their emancipation and development without negating their history and way of life.[58]

The possibility of detecting forms of resistance in the supposed backwardness of subaltern culture also excited Ginzburg, who had read Gramsci and de

---

56 This debate is documented in Pietro Clemente, Maria Luisa Meoni, and Massimo Squillacciotti, eds., *Il dibattito sul folkore in Italia* (Milan: Edizioni di cultura popolare, 1976) and in Carla Pasquinelli, ed., *Antropologia culturale e questione meridionale: Ernesto De Martino e il dibattito sul mondo popolare subalterno negli anni 1948–1955* (Florence: La Nuova Italia Editrice, 1977). Overviews of the debates are provided by Juan José Gómez Gutiérrez, *The PCI Artists: Antifascism and Communism in Italian Art, 1944–1951* (Cambridge: Cambridge Scholars Publishing, 2015), 82–107; Valerio Salvatore Severino, "Ernesto de Martino nel Pci degli anni Cinquanta tra religione e politica culturale," *Studi storici* 44 (2003): 527–553.

57 Mario Alicata, "Il meridionalismo non si può fermare ad Eboli," *Il dibattito sul folklore in Italia*, ed. Pietro Clemente, Maria Luisa Meoni, and Massimo Squillacciotti (Milan: Edizioni di cultura popolare, 1976), 183–198.

58 Raniero Panzieri, "Cultura e contadini del Sud: Prospettive nuove del meridionalismo dopo il convegno di Matera," in *Il dibattito sul folklore in Italia*, ed. Pietro Clemente, Maria Luisa Meoni, and Massimo Squillacciotti (Milan: Edizioni di cultura popolare, 1976), 235–240. On the position of the PSI see also Mariamargherita Scotti, "Il paradosso dell'autonomia: Traiettorie di intellettuali nel PSI tra anni Cinquanta e Sessanta," in *Aspettando il Sessantotto: Continuità e fratture nelle culture politiche italiane dal 1956 als 1968*, ed. Francesca Chiarotto (Turin: Accademia University Press, 2017), 222–237.

Martino in the 1950s.[59] Recalling the start of his research, Ginzburg pointed out that back then as a new student he found it inspiring to interpret the witch trials as a primitive form of class struggle. He explained how he searched inquisition protocols for the collision of two irreconcilable cultures and at same time drew parallels with the anticolonial independence movements in the underdeveloped zones and countries of what was then the Third World.[60] In his 1972 contribution to the anthology *Storia d'Italia*, Ginzburg applied a conceptual construct inspired by de Martino, Gramsci, and also Mikhail Bakhtin, according to which, beneath the "official religion" of the Catholic Church, there was a much older popular culture containing a "potentially revolutionary principle" nourished by hopes of deliverance and notions of justice – a popular culture which the clergy had always feared and had tried to appropriate or destroy, but had never managed to fully eradicate.[61]

The Political Traces of Microhistory

As Mariamargherita Scotti has recently found, the Marxist discussion about peasant and worker culture was also always concerned about the role of the party and its relationship to the masses. The discussion therefore always included the question of whether the class struggle of the proletariat could occur "spontaneously" and "from below" or whether it needed to be organised from above by the cadre party.[62] As the unity of action of the PCI and PSI began coming apart after 1956 and the onset of de-Stalinisation, Marxist historiographical formulations also eased their narrow orthodox focus on the party and its organisations. The end of the 1950s saw the arrival of a generation of heterodox Marxists who, following in the footsteps of Gramsci and de Martino, proceeded from the assumption of the autonomy of workers and peasants and wanted to strengthened their initiatives and also revise the theory of the party and its connection

59 Carlo Ginzburg, "Preface to the 2013 Edition," in *The Night Battles: Witchcraft and Agrarian Cults in the Sixteenth and Seventeenth Centuries*, ed. Carlo Ginzburg, trans. John and Anne C. Tedeschi (Baltimore: Johns Hopkins Universita Press, 2013), ix–xii, ix.
60 Ginzburg, "Preface to the 2013 Edition," *The Night Battles*, ix–xii.
61 Carlo Ginzburg, "Folklore, magia, religione," in *Storia d'Italia: I caratteri originali*, vol. 1, ed. Ruggiero Romano and Corrado Vivanti (Turin: Einaudi, 1972), 603–676, 611.
62 Mariamargherita Scotti, *Da sinistra: Intellettuali, Partito socialista italiano e organizzazione della cultura (1953–1960)* (Rome: Ediesse, 2011), 23–80, see also Nello Ajello, *Intellettuali e PCI: 1944–1958* (Rome: Laterza, 1979).

to the masses.[63] Going against established historical methods and institutions, they set about reconstructing the oppressed culture and the suppressed memories of the non-hegemonic classes.

Grassroots Counterculture and the History Workshops of the New Left

Associated with this interest in various and sometimes subconscious ways was a new Marxist Left. During the long 1960s, this Left developed not only new movements and forms of struggle but also new interpretations of the past, research practices and institutional structures. The latter included a network throughout northern Italy of history workshops self-described as *circoli di cultura* (cultural circles) or *leghe di cultura* (cultural leagues). They included, for example, the Incontri di Cultura circle, which formed in 1960 in Piacenza around Piergiorgio Bellocchio, who in 1962 began publishing the journal *Quaderni piacentini*, as well as the Lega di Cultura di Piadena started in 1967 by Giuseppe Morandi and Gianfranco Azzali. Also important was the Istituto Ernesto de Martino, established in 1966 in Milan by the historian Gianni Bosio and anthropologist Alberto Cirese and dedicated to the "critical knowledge and alternative presence of the popular and proletarian world." Ernesto de Martino figured here as an impulse behind historical initiatives dedicated to building up and cultivating a subaltern counterculture.[64] A brilliant representative was Gianni Bosio, who since the early 1950s (while still an editor of the journal *Mondo operaio*) had criticised the exclusions and narrow confines of an orthodox Marxist historiography concentrated on elites and the nation. Bosio consequently became a pioneer of Italian oral history and cultural organiser in search of new forms of intermediation between history and popular culture. He organised theatrical events and concert series, published phonograph records, and helped initiate the revival of Italian folk music.[65] Moving within this militant environment between political activism

63 Scotti, "Da sinistra," 425–447.

64 Matteo Rebecchi, "La lega di cultura di Piadena: Cronaca di un'esperienza," *Storie in movimento* 7 (2015): 108–111; Giacomo Pontremoli, *I "Piacentini": Storia di una rivista (1962–1989)* (Rome: Edizioni dell'Asino, 2017); Cesare Bermani, *Una storia cantata: Trentacinque anni di attività del Nuovo Canzoniere Italiano/ Istituto Ernesto de Martino (1962–1997)* (Milan: Jaca Book, 1997).

65 Alessandro Portelli, "Oral History in Italy," in *Oral History: An Interdisciplinary Anthology*, ed. David K. Dunaway and Willa K. Baum (Walnut Creek: AltaMira Press, 1996), 391–416; Pasquale Martino, "Pifferi e machine da scrivere. Intellettuali, letteratura, Nuova sinistra verso il Sessan-

and cultural work was also Alessandro Portelli, whose oral history portrait of his hometown of Terni appeared in 1985 in Einaudi's Microstorie series. Like many others of his generation, in the 1960s Portelli performed voluntary social work in the *borghetti* (working-class suburbs) of Rome, conducting interviews with resident southern Italian migrant workers and collecting their protest songs as part of the oppositional counterculture.[66]

Luisa Passerini belonged to a comparable milieu. In 1960, together with students and workers, she founded one of the leftist cultural circles that were then emerging in many places. As she recalled in an autobiographical retrospective on the Generation of 1968 in northern Italy, her group sought out former resistance fighters. They spent long evenings with them eating, drinking, singing political and old Piedmont folksongs and listening to their stories about their activities in the *Resistenza*. Although many former partisans were communists, they adopted a critical stance toward the party. They still had weapons hidden away because for them the war was not yet over. According to Passerini, this was the context that awoke her interest in oral culture – in the experiences and ways of seeing preserved in anecdotes and songs that cut against the grain of established history and did not fall in line with the official *Resistenza* narrative. In her case this interest, together with increasing politicisation, was one of the reasons why she began studying history and philosophy in 1961.[67] In Turin, Passerini soon became a member of a Situationist group that embarked on "revolutionising everyday life". In 1967, she travelled to Kenya, Tanzania, Zambia and Egypt for two years, supporting African liberation movements and documenting the "memory of resistance". At the university of Dar es Salaam, Tanzania, in collaboration with FRELIMO (the Mozambique Liberation Front), she wrote a book containing newspaper articles and leaflets as well as songs and oral history portraits of militant fighters. In 1969, she returned to Turin, where in various groups of the New Left she was able to deploy this form of historical writing in the service of political causes. Before joining the university as an assistant professor and the Turin group around Giovanni Levi in 1974, as a member of the workerist collective

totto," in *Utopie dal '68*, ed. Vincenzo Camerino, Pasquale Martino, and Silverio Tomeo (Lecce: Argo Editrice, 2009), 79–132.

66 Miroslav Vanek, "Alessandro Protelli," in *Around the Globe: Rethinking Oral History with its Protagonists*, ed. Miroslav Vanek (Prague: Charles University, 2013), 122–134.

67 Luisa Passerini, *Autobiography of a Generation: Italy 1968* (Middletown, Connecticut: Wesleyan University Press, 1988), 20–25; Luisa Passerini, "A Passion for Memory," *History Workshop Journal* 72 (2011): 241–250, 243.

Gruppo Gramsci she distributed leaflets before northern Italian factories and held courses on workers' history to educate the group's political cadres.[68]

From the Factory to Everyday Life: Giovanni Levi

As opposed to representations in numerous compendia and introductions to microhistory, in its founding years the pioneers of microhistory were not merely interested in a scholarly critique of structural-functionalist models of the French Annales School and American-style New Economic History. It is important to see that its analytical perspective was tied to militant intellectual practices in the political field. This also applied to Giovanni Levi.[69] Before he began studying history in Turin in 1958, Levi spent a few months as a nineteen-year-old in Palermo in Sicily, where he conducted interviews for the sociological study *Spreco* under the guidance of the social reformer Danilo Dolci.[70] Like Ernesto de Martino, Dolci wanted to use questionnaires and biographical narratives to enable the impoverished population of Sicily to bear witness to and break out of their difficult situation. He similarly wanted to strengthen the people's initiative from below and thereby contribute to solving the Southern Question.[71]

Giovanni Levi brought these survey and oral history techniques from the South to Turin, where fierce labour disputes had broken out in the factories. In those years the radical uprisings were led primarily by migrant workers from southern Italy. As a member of a PSI student group, Levi conducted experimental investigations in small enterprises into the living and working conditions of factory workers. In 1959, he became a member of the group associated with the journal *Quaderni rossi* in Turin around Raniero Panzieri, with whom he car-

68 Passerini, *Autobiography of a Generation*, 108–120; Passerini, *Passion for Memory*, 244.

69 On the experiences around 1960 of an entire generation of northern Italian intellectuals (including Danilo Dolci, Aldo Capitini, Ernesto Rossi, Manlio Rossi Doria, Raniero Panzieri and Vittorio Rieser) from Palermo to Turin, see Goffredo Fofi, *Strana Gente: Un diario tra Sud e Nord nell'Italia del 1960* (Rome: Donzelli Editore, 1993).

70 Danilo Dolci, *Specro: Documenti e inchieste su alcuni aspetti dello spreco nella Sicilia occidentale* (Turin: Einaudi, 1960). Evidently there were differences of opinion between Dolci and Levi, because according to Levi the group had to perform very inadequate work because of time constraints. See Paola Lanaro, "Intervista a Giovanni Levi," in *Microstoria: A venticinque anni da L'eredità immateriale*, ed. Paola Lanaro (Milan: Franco Angeli, 2011), 169–178, 172.

71 Giuseppe Barone, "Danilo Dolci e Carlo Levi: Il rapporto tra due settentrionali del Sud," *Meridiana* 53 (2005): 125–147. On the connection between ethnographic field studies and investigations of workers, see Marcelo Hoffmann, *Militant Acts: The Role of Investigations in Radical Political Struggles* (Albany: State University of New York Press, 2019) 68–79.

ried out activist workers' inquiries at Fiat.[72] In 1963 after the PSI fell in line to form a center-left coalition with the DC, Levi left the party, but as a university lecturer in Turin he joined a student-worker group that existed until 1973. As Levi stated in an interview, the group was anti-Leninist – basically anarchist – with positions very close to the Lotta Continua (Continuous Struggle) group, but less hierarchically organised.[73] According to this interview, Levi participated in the fierce workers' struggles and strikes that, starting in 1968, engulfed all of northern Italy. They were organised by rank-and-file *comitati di base* (base committees) in the factories with support from worker-student groups, which acted as pickets, conducted interviews and wrote pamphlets. In numerous interviews, Giovanni Levi traced his interest in microhistory directly back to this political milieu. Retrospectively he had a very clear picture of how his group studied the situation in the factories in order to stimulate the trade union struggle. In the early 1970s when campaigning in the Susa Valley and distributing leaflets on piecework wages, the reaction he received from one of the workers left him deeply disturbed. The recipient of the leaflet insisted, namely, that the issues it raised did not interest him, saying that the factory was by no means as central to workers as Levi and his comrades claimed, and that the most interesting part of his life occurred outside the factory walls. This small episode, Levi emphasised, revealed to him that he basically held a Leninist conception of reality. After that it became clear to him that one could only understand working-class people by investigating their daily life. Moreover, he also understood that to arrive at generalisations one must study reality in its small details, and not the other way around.[74] Based on such statements, one could say that for Levi microhistory was the logical scholarly consequence of these local political insights.[75]

Indeed, in 1975 Levi designed a large research project about Turin's working-class neighborhood of Borgo San Paolo during the interwar period. In contrast to early workerist studies, this project investigated not the work place but rather everyday life and anticipated key microhistorical imperatives – the reduction

72 Giovanni Levi, "Entrevista a Giovanni Levi," *Estudios sociales: Revista Universidad de Santa Fe Semestral* 9 (1995): 111–124, 113; Giovanni Levi, "Entrevista con Giovanni Levi," *Salud mental y cultura: Revista de la Asociación Española de Neuropsiquiatria* 71 (1999): 483–492, 487; Giovanni Artero, *Il punto di Archimede: Biografia politica die Raniero Panzieri da Rodolfo Morandi ai "Quaderni rossi"* (Cernusco sul Naviglio: Giovane Talpe, 2007), Romolo Gobbi, *Com'eri bella classe operaia* (Milan: Longanesi, 1989), 80–88.

73 Levi, "Entrevista a Giovanni Levi," *Estudios sociales* (1995): 115.

74 Giovanni Levi, "Il piccolo, il grande, il piccolo: Intervista con Giovanni Levi," *Meridiana* 10 (1990): 211–234, 223.

75 This interpretation follows Kroll, "Die Anfänge," 282.

of scale, focus on interpersonal relationships, and sensitivity to the actors' agency. Many members of the Turin group also participated in the research work, which was based on oral history interviews and led to an exhibition. In 1977 in a joint essay about the project, Giovanni Levi, Luisa Passerini and Lucetta Scaraffia made it clear that they were not writing a Marxist social history of parties, organisations, or forms of work but instead wanted to reconstruct the thought of a class before it was disciplined by party-Marxist relevance structures. Because such thought was passed down verbally and rarely left a written record, oral history promised the best access.[76] Quasi as a consequence of the Susa Valley episode described by Levi, the authors focused on everyday life and free time: on shared celebrations, games and theater. In the jokes, songs and spectacles cultivated here, the Turin group identified not only moments of community building and solidarity but also powers of rebellion and subversion that, referring back to Ernesto de Martino, they compared to the magical cults of the southern Italian peasants.[77] The authors did not need to make the political message of their research explicit. The plea to have popular culture and oral history sources taken seriously for historiographical reasons implicitly amounted to a demand to research – and mobilise – collective resistance not in the factory but in everyday life for political reasons. According to Maurizio Gribaudi, a participant in the research project, the predominant motive for the Turin group was political. The group wanted its research to shine light on the theoretical and practical dead ends of the Old Left's commitment to a teleological vision of history and its array of extremely conservative and economistic patterns of perception and criteria of relevance.[78] Years later in perhaps his most well-known case study, *Inheriting Power: The Story of an Exorcist* (originally published in Italian in 1985), Levi similarly criticised a functionalist economic history that disregarded core elements of the social world – culture and social relationships. Under debate in both cases were not only questions internal to scholarship but also questions about the agency of individuals and collectives when faced with seemingly overwhelming economic realities – in the past as well as in the present.[79]

---

76 Giovanni Levi, Luisa Passerini, and Lucetta Scaraffia, "Via quotidiano in un quartiere operaio di Torino fra le due querre: L'apporto della storia orale," *Quaderni storici* 12.35 (1977): 433–449.

77 Levi, Passerini, Scaraffia, "Vita quotidiana," 447.

78 Gribaudi, "La lunga marcia," 11.

79 Giovanni Levi, *Inheriting Power: The Story of an Exorcist*, trans. Lydia G. Cochrane (Chicago: University of Chicago Press, 1988).

Witch Hunt against Heretics: Carlo Ginzburg

The connections and transfers between political and historiographical culture can rarely be as vividly traced as in the case of Giovanni Levi and the Turin group. However, such ties are also strong in the case of Carlo Ginzburg, even though he mostly refrained from making explicit connections like those of Levi.[80] It is nonetheless obvious that Ginzburg took recourse to stories and figures of the past in order to comment on his own time. His famous book *The Cheese and the Worms* from 1976, which reconstructs the worldview of a sixteenth century Friuli miller named Menocchio, presents the miller as a witness of a popular culture that has something to say to the present. Building on the deliberations of de Martino, Gramsci and Bakhtin on the relationship between hegemonic and subaltern culture, Ginzburg was convinced that original ideas were not merely products of high culture that then seeped down into the lower class. Quite the contrary, as he sought to show with the example of Menocchio, progressive elements were often rooted in the 'deep layer' of popular culture. Thus, dominant culture cuts itself off from this bountiful source only at the cost of its own desiccation. According to Ginzburg, this is what happened in the Counter Reformation, which he saw as an attempt by the ruling class to once again ideologically safeguard its rule over the popular masses – using repression and witch trials, which cost Menocchio his life and made a rich popular culture disappear, and which functionalised any eviscerated remains of popular culture for the Catholic Church.[81]

By elucidating the Inquisition from the victim's perspective, Ginzburg became in a general sense an advocate of "the perspective of the victim", as he put it.[82] At the same time, he appointed himself a present-day prosecutor of the Catholic Church, Christian Democrats, and the class interests they upheld. In any case, it is difficult to avoid an analogy between Ginzburg's description of the crusade led by the Catholic Church in the sixteenth century against heterodox pieties and revival movements from below witch hunt it led during the Cold War against communists, who were excommunicated in 1949. It is also difficult to overlook the critical commentary directed at the two major parties that set course for the "historic compromise" in the early 1970s. Ginzburg's criticism targeted not only the dominant Christian-democratic ruling party and its forced exclusion of the Communists from the government coalition as of 1948. It was also

80 Keith Luria, "The Paradoxical Carlo Ginzburg," *Radical History Review* 35 (1986): 80–87.
81 Ginzburg, *The Cheese and the Worms*, 125–126.
82 Carlo Ginzburg, "Witches and Shamans," *New Left Review* 200 (1993): 75–85, 78.

directed against the PCI and its handling of the heterodox New Left of the 1960s and 1970s. Against this background, Ginzburg could say that Menocchio "is one of our forerunners" and comment on the present by drawing on his historical analysis.[83] As he noted in 1972, religion seemed less and less able to provide an outlet for the "longing for carnivalesque liberation" that had been swelling in popular culture for centuries. Instead this longing was being driven toward an explosion by a "mature capitalism" that rationalised more and more aspects of life. Ginzburg's disbelief that workers' parties and unions could serve as viable vehicles for channeling revolutionary energy did not even need to be mentioned. As he thought he recognised "from certain clues", the explosive need for carnival and liberation was finding a different outlet: through the political culture of 1968 and through art. This was especially clear for theater, where experimental workshops and street performances were being used to strive for a new relationship with the public. The goal was to create a carnivalesque relationship of cultural exchange between top and bottom that anticipated and experimentally created alternative models of society.[84] Ginzburg presumably understood his historiographical work as part of this spontaneous culture. Probably for this very reason, at the end of his essay he quotes neither Bakhtin nor Gramsci but recalls instead the observation of another "illustrious expert" for whom a revolution was a "long and tedious" process.[85]

Conclusion

It has since become commonplace to view microhistory as a method and ascribe it to a cultural turn marked by postmodern arbitrariness. But in terms of historiographical self-enlightenment, it is important to recall that the perspectives of microhistory gained their urgency as part of a Marxist culture, which while distancing itself critically from orthodox Marxism sought not to defeat but rather to

---

83 Ginzburg, *The Cheese and the Worms*, xxvi.

84 On the theme of carnival in the counterculture of Bologna in the 1970s, see Marco Belpoliti, *Settanta* (Turin: Einaudi, 2010), 283–329.

85 Ginzburg, "Folklore, magia, religione," 611. Presumably Ginzburg is quoting Friedrich Engels, who in a letter to Eduard Bernstein in 1883 wrote: "A revolution is a tedious process" and in another letter to Bernstein two months later noted again that "the major mistake of the Germans is imagining the revolution as a thing that can be arranged overnight. In actuality it is a multiyear developmental process of the masses under accelerating circumstances." On the quotes and context, see Roland Ludwig, *Die Rezeption der Englischen Revolution im deutschen politischen Denken und in der deutschen Historiographie im 18. und 19. Jahrhundert* (Leipzig: Leipziger Universitätsverlag, 2003), 284.

renew and expand the socialist project. The autonomist Marxism of the New Left played an important role in this change of perspectives. First developed within small groups, these approaches gained enormous momentum after 1968. In the case of the Turin group around Levi, the historiographical breakthroughs were associated with worker-student group experiences, factory militancy, and the imperatives of the Workers' Autonomy movement (*autonomia operaia*). Ginzburg, on the other hand, moved more vigorously in the spontaneous milieu of the Creative Autonomy movement (*autonomia creativa*) as expressed through the street theater, cultural centers and free radio of Bologna in the 1970s.[86] In both cases, historical thought was situated in a socially mixed and interdisciplinary community of thought and practice, a living political culture that included not only trade unions, history workshops and university seminars but also student-worker groups, concerts, journal projects and theatrical productions. Questions about popular culture, everyday life and the subjectivity of historical actors gained their urgency as part of the critical confrontation with the Marxist inquiry into revolutionary consciousness and agency. The goal was neither introspection for its own sake nor the celebration of private happiness. Quite the contrary, questions about the experiences of actors, about their self-conceptions and worldviews, were tied to questions about the conditions enabling resistance and emancipation. In this respect it is inaccurate to discuss microhistory in terms of the depoliticisation of historiography.

Nonetheless, it holds true that this microhistorical milieu collapsed in the late 1970s. While one can see the 1968 political awakening reaching its height, for example, in the Movement of 1977 (*Movimento '77*), the kidnapping and murder of Aldo Moro in 1978 and the subsequent mass arrests of militant leftists in the spring of 1979 marked the end of the movement.[87] These developments reinforced the tendency of many activists to withdraw from the public sphere, whether due to disillusionment, hostility, or growing state repression. In the case of microhistory, the *riflusso* went hand in hand with academic integration. In 1975, Giovanni Levi joined the editorial board of *Quaderni storici*. Directed by a committee that apart from Levi also included Edoardo Grendi, Carlo Poni and as of 1978 Carlo Ginzburg, the journal rapidly developed into one of academia's most innovative specialist publications, received well beyond the country's bor-

---

86 Nanni Balestrini and Primo Moroni, *L'orda d'oro: La grande ondata rivoluzionaria e creativa, politica ed esistenziale (1968–1977)*; Marco Belpoliti, *Settanta* (Turin: Einaudi, 2010).

87 Pierpaolo Mudu and Gianni Piazza, "Not only Riflusso: The Repression and Transformation of Radical Movements in Italy between 1978 and 1985," in *A European Youth Revolt: European Perspectives on Youth Protest and Social Movements in the 1980s*, ed. Knud Andresen and Bart van der Steen (Houndmills: Palgrave Macmillan, 2016), 112–126.

ders and becoming an international forum for social-historical debate. In 1981, Carlo Ginzburg and Giovanni Levi founded the Microstorie series with the Einaudi publishing house that in fact first gave microhistory its name. One paradox of developments since the 1980s is that even though microhistory failed to gain institutional footing in Italy and establish a school, it came to be Italy's perhaps most successful historiographical export product. Many of the actors who in the 1970s formed part of this community of thought and practice went to France, like Maurizio Gribaudi and Simona Cerutti, or to the United States, like Carlo Ginzburg, where they pursued academic careers.[88]

Although the process of scientification elevated microhistory into an academic framework and aligned it with social-scientific vocabulary, to a certain extent it also detached the methodology from the political issues and debates associated with its founding period. The transfer to France and North America reduced the Marxist dimensions of microhistory even further. The success of the microhistorical paradigm during the 1990s was also due to the fact that microhistory was not backed up by a 'school' that might have defended a 'proper' type of reading; this meant it could be adapted to very different historiographical milieus and applied in many variations. Whereas in India and Latin America microhistory fused with politically critical cultures of history such as subaltern studies, in Western Europe and North America it joined the repertoire of canonised historical approaches as a relatively innocuous method. Naturally, anyone who takes the imperatives of microhistory seriously must accept that the paradigm will be read and applied in very different ways. However, those who take it seriously will also recognise that today's popular version of applied microhistorical methodology ignores crucial components of this perspective. These include not only a historical awareness of the perspective's genealogy as part of the internal debates about the self-understanding of the Marxist Left but also more generally the perspective's heightened sensitivity to the politics of historical epistemology: its attentiveness structures, criteria for relevance and social functionality. This ties in closely with the will to embark on a comprehensive historical construction of meaning, which not only documents past events but also considers itself part of a democratic understanding about the present and about possibly better futures. While this chapter has endeavoured to historicise microhistory, the goal has not been to file it away as a phenomenon of the past. Quite the contrary, it is important to realise the approach's dual repeatedly– historiographical and political – aspirations, and to do so in repeatedly new ways.

88 Gribaudi, "La lunga marcia," 14–16.

Benjamin Zachariah

Antonio Gramsci's Moment of Arrival in India

Marxian thinking (I use the term 'Marxian' here instead of 'Marxist', which has more party-political connotations) has often been at its most creative in moments of defeat. One can look to the *18th Brumaire of Louis Bonaparte*, where Marx writes of the French longing "to return from the perils of revolution to the flesh-pots of Egypt", therefore voting and acting against their interests, the class consciousness of the French small-holding peasantry compared to potatoes in "a sack of potatoes": "Their mode of production isolates them from one another instead of bringing them into mutual intercourse".[1] This was itself a text that Antonio Gramsci (1891–1937) and Gramsci-influenced Marxians keep returning to, as possibly the first paradigmatic example of a bitter creativity in defeat; the common thread that people act against their own interests, and the obvious parallels between Bonapartism then and Fascism later were impossible to ignore. It is to this category of texts that Gramsci's *Prison Notebooks*, written in a Fascist prison, belongs.[2] But this collection of notes took a long time to reach a public,[3] and still longer to reach an English-reading one.[4] It would not be too much of an exaggeration to say that the English-speaking world by and large discovered Gramsci after 1971, the date of publication of the translated *Selections from the*

---

1 Karl Marx, *The 18th Brumaire of Louis Bonaparte* (Moscow: Progress Publishers, 1977) (1852), 105–106, 12.

2 A complete English translation now exists: Antonio Gramsci, *Prison Notebooks*, 3 vols: Vol. I ed. Joseph A. Buttigieg; trans. Joseph A. Buttigieg & Antonio Callari (New York: Columbia University Press, 1992) Vol. II ed. & trans. Joseph A. Buttigieg (New York: Columbia University Press, 1996); Vol. III ed. & trans. Joseph A Buttigieg (New York: Columbia University Press, 2007).

3 For a quick history of Gramsci's texts and their arrival in different linguistic contexts, see Joseph A. Buttigieg, "Foreword," to Carlos Nelson Coutinho, *Gramsci's Political Thought* (Leiden: Brill, 2012), first published in Rio de Janeiro in 1999, and translated from the Portuguese by Pedro Sette-Câmara, ix–xiv.

4 See Geoff Eley, "Reading Gramsci in English: Observations on the Reception of Antonio Gramsci in the English-speaking World 1957–82," *European History Quarterly* 14 (1984), 441–478; John Schwarzmantel, "Introduction: Gramsci in His Time and Ours", in *Gramsci and Global Politics: Hegemony and Resistance*, eds. Mark McNally and John Schwarzmantel (London: Routledge, 2009), 1–16, esp. 2–3.

https://doi.org/10.1515/9783110677744-006

Prison Notebooks;[5] one set of commentators refer, thus, to Gramsci's 'posthumous birth'.[6]

India, very much a part of that English-speaking world,[7] turned to Gramsci at around the same time, barring a few adepts who had an acquaintance with him earlier;[8] but Gramsci very quickly after that found a homeland in India, and several homesteads that all who claimed him insisted were his permanent address. This is not a particularly Indian phenomenon: it was noted by Chantal Mouffe in 1979 –"since his death in 1937, Gramsci has been subject to multiple and contradictory interpretations, ultimately linked to the political line of those who claimed or disclaimed him. So we have had the libertarian Gramsci, the Stalinist Gramsci, the social democratic Gramsci, the Togliattian Gramsci, the Trotskyist Gramsci and so on."[9] Gramsci wrote little and in passing on India, though much (and probably too much) has been made of his reference to Gandhian movements.[10] Gramsci's interest (and origins) in southern Italy, his reflections on its status as colony of northern Italy and on intra-Italian racisms, have, however, suggested to some writers on India an analogy they could follow.[11] His

---

5 Antonio Gramsci, *Selections from the Prison Notebooks*, ed. and trans. Quintin Hoare and Geoffrey Nowell Smith (New York: International Publishers, 1971).

6 Peter McLaren, Gustavo Fischman, Silvia Serra and Estanislao Antelo, "The Specters of Gramsci: Revolutionary Praxis and the Committed Intellectual," *Journal of Thought* 33(3): 9–41, 9.

7 A part at least of the reception of Gramsci in India started in Bengali journals such as *Anustup*, as part of ongoing debates on Marxism, Maoism, revolution, and the Naxalbari movement's aftermath; for obvious reasons, these were regionally debated and were not accessible to a wider audience without translation. Some of the articles I cite below in English acknowledge their origins in these Bengali debates.

8 For an attempt to track earlier Gramsci readings in India, see Vinayak Chaturvedi, ed., *Mapping Subaltern Studies and the Postcolonial* (London: Verso, 2000), viii–ix.

9 Chantal Mouffe, "Introduction: Gramsci today," in *Gramsci and Marxist Theory*, ed. Chantal Mouffe (London: Routledge, 1979), 1.

10 "Gandhism and Tolstoyism are naive theorisations of the 'passive revolution' with religious overtones": Gramsci, *Selections*, 107; Partha Chatterjee, *Nationalist Thought and the Colonial World: A Derivative Discourse?* (London: Zed Books, 1986), 50, 85–130; Neelam Srivastava and Baidik Bhattacharya, "Introduction," to *The Postcolonial Gramsci*, eds. Neelam Srivastava and Baidik Bhattacharya (London: Routledge, 2012), 1–14, on Gandhi, 'war of position' and 'war of movement', see 3–4. Chatterjee's reading of Gandhi via Gramsci is decontextualised and wrong: see Benjamin Zachariah, *Developing India: An Intellectual and Social History, c. 1930–1950* (Delhi: Oxford University Press, 2005), 160–162, 198.

11 Robert J.C. Young, "Il Gramsci meridionale," in *Postcolonial Gramsci*, 17–33. It does, however, seem to be somewhat essentialist to suggest that "There has always been something postcolonial about Gramsci" (17); or that "there is something innately postcolonial about Gramsci—be it his Sardinian origin, or his analysis of the Southern Question in Italy, or his engagement with con-

Marxist training and his presence as Italian Party representative at the first two Comintern Congresses, and especially at the Second, which discussed that theme intensively, gave him an awareness of the omnipresence of imperialism as a world phenomenon, in which venture Italy was a late but enthusiastic starter.[12] His world seemed therefore to offer analogies, parallels, or parables for Indian use; this Gramscian reception, however, appeared to forget a key concern from that world: fascism.

A number of key themes borrowed for India stand out in this respect: 'subalternity'; 'passive revolution'; a concern with 'hegemony' and resistance; 'spontaneity'; the 'national-popular', the nature and search for 'organic intellectuals'; 'civil society'; and of course the nature of the colonial and neo- or post-colonial state.[13] This chapter traces some of these concerns as they migrated from Gramsci's writing on Italy, in particular on southern Italy and its peasantry, to India; and addresses whether some of these concerns, or perhaps others from the Gramscian repertoire of ideas, are still productive of further scholarship.[14]

Much of the later scholarship on Gramsci was accessible to an English-speaking readership in India after his presence in the historiography of India had been established[15] and a pattern had been set, which meant that it was

---

temporary imperial issues, Gramsci was always a trenchant critic of imperial occupation and exploitation": Srivastava and Bhattacharya, "Introduction", 12. citing Robert J.C. Young from the same volume. As always, the word 'postcolonial' remains unclear – if the writers concerned would like to say 'anti-colonial' instead, it might make sense; but then they are also concerned with making identitarian claims related to Gramsci's southern origin (and disability, 18) – and it is teleological to suggest that Gramsci's *Prison Notebooks* were 'an early practical example of the broad perspective of what would become known as Cultural Studies': Young, "Il Gramsci meridionale," 21.

12 Hoare, "Introduction," *Selections from the Prison Notebooks*, xvii-xcvi; on the Comintern specifically, Young, "Il Gramsci meridionale," 20 – 21.

13 Thus for instance with the work of Ernesto Laclau and Chantal Mouffe, *Hegemony and Social Strategy: Towards a Radical Democratic Politics* (London: Verso, 1985).

14 Coutinho, *Gramsci's Political Thought*, in his prefatory remarks, asserts Gramsci's "universality" (and he therefore applies Gramsci's ideas to Brazilian history); and soon after, states that there is no such thing as "Gramscianism": xv, xvi. Both observations have their importance for this essay: the implication is that Gramsci's ideas are flexible enough to apply to a variety of contexts, but have not acquired, and should not acquire, something like a Party line.

15 The Workshop on 'Antonio Gramsci and South Asia' held at the Centre for Studies in Social Sciences, Calcutta, on July 1 – 2, 1987, the papers from which were published in the *Economic and Political Weekly* in a special issue of 1988 (several of which are cited below) could be identified as that moment. Sudipta Kaviraj's paper at that conference remains unpublished – and was entitled 'Gramsci and Different Kinds of Difference', perhaps an early engagement with the dangers of using Gramsci to create a form of South Asian exceptionalism? Personal communication with Sudipta Kaviraj, email of 16 January 2020.

not as thoroughly received and digested as the *Selections.*[16] It could be said, therefore, that the initial debates on Gramsci in India – Gramsci's Indian 'moment of arrival' – were the most productive, setting a trend and being a part of a creative engagement with a heterodox Marxism that was increasingly frustrated by the residual and still-Stalinised orthodoxy of Party-based Marxisms; but it could equally be said that the engagements with Gramsci paradoxically produced ways of thinking an Indian exceptionalism, which managed to emerge from what started as analogy and comparison.

Gramsci of course has after his death often left the realms of Marxism, in common with other political figures formerly known as Marxists such as Frantz Fanon,[17] and after becoming a postmodernist,[18] a postcolonial theorist,[19] a management guru[20] and a video games pundit,[21] is attracting the attention of right-wing pro-fascists,[22] in a curious parallel-worlds move that has also seen the Nazi legal theorist Carl Schmitt find his way into the pantheon of necessary political thinkers for the left to read.[23] Meanwhile, Gramsci scholarship on India has seen

---

16 See Francisco Fernández Buey, *Reading Gramsci* (Leiden: Brill, 2015), translated from the Spanish by Nicholas Gray, among various studies that bring together long-term engagements with Gramsci's work, and utilise close readings of Gramsci's correspondence; Marcos del Roio, *The Prisms of Gramsci: The Political Formula of the United Front* (Leiden: Brill, 2016), first published in Rio de Janeiro in 2005, and translated from the Portuguese by Pedro Sette-Câmara; also Peter D. Thomas, *The Gramscian Moment: Philosophy, Hegemony and Marxism* (Leiden: Brill, 2009) – the 'moment' was apparently in 1932; Anne Showstack Sassoon, *Gramsci and Contemporary Politics: Beyond Pessimism of the Intellect* (London: Routledge, 2000), which applies Gramsci to British politics from Margaret Thatcher to Tony Blair.

17 See Homi K Bhabha, "Foreword: Remembering Fanon," in *Black Skin, White Masks* by Frantz Fanon (London: Pluto Press, 1986), vi–xxvi; for instance (xvi) "For Fanon, like Lacan, the primary moments of such a repetition of the self lie in the desire of the look and the limits of language". See also Cedric Robinson, "The Appropriation of Frantz Fanon," *Race and Class*, 35, no. 1 (July 1993): 79–91.

18 Renate Holub, *Antonio Gramsci: Beyond Marxism and Postmodernism* (London: Routledge, 1992) acknowledged this trend quite early on, reading Gramsci as a literary critic.

19 See Srivastava and Bhattacharya, *The Postcolonial Gramsci*.

20 For an example, see Carole Elliott, "Representations of the Intellectual: Insights from Gramsci on Management Education," *Management Learning* 34/4 (2003): 411–427.

21 For an example, see Robert Cassar, "Gramsci and Games," *Games and Culture* 8, no. 5 (2013): 330–353.

22 See https://www.antifainfoblatt.de/artikel/marx-von-rechts-gelesen, accessed 3rd January, 2020. Also Tamir Bar-On, *Where Have All The Fascists Gone?* (Aldershot, Ashgate, 2007), Chapter Three.

23 See Giorgio Agamben, *Homo Sacer: Sovereign Power and Bare Life* (Stanford: Stanford University Press, 1998)(1995); Giorgio Agamben, *State of Exception* (Chicago: Chicago University Press, 2005)(2003).

later waves that have taken him further from his concerns. Since Gramsci as author has been not just figuratively dead for a while, he is ripe for such posthumous migration; and since much of what he left behind by way of writing was in fragments, there is less of a system to uphold, and the open-endedness can lead far away from what Gramsci wrote were his concerns. There are times and texts in which Gramsci is no more than a shibboleth.[24]

This chapter will not attempt to track these latter migrations, given that the volume of which it is a part restricts itself to a Marxist thematic, though it will trace some of the spillover. Much of the chapter is in the nature of delineating themes from Gramsci (or attributed to Gramsci) that have been important in Indian debates; in that sense, the piece is to a large extent in the nature of reportage, and is less concerned with 'what Gramsci really said', which in any case makes less sense for a series of fragments. This is also not to suggest that a clear line can be drawn between Marxist and non-Marxist concerns, nor is it necessary, in some Stalinist-vs-revisionist sense, to do so. But if the moment of transition to non-Marxist concerns is not always a clear line, the far ends of the trail show less of an interest in the larger concerns of a Marxist-influenced reading of Gramsci or a Gramsci-influenced reading of Gramsci: Why did the southern Italian peasantry not see the threat to itself from Fascism? What makes a Marxist fail to understand the life-worlds of the subaltern classes, thereby failing in all bids to organise them, indeed losing their support to the fascists? Is there a possible alliance between a working class and a peasantry, within or across the boundaries of metropole and (internal) colony, or does 'subaltern' leave the question of the socio-cultural consciousness of the persons concerned open to enquiry? The stakes of history, for the engaged intellectual, are never merely historical; and the local or 'national-popular' is always to be understood within an international(ist) context. Indian appropriations of Gramsci, relying as they did (at least as starting point) on analogies with the Italian situation and with Italian history, sometimes appear to have made precious little effort to understand Gramsci in his own context before borrowing fragments for their own use; but without that context, the analogies are pretty shaky.

24 This is a word used in an Austrian context: Walter Baier, "Gramsci was a Shibboleth," *International Gramsci Journal*, 3, no. 1 (2018): 55–67.

The Arrival of Antonio Gramsci in India: Subalternity, Consciousness, Passive Revolution

Gramsci found a ready readership in a political environment that found his writings a useful antidote to conventional Marxist narratives that seemed to imply a necessary and predictable link between economic 'base' and ideological-cultural 'superstructure'. This was also at a time when the classical 'proletariat' of the Marxist-revolutionary imagination was not doing as well as predicted. The best-known of the trends that bore the burden of Gramsci's travelling to India was the Subaltern Studies [hereafter *SS*] group, notably named after one of his key expressions;[25] but a wider engagement with him was evident in the historiography and social scientific literature on South Asia, and more particularly on India. *SS* has been written about *ad nauseam*, and has done a fair amount of polishing its own halo, which suggests that a short summary of their work in relation to the group's uses of Gramsci will suffice here;[26] and *SS* provided the occasion and impetus for much discussion of Gramsci in and for Indian usage, without all or the most provocative interpretations having come from the group itself.

Early *SS*'s engagement with a heterodox Marxism was influenced by Antonio Gramsci's concern (in the wake of the Fascist seizure of power in Italy) that the left had not really bothered to understand the (Italian) peasantry, which had seemingly betrayed its own interests by siding with the Fascists. The *SS* group translated this concern to India, in the aftermath of its own failed peasant revolution in the Naxalbari movement (c. 1967–1971)[27] and the state-led repression and murders that followed, and sought to study 'subaltern consciousness' – as an antidote to mainstream studies of Indian history which emphasised leadership – and this included communist-influenced histories, which centred the role of the Party.[28] In doing so it postulated an 'autonomous' domain of 'subal-

---

25 See Ranajit Guha, "Gramsci in India: homage to a teacher," *Journal of Modern Italian Studies* 16, no. 2 (2011) 288–295, for an internalist and retrospective account.

26 Many longer discussions on *SS* (c.1982–2000) can be found: for external readings of the school see for example David Ludden, "Introduction: A Brief History of Subalternity," in *Reading Subaltern Studies*, ed. David Ludden (Delhi: Permanent Black, 2002), 1–39; Benjamin Zachariah, *After the Last Post: The Lives of Indian Historiography* (Berlin and Boston: De Gruyter Oldenbourg, 2019), 21–55, esp. 30–37.

27 See Sumantra Banerjee, *In the Wake of Naxalbari: A History of the Naxalite Movement in India* (Calcutta: Subarnarekha, 1980).

28 David Arnold, "Gramsci and Peasant Subalternity in India," *Journal of Peasant Studies* 11, no. 4 (1984), 155–177.

tern' politics that was 'spontaneous', separate from, and resistant to organisation by elites.[29] As protagonists of peasant revolution, which came with the presentist concerns of the 1970s[30] that were then deferred from politics to historiography by the 1980s, many *SS* members were Gramscian and Maoist in their sympathies. "Yet, significantly, neither Mao's references to the need for 'leadership of the Party' nor Gramsci's strictures against 'spontaneity' featured with any degree of prominence in what we wrote", as one member put it in retrospect.[31] The term 'subaltern' was useful precisely for its lack of precision – Gramsci's attempt not to prejudge the issue of who the (revolutionary) subject might be – and it might be said that a self-issued warning was not taken seriously enough when Ranajit Guha paraphrased Gramsci as having said there was "no room for pure spontaneity in history".[32]

Allegedly following Gramsci, then, *SS* sought to understand 'peasant' consciousness, which was already an attempt to fix the 'subaltern' to a specific sociology; *SS* also set out to find popular versions of the 'nation', and popular contributions to 'nationalism'.[33] Expectations of a peasant 'national-popular' nationalism were of course defeated, and were more a product of many *SS* members' own hypernationalism, which was soon to express itself as a kind of nativist-indigenist consciousness, but that is a later part of the historiographical tale.[34] To the 'masses' or the 'subalterns', however, were attributed a life of their own; they were more or less autonomous in their actions, and were not to be seen as 'pre-political' in the sense of Eric Hobsbawm's 'primitive rebels',[35] but autonomous in their own right. In this respect, *SS* invoked a space where the 'subaltern' was separate and unhegemonised – the colonial state, and its successor state, could do no more than achieve mere 'dominance' over the Indian peasantry, not 'hegemony' in the Gramscian sense.[36]

29 Ranajit Guha, "On Some Aspects of the Historiography of Colonial India," in *Subaltern Studies I*, ed. Ranajit Guha (Delhi: Oxford University Press, 1982), 1–8.

30 See Zachariah, *After the Last Post*, 33–34.

31 Dipesh Chakrabarty, "Belatedness as Possibility: Subaltern History, Once Again," *Cadernos de Estudas Culturias* 3, no. 5 (2011): Subalternidade, 37–49, 45.

32 Ranajit Guha, *Elementary Aspects of Peasant Insurgency in Colonial India* (Delhi: Oxford University Press, 1983), 4.

33 Guha, "On Some Aspects."

34 See Zachariah, *After the Last Post*, 21–47.

35 Eric J. Hobsbawm, *Primitive Rebels: Studies in Archaic Forms of Social Movement in the 19th Century* (Manchester: Manchester University Press, 1959); Guha, *Elementary Aspects*, 5.

36 Ranajit Guha, "Dominance without Hegemony and its Historiography," in *Subaltern Studies VI*, ed. Ranajit Guha (Delhi: Oxford University Press, 1989), 210–309.

It was not immediately clear what the distinction between 'dominance' and 'hegemony' exactly was in this context; nor what was useful about writing about 'subaltern consciousness' as if it inhabited a parallel world. In 1978, the literary critic Edward Said had famously borrowed the term 'discourse' from Michel Foucault, in the sense of an implicit set of assumptions that disciplined how people within a social structure were able to think, and twinned it with Gramsci's concept of 'hegemony'. 'Hegemony' is a state of affairs where people are ruled with their apparent consent because an explicit resort to coercion is not required: people had internalised the disciplinary regime.[37] A later *SS*, once it discovered Said (and Said had discovered them back) would have more to do with a Saidian version of Foucault–Gramsci;[38] but at this point in *SS*'s development, hegemony was for elites and dominance was for subalterns. It might equally have been effectively argued that the open-endedness of the category 'subaltern' was quickly subsumed into an amalgamation of 'peasant-tribal-primitive-rebel', as Guha's peasant was all these things rolled into one, and so lacked specificity to the extent that he (almost always male in Guha's invocations) was an elementary peasant who could indeed have been from southern Italy as much as from the northern Gangetic plain or the Malabar Coast: the unintended message was that peasants would be peasants.[39] Really existing people were seldom able to appear in the historiographical recording of the historical record.

This theoretical blockage, which would eventually lead to a split in the *SS* group,[40] and a long march away from Marxism of any kind (although with a vestigial fondness for Gramsci intact), did not entirely rule out creative histories of really existing ordinary people, 'subalterns' in the sense of the residual of the population who were not obviously 'elite'.[41] Obviously, as a late wave of 'history from below', *SS* was also concerned with the British Marxist Historians' Group, led by E. P. Thompson (others within the *SS* group were interested in Louis Althusser, which at first glance seemed incompatible with Thompson[42]), and Gramsci offered to them another version of the concern with ordinary

37 Edward W. Said, *Orientalism* (New York: Pantheon, 1978).

38 Edward W. Said, "Foreword," *Selected Subaltern Studies*, ed. Ranajit Guha and Gayatri Chakravarty Spivak (New York: Oxford University Press, 1988), v–x.

39 That Guha's *Elementary Aspects* presented an undifferentiated peasant is a point many have made.

40 See Sumit Sarkar, "The Decline of the Subaltern in Subaltern Studies," and 'The Relevance of E.P. Thompson," in Sumit Sarkar, *Writing Social History* (Delhi: Oxford University Press, 1997), 50–81 and 82–108 respectively.

41 Guha, "On Some Aspects."

42 See Edward P. Thompson, *The Poverty of Theory* (London: Merlin Press, 1995) (1978).

lives. But other Gramscian influences, perhaps second-hand, could be seen in the model of *microstoria* that *SS*'s best contributions were able to provide, and Italian microstoria has often acknowledged its debts to Gramsci – such as Sumit Sarkar's *Kalki-Avatar of Bikrampur*[43] or Guha's *Chandra's Death.*[44] That is, outside of programmatic statements and theoretical debates, *SS* was indeed capable of subtle history (and of including women in their narrative, among other things). There would, however, remain the awkward question of the difficulties of dealing with 'popular culture' without romanticising or essentialising it – a problem that could be said to have a parallel in debates in Italy, following Gramsci and microstoria, on 'folklore' and 'progressive folklore' and the dangers of romanticising.[45]

However, this trend was assimilated very soon not to the understanding of the revolutionary subject that would not be a classical proletariat (which allegedly did not and could not exist in India[46]), but to a (postmodern?) assertion of the intrinsic value of 'the fragment' outside of the 'metanarrative'.[47] Separated from the activist idea of 'knowing the people', it was just that "we should remember that if history students all over the world could read about daily life in a single village in the French province of Languedoc in the 14th century or about the mental world of a solitary Italian miller in the 16th century, then in principle there is no reason why they should not do the same with a book about subaltern life in a village or small town in South Asia."[48] The device of

43 Sumit Sarkar, "The Kalki-Avatar of Bikrampur: A Village Scandal in Early Twentieth Century Bengal," in *Subaltern Studies VI*, 1–53, about a poor Brahmin *Sadhu* who was said to be the tenth *avatar* of Vishnu and his two lower-caste followers, who went on something of a rampage in the village of Doyhata in 1905.

44 Ranajit Guha, "Chandra's Death," in Ranajit Guha, ed., *Subaltern Studies V* (Delhi: Oxford University Press, 1987), 135–165, about the death of a Bagdi woman as the consequence of a failed abortion attempt in the Birbhum district of Bengal in 1849, which in Guha's close reading is turned to a study of sexuality, widowhood, caste and patriarchy in rural Bengal. Guha describes 'semi-feudal society' and 'feudal love' (p. 156), and the 'failure of the Raj to incorporate some of the most vital issues of indigenous social conflict within its hegemonic juricature' (p. 150) – the Gramscian clue in this piece.

45 See Brigitta Bernet's chapter in this volume.

46 Dipesh Chakrabarty, *Rethinking Working Class History: Bengal, 1890–1940* (Princeton: Princeton University Press, 1989).

47 Gyanendra Pandey, 'In Defence of the Fragment: Writing About Hindu-Muslim Riots in India Today', *Representations*, No. 37, Special Issue: Imperial Fantasies and Postcolonial Histories (Winter, 1992): 27–55.

48 Partha Chatterjee, "After Subaltern Studies," *Economic and Political Weekly* 47, no. 35 (September 1, 2012): 44–49, 49. The references are of course to Emmanuel Le Roy Ladurie, *Montaillou: Cathars and Catholics in a French Village, 1294–1334* (Harmondsworth: Penguin, 1980)

the 'fragment' potentially, and very soon actually, takes a set of studies out of the realms of the Marxian concerns from which the terminology and driving force of the earlier interventions originated; and we are not concerned here with attempting to follow an evasive device so far, even though the deconstructive gesture is differently productive in drawing our attention to the conceptual conflations we were once habituated to making, and to disaggregate them accordingly.[49]

However, the concerns that drove earlier discussions appear to be more politically relevant in this context: Thus, concerns with the non-'classical' nature of an 'Indian working class', the inadequacy of the Indian industrial economy to sustain and reproduce a 'proletariat' that was in part attached to the land and maintained agrarian, communitarian, communal and thus 'pre-capitalist' and pre-modern sentiments, ideological commitments and socialisation tendencies, once framed a number of these intellectual exchanges.[50] They followed on from the 1970s' 'mode of production' debate,[51] partly spurred on by a developmental imagination's interest in the economic fate of mankind and the place of India in it, and partly because, for a Marxist intellectual to intervene in the present of humanity with a view to changing its future, a proper and accurate view of the past was essential. 'Modes of production', here, as we are reminded often now, can co-exist and/or do not succeed one another in an orderly or linear manner; a 'dominant mode of production', or several that are not quite domi-

---

(1975), and Carlo Ginzburg, *The Cheese and the Worms: The Cosmos of a Sixteenth Century Miller* (London: Routledge and Kegan Paul, 1980) (1976).

49 Partha Chatterjee, *The Nation and its Fragments: Colonial and Postcolonial Histories* (Princeton: Princeton University Press, 1993).

50 Chakrabarty, *Rethinking*; Ranajit Das Gupta, "Material conditions and behavioural aspects of Calcutta working class 1875–1899," *CSSSC Occasional Paper* 22 (Calcutta: CSSSC, 1979). Ranajit Das Gupta, who was Chakrabarty's main interlocutor in a deepish labour history period, put it succinctly in his summary of trends: "The economic determinism alleged to be found in Marxist theories is replaced by a sort of cultural determinism." Ranajit Das Gupta, "Indian Working Class and Some Recent Historiographical Issues," *Economic and Political Weekly*, 31, no. 8 (Feb. 24, 1996): L27–L31, L29.

51 For a sense of this debate, see Utsa Patnaik, ed. *Agrarian Relations and Accumulation: The Mode of Production Debate in India* (Delhi: Oxford University Press/ Sameeksha Trust, 1990); Jairus Banaji, "For a Theory of Colonial Modes of Production," *Economic and Political Weekly* 7, no. 52 (Dec. 23, 1972): 2498–2502; M. V. Nadkarni, "The Mode of Production Debate: A Review Article," *Indian Economic Review* New Series, 26, no. 1 (January-June 1991), 99–104; and for the wider context of dependency theory, Aidan Foster-Carter, "The Modes of Production Controversy," *New Left Review* 1/107 (January-February 1978): 1–21.

nant, can give one the nature and characteristics of a social and political order (that can be named 'capitalist', 'feudal', 'semi-feudal' or 'colonial').[52]

Of particular importance in conceptualising this problem of 'incomplete transition' to capitalism in India – of which much more can be said[53] – was Gramsci's idea of a 'passive revolution' in which major social changes do not accompany the transition from (the remnants of) a feudal order to capitalism: an older elite assists in the transition with minimal or limited support from a working class, thereby presiding over its own continuity as an old aristocracy merges with and identifies with an emergent bourgeoisie, who in turn do not need to invoke solidarities (through the 'national' or 'national-popular') with, or mobilise, classes lower down the social order.[54] The resultant political order is devoid of the experience of popular participation in revolutionary change, as in the Italian or German case, in contradistinction to the 'classical' revolutionary trajectory of the French Revolution. Hence the 'passive revolution'.[55] This model was important in that it explained the top-down nature of the transition to 'modernity' in India (castes and estates rather than classes, a strong state, state capitalism, 'pre-capitalist' survivals). Gramsci's idea of a 'passive revolution' seemed to explain the top-down nature of the Indian state and the inadequate development of a national-popular consciousness, in which the limited participation of the 'masses' in revolutionary activity led to the continuation of pre-independence and pre-capitalist institutions and elites rather than their displacement in the new, non-revolutionary order.[56] It was also extended by Asok Sen[57] and Partha Chatterjee:[58] What if 'passive revolution' was the rule, and not the exception to the rule? After all, many if not most major social changes or 'revolutions' had happened without a capitalist revolution, merely a 'passive revolution' preserving the main characteristics of the pre-existing social order. India, then, would be part of the centrality of the model, and not the exception. But again, the concern with political economy that might have needed to accompany

---

52 Jairus Banaji, *Theory as History: Essays on Modes of Production and Exploitation* (Leiden: Brill, 2010); see especially chapter 10, 'Modes of Production – a Synthesis', 349–360; also Amar Baadj's essay in this volume.

53 See also Mohajer and Yazdani's essay in this volume.

54 The clearest explanation of its potential for use in the Indian context was in Sumit Sarkar, *Popular Movements and Middle-Class Leadership: Perspectives and Problems of a History from Below* (Calcutta: KP Bagchi, 1988)

55 Gramsci, *Selections*, 106 ff.

56 Chatterjee, *Nationalist Thought and the Colonial World*, 43–49.

57 Asok Sen, "The Frontiers of the *Prison Notebook*," *Economic and Political Weekly*, 23, no. 5 (January 30, 1988): PE31–PE36: PE34.

58 Chatterjee, *Nationalist Thought and the Colonial World.*

such a debate, and once did, was not sustained in what swiftly became only a political model. Here too, Gramsci, who wrote very little on political economy himself while in prison, would not necessarily have been helpful.[59]

It was not immediately apparent even from this model why 'subaltern' politics had to inhabit a 'separate and autonomous' domain, as the SS group seemed to suggest in its manifesto and in its theoretical insistences (though not in its historical work: Shahid Amin's *Gandhi as Mahatma*, for instance, was concerned with instances of peasants interpreting Gandhi through what Amin interpreted as 'traditional' peasant culture, but refracted through the colonial reportage that Guha had called "the prose of counter-insurgency"; and Amin read very much 'with the grain' rather than 'against the grain', the latter being what Guha recommended[60]). Indeed, dissenting voices seemed to hone in on the assertion of a separate subaltern consciousness, especially in the pages of the journal *Social Scientist*,[61] which was close to the official Communist Party of India (Marxist), the CPI(M) being the pro-Beijing party in India rather than the old Communist Party of India (CPI), which was pro-Moscow (the two parties split in 1964), and therefore more interested in what might be called a 'peasant question'. The 'autonomous domain' argument was seen as "a kind of metatheoretical position", a "presupposition" rather than something actually emerging from the study of really existing situations.[62] The contention that Gramsci's "entire project had the single purpose of reconstituting a Leninism that would be appropriate to the conditions of a backward, largely peasant, indifferently industrialised society – in the face of fascism", might also have been an exaggeration.[63] But the erasure of that political context from readings of Gramsci in India seemed at least to be questionable, in the context of the rise, from the 1980s and through the 1990s till today, of right-wing forms of nationalism that scholars working on India are only reluctantly agreeing to call fascism.[64]

---

59 David F Ruccio, "Unfinished Business: Gramsci's *Prison Notebooks*," *Rethinking Marxism* 18, no. 1 (January 2006), 1–7.

60 Amin, "Gandhi as Mahatma;" Guha, "The Prose of Counter-Insurgency".

61 See Suneet Chopra, "Review Article: Missing Correct Perspective," *Social Scientist* 10, no. 8 (August 1982): 55–63; Javeed Alam, "Peasantry, Politics and Historiography: Critique of New Trend in Relation to Marxism," *Social Scientist*, 11, no. 2 (1983): 43–54; for a later example, see Aijaz Ahmad, "Fascism and National Culture: Reading Gramsci in the Days of Hindutva," *Social Scientist* 21, 3/4 (March–April 1993): 32–68.

62 Alam, "Peasantry, Politics and Historiography," 43.

63 Ahmad, "Fascism and National Culture," 38.

64 See, for historians' attempts to use this term and its historiography to bear on India, *Fascism: Essays on Europe and India*, ed. Jairus Banaji (Gurgaon: Three Essays Press, 2013); Benjamin Zachariah, "Rethinking (the absence of) fascism in India," in *Cosmopolitan Thought Zones: South*

And indeed, it has appeared to readers more than a few times that a reading of Gramsci in India was against the spirit as well as the letter of Gramsci's reading of Italian history, and that the critics of the (admittedly self-appointed) Gramscians in India had read Gramsci more thoroughly in his Italian contexts as well as with an eye to Indian analogous situations or internationalist solidarities.

In addition, differences were also voiced within the pages of *Subaltern Studies* itself: one such internal-external critic, whose contribution to *SS*'s discussions has been underplayed or overlooked, pointed out that the *SS* group's "principal interest" was "the analysis of subaltern consciousness in a pure form, unadulterated by the outside interference of organised political parties".[65] *SS* had as a group apparently decided not to read or cite Vladimir Lenin, who saw the working class movements building on and absorbing the gains of bourgeois cultural progress; and were also uninterested in Rosa Luxemburg, who was closer to *SS* than they would know. Luxemburg, the critic continued, "locates socialist consciousness within the internal dynamics of subaltern consciousness. Socialist consciousness, according to this conception, can be reached without critically absorbing bourgeois consciousness. This idea, radical as it may sound, becomes entrapped by the false consciousness projected by the ruling class. In the ultimate analysis it succumbs to untaught spontaneity … ."[66] The idea of 'subaltern consciousness' could be seen as in the tradition of Russian populism or a form of neo-Gandhism, which believes that Western-imported political institutions do not sit well with the 'traditions' of the people. Luxemburg exalts and somewhat romanticises proletarian consciousness, whereas for Lenin, a socialist consciousness needs to be more than a "trade union consciousness",[67] and cannot arise somewhat spontaneously from within a working class. "The progressive bourgeoisie … are at the initial stages better equipped to understand the limitations of fragmented struggles."[68] And it is debatable what if at all can be attributed to a consciousness of an undefined, amorphous entity that is not even a class, the undifferentiated 'subaltern'. Thus, the beginnings of a critique of a romantic-

---

Asia and the Global Circulation of Ideas, ed. Sugata Bose and Kris Manjapra (New York: Palgrave Macmillan, 2010), 178–209; and Benjamin Zachariah, "A Voluntary *Gleichschaltung?* Perspectives from India towards a non-Euro centric understanding of fascism," *Transcultural Studies* (December 2014): 63–100.

65 Ajit K. Choudhury, "Discussion: In Search of a Subaltern Lenin," in *Subaltern Studies* V, ed. Ranajit Guha (Delhi: Oxford University Press, 1987), 236–251; quote from 237.

66 Choudhury, "In Search of a Subaltern Lenin," 239.

67 Choudhury, "In Search of a Subaltern Lenin," 247.

68 Choudhury, "In Search of a Subaltern Lenin," 245.

mystic use of the category 'subaltern', whether the category was actually attributable, in *SS*'s use of it, to Gramsci or not, was expressed quite early.

It was indeed once commonly asserted that Gramsci's use of the term 'subaltern' was one of his attempts to evade Fascist censors,[69] and there was no need to use the term if conditions of censorship were not prevalent – but indeed, this is now not considered to be the case, with the open-endedness of 'subaltern' being considered part of its usefulness as a category.[70] Many of the *SS* expositions, in fixing 'subaltern' as 'peasant', or as 'not-yet-proletarian', could then be said to be mistheorising altogether. However, exploring or exploding the vicissitudes or mythologies of spontaneity required an understanding of the role of intellectuals, and therefore a discussion of Gramsci's categories of 'traditional' and 'organic' intellectuals; of spontaneity,[71] and also a return to the first available Gramsci text in the English-speaking world: the *Modern Prince*, who is a personification of the Communist Party.[72] This was connected with "the formation of a national-popular collective will, of which the modern Prince is at one and the same time the organiser and the active, operative expression."[73] The Party, if it had to undertake the role of the (collective) organic intellectual of the working classes, also had a responsibility to mobilise intellectuals of the non-working classes too; and it could fail miserably in that. "It was evident that the [First World] war, with the enormous economic and psychological confusion it caused, especially among minor intellectuals and the petty bourgeois, would have radicalised those strata. Instead of making them its allies, the party turned them gratuitously into enemies; that is, it drove them back to the ruling class."[74]

---

69 The censorship question is raised by Hoare and Smith in their "Preface" to *Selections from the Prison Notebooks*, xi. They do not specifically refer to the term 'subaltern' here.

70 Marcus E Green, "Rethinking the subaltern and the question of censorship in Gramsci's *Prison Notebooks*," *Postcolonial Studies*, 14, no. 4 (2011): 387–404. Green attributes the mistake to David Arnold and Gayatri Spivak, neither of whom bothered to refer to Gramsci's text when speculating in this manner, and with Spivak compounding the error and passing it on by repetition and by virtue of her authority: 390.

71 Denzil Saldanha, "Antonio Gramsci and the Analysis of Class Consciousness: Some Methodological Considerations," *Economic and Political Weekly*, 23, no. 5 (January 30, 1988): PE11–PE18; Arun K. Patnaik, "Gramsci's Concept of Common Sense: Towards a Theory of Subaltern Consciousness in Hegemony Processes," *Economic and Political Weekly*, 23, no. 5 (January 30, 1988): PE2–PE5+PE7–PE10.

72 Antonio Gramsci, *The Modern Prince and other Writings* (London: Lawrence and Wishart, 1957).

73 Gramsci, *Selections*, 133.

74 Gramsci, *Prison Notebooks*, vol. II, 44.

In later versions, when 'subaltern' was allowed by subalternists to unfix itself again, it became somewhat over-flexible. The "subalternity of an elite" was invoked;[75] and it would not be difficult to agree that "in its various deployments, the term 'subalternity' becomes so mobile and indeterminate that virtually everyone becomes, in one situation or another, a subaltern."[76] The 'subaltern', in *SS* at least a residual category of 'non-elite',[77] but relationally therefore a term usable for an elite that is subaltern in relation to another elite, also became the route to a romanticised indigenism, which invoked Gramsci in a scarily decontextualised and instrumental manner. Gramsci was now enlisted as an ally against (western) modernity: it allegedly became important, via Gramsci, to "ask a question that Gramsci does not ask. What would happen to our political imagination if we did not consider the state of being fragmentary and episodic as merely disabling?"[78] Considerations of the nature of subaltern consciousness and its relationship to the state, to the ruling classes, and to coercion, consent, hegemony, were dispensable.

And the answer:

> Thinking the fragment radically changes the nature of the political agent whom we imagine. The subaltern, on this register, is no longer the citizen in the making. The subaltern here is the ideal figure of the person who survives actively, even joyously, on the assumption that the statist instruments of domination will always belong to somebody else and never aspires to them. This is an ideal figure. No actual member of the subaltern classes would resemble what I imagine here.[79]

This theoretical and authentic subaltern might indeed, the author concedes, remind some readers of an essentialised, romanticised (völkisch-Nazi?) version of the figure of the peasant, especially since he is not a real person any longer. It might also be said that the romanticised and essentialised subaltern might be reminiscent of Gandhi's or Leo Tolstoy's authentically free commune-living peasant, in a Narodnik sense of the term; that form of self-regulating and allegedly stateless subaltern still persists in the writing of a James Scott. The völkisch subaltern is promoted, on the other hand, by the strong state that seeks to realise its fascist control – but this distinction was not raised by participants in this exchange. However, in the author's opinion, this recognition of the subaltern as po-

---

75 Chatterjee, *Nationalist Thought and the Colonial World.*

76 Ahmad, "Fascism and National Culture," 46.

77 Guha, "On Some Aspects," a note on terminology.

78 Dipesh Chakrabarty, *Habitations of Modernity: Essays in the Wake of Subaltern Studies* (Chicago: University of Chicago Press, 2002), 35.

79 Chakrabarty, *Habitations of Modernity,* 36.

tentially völkisch-fascist by others is itself to be deplored, since it is a pathological condition of their own condition. "It is also true that the experience of fascism has left a certain trauma in leftist intellectuals in the West. They have ceded to the fascists all moments of poetry, mysticism, and the religious and mysterious in the construction of political sentiments and communities (however transient or inoperative). Romanticism now reminds them only of the Nazis."[80] And that would be a surrender, if Indian intellectuals (or intellectuals concerned with India? The distinction is not made) followed this trend, to 'Eurocentrism', because 'romantic nationalism' in India had led to other things than fascism (and the author claims Gandhi and Rabindranath Tagore for this romantic nationalism, without any suggestion as to why they both fit in this framework). In the realms of mystic-fascist poetry, we are a long way away from Gramsci's anti-Fascist concern with subaltern consciousness. And somehow, the state itself, colonial, neo-colonial, postcolonial or any other variation thereof, starts to disappear from view.

Conceptual Clarifications, Indian Usage: Hegemony, Intellectuals and the 'National-Popular'

It would not be the first time within Marxian debates that an attempt to move beyond mechanistic base-superstructure models, economic determinism, or rigid stageism, seemed quickly to move the neophytes, or at least the neophytes of the neophytes, beyond the boundaries of Marxian concerns altogether – another of *SS*'s role models, Thompson, could be said to have achieved this for social-historical analyses of 'working class' formations, where if a 'working class' could be 'English' (and parochial), it was certainly not the universal class of a future communism (yet) – and could be seen as more 'English' than 'class'.[81] In these circumstances, if Gramsci was well received relatively early among an emergent New Left in Europe[82] (but not immediately among the Italian New

80 Chakrabarty, *Habitations of Modernity*, 37.
81 Edward P. Thompson, *The Making of the English Working Class* (London: Victor Gollancz, 1963).
82 See for instance James Merrington, "Theory and Practice in Gramsci's Marxism," *Socialist Register* 1968: 145–176; and a longer, critical interpretation by Perry Anderson, "The Antinomies of Antonio Gramsci," *New Left Review* 100 (1977): 5–78. For a more thorough list of titles see Eley, "Reading Gramsci in English."

Left),[83] the 1980s wave of Gramsci-catalysed discussions in India could be said to have been interrupted by the end of 'really existing socialism' in 1989–1990, which quickly put discussions of Marxian thinking altogether on the defensive, leading to self-censorship among an older generation and ignorance among a younger generation on matters of Marxian concern. Gramsci, then, arrived in India at a point when the dead man had a small window of opportunity to make an impact within a Marxian framework.

It is worth remembering that Gramsci saw the Bolshevik Revolution of 1917 as itself a corrective to a rigid stageism, because it had (even in Lenin's assessment of a little while before) arrived too soon: a (Second International?) belief in historical trajectories had been superseded by a revolution that had surprised itself; and the 'vanguard party' sought to catch up with events. This connected to the crucial question of consciousness, leadership (by the 'modern Prince'?), and of intellectuals. As Gramsci put it,

> The distinction between intellectuals and nonintellectuals, in reality, refers only to the immediate social function of the professional category of intellectuals. In other words, it takes into account the preponderant aspect of a specific professional activity: whether it is weighted more heavily toward intellectual elaboration or toward muscular nervous effort. This means that while one can speak of intellectuals, one cannot speak of nonintellectuals, because nonintellectuals do not exist. Yet, the relation between the effort of intellectual cerebral elaboration and muscular-nervous effort is not always the same; hence there are different levels of specific intellectual activity. There is no human activity that is totally devoid of some form of intellectual activity; *homo faber* cannot be separated from *homo sapiens.*[84]

As an early commentator on Gramsci noted:

> Central to Gramsci's schema is the concept of egemonia. Since this is itself the subject of controversy, it is as well to begin by formulating it in the most general terms. By 'hegemony' Gramsci seems to mean a socio-political situation, in his terminology a 'moment,' in which the philosophy and practice of a society fuse or are in equilibrium; an order in which a certain way of life and thought is dominant, in which one concept of reality is diffused throughout society in all its institutional and private manifestations, informing with its spirit all taste, morality, customs, religious and political principles, and all social relations, particularly in their intellectual and moral connotation. An element of direction and con-

83 Paolo Capuzzo and Sandro Mezzadra, "Provincializing the Italian Reading of Gramsci," *The Postcolonial Gramsci*, eds. Srivastava and Bhattacharya, 34–54.

84 Joseph A. Buttigieg, "Antonio Gramsci: From the Prison Notebooks," *Daedalus* 131, no. 3, On Education (Summer, 2002): 71–83, 82.

> trol, not necessarily conscious, is implied. This hegemony corresponds to a state power conceived in stock Marxist terms as the dictatorship of a class.[85]

The state, according to Gramsci's notes, consisted of 'political society', mostly in and around organised state power, and 'civil society', outside that 'political society'. "The main value of Gramsci's concept of civil society, which is intertwined with his theory of hegemony, resides in its exposure of the mechanisms and modulations of power in capitalist states that purport to be democracies."[86] 'Civil society', in such a reading, is where hegemony is produced, reproduced, sustained, and not, as in much post-1990s usage, a space where active civic life, or a Habermasian 'public sphere',[87] curtails the excesses of a state that would otherwise be undemocratic. Later commentaries on Gramsci's idea of hegemony would paraphrase it into a more recognisable (by today's standards) language of cultural studies, even while trying to preserve some of its radical potential: "Hegemony invents a co-incidence among four relevant sites of ideological production: identity politics; 'imagined' communities; the state administration; and social relations of production."[88] Chatterjee's late attempt to turn 'political society' into a residual category of a residual category ('civil society'), never quite achieved explanatory power, even as it sought to introduce another exceptionalist reading into Indian history and politics via a posthumously post-Italian Gramsci.[89] For a while, however, the Marxian context of Gramsci maintained its link with social transformation and revolutionary change: "The struggle against capitalism can never be a matter of merely smashing the state. It calls for the achievement of counter-hegemony in civil society. Indeed, such hegemo-

85 Gwyn A. Williams, "The Concept of 'Egemonia' in the Thought of Antonio Gramsci: Some Notes on Interpretation," *Journal of the History of Ideas*, 21, no. 4 (Oct.–Dec., 1960): 586–599, 587.

86 Buttigieg, "Gramsci's Concept of Civil Society," *Boundary* 2, 22, no. 3 (Autumn, 1995): 1–32, esp. 3. Among other things, Buttigieg is concerned with the way the concept has been misused to explain the end of 'really existing socialist states' that were allegedly defeated by their 'civil societies'.

87 Jürgen Habermas, *The Structural Transformation of the Public Sphere* (Cambridge, MA: MIT Press, 1989) (1962). See also Craig Calhoun, ed. *Habermas and the Public Sphere* (Cambridge, MA: MIT Press, 1992).

88 McLaren et al., "Specters of Gramsci," 15.

89 Partha Chatterjee, *The Politics of the Governed: Reflections on Popular Politics in Most of the World* (New York: Columbia University Press, 2004); see 41 for his turning 'political society' into a residual of a residual: 'civil society', which he, peculiarly, seems to associate with the Lumpenproletariat (p. 47). Also see Partha Chatterjee, *Lineages of Political Society: Studies in Postcolonial Democracy* (New York: Columbia University Press, 2011).

ny is often implied as a pre-condition for the building of a historical bloc to go for the seizure of state power."[90] Paraphrased, this might be a case for the realisation of 'socialist (wo)man' or a 'socialist humanism' as a precondition to the transition from capitalism to socialism – if that goal was indeed still even a distant aspiration. There might productively be a dialogue here between a Gramsci-influenced idea of hegemony and Alexandra Kollontai's argument with Lenin about the slow change to workers' consciousness on matters of gender equality even after the revolutionary reorganisation of production relations.[91]

Guha's reading of hegemony builds on, and departs from, Gramsci: 'dominance without hegemony' is what the colonial state and its would-be bourgeois nationalist successor can possess. 'Hegemony' – the rule by apparent consent of the ruled – does not occur in India. 'Dominance' can include 'hegemony' – which is a special kind of dominance, according to Guha – but does not do so in the Indian context. Indian bourgeois nationalists aspire towards hegemony, in anticipation of a future state, trying to speak for and capture the imagination of the people-nation, but they do not. The colonial state similarly did not. The bourgeois nationalists 'discipline and mobilise' and cannot attain hegemony because they learned their language – of nationalism – from the coloniser. This still postulates an 'autonomous domain' of the subaltern, it is worth noting; "hegemony as we understand it is a condition of dominance in which the moment of persuasion outweighs that of coercion",[92] and even in the course of 'nationalist' struggles such as the Swadeshi Movement of 1903–1908, or in 'Gandhian' Non-Cooperation in 1920–1922, (bourgeois) mobilisers had to coerce ordinary people into accepting their programme, via such measures as caste sanctions or social boycotts. Persuasion had clearly not succeeded; and the need to discipline the people(-nation?) they sought to mobilise showed that the nationalist elite had failed to achieve hegemony. Guha is careful to dismiss the idea of the 'non-coercive state' as an absurdity: even a hegemonic state that relied mostly on persuasion would clearly contain *some* coercive elements, else it would not be a state at all. To that extent, Guha was very clear about his roots in a Marxian tradition.[93]

However, this leaves an awkward space for Gramsci's discussion of intellectuals in the formulation. The 'traditional intellectual', being one whose pro-

---

90 Sen, "The Frontiers," PE35.

91 Alexandra Kollontai, *Sexual Relations and the Class Struggle* (1921); Alexandra Kollontai, *Love of Worker Bees* (1924) and Alexandra Kollontai, *A Great Love* (1929) fictionalises this theme.

92 Ranajit Guha, "Discipline and Mobilise," in *Subaltern Studies VII* ed. Partha Chatterjee and Gyanendra Pandey (Delhi: Oxford University Press, 1992), 69–120, 72. Also Guha, "Dominance without Hegemony," 231.

93 Guha, "Dominance without Hegemony," 231–232.

fession is 'traditionally' an intellectual one, and possibly a pre-modern or pre-bourgeois intellectual profession, tends to defend the status quo; the 'organic intellectual' is one who articulates the consciousness and needs of his own class from within his class (most obviously the bourgeoisie). What is needed is an 'organic intellectual' from the working class and/or peasantry: a 'subaltern' intellectual, or a "subaltern Lenin".[94] As Gramsci put it: "The political party for some social groups is nothing other than their specific way of elaborating their own category of organic intellectuals directly in the political and philosophical field and not just in the field of productive technique."[95] In one view, then, the idea of the 'organic intellectual' can be an attempt to "transcend the antimonies of populism and vanguardism".[96] If again it is possible to read that the "national-popular collective will" is what Gramsci associates with "a social revolution that incorporated the peasant interest as the focal point of national interest",[97] it is also fair to suggest that this search for a hegemonic 'nationalism' that is more than just nationalism – and the unresolved, polemicised Luxemburg versus Lenin exchange returns here,[98] with the possible addition of Fanon's search for a nationalism in Algeria that is effectively also a socialist revolution[99] – is one that imprisons Marxism in the 'national-popular' (for a period of time? Or longer?). This is where the difficulties of a Gramsci out of time and place become evident – because there might here be an actor missing: the figure of the fascist. An almost throwaway remark, also in a retrospective analysis of itself by a member of SS, suggests a clue: "In the years following the Emergency, when Subaltern Studies was born, we were thoroughly convinced that the political order in India lacked foundation in popular consent and that the facade of electoral democracy would be thrown aside once more should it become inconvenient again for the rulers."[100] Possible resemblances to the situation today might well be found.

On nationalism and its (hegemonic or non-hegemonic) connection with the 'people-nation', not much by way of cogent analysis appeared from these debates, though much was written on elite nationalism, its 'moments', its construc-

94 Chaudhuri, "In Search of a Subaltern Lenin."
95 Gramsci, *Selections*, 15.
96 McLaren et al., "Specters of Gramsci," 26.
97 Ahmed, "Fascism and National Culture," 53.
98 Rosa Luxemburg, *The National Question* (1909); Vladimir I. Lenin, *The Right of Nations to Self-Determination* (1914).
99 Frantz Fanon, *The Wretched of the Earth* (Harmondsworth: Penguin, 1967) (1961); see Benjamin Zachariah, *Playing the Nation Game: The Ambiguities of Nationalism in India* (Delhi: Yoda Press, 2011), Chapter One.
100 Partha Chatterjee, "After Subaltern Studies," *Economic and Political Weekly* 47, no. 35 (September 1, 2012), 44–49, 45.

tions, or its 'failures'.[101] Sudipta Kaviraj wrote that Gramsci had acknowledged for Italy a problem relevant to the Indian context – the existence of a romantic and "immemorialist" nationalism that goes back to earliest times, and a trend of acknowledging the modern and constructed nature of the national. Kaviraj points out, however, that the 'immemorialist' tradition is more attractive; and that even a constructed entity acquires reality.[102] But the failure of 'elite' nationalism in this reading might have been prompted by a too-strong initial assertion of the 'autonomous and separate domains of subaltern consciousness' argument. It was also necessary to treat "religion as a constitutive force in subaltern consciousness" – this was attributed by Chatterjee to Gramsci, begging the question of what 'religion' might mean in this context.[103] He glossed this later with a conjunction that is of course not an explanation – "the emergence of new philosophies *and* religions ... will have its impact [on the common people] through the borrowed element in common sense."[emphasis mine][104] Apparently, the "common sense" of ordinary people has (as yet) "no clear theoretical consciousness of his practical activity." Chatterjee writes that this "common sense" is comprised of an "autonomous element" and an "element which is borrowed from the dominant classes and which expresses the fact of the ideological submission of the subaltern group".[105] "For the subordinate masses religion enters their common sense as the element which affords them an access to a more powerful cultural order"; and since religions are also class-stratified, "the one religion will then appear among different social groups and strata in several distinct and particular forms".[106] A critique of caste would have to be grounded in a "struggle ... to resist the dominating implications of this code" of elite interpretations of the [one?] religion.[107] Chatterjee here, though he could be accused of attributing a spurious unity to that which is called 'Hinduism' (in a way that B. R. Ambedkar, for instance, systematically opposed)[108] and thereby forcibly incorporating 'lower' castes into 'Hinduism' within a hierarchy, does at least get away in part from the mythologised 'autonomous domain' of the subaltern:

---

101 Chatterjee, *Nationalist Thought*; later Chatterjee, *The Nation and its Fragments*.

102 Sudipta Kaviraj, "The Imaginary Institution of India," in *Subaltern Studies VII*, 1–39; citation from 8–9.

103 Partha Chatterjee, "Caste and Subaltern Consciousness," in *Subaltern Studies VI*, 169–209, 169.

104 Chatterjee, "Caste and Subaltern Consciousness," 170.

105 Chatterjee, "Caste and Subaltern Consciousness," 170–171.

106 Chatterjee, "Caste and Subaltern Consciousness," 172.

107 Chatterjee, "Caste and Subaltern Consciousness," 174.

108 B. R. Ambedkar, *What Congress and Gandhi have done to the Untouchables* (Delhi: Gautam, 2009) (1945), for instance.

> Perhaps we have allowed ourselves to be taken in too easily by the general present of an abstract negativity in the autonomous domain of subaltern beliefs and practices and have missed those marks, faint as they are, of an immanent process of criticism and learning, of selective appropriation, of making sense of and using on one's own terms the elements of a more powerful cultural order.[109]

The relatively weak influence of themes of political economy in these debates should also be noted. One of the strong questions of Marxist debates on India was the nature of the Indian political economy, how to characterise its 'mode(s) of production', and relatedly, what many regarded as the 'incomplete transition' to capitalism in India. The central point in these debates was that capitalism had not reproduced itself in a colony adequately in its own image. The suggestion that 'backward' formations or social formations apparently outside capitalism were themselves produced by capitalism[110] (in the manner suggested, for instance, by dependency theorists or by World Systems theory following Immanuel Wallerstein) was not always taken as seriously as it ought to have been, though by about 1982, the year of the publication of volume 1 of *SS*, Amiya Bagchi, not of the *SS* collective, had brought these debates to bear on the Indian situation.[111] The remark made in Kalyan Sanyal's conversation with Chatterjee (translated from the journal *Baromas* and originally in Bengali), pertains to this somewhat: "Marxists are still utterly enthralled by the transformative power of capital, which is why they feel compelled to call every lack of transformation an incomplete transition. But if we can get rid of this idea of transition, perhaps a bridging might be possible."[112] What Gramsci readings had to do with this is not immediately apparent, but as Sanyal put it earlier, in what is both an apt summary and a critique of Nehruvian 'socialism':

> The bourgeoisie, while striving for hegemonic position, wants the separation of civil society from the state. The need for this separation arises out of the fact that in a transitional economy, interest groups located within the domain of pre-capital may have considerable influence on the state and these groups may use their power to thwart the expansion of capital if the state is allowed to intervene in civil society. The demand voiced by the bourgeoisie for the 'minimal state' is based on this fear of negative intervention. The state, according to the

109 Chatterjee, "Caste and Subaltern Consciousness," 206.

110 Kalyan K. Sanyal, "Accumulation, Poverty and State in Third World: Capital/Pre-Capital Complex," *Economic and Political Weekly*, 23, no. 5 (Jan. 30, 1988): PE27–PE30.

111 See Amiya Kumar Bagchi, *The Political Economy of Underdevelopment* (Cambridge: Cambridge University Press, 1982).

112 Partha Chatterjee and Kalyan Sanyal, "Rethinking Postcolonial Capitalist Development: A Conversation between Kalyan Sanyal and Partha Chatterjee," *Comparative Studies of South Asia, Africa and the Middle East*, Volume 36, Number 1 (May 2016): 102–111, 103.

> bourgeois, should confine itself to the task of creating an atmosphere most conducive to the process of accumulation. This includes the creation of infrastructural facilities through public investment. Private investment is possible and profitable only when such facilities are available, and the market created by public investment also helps capital to solve the effective demand problem. Apart from this, the state is just the guardian of 'fair play' and the 'rules of the game'.[113]

Sen also raises this question: "The reality of a passive revolution, as Gramsci elaborates it with several examples, opens up questions about the nature and role of capitalism in history. Its progressive role in making for the pre-conditions of a socialist transition no longer appear to be self-evident."[114] The struggle, in their writing, still appears to require a disaggregation of the 'inside' and 'outside' of 'capital' – though both, according to Sanyal, would be within 'capitalism' (dependency or world systems theorists would not have disagreed), while showing the difficulties with understanding the dynamics of co-existing modes of production, and forms of society that emerge from dominant modes of production that do not follow each other in the predicted Marxist stages. "The joke is that there was a transition from feudalism to capitalism via socialism", Sanyal was to say later[115] – a remark that fits his earlier remarks about India,[116] and his later book on the 'postcolonial capitalism',[117] but in this case, was a general comment that also reflected on the experiences of the Soviet Union and China.

What's Left of Gramsci

A number of the questions that Gramsci raises, that *SS* linked itself to, remain open to further development. It might be said that Gramsci's post-Marxist avatars took over very quickly after the window of opportunity to discuss Gramsci from the English translation and still within a Marxian framework was open from 1971 to 1989, and then only slightly ajar, or open only in the sense of the gaps in the Indian adaptation of Venetian blinds that are allowed by Indo-Saracenic architecture. A flaw in an attempt to understand the nature of an Indian, or a colonial Indian, state or political order with assumptions of subaltern 'autonomy' and the lack of hegemony of state formations in India might be noted in this regard.

113 Sanyal, "Accumulation, Poverty and State," PE28.
114 Sen, "The Frontiers," PE34.
115 Chatterjee and Sanval, "Rethinking Postcolonial Development," 105.
116 Sanyal, "Accumulation, Poverty and State."
117 Kalyan Sanyal, *Rethinking Capitalist Development: Primitive Accumulation, Governmentality, and Postcolonial Capitalism* (London: Routledge, 2007).

There might indeed be a more urgent question: to study a social order, any social order, in fragments, makes little sense if one is interested at all in larger questions of social stability and social change, whether one is within or without a Marxian framework. The questions of 'subaltern consciousness', 'hegemony', or 'passive revolution' that were raised for India via Gramsci and Italian analogies make little sense unless read without being overdetermined by the quest for 'nationalism' or the 'national-popular'. To that extent, the modest question of historians understanding the life-worlds of ordinary people, the history-from-below question, makes more sense on its own and as completely open-ended.

Can we reread Gramsci now and is he relevant in a time of right-wing populism and fascism? This is not as contemporary a question for India as might be assumed; for fascist social mobilisation is nearly a hundred years old in India now. This would also require us to restore the central, and often implicit, figure in the Gramscian world of the *Prison Notebooks:* the fascist, whose surprising near-erasure in Indian readings of Gramsci has been a recurrent theme in this piece. A demobilised 'national-popular' that has never been properly mobilised in pursuit of major social or revolutionary change, in this perspective, because change has taken 'passive revolutionary' forms, cannot be assumed (because the fascists have been trying to mobilise, and to some extent have successfully mobilised, 'the subaltern'). And historical enquiry that presupposes separate worlds – of 'religions', 'castes', 'intellectuals', 'subalterns' – cannot begin to address this question without resort to a version of nostalgia, essentialism, and an inability to see the implications of the past for the future.

Kavita Philip

The Science Problem in Marxism

On a loose sheet of paper, sometime between 1873 and 1882, Friedrich Engels scribbled some notes about a late-eighteenth-century shift in the meaning of scientific materialism:

> At the end of the last century, after the French materialists who were predominantly mechanical, the need became evident for an encyclopaedic comprehensive treatment of the entire natural science of the old Newton-Linnaeus school, and two men of the greatest genius undertook this, Saint Simon (uncompleted) and Hegel.[1]

In the aftermath of the Scientific Revolution of the sixteenth and seventeenth centuries, the eighteenth century Enlightenment and the Industrial Revolution, previous understandings of the natural and physical worlds had been overturned. Engels continued, referring to an ongoing late nineteenth century scientific conversation: "Today, when the new outlook on nature is complete in its basic features, the same need makes itself felt, and attempts are being made in this direction."[2] Here Engels was identifying the still-incomplete task of integrating all of revolutionary discoveries in natural and physical sciences, and of connecting these, in turn, with social, economic, and philosophical investigations.

This 'new outlook on nature' was emerging in scientific contexts, which Engels avidly studied. On many other sheets of paper like this one, contemporary scientific findings were described, debated and summarised with as much detail and attention as we find in Engels's more well-known investigations of the working classes or of political economic theory. No clear conclusion nor any integrated vision for a political economy of science emerges in these sheets, however. They were transcribed, decades later, simply labelled 'Notes,' and appended to other excerpts and notes on 'Heat,' 'Electricity,' 'Natural Science and the Spirit World' and 'The Part Played by Labour in the Transition from Ape to Man.' Together with an appendix containing previously unpublished 'Notes to Anti-Dühring,' these constituted fragmented chapters of the rather abstruse book known as *The Dialectics of Nature.*

---

1 Friedrich Engels, *The Dialectics of Nature* (New York: International Publishers, 1940), 178–179. These notes appear in a paragraph titled "The classification of sciences," in Chapter VII, "Notes."

2 Engels, *Dialectics of Nature*, 179.

https://doi.org/10.1515/9783110677744-007

This chapter suggests that we pay close attention to this vast, untapped vein of scientific study in the work of Karl Marx and Engels. A problem immediately arises, however, as we attempt to formulate the question of science in Marxism. Ahistorical models of science, tied to assumptions of deterministic social models of transition, and technocratic histories of technique, tied to Promethean systems of extraction and labour-control, have shaped the more deterministic and scientistic strands of Marxism. The political economic analysis of science and technology as a historical form of knowledge, however, has not been a significant part of mainstream humanist legacies in Marxism. This is the 'science problem' that this chapter sets out to address.[3]

In order to bring Marxist science back into focus, we have not only some understudied and fragmentary texts, such as *The Dialectics of Nature* and Marx's scientific notebooks, but also a rich historical record of the ways in which these fragments inspired shifts in scientific practice and planning. Marxist humanists have not considered the lab, the scientific conference, technological objects, infrastructure, or logistics as sites of Marxist theorising. But small, scattered groups of Marxist scientists have, at different periods in the twentieth century, been intrigued by Engels's radical approach to the practice of science. Although they are largely neglected in cultural and economic history, these 'red scientists' are well known in the history of science, and their work still circulates globally in science- and technology-oriented activist networks. We will draw on their history to understand both the mechanistic dead-ends and the potentially dynamic futures of radical anti-capitalist science.

The call for a new, non-mechanical materialism, rooted in a new understanding of nature, but going beyond the dialectics of Georg Wilhelm Friedrich Hegel (1770–1831) and the industrial optimism of Henri de Saint Simon (1760–1825), was critical to Marx and Engels's work from their earliest collaboration in the early 1840s. Marx's scientific excerpt notebooks, contemporaneous with his unfinished work on the second and third volumes of *Capital*, have thus far been the interest only of scholars of archival marginalia. The meaning of these notes has remained cryptic to humanist interpreters of the Marxist legacy. Today, with Marx's extensive notes on science being prepared for publication in the new MEGA editions, we have, for the first time, an archive that helps us understand the significance of science for Marxist political economy and philoso-

---

3 The most comprehensive treatment of Engels's legacy is Helena Sheehan, *Marxism and the Philosophy of Science: A Critical History, The First Hundred Years* (New Jersey: Humanities Press, 1985). The planned second volume (covering post-1945 developments in the dialectics of nature debate) was never completed.

phy.[4] While this archive in its entirety is not yet widely available, we must prepare ourselves to read it by revisiting the problem that science has posed for Marxists. Without a framework for understanding how and why science has been a problem in the Marxist legacy, we are likely simply to reproduce some of the anachronisms and stereotypes that have dogged this issue since its inception. And without paying attention to the details of the scientific changes of the late nineteenth century, we would miss an important aspect of the changes in Marx's models of materialism and nature. This chapter attempts to retrieve a historiographic framework to help reformulate questions about science, technology and capitalism, a century and a half after Marx and Engels began studying this conjuncture.[5]

The 'science question' for Marxists, then, is twofold: What was the role of science in Marx and Engels's formulation of philosophical critique and political

---

4 Begun in the 1920s in Moscow and still ongoing, the MEGA project in different forms has encountered many historical and geopolitical obstacles. Its current status can be accessed at http://mega.bbaw.de/projektbeschreibung. Accessed April 21, 2020. My comments in this chapter are thus provisional, based on a few scholars' pioneering work using the newly edited scientific and technical excerpt-notebooks, which are by no means complete or conclusive yet. The point is not to arrive hastily at a conclusive view of this newly-edited archive, but to begin, here, to put it in its proper historical context. We have a fresh chance to properly historicise these nineteenth-century writings rather than continue in the variously teleological and politically motivated readings we have inherited from a complex twentieth century.

5 It is important to note that science has a place in Marx's corpus that goes far beyond the influence of scientific work on Marx and Engels, and their uptake by scientists. I restrict this chapter to this narrow focus for reasons of space. I am in agreement with Saito's claim in his path-breaking analysis of the notebooks, where he shows how Marx's scientific interests were key to the political economic arguments he was working on, slated to appear in *Capital,* Volumes 2 and 3. As Saito writes: "[I]t is essential to emphasize that Marx's notebooks need to be analyzed in close connection with the formation of his critique of political economy rather than as a grandiose materialist project of explaining the universe. In other words, the notebooks' meaning cannot be reduced to his search for a scientific worldview. Earlier literature often claims that through new discoveries in natural sciences Marx followed the classical tradition of the philosophy of nature by Hegel and Schelling, trying to figure out the universal laws that materialistically explain all phenomena within the totality of the world. In contrast, I inspect Marx's research on natural science independent of any totalizing worldview but examine it in close relation to his unfinished project of political economy." See Kohei Saito, *Karl Marx's Ecosocialism: Capital, Nature, and the Unfinished Critique of Political Economy* (New York: Monthly Review Press, 2017), 19. Marx's wide-ranging attention to the intersection of science, technology, and human subjectivity requires historians to expand their own analytical frames. A reconstruction of Marxist science studies would include, for example, the Frankfurt School tradition of Marxist sociology of science and its critiques of technocratic instrumentalism and fascism. Such an exploration (which awaits the publication of MEGA IV) would link the "science question," as articulated here, to the issues of political economy raised by Saito.

economic methods? And how did scientists themselves understand the significance of Marx and Engels's insights into scientific method and practice? Science after Charles Darwin was bringing about a revolution in understandings of nature, which could now be analysed as historically dynamic, proceeding through shifting material conditions, rather than created *ex nihilo* or understood via static essences. Marx and Engels were fascinated by this, and believed it held the key to their own revision of bourgeois political economy and humanist philosophy. They both made extensive notes consisting of excerpts from the world of scientific research. They corresponded with each other, and with scientists of their day, seeking to revise the mechanical, determinist analytics that spilled over from eighteenth century French and British materialism. As Eric Hobsbawm observes, Engels recognised that "diachronicity, that is, history, inevitably entered the sciences with the theory of evolution." The dialectical materialist method, in this context, addressed the task of constantly historicising both scientific and political categories of analysis. Marx and Engels's notion of dialectics, drawn from science, "was essentially historical, and its concern was with change and transformation."[6]

Retrieving the Science Question

Reading these 'excerpt notebooks' and scientific correspondence entails dipping into a history of science that has seemed positivist and technical to humanists.[7] Discussions of science have seemed abstruse and marginal to mainstream humanist interpreters of the Marxist tradition. However, this seemingly internalist history has spoken, over the years, to radical scientists who find inspiration in the kind of truth-making that science promotes, while simultaneously seeking

---

6 Eric Hobsbawm, "Preface", in *J.D. Bernal, Life in Science and Politics* eds. Brenda Swann and Francis Aprahamian (London: Verso, 1999), ix–xx.

7 MEGA Section IV ("Exzerpte, Notizen, Marginalien") contains miscellaneous notes that are in the process of being edited for wider circulation. Kohei Saito is editor of Volume 18, in process. His compelling book, *Karl Marx's Ecosocialism: Capital, Nature, and the Unfinished Critique of Political Economy* (New York: Monthly Review Press, 2017) is based on his initial readings of this archive. Some further notes on Marx and Engels's scientific writings are available in scattered contexts. See, for example, Kaan Kangal, "Engels' Intentions in Dialectics of Nature," *Science & Society* 83, no. 2 (2019): 215–243 and Pradip Baksi, "MEGA IV/31: Natural-Science Notes of Marx and Engels, 1877–1883," *Nature, Society, and Thought: A Journal of Dialectical and Historical Materialism* 14, no. 4, October 2001: 377–390. Baksi notes that MEGA IV, Volume 31 "provides new materials related to the hitherto little-noticed natural-science studies of Marx, and some materials related to Engels's Dialectics of Nature."

a way to put their daily modes of knowledge-making practices into political economic contexts. Exploring the science question in Marxism can prompt not only historicist revision but activist reorientations as well. The beginning of the twenty-first century has witnessed an explosion in progressive social movements calling for attention to the way scientific and technological systems were being reshaped and deployed by state and corporate forces. This proprietary corporate/imperial capture of science has seemed, to many scientists and technologists, to betray the potential of the new techno-sciences of the late twentieth century, from the human genome project to the internet. Challenging this capture, and suggesting that the potential of science and technology should be turned to the needs of the people, the creativity and resistance of progressive movements in the techno-scientific domain grew vigorously in the first two decades of the twenty-first century. However, for the most part, their ethical and social justice demands were not articulated in Marxist terms. In this context, there is a need for a broader engagement with Marx and Engels's writings on science that offer us a *longue durée* understanding of capitalist science and help us speculate about the futures of anti-capitalist science.

Marx had been interested, since his earliest political investigations, in the political significance of antagonisms between metaphysics and materialism.[8] For example, in his doctoral dissertation, *Differenz der demokritischen und epikureischen Naturphilosophie,* Marx explored the roots of contingency in the philosophies of science of Democritus and Epicurus. Under the guidance of Young Hegelian scholar Bruno Bauer, Marx argued that theology would inevitably give way to philosophy. However, a few years later, in *The Holy Family,* Marx articulated a more robust commitment to materialism, rejecting Bruno Bauer's philosophical idealism. *The Holy Family* included a key section on scientific materialism. Engels later described this section as the expression of their collaborative realisation that "the cult of abstract man, which formed the kernel of Ludwig Feuerbach's new religion, had to be replaced by the science of real men and

---

8 See Karl Marx, "Debates on the Law on Thefts of Wood," a series of articles first published in the Supplement to the Rheinische Zeitung Nos. 298, 300, 303, 305 and 307, October 25, 27 and 30, November 1 and 3, 1842. Translated Clemens Dutt, archived at https://www.marxists.org/archive/marx/works/download/Marx_Rheinishe_Zeitung.pdf, accessed April 21, 2020 and Karl Marx, "The Difference Between the Democritean and Epicurean Philosophy of Nature," Doctoral Thesis, March 1841, in Marx-Engels Collected Works, Volume 1 (Progress Publishers, 1902), archived at https://www.marxists.org/archive/marx/works/1841/dr-theses/index.htm, accessed April 21, 2020.

of their historical development."[9] Marx's understanding of materialism grew systematically away from the humanist idealism of Feuerbach and Bauer and towards a philosophy grounded in experimental science.[10] The notion of material exchanges, which was revolutionising the natural sciences of the late nineteenth century, would offer Marx a way to get beyond both the idealist theological models of abstract humans and the ahistorical, mechanistic models of nature that were legacies of eighteenth century philosophy.

For example, Marx' and Engels' claims about all matter being in motion grew out of their anti-theological politics. By arguing that all matter began in motion rather than in stasis, they were arguing against a theological, static first-cause position, and thus putting their weight behind a materialist chemistry-based understanding of life rather than a metaphysical, God-created notion. Returning to a well-known critique of religious teleology in *The Dialectics of Nature*, we note Engels's anti-teleological argument linking matter and mind:

> The old teleology has gone to the devil, but it is now firmly established that matter in its eternal cycle moves according to laws which at a definite stage – now here, now there – necessarily give rise to the thinking mind in organic beings.[11]

---

9 Friedrich Engels (from "Ludwig Feuerbach and the End of Classical German Philosophy"), cited in the introduction (by the Institute of Marxism-Leninism), in Marx and Engels's first joint work, Karl Marx and Friedrich Engels, *The Holy family, or Critique of Critical Critique. Against Bruno Bauer and Co.* (Moscow: Foreign languages Publishing House 1956), 11.

10 Humanities theorists John Clark and Andreas Malm have found in the early Marx evidence of a technological optimism, and a "promethean" attitude towards nature. Judith Butler has recently responded to this argument, exploring Marx's model of nature in the 1844 Economic and Political Manuscripts, finding evidence of more than simple instrumentalist anthropocentric models of nature. Kohei Saito explores a longer history of shifting notions of nature in Marx. He traces the changes in Marx's model of labor and nature after the publication of *Capital* Volume I. He shows that the notion of "species being" in the 1844 manuscripts owed its origin to Feuerbach. Marx later discarded this, argues Saito, moving far beyond his early Prometheanism and developing a more complex, material, "ecological" view influenced by soil science and organic chemistry. See John P. Clark, "Marx's Inorganic Body," *Environmental Ethics* 11:3 (Fall 1989), 243–58, and Judith Butler, "The inorganic body in the early Marx: A limit-concept of anthropocentrism," *Radical Philosophy* 2, no. 6 (Winter 2019), 3–17. The "Promethean v. Ecosocialist" Marx debate was framed by Paul Burkett and John Bellamy Foster, and extended by Kohei Saito. I draw on their scholarship in the following section on *Stoffwechsel*/material exchange. See John Bellamy Foster, *Marx's Ecology: Materialism and Nature* (New York: Monthly Review Press, 2000); Paul Burkett, *Marx and Nature: A Red and Green Perspective* (Chicago: Haymarket Books, 2014); Saito, *Karl Marx's Ecosocialism*.

11 Karl Marx and Frederick Engels: *Collected Works*, Vol. 25 (London: International Publishers, 1987), 475–476.

Kohei Saito, in *Karl Marx's Ecosocialism*, demonstrates that Marx and Engels found support for this argument in post-Darwinian natural sciences and organic chemistry. Chemistry was a field that came into existence at the intersection of philosophical and theological theory, agricultural practice, capitalist agriculture and laboratory experimentation. It is only when seen in the context of the fierce nineteenth century arguments over metaphysics, nature and science that the 'matter in motion' phrase reveals its historical significance. As an abstract rule for contemporary scientists, the admonition to see all matter as being perpetually in motion is not practically useful, especially through much of the twentieth century when theology is not the main political enemy of science.

Marx, as we know, commonly produced polemics against the theories of bourgeois economists and philosophers, finding in their theories too much of the theological impulse, resistant remnants of mystical views of life and resurgent metaphysical notions of self. His own articulations of radical political economy were rooted in the processes of labour. In order to understand changes in the ways in which labour operated on nature, and production shifts in technology that rendered workers less and less able to control the terms of their labour or the products of their work, Marx studied not only the sciences of life but also the technologies of production (particularly factory machines), to understand how workers and machinery competed for power. In Chapter 15 of *Capital*, Volume I, "Machinery and Modern Industry", Marx and Engels argue: "But machinery not only acts as a competitor who gets the better of the workman, and is constantly on the point of making him superfluous. It is also a power inimical to him ... It is the most powerful weapon for repressing strikes ... It would be possible to write quite a history of the inventions, made since 1830, for the sole purpose of supplying capital with weapons against the revolts of the working-class."[12] In this chapter they lay out the framework for a philosophy and history of technology, issuing a challenge that few philosophers or historians have fully taken up. Marx's labour theory of value was indebted to, and inextricable from, a historiography and philosophy of science and technology.

12 Karl Marx and Frederick Engels: *Collected Works*, Vol. 35, Capital Volume I (London: Lawrence & Wishart, Digital Edition, 2010), 438–439.

Material Exchanges[13]

"Capitalist production ... disturbs the circulation of matter between man and the soil"[14]

Marx borrowed terms like 'Stoffwechsel' (or the exchange of materials) from the chemistry of metabolism. This term became central to the ways in which he understood all kinds of material exchange, from agricultural production to circulation.

---

13 A particular idea of materialism, emerging from scientific debates of the time, underpins Marx's political economy. Marx borrowed the word *Stoffwechsel* from Justus Liebig. Friedrich Tiedeman (1830) in *Physiologie des Menschen* used it to describe the chemistry of life, although it might have been in general use before that. As early as 1796, J. C. Reil uses the term "Wechsel der Materie" (Reil, "Von der Lebenskraft," *Archiv für Physiologie*, i, Part 1 (1796), 8–162, cited in Bing 1971). Bing comments: "Through a veil of mysticism he seems to have seen that life consists of changes which obey the laws of chemistry." It is precisely this momentous shift from mysticism to science that was in progress while Marx was writing. Liebig used the term Stoffwechsel less often than the term Metamorphose. There were many other phrases in use to describe the exchange of materials and transformations of energy forms in living things. Bing explains that the "richness of expressions for the idea of metabolism may be related to the intellectual vigor in Germany during the middle of the nineteenth century." Bing notes that in eighteenth-century scientific texts, the term "animal economy" (*die thierische Oekonomie*) is used for "what we today would call 'metabolism' ... It could have been said that [medical scholars] made studies of the economy of their bodies." F. C. Bing, "The History of the word 'metabolism,'" in *Journal of the History of Medicine and the Allied Sciences* 26, no. 2 (April 1971): 158–180 can see here that the familiar eighteenth- and nineteenth-century notion that metaphors could be borrowed between the spheres of science and society to elucidate, discover, and systematise theories of each, while also elucidating the term itself, in its technical meanings. After the specialisations of the nineteenth century were complete, however, terminology and theory in each field became insulated, and, when borrowings did occur, scientific terms tended to be more static, having settled more firmly into specialised disciplinary significations after the 1920s.

14 "Die kapitalistische Produktion ... stört sie andrerseits den Stoffwechsel zwischen Mensch und Erde." Marx and Engels, Das Kapital, Vol. II (Hamburg: O. Meissner, 1883), 517. Marx explains this borrowing from science, and makes the link to economic exchange in the C-M-C equations. See the note in one of his last economic writings [Randglossen zu Adolph Wagners "Lehrbuch der politischen Ökonomie" (Zweite Auflage), Vol. I, 1879]: "wo der "*Wechsel in den (naturalen) Bestandteilen der Gütermasse*" {einer Wirtschaft, alias bei Wagner getauft "*Güterwechsel*" für Schäffles "*sozialen Stoffwechsel*" erklärt wird—wenigstens ein Fall desselben; ich habe das Wort aber auch beim "naturalen" Produktionsprozeß angewandt als Stoffwechsel zwischen Mensch und Natur} von mir *entlehnt* ist, wo der Stoffwechsel zuerst auftritt in Analyse von W-G-W und Interruptionen des Formwechsels". Available in German and English at https://www.marxists.org/archive/marx/works/1881/01/wagner.htm. accessed April 21, 2020.

A year after the publication of *Das Kapital, Volume I*, Karl Marx wrote to Friedrich Engels:

> I would like to know from Schorlemmer what is the latest and best book (German) on agricultural chemistry. Furthermore, what is the present state of argument between the mineral-fertilizer people and the nitrogen-fertilizer people? ... For the chapter on ground rent I shall have to be aware of the latest state of the question, at least to some extent.[15]

In *Capital* Volume I, Marx had drawn on the scientific debate over the chemical origins of life, the agrarian debate over fertilisers, and the link between science and craft. But he had only drawn out a fraction of the implications of these, and was already starting to extend his reading in order to address, in future volumes, the precise ways in which he saw craft and technique, science and the state, agrarian production and soil fertility, labour and machinery, the worker and bourgeois subjectivity, as historically interconnected. Organic chemistry was at the time a new field, founded in the radically experimental context of the late eighteenth and early nineteenth centuries, when ancient theories of the natural world were being overturned by experimental findings. Engels saw the communist commitment to totality and dialectics at the core of this vast intellectual scope that synthesised history, philosophy and scientific method.

Organic chemistry had originated in 1828 when German chemist Friedrich Wöhler experimentally disproved the doctrine of vitalism. Vitalism, the belief that organic matter was endowed with an inherent, vital life force, can be traced back to antiquity, through Aristotle and Galen. Marx and Engels were engaged with the revolutions that from the sixteenth through the eighteenth century had brought a confrontation between ancient vitalist theories (seeing life in terms of spirit, force, or *telos*) and a modern mechanistic view.

Many of the chemists Marx and Engels admired were influenced by early years in craft or practice of some kind. Organic chemistry by the 1870s was a battleground for theory and praxis. This battleground was the same one in which Marx and Engels were formulating, testing and changing their theories of political economy and history. Marx's inquiries after nitrogen fertiliser were likely to have been part of his attempt to understand the intense agrarian de-

---

15 Marx, letter to Engels, 3 January 1868. The letter is cited in Ian Angus, Marx Engels and The Red Chemist https://monthlyreview.org/2017/03/01/marx-and-engels-and-the-red-chemist/ and in Saito, Marx's Ecological Notebooks https://marxismocritico.com/2016/02/24/marxs-ecological-notebooks/ accessed April 21, 2020. On Marx's funeral, see *Der Sozialdemokrat* March 22 1883 https://www.marxists.org/archive/marx/works/1883/death/dersoz1.htm, accessed April 21, 2020.

bates over the practical implications of Justus Liebig's *Agricultural Chemistry.*[16] The centrality of Liebig's work to Marx's work in *Capital* Volume I has been well established.[17] For example, Marx was taken by Liebig's characterisation of modern cultivation as a *Raubbau,* or 'robbery system,' a term that resonated with Marx's notion of exploitation, linking his economic analysis with new findings in agrarian science. Thus it seemed to Marx that whether individual scientists were explicitly socialist or not did not matter; new scientific findings were proving that theory and practice were inseparable, that materialist concepts linked different specialisations to offer a unity of natural and cultural analytics, and thus that science of the time had 'unconscious' socialist tendencies. It remained to the revolutionary political economist to thread these tendencies together with historical dynamics while striving for a materialist analytic that pushed back against the resurgence of vitalism and other new forms of Romanticism, paired as they were with post-1871 German nationalism.[18]

Justus Liebig (1803–1873), a Darmstadt-born scientist, whose fascination with chemistry had begun in his father's hardware shop where pigments were compounded, is considered the founder of organic chemistry. Recent archival work suggests that Marx wanted, in Volume 3, to analyse the relationship between the "declining productivity of the soil" and the falling rate of profit.[19] Saito's reading of Marx's "ecological notebooks" reveals that Marx was, by 1868, following the critical debate in which many of Liebig's supporters had descended into Malthusianism, linking declining productivity to the need for reducing population. This Malthusianism outraged Marx – who saw capitalist exploitation to blame for reduced productivity – and altered his science-reading trajectory. He began to follow a new crop of critical botanists and agricultural physicists such

---

16 Justus Freiherr von Liebig and Lyon Playfair, *Organic Chemistry in Its Applications to Agriculture and Physiology* (London: Taylor and Walton, 1840). Enormously influential, the book was commonly referred to by the short title *Agricultural Chemistry.*

17 J. D. Bernal noted this link as early as 1935. See also John Bellamy Foster, *Marx's Ecology: Materialism and Nature* (New York: Monthly Review Press, 2000).

18 Irrationalism and anti-science attitudes do not, of course, entail fascism, as Anne Harrington has shown. The relationships between authoritarianism, rationalism, holism, and socialism cannot be deduced from formalisms, but must be unraveled through their historical specificity. See Anne Harrington, *Reenchanted Science: Holism in German Culture from Wilhelm II to Hitler* (Princeton: Princeton UP, 1996).

19 See Kohei Saito, "Marx's Ecological Notebooks," *Monthly Review* 67, no. 9 (2016): 25–42, and Kohei Saito, *Karl Marx's Ecosocialism.*

as Carl Fraas, whose theories of agrarian crisis and climate became interesting to him as representing an "unconscious socialist tendency."[20]

Marx and Engels critically engaged with the findings of science as they occurred, followed debates, and historicised the terms and implications in conversation with both scientists and economists. They did not simply accept scientists' opinions as theirs; rather, they evaluated scientific claims in the light of arguments from theology, metaphysics and political economy.

Saito reports that "in the final fifteen years of his life Marx filled an enormous number of notebooks with fragments and excerpts. In fact, a third of his notebooks date to this period, and almost one half of them deal with natural sciences."[21]

These notebooks show that, contrary to common assumptions about the divisions of labour between Marx and Engels, positing a humanist Marx and a scientistic Engels, both Marx and Engels were fascinated with the ways in which the new sciences were overturning ancient philosophical foundations and traditional economic assumptions about the organisation of life. As in all their work, they attempted to theorise from the ground up in their work on scientific method, building expertise by reading and engaging with scientists in every sphere. Because this was such a huge task, and because recent revolutions had occurred in almost every field of science, this was literally unending work – it never ended for Marx, and although Engels's editing and publishing of *Capital* Volume III had been expected to integrate these studies with their theories of labor, subject-formation, and knowledge, it failed to do so.

The Taming of Early Scientific Speculation: Specialisation, Positivism and Anti-Science Politics

Marx and Engels's research notebooks show what scholars have seen as an astonishing level of engagement between scientific research and social and humanist thinking. Historians of science show us that this kind of interchange was not unusual between the seventeenth and mid-nineteenth century. The nineteenth century saw a number of contradictory trends in science, some extensions

20 Marx to Engels in a letter dated March 25, 1868, praising Fraas's book *Climate and the Plant World Over Time*, as cited in Kohei Saito, "Marx's Ecological Notebooks." *Monthly Review* 67, no. 9 (2016): 25–42. https://marxismocritico.com/2016/02/24/marxs-ecological-notebooks/

21 Kohei Saito, "Marx's Ecological Notebooks," *Monthly Review* 67, no. 9 (2016): 25–42.

of the past two centuries, and others the beginning of new trends that would shape twentieth century academic disciplines and industrial development. By the end of the nineteenth century, institutional changes favored the specialising and narrowing tendencies that had begun to characterise scientific research since the 1850s. Specialisation was good for the progress of science in precisely delineated problem areas, in which standardised assumptions and constraints made it easier to accumulate usable insights. Powerful scientific and technological findings powered the industrial revolution. But institutional specialisation constrained the wide, sweeping sorts of scientific and humanist speculation that had characterised the revolutions in physics, chemistry, agrarian science, mathematics and biology of the seventeenth and eighteenth centuries.[22] Indeed, the very proliferation of specialised forms of knowledge, and the generalised acceptance of specialisation that followed, is what made Engel's attempt to follow multiple sciences in their own terms and using their specific notations seem abstruse to twentieth and twenty-first century readers.[23] The fading of early modern cultures of intermingled scientific and humanist speculation brought more than a philosophical loss. The everyday effects of separating religious, technical, poetic and humanist spheres would come to define, in a popular cultural sense, the disenchantment of the industrial age.

The scientific and philosophical work of Austrian physicist and philosopher Ernst Mach (1838–1936) for example illustrates both this shift in the relationship between science and the humanities and the ongoing centrality of science to Euro-American political philosophies of the late nineteenth century, as well as its confusing legacy in the twentieth century. Mach has been credited for bringing socialist, pragmatist, positivist, constructivist and even Buddhist commitments to his influential work on the epistemic implications of the seismic shifts

---

22 For an influential analysis of the separation of disciplines in eighteenth-century Prussia, see Immanuel Kant, trans. Mary J. Gregor, *The conflict of the faculties (Der Streit der Fakultäten)* (Lincoln: University of Nebraska Press, 2011) (1798). Thomas Kuhn in *Structure of Scientific Revolutions* argues that specialisation is part of the natural process of scientific progression. However, the question of which parts of science do progress, when, and why are also connected to politics and funding. This something Kuhn acknowledged, but never developed. These links between science and the histories of nationalism, imperial politics, and political economy were taken up by scholars of science and technology studies (STS) after the Cold War.

23 This was precisely the kind of scholarship that was expected from historians of science until recently. Until the 1990s, scholars of science and society tended to be trained in some scientific or technical field in addition to being trained in history, philosophy, or sociology. With the rise of STS, a unified methodological canon has to some extent replaced the older model of multiple disciplinary trainings.

in scientific knowledge that he lived through, and participated in.[24] Historian of science Gerald Holton suggests that Mach's anti-metaphysical arguments were crucially important for nineteenth-century experimental and theoretical work that sought to describe natural and physical systems through their observation and description rather than by recourse to transhistorical theological assumptions. This required a strong break with tradition (understood as continuous with ancient or classical knowledge). A guide for breaking with abstract, theological, received knowledge seemed to be provided by Mach's grounded science and its immanent philosophy (a mixture of atheism, socialism, empiricism and pragmatism), seen as radical "in the last third of the nineteenth century, when some German textbooks in physics still implied that the meaning of concepts was to be sought on a higher, metaphysical plane."[25] It was this radical break with abstract theory that was so new in the late nineteenth century but would soon appear antiquated in the light of the new physics and its irreducibly complex intermingling of theory and experiment, abstract concepts and measurable data.

Mach is known to the public for his scientific work on the speed of sound, but his philosophical work even was more far-reaching. He influenced almost the entire range of philosophy forged at the turn of the century, from pragmatists like William James to the 1911 Gesellschaft für positivische Philosophie (Society for Positivist Philosophy) and its successor, the 1929 Vienna Circle.[26] Philosophers from Mach to the Vienna Circle, notes historian of science Helena Sheehan, "strove to set science upon secure foundations ... to subject all belief to the clear light of reason and the rigor of experiment."[27] As physicist Philipp Frank recalled: "An attempt was made by a group of young men to retain the most essential points of Mach's positivism, especially his stand against the misuse of metaphysics in science."[28]

---

24 See John Thomas Blackmore, *Ernst Mach: His Work, Life and Influence* (Berkeley: University of California Press, 1972); Gerald James Holton, *Science and Anti-science* (Cambridge, Massachusetts: Harvard University Press. 1997).

25 Gerald J. Holton, *Science and Anti-Science*, 4.

26 Gerald J. Holton, *Science and Anti-Science*, 12–14. Holton reproduces the 1911 "Aufruf" from the 'Gesellschaft für positivische Philosophie', which begins: "Eine umfassende Weltanschauung auf Grund des Tatsachenstoffes vorzubereiten, den die Einzelwissenschafter aufgehäuft haben, und die Ansätze dazu zunächst unter den Forschem selbst zu verbreiten, ist ein immer dringenderes Bedürfnis vor allem für die Wissenschaft geworden, dann aber auch für unsere Zeit überhaupt, die dadurch erst erwerben wird, was wir besitzen."

27 Sheehan, *Marxism and the Philosophy of Science*, 43.

28 Philipp Frank, cited by Thomas Uebel, "On the Austrian Roots of Logical Empiricism," in *Logical Empiricism – Historical and contemporary Perspectives*, ed. Paolo Parrini, Wesley C. Salmon, Merrilee H. Salmon (Pittsburgh: University of Pittsburgh Press, 2003), 76–93. Citation 70. Franck

The effort to reinforce scientific facts against idealist philosophy was linked to Mach's early understanding of the mid-nineteenth century traditionalist threat to science. Mach, as well as his followers whose work extended into the late twentieth century, failed to understand that the philosophical and political implications of scientific observation had changed by the 1920s. Yet even as his philosophical influence grew stronger, beyond the nineteenth century, Mach literally could not understand what was going on in physics by the 1920s – for example, in his correspondence with younger physicists it is clear that he did not have the required mathematical literacy to even read Einstein's papers, let alone formulate adequate philosophical frameworks for the new sciences.

The turn to description had run its course by the 1920s; twentieth-century physics as well as the century's global anti-imperial political cultures suggested that all facts are theory-laden.[29] But Mach's influence on two continents and across almost all philosophical specialisations meant that his followers – many of whom lived and worked throughout the twentieth century, like behavioral psychologist B. F. Skinner (1904–1990) – would extend a nineteenth century empiricism far beyond its expiry date. Machism's fuzzy domain suggests both the sheer productivity of this fuzzy metaphor.[30] In Otto Blüh's words, Mach wished to keep "the door between laboratory and church firmly shut" and so he "barred the door of the laboratory from within."[31] Many attempts have been made to batter down this laboratory door since then. But the effects of this positivist overreach are still with us.

---

was part of this group that grew into the Vienna Circle. Philipp Frank's Machism was vigorously criticised in the Soviet version of scientific dialectics.

29 The implications of this radical intermingling of theory and fact were to reverberate through the first half of the twentieth century. Initially, physicists were also philosophers (see Werner Heisenberg, *Physics & Philosophy: The Revolution in Modern Science* (New York: Harper Perennial, 2007 (1958)), and almost all physicists were conversant with the philosophical questions about representation, reality, correspondence, and models. By mid century, however, questions about observation and measurement were to be disciplinarily separated from questions about meaning and reality.

30 Historian of science Nancy Stepan has argued that metaphor is not a removable overlay over scientific observation; it is an integral part of scientific thinking. Loose metaphors are not a sign of faulty thinking; on the contrary, scientists need capacious metaphors to understand, to speculate, or to test new hypotheses. Nancy Leys Stepan, "Race and Gender: The Role of Analogy in Science," *Isis* 77, no. 2 (1986): 261–77.

31 Otto Blüh, Ernst Mach: Physicist and Philosopher (1970), 18, as cited in Sheehan, *Marxism*, 267.

Experiments in Marxist Science

The extensive twentieth-century changes in science, technology, and their roles in global capitalist production mean that it is insufficient simply to pick up Marx and Engel's late-nineteenth-century scientific observations and celebrate their prescience. Methodologically, it is their approach to the historiography of science that has been the missing element in scholarly treatments of Marxist science. When scientific practice and historiography are carried out within the same frame, they can offer radical insights into both science and history, as well as into a range of political and philosophical questions. Their methodology grew from critically weaving together three different problem areas: labour and economic change, scientific theories and technological machinery and the history of science and technology. Each of these were of course already of interest to bourgeois thinkers in the nineteenth century; but Marx and Engels differed from them in that they were historicizing their categories of analysis in all three areas.

The most prominent attempt to situate *The Dialectics of Nature* at the heart of state policy and scientific practice was in the Soviet Union. In the brief period after the revolution and before Stalin's purges, Soviet science soared. Cold War historiography has left us with the notion that Lysenkoism, the term almost synonymous with pseudoscience, resulted from the application of dialectical materialism to the everyday practice of science. Lysenkoism's disastrous results, politically and scientifically, are held to falsify dialectical materialism as a philosophy and methodology. But as historian Nikolai Krementsov notes: "We know now that the problem with genetics wasn't dialectical materialism or the relationship of Mendelian inheritance to agriculture; the problem with genetics was Stalin."[32]

Soviet science through the twentieth century was to fail on many counts; but in the 1930s a paradigmatic intertwining of Marxist science, history of science and political economic analysis might have helped fuel one of the most influential western periods of scientific engagement with Engels.

In 1931, a delegation of scientists and historians of science led by Bukharin attended the Second International Congress of the History of Science and Tech-

32 Nikolai Krementsov, *Stalinist Science* (Princeton, NJ: Princeton University Press, 1997), 25. I do not touch here on the considerable Soviet achievements in rocketry and computer science; see Asif A. Siddiqi, *The Red Rockets' Glare: Spaceflight and the Soviet Imagination, 1857–1957* (Cambridge University Press, 2013); Benjamin Peters, *How Not to Network a Nation: The Uneasy History of the Soviet Internet* (Cambridge, MA: MIT Press, 2017).

nology in London. Gary Werskey, a Marxist involved in the British post-1968 radical science movement, wrote a 1971 introduction to the re-issue of the papers presented by the 1931 Soviet delegation. Looking back from 1971, he wrote: "What they wished to communicate above all else was the intellectual vitality, self-awareness, social usefulness and sheer prosperity of science in a socialist society."[33] As Joseph Needham (one of the only surviving attendees of the 1931 meeting) noted in the same volume, most of the Soviet scholars he had admired in 1931 had since then perished in the Stalinist purges or been banished from mainstream Soviet science. He had been one of a small group of British Marxist scientists who were taken with the 1931 Soviet delegation's scholarship.[34] Most profoundly, they were attracted by the ways in which science and the history of science were intertwined in the Soviet model. Many of them had already moved towards socialism, but this was their first encounter with the way historiography of science, embedded in contexts of scientific practice, and could offer a new perspective on the current forms of science, society, and state interactions. Werskey notes that "Unlike most of the historians, philosophers and scientists whom they were eventually to confront in London, the Russians offered their scholarship as a contribution to a programme of socialist reconstruction which relied heavily on the work of natural scientists."

The Soviet scholars, particularly Boris Hessen, who presented a paper on the socio-economic history of Newton, set out "a sustained Marxist treatment of social and economic factors as elements in scientific and technological development."[35] In this framework, historiography and scientific practice were inextricable from each other, and both were linked to State planning. Socialist planning depended on both science and history. Sheehan reports that Antonio Gramsci read the Russian conference paper collection in prison, and that it influenced Marxist physicist Christopher Caudwell's work on science and society.[36] Although Hessen, Bukharin, and most of the delegation were soon to fall out of fa-

---

33 Gary Werskey, "The Marxist Critique of Capitalist Science: A History in Three Movements?" *Science as Culture* 16, no. 4 (2007): 397–461.

34 On Needham as an unknown classic in modern historical scholarship see: Hans Ulrich Vogel, "Joseph Needham (1900–1995)," in *Klassiker der Geschichtswissenschaft, Vol. 2*, ed. Lutz Raphael, (München, Beck, 2006) 27–44.

35 "Editors Note", in *Science at the Cross Roads: Papers Presented to the International Congress of the History of Science and Technology Held in London from June 29th to July 3rd, 1931*, ed. by the Delegates of the USSR, with a new Foreword by Dr Joseph Needham and a new Introduction by P. G. Werskey. (London: Frank Cass & Co, 1971), v.

36 Delegates of the USSR, ed., *Science at the Cross Roads: Papers Presented to the International Congress of the History of Science and Technology Held in London from June 29th to July 3rd, 1931* (London: Kniga Ltd, 1931).

vour with the Stalinist regime, the 1931 conference is believed to mark the origin of Marxist science studies in Britain. The British 'red scientists' active in the 1930s included Conrad Waddington, J. D. Bernal, J. B. S. Haldane, Lancelot Hogben, Hyman Levy, Joseph Needham, Christopher Caudwell and others. The story of Marxist science in the twentieth century inextricably links Soviet, US and European histories, and a truly global history is yet to be written.[37] In retrospect, the founding of British Marxist science studies in the 1930s was both an unprecedented opportunity to develop Engels's ideas in a different political context as well as a tragic failure to do so.

In the same decade, John Desmond Bernal would elevate Francis Bacon as the ideal philosopher-scientist while Adorno and Horkheimer would lay much of the blame for an instrumentalised, imperialist, mathematical imagination at Bacon's feet. Each group took up vital elements of Marx and Engels's legacy, but the half-century since Marx's death, and the political and philosophical impacts of science, war, and empire brought into question the very categories of their analysis – reason, observation, subjectivity, ethics. Marxist scholars of science and society diverged from Marxist scholars of culture and philosophy. The two Marxist worlds of science studies and critical theory separated in the 1930s, and would not agree on the role of reason in the world for the next century.

The British 'red scientists' spent the 1930s and 1940s attempting to do three things together: practice cutting edge science, publish historical analyses of science and society and work within the State to bring scientific planning to center stage. They succeeded in the first, had mixed results with the second, and succeeded so well with the third that they would rethink some of their convictions about the inherent progressiveness of science. Through the 1930s and 1940s, many of the British leftist scientists were to become Fellows of the Royal Society and win accolades for their fundamental contributions to physics, biology, chemistry and mathematics. The red scientists of the 1930s were pioneers in their scientific disciplines as well as public intellectuals who, following Engels and inspired by the Soviet 1920s model of dialectical materialist historiography of science, laid the western foundations for the integrated study of science, technology and society.

---

37 Sheehan's *Marxism and the Philosophy of Science* is the best Marxist treatment of dialectics and science from Engels through Lukacs. Loren Graham, Elena Aronova and Audra Wolfe have written extensively on Cold War science. An oral history of 1930s red science is Gary Werskey, *The Visible College: A Collective Biography of British Scientists and Socialists of the 1930s* (London: Free Association, 1988). There is a need for more global history that can take into account not only Russia and the US but put them in the context of post-colonial scientific and historiographic debates after 1945.

In pre-World War II Cambridge, scientists formed the second largest academic group (after historians) on the Left.[38] Because of their influence, the study of the 'social relations of science' grew into a separate division by 1938 in the British Association for the advancement of Science. There were French and Dutch leftist science movements as well, and the European scientists' leftism influenced the US Marxist journal *Science and Society.*[39] It seemed as if Engels's approach had found its moment. J. D. Bernal wrote in *The Labour Monthly*: "After half a century of neglect, the methods of Engels and Marx are at last coming into their own in the scientific field."[40]

J. B. S. Haldane's *The Marxist Philosophy and the Sciences* explicated Marx and Engels's dialectical principles, arguing that Marxism was an open-ended philosophy of science, not an economic-determinist toolbox. The following year he completed his introduction to the first English edition of Engels's *Dialectics of Nature.* Soon after the Suez crisis of 1956, he departed for India with Helen Spurway, leaving angry denunciations of British imperialism and looking forward to joining a diverse postcolonial scientific context. J. D. Bernal, deeply influenced by conversations with Bukharin and Hessen in 1931, would go on to strongly advocate for the role of planning in science. His 1939 book, *The Social*

38 Gary Werskey, "The Marxist Critique of Capitalist Science: A History in Three Movements?" Science as Culture. 16, no. 4 (2007): 397–461, 407

39 Gary Werskey, "The Marxist Critique of Capitalist Science," 408; David Caute, *Communism and the French Intellectuals, 1914–1960* (London 1964); Mary Jo Nye, "Science and Socialism: The Case of Jean Perrin in the Third Republic," *French Historical Studies* 9, no. 1 (1975): 141–69.

40 John D. Bernal, "Engels and Science," *Labour Monthly Pamphlets,* No. 6 (1935) https://www.marxists.org/archive/bernal/works/1930s/engels.htm, accessed April 21, 2020. For a sample of the extensive social and cultural analyses of science produced by scientists, see, e.g., P. M. S. Blackett, *The Military and Political Consequences of Atomic Energy* (London: Turnstil Press, 1948), P. M. S. Blackett, *Studies of War: Nuclear and Conventional* (Edinburgh: Oliver & Boyd, 1962), M. Prenant, *Biologie et Marxisme* (Paris: Editions Société Internationale, 1935); H. Levy, *The University of Science* (London: Watts, 1932); H. Levy, *A Philosophy for Modern Man* (London: Watts, 1938); J. B. S. Haldane, *The Marxist Philosophy and the Sciences* (London: Allen and Unwin, 1938); C. H. Waddington, *The Scientific Attitude* (West Drayton, Middlesex: Penguin Books, 1948), Jean Baptiste Perrin, *Pour la Libération* (New York 1942). Their scientific findings were often far ahead of their time. For example, Waddington introduced the term "epigenetics" into biology, indicating the role of historical development that a narrow, deterministic focus on genetics had obscured. For an analysis of the once-obscure, now newly important importance of history in biological development, see Jessica Riskin, "The Naturalist and the Emperor, a Tragedy in Three Acts; Or, How History Fell Out of Favor As a Way of Knowing Nature," *Know: A Journal on the Formation of Knowledge* 2, no. 1 (2018): 85–110. For a contemporary science studies perspective on the importance of epigenetics, see Hannah Landecker, "Food As Exposure: Nutritional Epigenetics and the New Metabolism," *Biosocieties* 6, no. 2 (2011): 167–194.

Function of Science, set out the red scientists' dream of a progressive, vanguardist, science-driven nation whose policies and education were structured around research and the improvement of everyday life through science. Much of this vision did in fact become central to the post-war capitalist landscape, due partly to the effects of the work of scientists as public intellectuals and immediately after the war, as advisors to governmental agencies.

During the war years, many red scientists served the British military, seeing the fight against fascism as their generation's duty. But their public influence dwindled as a Cold War anti-communism took hold,[41] and their theories of science as a progressive force seemed oddly misguided as scientific and technological changes defined newer, more powerful, profitable, and penetrative modes of capitalism. The marginalisation of socialist scientists in the 1950s, and the growth of a US-State Department-funded narrative of science being the harbinger of free markets in the developing world, resoundingly defeated the red scientists' discourse of scientific socialism. Although Bernal's *Social Function of Science* was lauded as his magnum opus and re-issued in 1964, by then it had largely antiquarian interest, much as Engels's *Dialectics of Nature* had seemed quaint to Einstein in 1920. One again, three decades had brought a dramatic change in the framework of understanding science, technology, and society.

The Cold War facilitated a conservative wave in historiography of science. Conservative scholars took back their institutional privilege by a variety of means, including press campaigns against the Marxist scientists. They succeeded in marginalizing what they saw as a vulgar Marxist 'externalist' method, returning to internalist readings of science that rejected the notion that politics and economics shaped scientific fact. Yet, in his 1964 update on *The Social Function of Science*, Bernal reiterated his confidence that a technological future led by the principles of science would necessarily be socialist: "The scientific and com-

---

41 Werskey describes the red scientists' "swift and hard fall from political grace and influence after 1948." Bernal and Blackett would later be denied entry into the US as dangerous subversives. Eric Hobsbawm estimated that between 1948 and 1958, "no known communists were appointed to university posts … nor, if already in teaching posts, were they promoted." (Eric Hobsbawm, *Interesting Times*, 182, as cited in Werskey, *The Marxist Critique of Capitalist Science*, p 455, footnote 101). There were disciplinary shifts as well: Blackett abandoned nuclear physics for geophysics, Needham switched from biochemistry to the history of Chinese science. Haldane and his wife Helen Spurway left for India, which was to be a grand experiment in supporting postcolonial science, but ended with little more than Haldane's clever adaptation of an upper-caste Brahmin scientific imagination. See Gordon Mcouat, "J. B. S. Haldane's Passage to India: Reconfiguring Science," *Journal of Genetics* 96, no. 5 (2017): 845–852.

puter age is necessarily a Socialist one," he boldly announced.[42] He was spectacularly wrong. The computer age was to usher in a new age of exploitation and profits, and the corporatisation of the state in the interest of technological advancement.

Why did the red science view fail so spectacularly, twice in less than a century? Shortly after Marx and Engels' lifetimes, the troubled histories of nationalism coupled with the paradigm shifts that overturned Newtonian science made their notes on science age poorly, and they fell into the overlooked marginalia of Marxist archives. The well-funded agendas of anti-communism had, of course, much to do with the second marginalisation of red science, in the 1950s. But additionally, there was an inadequate set of skills on the left to simultaneously historicise and politicise scientific theory and practice. Bernal, Haldane and other red scientists worked outside their day jobs, reading histories of science and carrying out social analyses of science while doing full-time, cutting edge laboratory and theoretical science. Given the lack of institutional support for this combination of disciplinary activities, their achievements were remarkable. However, their skills were inadequate to the triple task that Marx and Engels had outlined: the task of braiding together scientific practice, political economic analysis and historiography of science. They combined the daily practice of science with the study of the relations between science and society; they were highly trained in science; and they had no training at all in analysing the social. Although they had a deep understanding of the dynamism of scientific processes in their own specific areas of expertise, they had no historical skills by which to locate primary sources, assess historiographic arguments, and synthesise social scientific and philosophical debates. Instead of historicising their categories of analysis, they transposed their own social habits in scientific communities largely composed of educated, liberal humanist white men onto their model of scientific progress:

> "In science men have learned consciously to subordinate themselves to a common purpose ... In science men collaborate not because they are forced to by superior authority or because they blindly follow some chosen leader, but because they realise that only in this willing collaboration can each man find his goal. Not orders, but advice determines action. Each man knows that only by advice, honestly and disinterestedly given, can his work succeed, because such advice expresses as near as may be the inexorable logic of the material

42 J. D. Bernal's essay, "After Twenty-five Years" was included in the reissue of *The Social Function of Science* (Cambridge, MA: MIT Press, 1967), xvii–xxxvi. It was originally published in *The Science of Science*, eds. Maurice Goldsmith and Alan McKay, (London: Souvenir Press, 1964).

> world, stubborn ... These are things that have been learned painfully and incompletely in the pursuit of science. Only in the wider tasks of humanity will their full use be found."[43]

The figure of selflessly collaborating men was rarely understood as an outcome of a long history of male privilege in science.[44] Theirs was an inspiring but deeply limited understanding of the power of science to improve humanity. The processes of collaboration and mutual advice were assumed to simply mirror the 'inexorable logic' of nature; thus, for example, the labour of secretaries or the politics of the State seemed merely background work that followed dutifully in the heroic footsteps of Nature and Scientific Man.

The red scientists excelled in scientific practice but lacked training in historiography. They did manage to learn an impressive array of skills by attending conferences and reading widely. But they were tripped up by the assumption that their scientific day-jobs could simply be combined with self-taught historiographic skills. Both science and history, as disciplines, had evolved beyond the amateur contexts of Enlightenment gentlemen's pursuits. The red scientists produced remarkable texts in the historical and social analysis of science given that they were amateurs in the field. Even their Soviet-inspired socio-economic skills had aged poorly, in the light of the nuanced archival and historiographic developments that had resulted, in part, from the very specialisation and disciplinary focus that had grown in Anglo-American humanities institutions. As Needham recalled in 1971, Soviet historian Boris Hessen had stunned the red scientists with his "trumpet-blast" of an essay on Isaac Newton's bourgeois scientific production. Hessen's "externalist" model of studying science in the context of social and economic activity was threatening to the influential Oxbridge school and its "internalist," Great Men of Science model. But Hessen also made "mistakes of detail on the way," and his work suffered, Needham recalled, from an "unsophisticated bluntness."[45]

---

43 Bernal, *The Social Function of Science*, xxxv–xxxvi.

44 There are reports that Rosalind Franklin found Bernal's laboratory at Birkbeck College a refuge from the sexism she experienced from male DNA-researchers who appropriated her work in X-ray crystallography. Their individual heroism, however, seemed to substitute for social and historical critique. The story of the women who supported and enabled the lives of the red scientists has yet to be told – see Hilary Rose and Steven Rose, "Red Scientist: Two Strands from a Life in Three Colours," in Swann and Aprahamian, eds., *J.D. Bernal: A Life in Science and Politics*, 132–159.

45 Joseph Needham, "Foreword", in *Science at the Cross Roads* ed. by the Delegates of the U.S.S.R., viii.

There was much to appreciate in the ad-hoc historiography that the red scientists adapted to their ends. But by the 1960s, it was also clear that they had insufficiently complex understandings of the constitutive role of science and technology in new forms of capitalism. Nor could they understand the ways in which Cold War funding had facilitated a fresh rhetoric about 'neutrality' of science, deployed in the developing world as an anti-Communist strategy. In 1953, Michael Polanyi, invited by the physicist Alexander Weissberg to chair the Committee on Science and Freedom for the Congress for Cultural Freedom, would begin a movement to end ideology and ground the future in data management.[46] The 'end of ideology' was a phrase coined by Daniel Bell. Polanyi and Edward Shils (founder-editor of the 1945 *Bulletin of Atomic Scientists*) would make it the slogan of the Congress for Cultural Freedom (CCF) from the mid-1950s, using science in opposition to ideology in a plan to "secure a post-Marxian basis for liberalism throughout the world."[47] The CCF's Committee on Scientific Freedom as well as the Committee for Economic Development sought to turn the social study of science into a key driver of anti-Communism. Several post-World War II CCF Study Groups were created to discuss "the dramatic changes in the role of technology and science."[48] The CCF aimed to frame data as the foundation of international policy advice. Data and scientific detachment were held up in opposition to political struggle and ideological debate.

The notion of data-driven social policy foreshadowed the future rise of data and algorithms as a substitute for the messiness of democratic public participation in the agendas of development. If science studies was inaugurated with Bernal's 1939 *The Social Function of Science* as a Marxist return to Engels, it was transformed in less than two decades to a CIA-sponsored discourse about anti-Communist global development. This was an even more dramatic shift than the 1920s' conversion of an anti-metaphysical nineteenth-century empiricism into logical positivism.

---

46 See Elena Aronova, "The Congress for Cultural Freedom, Minerva, and the Quest for Instituting 'Science Studies' in the Age of Cold War," *Minerva* 50, no. 3 (2012): 307–337. Hilary Rose and Steven Rose mark Bernal's *Social Function of Science* as the founding intellectual moment of the study of Science Technology and Society. "Even today, one of the most prestigious awards of the US Society for the Social Studies of Science is an annual Bernal prize; that all too many of its recipients have been the narrow professionals of whom his life as a public intellectual stands in contempt is just one of life's ironies." Rose and Rose, in Swann and Aprahamian eds., *J. D. Bernal: A Life in Science and Politics*, 136.

47 Aronova, "The Congress for Cultural Freedom," 312.

48 Aronova, "The Congress for Cultural Freedom," 314.

There would be one last western attempt before the end of the twentieth century to reconfigure the discussion of Marxist science and historiography. A group of largely American and British science students involved in the campus protests of the 1960s and inspired by the anti-imperialist solidarities of the 1970s, began radical science collectives in the early 1970s (see Fig. 1 below, *Science for the People* magazine) This group had a more precise understanding of the ways in which the nature and practices of science and tech were shaped by their political economic context. They did not believe that science embodied only collaborative and progressive values, shored up by the stubbornness of facts and reality. They entered into partnerships and coalitions with activists, and challenged the State rather than working along with it to increase the status of science. Unlike the 1930s red scientists, their careers did not lead to Fellow of the Royal Society or State science advisor roles. They took an internationalist perspective further than the anti-fascist generation had been able to.

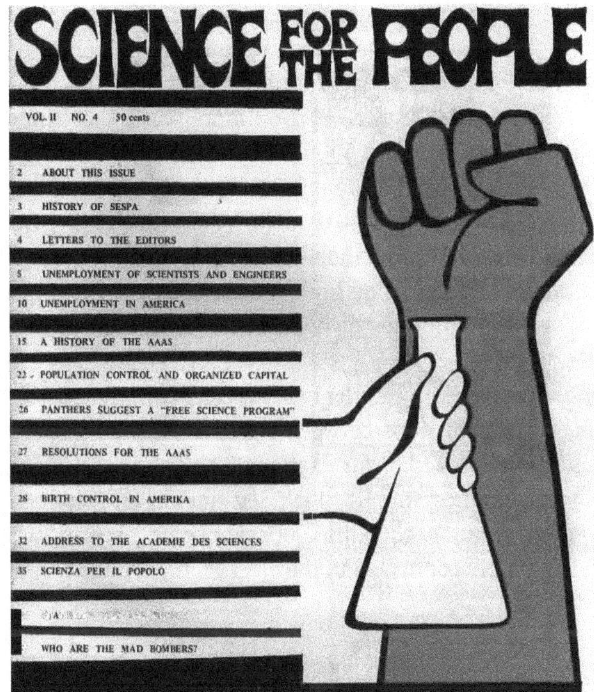

Fig. 1: "Science for the People" Magazine Cover, December 1970. Published by Scientists and Engineers for Social and Political Action (SESPA). Artwork by Elizabeth Fox-Wolfe. Reproduced with thanks to Herb Fox and the Artwork Working Group of Science for the People.

The American-born Robert Young, co-founder of the *Radical Science Journal*, emerged as a Bernal-like figure of the 1970s.[49] He abandoned a prestigious career in the history of science at Cambridge, becoming a full-time science activist and later entirely changing fields to retrain as a psychotherapist. Les Levidow, after receiving a US Master's degree in Biology, became part of the British collective in the mid-1970s, and the founding editor of the journal *Science as Culture* in 1987. The participants in this movement were quite different from 1930s red scientists, in that they spurned eminent science positions and mainstream recognition, instead supporting social movements against nuclear power, the rise of genetics, corporate agriculture and new sociobiological racisms, while articulating feminist approaches to reproductive rights and anti-imperialist critiques of population control, in the two decades following the 1968 student uprisings. They pushed for curriculum reform and democratic participation in science. They raised more feminist concerns than the 1930s red scientists did, and engaged with manifestos of groups like the Black Panthers, attempting to call attention to structural racism in science and technology. They were more engaged with grassroots struggles, much more likely to reject the mantle of vanguardist expert, and less convinced that science was inherently a model for progressive practice. Werskey recalls that "In some respects, the 'events' of 1968 more closely resemble the revolutions of 1848 than the Popular Front politics of the 1930s."[50] These activist-scientists were more influenced by the Frankfurt School's critique of science than by red scientism, closer to Gramsci than to Mach, and took their lead from counter-cultures rather than from nation-states. These popular movements would run aground on the neo-liberal defunding of public education, but they laid the foundations for future critiques of populist authoritarianism in a different era.[51]

By the 1970s there were vigorous science-oriented movements in the postcolonial world. Yet there were few interactions between western and non-western science movements in this period. In India, for example, the Peoples' Science Movement (PSM), officially inaugurated in 1978, included among its subcontinent-wide chapters a movement dating back to the 1960s whose slogan was "science for social revolution," explicitly connected to the election of a Marxist state

49 Werskey, "The Marxist Critique of Capitalist Science," 433.

50 Werskey, "The Marxist Critique of Capitalist," 429.

51 In 2014, Science for the People (SftP) in the US was re-launched, in response to the rise of anti-science and right-wing nationalist movements in the 2010s.

government in Kerala.[52] The Indian PSMs rejected hierarchies between indigenous and expert knowledge, and mobilised education, health and other campaigns to address the problems of development that confronted a young postcolonial nation. Movements across the former colonial world were raising issues of land, food, resources and survival, but these were separated from Anglo-American 'science and society' studies by invisible assumptions about identity and knowledge formations. Western studies of science were considered to be complex second-order engagements with theory, history, and knowledge-production, while developing world studies were considered to be first-order questions of poverty, survival or tribal identity.[53]

When there was a recognition of the existence of Third World Science movements, there was rarely western acknowledgement of their role as theorising or originating a new conversation about Marxist science, or as bringing the challenge of decolonisation to the fore for the first time, despite assertions of anti-imperialist sentiments since Marx and Engels's original writing. Science was still taken for granted, in all the Euro-American twentieth century movements, as a western form of thought. Even progressive scholars contested mainly its diffusion and application in the peripheries, rather than its very origin story. The his-

---

52 The KSSP (Kerala Shastra Sahitya Parishad), founded in 1957 or 1962 according to different reports. See Shiju Sam Varughese, *Contested Knowledge: Science, Media, and Democracy in Kerala* (New Delhi: Oxford University Press, 2017) and Anwar Jaffry, Mahesh Rangarajan, B. Ekbal and K. P. Kannan "Towards a People's Science Movement", *Economic and Political Weekly* 18, no. 11 (Mar. 12, 1983), 372–376. See also Roopali Phadke, "Reclaiming the Technological Imagination: Water, Power, and Place in India," in *Knowing Nature: Conversations at the Intersection of Political Ecology and Science Studies*, eds. Mara Goldman, Paul Nadasdy, and Matt Turner (Chicago: University of Chicago Press, 2011), 244–263.

53 While the historiography of science was largely a Eurocentric diffusion story in the 1970s, the growth of development studies and political ecology produced a vigorous scholarly/activist discourse on nature and culture, albeit in fields that rarely intersected with history of science. See, e.g. Susan George, *How the Other Half Dies: The Real Reasons for World Hunger* (New York: Dover, 1991); Michael Goldman, *Imperial Nature: The World Bank and Struggles for Social Justice in the Age of Globalization*. (New Haven, Conn: Yale University Press, 2006); Judith A. Carney and Richard N. Rosomoff, *In the Shadow of Slavery: Africa's Botanical Legacy in the Atlantic World* (Berkeley, Calif: University of California Press, 2011). The histories of science, technology, and the philosophy of dialectical materialism in China and the Soviet Union are also extensive, and specific to their shifting political contexts. See Lu Gao, "From Dialectics of Nature to STS: The Historical Evolution of Science Studies in China," in *Science Studies during the Cold War and Beyond*, ed. E. Aronova and S. Turchetti (New York: Palgrave Macmillan, 2016), 267–88; Loren R. Graham, *Science, Philosophy, and Human Behavior in the Soviet Union* (New York: Columbia University Press, 1987).

toriography of global science in the 1970s remained largely a story of western knowledge diffusion.

Both the 1930s and the 1970s saw a surge in interest among scientists to take up the questions Marx and Engels had begun to pose about science and technology, and the creation of activist-academic experiments in turning science to the cause of liberation. Both efforts lasted a decade or so before being pushed to the margins by new geopolitical forces: Cold War anti-communism marginalised red scientists in the 1950s, and neo-liberalism in the 1980s undermined the power of most post-1968 science-activism experiments.

Why Revisit the Science Problem in Marxism?

Biologists Richard Lewontin and Richard Levins argue: "The history of our science must include also its philosophical orientation, which is usually only implicit in the practice of scientists and wears the disguise of common sense of scientific method."[54] These biologists, influenced by post-1968 social movements, spent their careers devising ways to combine their everyday scientific practice with the historicist task of setting ideas in their social context as well as the critical philosophical task of studying truth alongside power. Many systematisations of Engels miss this historicising move.

Today, reading Engels's notes along with Marx's scientific notes and correspondence is both fascinating (in terms of offering accounts of contemporary discoveries) and frustrating (in terms of the absence of a complete, convincing philosophical argument).[55] On the other hand, we read other kinds of fragments: Gramsci's Prison notebooks or Michel Foucault's 1973 lectures on The Punitive

---

54 Richard Levins and Richard C. Lewontin, *The Dialectical Biologist* (Cambridge, Mass: Harvard University Press, 1985), 286.

55 Helena Sheehan has written a memoir in which she chronicles her attempt to unravel the mysterious forgetting of this legacy. She recalls her time in the 1970s at Trinity College Dublin, while traveling to London and later to Moscow for research: "Living as if in some parallel universe much of the time, parts of academe proceeded as if the only story in philosophy of science was the one proceeding from the Vienna Circle through Popper, Lakatos, and Kuhn ... The work of Engels, Bukharin, Hessen, Bernal, Haldane, Langevin, Hörz, and many others was never mentioned. I found adjusting to the philosophy department of Trinity strange every time I returned from Moscow or Berlin or Dubrovnik or even London." (Helena Sheehan, "Marxism and Science Studies: A Sweep through the Decades," *International Studies in the Philosophy of Science* 21, no. 2 (July 2007): 197–210. https://doi.org/10.1080/02698590701498126, p 202) accessed April 21, 2020. See also Helena Sheehan, *Navigating the Zeitgeist: a Story of the Cold War, the New Left, Irish Republicanism, and International Communism* (New York: Monthly Review Press, 2019).

Society are examples of notes that were never fully revised into a manuscript by the author.[56] As MEGA IV is prepared for publication and this neglected archive reaches a wider global readership, is it possible to return to Marx and Engels's scientific fragments with a new open-mindedness, and to re-purpose these fragments into a new interdisciplinarity?

In his 1940 Preface to Engels's *Dialectics of Nature,* J. B. S. Haldane noted that its content "refers to the science of sixty years ago. Hence it is often hard to follow if one does not know the history of the scientific practice and theory of that time."[57] This descriptive statement holds a clue to the seeming unreadability of *Dialectics of Nature.* I have suggested that Saito's and other archival findings in MEGA (IV) help us put *The Dialectics of Nature* in its proper scientific context. But apart from the unfinished nature of the textual fragments in both Marx's notebooks and Engels's *Dialectics of Nature,* there is a disciplinary problem that poses challenges for our next steps in this urgent yet recondite debate. Marx and Engels's scientific notes seem unreadable because their requisite reader has not existed for most of the hundred and fifty years since their creation. In order to critically read and engage with these notes on science, method and history, readers would need simultaneously to draw on scientific training, methodologies from the historiography of science and a Marxist political perspective. In addition, they should have some experience in the overlapping zones of scientific research and anti-capitalist activism – this would allow the integration of non-western experiences of colonialism in the same frame as Euro-American accounts of knowledge production. But today, even Marxist studies follow scholarly models of disciplinarity that package Marx and Engels's economic theories and humanist philosophies cleanly separated from the nineteenth-century historiographies of science and rationality in whose context they had originally emerged.

Thus far, the most common systematisations of Engels's project formulate 'rules' for carrying out dialectical materialist science. So, for instance, we are encouraged to understand nature in terms of transformations from quantity to quality (illustrated by a famous passage describing the boiling of water), or to

56 Gramsci's thirty unsystematic notebooks, smuggled out of prison in the 1930s, were edited and published more than a decade after his death. Foucault's 1973 *Punitive Society* lectures were recorded and then erased, because the tapes were re-used for a subsequent lecture. The transcript later retrieved and used for publication was an early version, done privately for Foucault's own use and heavily annotated by him, and were the only extant copy after his death.

57 J. B. S. Haldane, "Preface," in Frederick Engels, *The Dialectics of Nature*, ed. and transl. Clemens Dutt, with a preface and notes by J.B.S. Haldane (New York: International Publishers, 1940), ix.

see the centrifugal and centripetal forces in planetary motion in terms of inherent contradiction. As Marxist scientists have found, however, there is no rule-based method that one can systematise from *The Dialectics of Nature* that makes sense to use in everyday scientific practice. For example, the law of transformation of quantity into quality does not help us to discover the temperature at which water boils. While it is true that Marx and Engels's notes on science do contain many passages advocating a rule-based understanding of dialectical scientific method, these are not the most usable insights in this corpus.

Activist scientists, again, are our best guide to this issue. In a chapter on dialectics, Lewontin and Levins, reflecting on a lifetime of doing science and politics dialectically, reject "the illusion that dialectics are rules derived simply from nature."[58] They study nature through its historicity, heterogeneity and contingency, rejecting Cartesianism's errors of reductionism, reification and alienation. They do see quantity, quality, contradiction and motion in the terms that Marx and Engels explicated, but they do not use these ideas as a priori laws: "Formalizations of the dialectic have a way of seeming rigid and dogmatic in a way that contradicts the fluidity and historicity of the Marxist world view. This is especially the case when it is set out as 'laws', by analogy with the laws of natural science."[59] They historicise *The Dialectics of Nature*: "Engels's understanding of the physical world was, of course, a nineteenth-century understanding, and much of what he wrote about it seems quaint."[60] Stephen Jay Gould, who did not identify himself as a Marxist (but did acknowledge Marxist influence from his father) sees Engels's laws of dialectics as "guidelines for a philosophy of change" rather than "dogmatic precepts true by fiat."[61]

Levins lists the dialectical scientific worldview: "(1) the truth lies in the whole; (2) parts are conditioned and even created by their wholes; (3) things are richly connected; (4) each level is relatively autonomous but is also linked to other levels; (5) things are the way they are because they got that way; (6) things are snapshots of processes; (7) the dichotomies into which we split

---

58 Levins and Lewontin, *The Dialectical Biologist*, 268.

59 Levins and Lewontin, *The Dialectical Biologist*, 267.

60 Levins and Lewontin, *The Dialectical Biologist*, 279.

61 Stephen Jay Gould, *An Urchin in the Storm: Essays about Books and Ideas* (New York: Norton, 1988), 154, as cited in Poe Yu-ze Wan, "Dialectics, Complexity, and the Systemic Approach: Toward a Critical Reconciliation," *Philosophy of the Social Sciences* 43, no. 4 (2013), 411–452, 438. See also Stefano B. Longo, "Book Review: The Science and Humanism of Stephen Jay Gould," *Human Ecology Review* 18, no. 1 (2011): 88–89.

the world are ultimately misleading."[62] Ernst Mayr, "a great non-Marxist biologist," claimed to share "at least six beliefs with dialectical materialists."[63] Paul Feyerabend sums up the problem for scientists with the simple borrowing of a historicist explication of dialectical materialist laws:

> It is not easy to judge the concrete work of a scientist according to the standards of dialectical materialism. The reason is that the philosophy of dialectical materialism has until now failed to develop a methodology that might guide scientists in their research. Of course, one frequently hears that good scientists have proceeded in accordance with dialectical principles, but just what these principles are and how a person who has not yet achieved greatness is supposed to proceed - this is left undetermined.[64]

There is a great deal of literature critiquing the transposition of natural laws into the humanities, and the resulting scientistic wrong turns in humanist and social scientific theorising. But we have not explored the significance of scientific practice for historiography, nor forged a nuanced Marxist historiography for the study of the social relations of science and technology.[65]

Scientists, philosophers of science and cultural historians commonly make post-hoc judgements of good or bad science, real or pseudoscience. But the historiography of science teaches us that such judgements are more complicated if one attempts to define scientific truth in its own historical context rather than by the consensus that emerges a century later. This is not to let 'bad science' off the hook. Rather, it is to insist that we more deeply historicise science, asking more questions about the social effects of truth-making practices, for example, than transhistorical ethical questions about 'pseudo' or 'real' science. Without a method by which to understand scientific practice within its political contexts, we have no way of seeing science and technology – as historically-specific practices, not as a set of axioms assumed to be transhistorically true – as part and parcel of human practices in social, cultural and political spheres. Contemporaneous arguments about the political implications of scientific experiments in their own

62 As cited in Wan, *Dialectics, Complexity, and the Systemic Approach*, 427–428.
63 Wan, *Dialectics, Complexity, and the Systemic Approach*, 428.
64 Paul K. Feyerabend, "Dialectical Materialism and the Quantum Theory," *Slavic Review* 25, no. 3 (1966): 414–417, 415.
65 The western humanist critical tradition stemming from Lukacs is summarised in Sheehan, *Marxism and the Philosophy of Science*. The other humanist tradition, stemming from the Frankfurt School, and its relationship with mathematics has recently received an original treatment in Matthew Handelman, *The Mathematical Imagination: On the Origins and Promise of Critical Theory* (New York: Fordham University Press, 2019). See also Andrew Feenberg, *Critical Theory of Technology* (New York: Oxford University Press, 1991).

time can offer valuable lessons in interdisciplinary analysis. This is what Marx and Engels's notes on science, however fragmentary, offer us. The fragments illustrate how we might build such a conversation today, bringing the everyday findings and practices of science out of their ivory tower and into the public sphere for discussion and debate.

To begin with, these fragments and notes might be read more robustly along with Marx and Engels's extensive work on labour, technology and the making of the family and the working class. Secondly, the claims relating to 'human nature' and to ecologies must be historicised: it is pointless to ask whether Marx and Engels were ecologists or interdisciplinarians in a twentieth century academic sense; we must understand them as living contemporaneously with nineteenth-century advances in physics and chemistry, rather than criticise them for not adhering to the norms of Cold War philosophers of science. Third, we might take up anew the insight of science and technology's global and cultural embeddedness (a central insight of non-Marxist twentieth century science and technology studies) while returning to Marx and Engels's insights that science and technology are neither transhistorical abstractions floating above political practice nor brute instrumentalisms undergirding the protean complexity of human politics.

When Marx and Engels's writing on science is read as a rule-book for scientists across historical periods, it fails to inspire either scientists or political philosophers. When, on the other hand, it is read as part of a historical, philosophical and activist project that historicises modes of rationality in relation to systems of production and labour relations, it illuminates interdisciplinary insights that modern disciplinary structures have obscured. It is the latter reading that constitutes an under-theorised yet newly relevant part of the Marxist legacy today.

Marx and Engels leave us with a model of scientific knowledge production that is inseparable from global analyses of capitalism. New archival explorations have begun to investigate these approaches. New social movements against the technological accelerations of capital have, several times in the last century and a half, attempted to articulate what a 'science for the people' might look like. Despite the many wrong turns and obfuscations, the science question in Marxism must be revisited, yet again, as there is no field that exemplifies the production of power and inequality more vividly than technoscience in the twenty-first century.

Part Two: **Marxism and the Pre-Modern Worlds of the Near East and North Africa**

Mohammed Maraqten

Marxist Historiography and the Ancient Near East

The Impact of Marxist Writings on the Historical Interpretation of the Ancient Near East in Retrospect

The ideas which Karl Marx and Friedrich Engels formed, and their abundant works can be understood in several ways. As a result, they have presented the groundwork for different schools of thought to understand the world-historical process.[1] Marx carried out wide-ranging historical inquiries, examining a substantial part of what was considered as 'world history' in his time.[2] Although many studies have been written concerning Marx and classical antiquity,[3] little has been written about Marx and the Ancient Near East.[4]

The contributions of Marxist scholars to the study of the Ancient Near East are very significant, especially those studies written between 1960 and end of the 1980s. These studies concentrated on socio-economic analyses, origins and formations of the state and the social structure of society and cities.

After 1990s and the collapse of the Soviet Union and other socialist countries, the Marxist historians lost the institutional bases of their studies. This collapse seriously reduced the credibility of Marxism as a general theory of history and society among scholars. In the light of these developments, the 1990s saw a retreat from Marxist interpretations of history, and this had an impact on the reassessment of the history of the Ancient Near East by both Marxist and non-Marxist scholars. Parallel to these changes the field of Ancient Near Eastern studies has progressed and the international scholarship in this discipline has achieved brilliant results.[5]

---

1 See Eric Hobsbawm, "Marx and History," *Diagnoses* 32, no. 125 (1984): 103–114.

2 Michael R. Krätke, "Marx and World History," *International Review of Social History* 63, no. 1 (2018): 91–125 see also the article of Matthias Middell in this volume.

3 See for instance Richard I. Frank, "Marxism and ancient history," *Arethusa* 8, no. 1 (1975): 43–58 and Konstantinos Vlassopoulos, "Marxism and Ancient History," in *How to Do Things with History: New Approaches to Ancient Greece*, eds. Danielle Allen, Paul Christesen and Paul Millett (Oxford: Oxford University Press, 2018), 209–235.

4 Andrej Kreutz, "Marx and the Middle East," *Arab Studies Quarterly* 5, no. 2 (1983), 155–171; Frank, "Marxism and ancient history," 50–51.

5 Daniel C. Snell, *A Companion to the Ancient Near East* (Oxford, Malden: Wiley-Blackwell, 2005); Eckart Frahm, *A Companion to Assyria* (London: Wiley-Blackwell, 2017); Gwendolyn Leick, *The Babylonian World* (London: Routledge, 2007).

https://doi.org/10.1515/9783110677744-008

In the light of these developments, the 1990s saw a retreat from Marxist interpretations of history, and this had an impact on the reassessment of the history of the Ancient Near East by both Marxist and non-Marxist scholars.

In this chapter, an outline of the significance of the Marxist studies on the Ancient Near East will be presented along with a discussion of those Marxist ideas that are still regarded as valid by the international community of Ancient Near East specialists and a consideration of the extent to which these Marxist studies have inspired the scholarly community.

Karl Marx and the Impact of the Marxist Writings on the Historical Interpretation of the Ancient Near East

Specific attention should be paid to the fact that in 1883 when Karl Marx died, the cuneiform writing system had only recently been deciphered and only the Akkadian language was slightly known. Historical knowledge of the Ancient Near East was at that time very limited since the cuneiform sources were not available and hitherto only a very small number of socio-economic documents in Sumerian and Akkadian were published. In fact, at this time most of the historical accounts of the Ancient Near East were based primarily on the Classical authors and the Biblical accounts.[6]

Thus, it is clear that Marx and Engels had only very limited knowledge of the Ancient Near Eastern civilisations,[7] and Marx was aware of the historical knowledge of his time.[8] However, their major concepts on economy and society in antiquity have been enormously significant for the later scholarship of Mesopotamia, and these concepts continue to function as a convenient framework of orientation.[9]

Marxist thought has influenced not only the archaeological theories of the historical periods but also those of the prehistoric and protohistoric eras. Marx

6 Marc Van De Mieroop, *Cuneiform Texts and the Writing of History* (London, New York: Routledge, 1999), 100–113.

7 On the writings of Marx and Engels on the ancient Near East see Burchard Brentjes, "Marx und Engels in ihrem Verhältnis zu Asien," in *Karl Marx und Friedrich Engels zur Geschichte des Orients*, ed. Burchard Brentjes (Halle: Martin-Luther-Universität, 1983), 3–30.

8 Krätke, 'Marx and World History', 91–125.

9 On the pre-Capitalists Formations by Marx see Eric Hobsbawm, *How to Change the World: Reflections on Marx and Marxism* (New Haven: Yale University Press, 2011), 127–175.

carried out the study of the origins and dynamics of capitalist society and the societies of the pre-capitalist period. He used his materialist framework and his treatment of ancient societies was, however, sketchy at best for this phase. Nonetheless, he revealed the features of social change in the historical and pre-historical periods.[10] The basic orientation of Marxist scholars for the study of the formation of the state in the Ancient Near East has been provided by Engels' study entitled *Der Ursprung der Familie, des Privateigentums und des Staats.*[11] He relied on the notion of the primitive Mode of Production in the book, *Ancient Society*[12] by the American anthropologist L.H. Morgan. In this book Morgan illustrated a pre-class social structure of society where the measures of production were possessed by the community and integrated important evidence about the emergence of class society.[13]

The key influence of Marx in historical studies on the Ancient Near East was in the area of theory. As is well known, his historical materialism is based on a specific concept of society and social change. He was mainly concerned with the ways in which contradictions between forces and relations of production happen and lead dialectically to transformations of society.[14]

Substantial Marxist studies on the Ancient Near East started with the Soviet Marxist historiography on Antiquity. By the 1920s, Soviet scholars started using Marxist historical ideas in archaeology and in the interpretation of Ancient Near Eastern history.[15] They applied what has been defined as orthodox Marxist theo-

---

10 Karl Marx, *Formen, die der kapitalistischen Produktion vorhergehen* (Berlin: Dietz, 1952); See also Ph.L. Kohl, and C. Fawcett, "Archaeology in the service of the state: theoretical considerations," in *Nationalism, politics, and the practice of archaeology*, eds. Philip L. Kohl and Clare Fawcett (Cambridge: CUP, 1996) 3–18.

11 See also Friedrich Engels, "The Origin of the Family, Private Property and the State," in *The Marx-Engels Reader*, ed. Robert C. Tucker (New York: W.W. Norton, [1884], 1978), 734–759.

12 Morgan, L. H., *Ancient Society; or, Researches in the Line of Human Progress from Savagery through Barbarism to Civilization* (Chicago: Charles H. Kerr & company, 1877).

13 Friedrich Engels, *Der Ursprung der Familie, des Privateigentums und des Staats: Im Anschluss an Lewis H. Morgan's Forschungen* (Hottingen-Zürich: Verlag Schweizerische Volksbuchhandlung, 1884).

14 Jerzy Topolski, *Methodology of History* (Warszawa: Polish Scientific Publishers, 1976), 197–216; Igor M. Diakonoff, ed., *Early Antiquity I*, trans. Alexander Kirjanov (Chicago: University of Chicago, 1991), 4–13.

15 On archaeology in general see Bruce G. Trigger, *A History of Archaeological Thought* (Cambridge: CUP, 2006). and Norman Yoffee and Andrew Sherratt, *Archaeological theory: who sets the agenda?* (Cambridge: CUP, 1997). On Marxist archaeology see the discussion in Thomas C. Patterson, *Marx's Ghost: Conversations with Archaeologists* (Oxford, New York: Berg Publishers, 2003), 1–32 and Randall H. McGuire, *A Marxist Archaeology* (Orlando: Academic Press, 2002), 9–17.

ry by the Bolshevik Party and adopted a well-defined framework of key notions to Ancient Near Eastern history and archaeology: (1) Dialectical and Materialist Standpoint, (2) Distinct Phases of Human Society, (3) Infrastructure (Forces of Production, Relations of Production), (4) Superstructure.

Soviet scholars and later their colleagues in the socialist countries studied the economic structures and the contradictions inside these societies.[16] The continuity of the historical process was an important aspect of their approach but at the same time Marx's idea of class struggles as the prime movers of change was a central element in their studies on the contradictions and causes of change in society and history.[17]

The Soviet orientalist Vasiliy V. Struve (1889–1965) made pioneering efforts.[18] The studies of Struve on the Ancient Near East were fundamental not only for Soviet scholars, but for Marxist historians in general.[19] A specific conventional form appears in which governments such as those of the Soviet Union and GDR (German Democratic Republic) managed historical and archaeological writing according to Marxist dogmas.[20] The governmental statement on the use of Marxist-inspired methodology and theory, that is, historical materialism and dialectical materialism, as the only method to analyse historic events is accurately seen as a detrimental approach.[21] In East Germany, the government arranged for the chapter on the Ancient Near East in school textbooks to be written by specialists in the field.[22]

Independent from Soviet scholarship, the Australian archaeologist V. Gordon Childe (1892–1957) also played a pioneering role in establishing Marxist archae-

---

16 On the rise of the historical materialism see Topolski, *Methodology of History*, 176–181.

17 Topolski, *Methodology of History*, 208–213.

18 Diakonoff, *Early Antiquity*, 7.

19 The standard work for Marxist's Soviets historians is Marschall Shukow, ed., *Weltgeschichte in 10 Bänden* (Berlin: Deutscher Verlag der Wissenschaften, 1961–1968). The contribution on the ancient Near East is written by V. V. Struve.

20 Elke Gringmuth-Dallmer, "Between Science and Ideology: Aspects of Archaeological Research in the Former GDR Between the End of World War II and the Reunification," in *Archaeology of the Communist Era: A Political History of Archaeology of the 20th Century*, ed. Ludomir R. Lozny (New York: Springer, 2017) 235–273; on the Marxist methodology of ancient history in the GDR see for instance Isolde Stark, *Elisabeth Charlotte Welskopf und die Alte Geschichte in der DDR: Beiträge der Konferenz vom 21. bis 23. November 2002 in Halle/Saale* (Stuttgart: Franz Steiner Verlag, 2005).

21 On the rise of the historical materialism see Topolski, *Methodology of History*, 176–181 and McGuire, *A Marxist Archaeology*, 9–17, on critical approach see Gringmuth-Dallmer, Between Science and Ideology, 235–273.

22 Hans Neumann, "Der Alte Orient in der Schule: Erfahrungen (und Perspektiven?) beim Verfassen von Geschichtslehrbüchern," *Altorientalische Forschungen* 43, no. 1–2 (2016): 170–188.

ology.[23] Childe emphasised cultural evolution and expressed his criticism of the methodology of Soviet archaeology and did not agree with the whole agenda of Soviet archaeology. He refused its comprehensive scheme of socio-economic formations and any other unilinear expression of social evolution.[24] His publications stand out from those of his contemporary archaeologists. He developed an outstanding vision and found the best satisfactory framework for the explanation of his theory of prehistoric and historic past in Marxism and was able to analyse archaeological artefacts using Marxist thought.

He interpreted the transition from hunter-gathering to settled agriculture and pastoralism as the first great social revolution, and called it the *Neolithic Revolution*, also known as the Agricultural Revolution or the First Agricultural Revolution. Childe presented the results of his reflections in 1936 in his book *Man Makes Himself.* The concept of a Neolithic Revolution is still used by the international scholarly community.[25]

His idea started with the question of why Man had decided to settle in dwellings. What had inspired him to do this? Was he compelled by external powers or was it a spontaneous initiative that became particularly beneficial? Hunting–gathering must have become unsatisfactory at some point and Man had to look for a better situation. This better condition was found in sedentary farming, which was associated with the domestication of animals and plants. Childe assumed that the origins of sedentarisation should be sought in the area of the Near East. According to him, agriculture requests water. Once it goes further than the most basic production on a sustenance level, it requires irrigation techniques, digging, constructions of dams and water distribution channels on a large-scale.[26] These are social duties. This account goes right to the heart of historical materialism.[27]

Further, in his later book *What Happened in History*, Childe tried to develop a more obviously Marxist style to express accounts of cultural change that were centred not on technological knowledge as a prime mover but on social, politi-

---

23 See for instance Vere G. Childe, *What Happened in History* (rev. ed.) (London: Penguin Books, 1954); Patterson, Marx's Ghost, 33–62.

24 Vere G. Childe, *Man Makes Himself* (New York: Mentor Books, 1958).

25 See for instance Alan H. Simmons, *The Neolithic Revolution in the Near East: Transforming the Human Landscape* (Tucson: University of Arizona Press, 2007), 11–13.

26 Vere G. Childe, *Social Evolution* (London: Watts, 1951).

27 On the rise of historical materialism see Topolski, *Methodology of History*, 176–181.

cal, and economic institutions and the role they played in bringing about change.[28]

The Marxist historians of the Ancient Near East were led by Igor M. Diakonoff (1915–1999)[29] and the other members of the Soviet school of the socio-economic history of the Ancient Near East such as Muhammad A. Dandamayev (1928–2017).[30] These scholars made very important contributions to the study of the Ancient Near East. The international scholarship of the Ancient Near East had to take into account these Marxist works from the mid-1960s and onward, and not only the Soviet studies but also the studies of other non-Soviet Marxist historians such as the East German studies on the Ancient Near East.[31] Among the East German scholars are Horst Klengel[32] and Joachim Oelsner.[33] Joachim Herrmann was one of the most prominent archaeologists in East Germany.[34] Marxism's impact on archaeology was especially pronounced in the periodisation of history.[35] Of great significance are the studies of the East German scholar Holger Preißler on the socio-economic structures in ancient Yemen, in which he gave several specific examples on the free and unfree status

---

28 Gordon Childe accomplished the difficult task of developing a more thoughtful and less dogmatic consideration of Marxism as a methodical apparatus and was able to apply it to the analysis of archaeological data, see Trigger, *A History of Archaeological Thought*, 344.

29 Igor M. Diakonoff, ed., *Ancient Mesopotamia, Socio-economic History: a Collection of Studies by Soviet Scholars* (Moscow: Nauka, 1969); Igor M. Diakonoff, *The Paths of History* (Cambridge: CUP, 1999).

30 Muhammad A. Dandamayev, *Slavery in Babylonia: From Nabopolassar to Alexander the Great* (DeKalb: Northern Illinois University Press, rev. edition, 1984).

31 Hans Neumann, "Altorientalistik in der DDR (1986–1990) und ihre inhaltlich-strukturelle Umgestaltung in den neuen Bundesländern (1990/91–1995)," in *Wissenschaft und Wiedervereinigung. Asien – und Afrikawissenschaften im Umbruch: Studien und Materialien der Interdisziplinären Arbeitsgruppe Wissenschaften und Wiedervereinigung der Berlin-Brandenburgischen Akademie der Wissenschaften*, eds. Wolfgang-Hagen Krauth and Ralf Wolz (Berlin: Akademie Verlag, 1998), 165–268, 209–212.

32 Horst Klengel, ed., *Kulturgeschichte des alten Vorderasien* (Berlin: Veröffentlichungen des Zentralinstituts für Alte Geschichte und Archäologie der Akademie der Wissenschaften der DDR 18, 1989).

33 Joachim Oelsner, *Materialien zur babylonischen Gesellschaft und Kultur in hellenistischer Zeit* (Budapest: Eötvös University, 1986).

34 In 1969 J. Herrmann (1932–2010) was employed as a head of the newly created Central Institute for Ancient History and Archaeology of the GDR Academy of Sciences. Most of his research contributions related to Karl Marx, Friedrich Engels and Lenin and their theories, as is frequently the case with other GDR archaeologists. Herrmann was a productive publisher and author, see Gringmuth-Dallmer, *Between Science and Ideology*, 235–273.

35 Irmgard Sellnow, *Grundprinzipien einer Periodisierung der Urgeschichte: Ein Beitrag auf Grundlage ethnographischen Materials* (Berlin: Akademie-Verlag, 1961).

of individuals and groups in the Sabaean kingdom.[36] In addition, several Russian Marxist scholars contributed to the studies of ancient South Arabian civilisations. Among them were N. Pigulevskaja, A. G. Lundin and M. B. Piotrowski.[37]

In general, the forces, the means and the relations of production were a favourite topic among Marxist historians,[38] alongside the study of the social and economic life of the common man.[39] In the 1960s, the emphasis was on the origins of states or more complex political structures that were seen as the seeds of modern nation-states. The nationalistic flavour of such research is obvious in several countries of the Near East. Despite certain common patterns in the applied theory, methodology, and the organisation of archaeology, there are also certain regional peculiarities, hence the term 'Marxist-inspired ideologies'.[40]

Among Western scholars, Karl Wittfogel's work *Oriental Despotism* attracted a great deal of attention.[41] Actually, Karl Wittfogel (1886–1988) was more concerned with the totalitarian systems of his day than with ancient history. He tried to relate the evolution of absolute power in regions outside Europe to the organisation of hydraulic resources. The ex-Marxist Wittfogel employed Marx's original terms as a polemical reflection of the Soviet state, which he counted as a manifestation of totalitarianism similar to Asia's 'hydraulic civilisations'.[42] He presents a clear analysis of the central role of irrigation systems in Egypt,

---

36 Holger Preißler, "Abhängigkeitsverhältnisse in Südarabien in mittelsabäischer Zeit (1. Jh. v. u. Z. – 4. Jh. u. Z.)," *Ethnographisch-Archäologische Zeitschrift (EAZ)* 25, no. 1 (1984): 75–83; Holger Preißler, *Das kulturelle Niveau von Abhängigen in mittelsabäischen Inschriften, in Aktualisierte Beiträge zum 1. Internationalen Symposium Südarabien interdisziplinär an der Universität Graz mit kurzen Einführungen zu Sprach- und Kulturgeschichte. in Memoriam Maria Höfner*, ed. Roswitha G. Stiegner (Graz: Verlag Leykam, 1997), 133–142.

37 Walter W. Müller, *Südarabien im Altertum: Kommentierte Bibliographie der Jahre 1997 bis 2011* (Tübingen, Berlin: Wasmuth Verlag, 2014), 180–185, 235.

38 Diakonoff, *Early Antiquity*, 57; Elisabeth Ch. Welskopf, *Die Produktionsverhältnisse im alten Orient und in der griechisch-römischen Antike* (Berlin: Akademie-Verlag, 1957), 114–118, 158–177.

39 Joachim Herrmann and Irmgard Sellnow, eds., *Die Rolle der Volksmassen in der Geschichte der vorkapitalistischen Gesellschaftsformationen. Zum XIV. Internationalen Historiker-Kongreß in San Francisco 1975* (Berlin: Akademie Verlag, 1975).

40 Henri J. M. Claessen and Peter Skalnik, eds., *The Early State* (Berlin: de Gruyter Mouton, 1978); Norman Yoffee, *Myths of the archaic state: evolution of the earliest cities, states and Civilization* (Cambridge: CUP, 2005); Horst Klengel, "Einige Erwägungen zur Staats-Entstehung in Mesopotamien," in *Beiträge zur Entstehung des Staates*, eds. Joachim Herrmann and Irmgard Sellnow (Berlin: Akademie-Verlag, 1973), 36–55.

41 Karl A. Wittfogel, *(1957): Oriental Despotism: A Comparative Study of Total Power* (New Haven, London: YUP, reprint 1967).

42 Peter J. Perry, "Thirty years on: or, Whatever happened to Wittfogel?," *Political Geography Quarterly* 7, no. 1 (1988): 75–80.

Mesopotamia, India and China to explain the basic differences between the state-ruled societies of Asia and the pluralist societies in the West.[43]

Wittfogel presents in his hypothesis a well-defined investigation of the key role of irrigation systems to the rise of the state in Mesopotamia, Egypt, India and China. In his view, the origin of the state stemmed from the requirement of building and managing large-scale irrigation systems. This hydraulic hypothesis of Wittfogel has gained attention in regard to ancient state formation.[44] However, it has since been proved that the formation of the earliest states in the world did not depend on large-scale irrigation systems.[45]

Marxist Studies on the Ancient Near East since the 1970s

The progress of our knowledge of the Ancient Near East is due to the discovery of thousands of written records since the middle of the twentieth century and other archaeological discoveries.[46] Essentially, there are some enormous contributions on these topics, not only by Marxist historians themselves but also by many other scholars, who were inspired by Marxism. Among these contributions are surveys of the history and culture of the Ancient Near East, studies on legal systems, social institutions, economic structures, ethnic relations and religions from the third to the end of the first millennium BCE.[47]

It should be emphasised that after World War II a new surge of Marxist studies in the field of ancient history and in particular on the Ancient Near East occurred. These Marxist studies on Antiquity flourished in the 1970s and continued until the end of the 1980s, especially in the GDR.[48] It must be emphasised that the Marxist studies on the Ancient Near East in this period constituted a challenge for Western scholarship in the field. As before, the great impact of the Marxist school of Ancient Near Eastern Studies was primarily in the field of eco-

43 Udo Witzens, "Kritik der Thesen Karl A. Wittfogels über den "hydraulischen Despotismus" mit besonderer Berücksichtigung des historischen singhalesischen Theravāda-Buddhismus" (Dissertation, Universität Heidelberg, 2000), 8–33.

44 Wittfogel, *Oriental Despotism.*

45 David H. Price, "Wittfogel's Neglected Hydraulic/Hydroagricultural Distinction," *Journal of Anthropological Research* 50, no. 2 (1994): 187–204.

46 Snell, *A Companion to the Ancient Near East*; Frahm, *A Companion to Assyria*; Leick, *The Babylonian World.*

47 Snell, *A Companion to the Ancient Near East*; Leick, *The Babylonian World.*

48 Neumann, "Altorientalistik in der DDR," 165–268.

nomics and socio-economic developments as well as on the origins of the state, etc.[49]

In general, it seems that at first Western scholars of the Ancient Near East did not concern themselves much with Marxist historical studies. However, by the mid-1970s, the debate on Marxist concepts by scholars in the field was no longer prohibited in Western countries, and Marxism started to enter the theories of prehistoric archaeology and historical studies in the United States as well as in Britain.[50] Marxist scholars of the ancient historical fields, especially in Italy and France, had started already in the 1960s to develop new approaches to the study of ancient history. Some of these historians identified themselves as Marxists, while others employed Marxist categories and drew on Marxist theory while refusing to be classified as Marxists.[51]

In the Communist Bloc, the Marxist and the Marxist-inspired approaches and theories were challenged after the collapse of the Soviet Union and the other socialist countries. Marxist historiography and theory experienced a decline after these events since these studies were associated with the state institutions and academies that belonged to the political systems and ideologies of these countries.[52] However, in the Western countries, the Marxist historians and archaeologists as well as scholars who were inspired by Marxism elucidated the historical phenomena from the past without being put under political or administrative pressure and they continued their activities. It should be noted that in the Western countries, although the governments had limited control over the organisation and practice of archaeology and history, this research was often governed by religious and colonial assumptions and it is not correct to claim that such research in the West had no ideological background and

49 Vlassopoulos, "Marxism and Ancient History," 209–212; see also Joachim Herrmann and and Jens Köhn, *Familie, Staat und Gesellschaftsformation. Grundprobleme vorkapitalistischer Epochen einhundert Jahre nach Friedrich Engels' Werk Der Ursprung der Familie, des Privateigentums und des Staats* (Berlin: Akademie Verlag, 1988).

50 McGuire, *A Marxist Archaeology*, 1–17; Vlassopoulos, Marxism and Ancient History, 209–212; Ludomir R. Lozny, "Sickle, Hammer, and Trowel: Theory and Practice of Archaeology Under Communism" in *Archaeology of the Communist Era: A Political History of Archaeology of the 20th Century*, ed. Ludomir R. Lozny (New York: Springer, 2017), 9–58.

51 Patterson, *Marx's Ghost*, 33–62.

52 Sergey Krikh, "Assyriology and Stalinism: Soviet Historiography and the Invention of Slavery in the Ancient Near East," *Journal of Ancient Near Eastern History* 3, no. 2 (2018): 191–209; Leo S. Klejn, "Archaeology in Soviet Russia," in *Archaeology of the Communist Era: A Political History of Archaeology of the 20th Century*, ed. Ludomir R. Lozny (New York: Springer, 2017), 59–99.

that only the goals of archaeology were somewhat different.[53] In many cases historiography in the West is governed by the ideologies of Orientalism[54] and Eurocentrism.[55] Even though Orientalism as a scientific perspective has shown various hints of interior crisis and indications of collapse, Orientalism has been preserved by extensive and organised institutional support. However, it should be distinguished between Orientalism as an ideological approach and Oriental studies and the great and important contributions of Western scholars on history and archaeology of the Middle East.

Since the 1990s, Marxist studies have slowly declined in current writings on the economic and social history of the ancient world. If one comes across the name of Marx or the term Marxism, it is mostly stated within the within the context of a polemical statement.[56] However, in recent years Marxist ideas have established new impetus and new approaches have been developed.[57] Some of the concepts were developed by two of the greatest Marxist scholars of the Ancient Near East, namely the Russian Igor M. Diakonoff and the Italian historian Mario Liverani.[58] Marxist theories of culture have generally emphasised that ideas and institutions depend on a society's basic relations of production. Marxist studies on these topics such as those of Dandamayev have had a guiding impact in the field.[59]

Many Marxists or former Marxist historians have changed their positions from purely materialist ones to more idealist ones and they have abandoned some of their orthodox Marxist ideas.[60] Although the theoretical approaches of the Marxist historians are still important in this discussion,[61] several classical notions of Marxist historical thought such as the six stages of development or

---

53 Mogens T. Larsen, "Orientalism and Near Eastern archaeology," in *Domination and Resistance*, eds. Daniel Miller, Michael Rowlands and Chris Tilley, (London: Routledge, 1989), 228–238; Bruce G. Trigger, "Alternative Archaeologies: Nationalist, Colonialist, Imperialist," *Man* (New Series) 19, no. 3 (1984): 355–370.

54 Said, *Orientalism.*

55 Mario Liverani, "Ancient near Eastern History from eurocentrism to an Open World," *ISIMU: Revista sobre Oriente Próximo y Egipto en la antigüedad* 2 (1999): 3–9.

56 Neumann, "Altorientalistik in der DDR," 165–268.

57 Eric Hobsbawm, "Marxist Historiography Today," in *Marxist History- Writing for the Twenty-first Century*, ed. Chris Wickham (Oxford: OUP, 2008), 180–187.

58 Diakonoff, *The Paths of History*; Mario Liverani, *The Ancient Near East: History, Society and Economy* (London, New York: Routledge, 2013).

59 Muhammad A. Dandamayev and Vladimir G. Lukonin, *The Culture and Social Institutions of Ancient Iran* (Cambridge: CUP, 2004).

60 McGuire, *A Marxist Archaeology*, 9–17; Trigger, *A History of Archaeological Thought*, 33–34.

61 Paul Wetherly, *Marxism and the State: An Analytical Approach* (New York: Palgrave Macmillan, 2005).

'formations', slaveholding, and the Asiatic mode of production have been abandoned.[62] In general, though historical materialism and historical determinisms are now doubted, many of the ideas of Marx are still relevant today.[63]

Contemporary Revisions of Classic Marxist Concepts

After the decline of state-sponsored orthodox Marxism, the other ways in which Marx's ideas have been taken up and developed became more important in the field. We have mentioned the importance of the Australian archaeologist Childe. Marxian ideas on history were supplemented by Marxist-inspired historians and social scientists who were also able to draw upon such non-Marxist thinkers as Max Weber.[64] Marxist thought can still be turned into a useful tool by contemporary historians to deal with Ancient Near Eastern history. We will try to answer the question of what is still relevant from the Marxist studies on the Ancient Near East and what are the current approaches of Marxist studies relating to the Ancient Near East. There are some traditional Marxist topics which have continued to be relevant and other Marxist positions which have been modified. These include the traditional Marxist themes and positions, or those in need of modification, which are discussed hereafter: Historical stages of humanity; oriental despotism and the Asiatic mode of production; slaveholding societies.

Historical stages of human history: The ideas of social formation and the stages of history were among the principle Marxist ideas which were applied to the Ancient Near East by Marxist historians.[65] The traditional Marxist pattern of the phases of history, that is, the six stages of development or 'social formations': the pre-class formation (the primitive community), then three classes: slaveholding, feudalism and capitalism, socialism and communism is now, in general, no longer popular with historians.[66]

Historians have been forced to reconsider these stages and to develop new valid historical concepts and periodisation. Even Marxist scholars of the Ancient Near East represented by the great authority in the field, Diakonoff, considered the Marxist theory of historical materialism as old-fashioned. In the 1990s, the

62 Neumann, "Altorientalistik in der DDR," 209–212.
63 Topolski, *Methodology of History*, 208–218.
64 Hobsbawm, Marxist Historiography Today, 180–187.
65 Diakonoff, *Early Antiquity*, 4–13.
66 See Diakonoff, *The Paths of History*, 2–4; Topolski, *Methodology of History*, 295–301.

Marxist theory of historical process proved that this theory as it had been represented by the Marxist historians of the twentieth century was totally out-dated. Marxist scholars declared in the 1990s that the theory of historical phases was in need of reconsideration due to the realities of the twentieth century They believed that the hypothesis of the awaiting Communist step is poorly proved and pointed to other weaknesses, both theoretic and pragmatic.[67]

Diakonoff developed new perspectives in his work *The Paths of History* (1999). According to him, the historical stages of history are not six stages as was maintained by traditional Marxist theory, but rather eight. These are as follows: First Phase (Primitive); Second Phase (Primitive Communal); Third Phase (Early Antiquity); Fourth Phase (Imperial Antiquity); Fifth Phase (the Middle Ages); Sixth Phase (the Stable Absolutist Post-Medieval Phase); Seventh Phase (Capitalist); Eighth Phase (Post-Capitalist).[68]

Marx and Engels explained in the *Communist Manifesto* that a continuous component throughout recorded history is that social change occurs as a result of the class struggle.[69] According to recent studies of Marxist historians such as Diakonoff, class struggle is no longer considered to be a prime-mover for social struggle and social culture changes.[70] It is now evident that in the Ancient Near East transitions between historical stages have often taken place in a peaceful and gradual manner and that they were settled through consensus.[71] As a result, class struggle – which was considered as the key social contradiction – is in many cases doubtful. In addition, despite the invasions and migration movements that are well-known in history, the processes of assimilation and acculturation of social groups allowed an autochthonous habitat to continue.[72] This means that class struggle and the issue of class antagonism as a historical event are now doubtful.[73] The challenge remains for historians to know and understand how social changes function and happen. On the other hand, some historians have accepted the notion of class struggle as a determining factor in the history of Ancient Greece.[74]

---

67 Diakonoff, *The Paths of History*, 3.

68 The whole book of Diakonoff, *The Paths of History* is a discussion of the eight stages.

69 Karl Marx and Friedrich Engels, *Manifesto of the Communist Party* (Moscow: Progress Publishers, 1986), 34.

70 The notion class struggle disappeared from the last studies of Diakonoff, *Early Antiquity* and The *Paths of History.*

71 Topolski, *Methodology of History*, 287–294.

72 Diakkonoff, *The Paths of History*, 17.

73 Trigger, *A History of Archaeological Thought*, 449.

74 See Geoffrey E. M. de Ste. Croix, *The Class Struggle in the Ancient Greek World* (London: Cornell University Press, 1981).

Oriental despotism and the Asiatic mode of production: Both notions are now considered old-fashioned.[75] However, the concept of Oriental despotism which belongs more to the legacy of Eurocentrism is still in the minds of many in the West.[76] A traditional view of the Oriental despotism of oriental rulers has dominated European conceptions of the Orient, at least since the eighteenth century.[77]

Marx, Engels and Marxist scholars considered the 'Orient' and Africa, etc. as having experienced a different process of development than Classic Antiquity and Europe.[78] According to some writers, this signified that the whole world had passed through the same stages of progress except for the 'Orient'[79] (but this would probably also apply to other regions of the world, such as Africa or Latin America). Thus, the Orient was considered in this case as 'the Other' of Europe, which became an orthodoxy among those who studied the ancient world and excluded the Orient from the developments in Europe.[80]

The notion of the Asiatic mode of production was formulated for understanding Asiatic societies. It was developed primarily by Marxist historians and applied to the study of the Ancient Near East.[81] This model of the Asiatic mode of production has subsequently been an essential feature in Marxist theory and politics. There is no agreement about it among the Marxist historians themselves, but it has mostly been criticised by Western scholars.[82]

The Asiatic mode of production is based on the idea of a fundamental difference between the East and the West including the absence of the private property of land in the Orient, self-ruling village communities and a despotic centralised state in charge of public buildings, especially large-scale irrigation systems, that

---

75 Neumann, "Altorientalistik in der DDR," 165–268.

76 See for example Manfred F.R. Kets de Vries, "The spirit of despotism: Understanding the tyrant within," *Human Relations* 59, 2 (2006), 195–220.

77 Vicesimus Knox, *The Spirit of Despotism* (London: W. Hone, 1821), 12–18; Kets de Vries, The spirit of despotism, 195–220; Perry Anderson, *Lineages of the Absolutist State* (London: Verso Books, 1974), 462–549.

78 Marx, Formen; Umberto Melotti, *Marx and the Third World* (London: Palgrave Macmillan, 1977), Andrej Kreutz, "Marx and the Middle East," *Arab Studies Quarterly* 5, no. 2 (1983): 155–171.

79 On the Concept of Eurocentrism and the question of Marx's and Marxist historians Eurocentrism see Kolja Lindner, "Marx's Eurocentrism: Postcolonial Studies and Marx Scholarship," *Radical Philosophy* 161 (2010): 27–41.

80 Kreutz, *Marx and the Middle East*, 155–171.

81 Marian Sawer, *Marxism and the Question of the Asiatic Mode of Production* (The Hague: Martinus Nijhoff, 1977), 40–146; Anderson, *Lineages of the Absolutist State*, 462–549.

82 Anderson, *Lineages of the Absolutist State*, 462–549.

is responsible for the financing of public infrastructure and state institutions, mainly through power and the control of the armed forces.[83]

Marx's concept of the Asiatic mode of production was primarily formulated in terms of the absence of strong economic structures and processes. The Asiatic mode of production was also a version of the conventional political notion of 'Oriental despotism'. It has been applied by the Soviet historian Diakonoff to Mesopotamia.[84] This mode of production has been defined also as 'despotic-village community',[85] and is described as a despotic monarchic ruling class who lived in central cities and directly appropriated surplus from countryside communities belonging to them. This means that the Asiatic mode was also a type of the traditional political concept of 'Oriental despotism'.[86]

The Asiatic mode of production is a concept that has been the topic of much debate by both Marxist and non-Marxist historians and it has been energetically criticised for its absence of an empirical foundation and for drawing on the Orientalist idea of Asiatic stagnation.[87] It is still sometimes applied by classical historians who seek a way to exclude the Near East from their field of study.[88] The Marxist Orientalist Maxime Rodinson considered the concept of the Asiatic mode of production to be weak and too simplistic for the study of highly complex societies.[89] Furthermore, the field of postcolonial studies has rejected the Asiatic mode of production concept, following Edward Said's *Orientalism*, seeing it as a reflection of the cultural stereotypes that encouraged European colonial expansion.[90]

The hypotheses of Wittfogel on Oriental despotism were sharply criticised from the beginning, but his hydraulic hypothesis has recently been revisited

---

83 Melotti, *Marx and the Third World*, 73–76; Diakonoff, *Early Antiquity*, 5–6, 9–11.
84 Igor M. Diakonoff, "Early Despotisms in Mesopotamia," in *Early Antiquity*, trans. Alexander Kirjanov, Igor M. Diakonoff, ed. (Chicago: University of Chicago, 1991), 84–97; Kreutz, Marx and the Middle East, 159–162.
85 Diakonoff, *Early Antiquity*, 9.
86 Edward W. Said, *Orientalism* (New York: Vintage, 1979), 32–33; Stephen P. Dunn, *The Fall and Rise of the Asiatic Mode of Production* (London, New York: Routledge, 2012).
87 Bryan S. Turner, *Marx and the End of Orientalism* (London: Routledge, 2014), 39–52.
88 Anderson, *Lineages of the Absolutist State*, 462–549; Dunn, *The Fall and Rise of the Asiatic Mode of Production*; Sawer, *Marxism and the Question of the Asiatic Mode of Production*, 40–146; Lindner, "Marx's Eurocentrism," 27–41.
89 Maxime Rodinson, *Islam and capitalism* (New York: Pantheon, 1974), 58–68.
90 Said, *Orientalism*, 9, 153–166. This book criticises and fixes on the colonial aspects of Western intellectual and academic legacies and influenced scholars to pay attention to the miscalculated misinterpreting of the oriental culture in Marxist historiography and neo-Marxist economic theories of imperialism.

for understanding ancient societies.[91] However, there are some scholars who still use the Marxist economic approaches such as the concept of Modes of Production and apply them to Ancient Near Eastern studies, including Biblical studies.[92]

Some Marxist historians make the useful difference between the mode of production as a general concept and a social formation that concerns specific societies which may combine various modes of production.[93] In this case, mode of production expresses a specific phase of history epitomised by the main common form of production, for example, primitive communism, Asiatic mode of production, the ancient mode of production, feudalism, capitalism, socialism and communism.[94]

It has been suggested recently that theories on the Asiatic mode of production and its relations to other modes (such as the Slaveholding and Feudalism modes) belong to the field of Marxist studies rather than to the study of the Near East.[95] Liverani developed a new perspective in dealing with the socio-economic relations in the Ancient Near East, which makes use of the concept of 'modes of production'. He compares the domestic mode of production in the village societies to the palace mode of production in the cities. The latter derives its resources from the villages for non-productive reasons and intrudes upon the rights of the community through the commercialisation of the land. [96]

The existence of an 'Oriental' or 'Asiatic' mode of production seems to be an extremely misleading notion. It has no foundation and was based on a seriously faulty knowledge of the Oriental world and it is doubtful to be of any value in sociological or historical assessment.[97] As a result, the concept of Oriental des-

---

91 Witzens, "Kritik der Thesen Karl A. Wittfogels"; Michael J. Harrower, "Is the hydraulic hypothesis dead yet? Irrigation and social change in ancient Yemen," *World Archaeology* 41, no. 1 (2009): 58–72.

92 See for instance the study of Gerald West, "Tracking an ancient Near Eastern economic system: The tributary mode of production and the temple-state," *Old Testament Essays* 24, no. 2 (2011): 511–532, in which he gave a model depending on Marxist economic analysis that he gathered and then used to study the economic system in the Ancient Near East comparing that with the Classical world and biblical history. On Economic system in the ancient Near East see Kajsa Ekholm and Jonathan Friedman, "Imperialism and Exploitation in Ancient World- Systems," *Review* (Fernand Braudel Center) 6, no. 1 (1982): 87–109.

93 Dunn, *The Fall and Rise of the Asiatic Mode of Production.*

94 Sawer, *Marxism and the Question of the Asiatic Mode of Production*, 40–146.

95 Diakkonoff, *The Paths of History.*

96 Liverani, *The Ancient Near East.*

97 For current sources on the ancient Near East see for example Snell, *A Companion to the Ancient Near East*; Frahm, *A Companion to Assyria*; Leick, *The Babylonian World.*

potism, which was associated with the Asiatic mode of production, is regarded as doubtful according to Marxist historians.[98]

Slaveholding societies: The written records of the Ancient Near East give us information about the experience of slavery from the beginning of the third millennium until the end of the first millennium BCE. Although there was a high number of slaves in Mesopotamian society, there was no system of slaveholding in ancient Mesopotamia.[99] Since important data about slaves is to be gained from many cuneiform economic and legal documents and from the Mesopotamian law codes such as the Code of Hammurabi,[100] this topic received much attention from researchers, and its study is still influenced by Marxist thought.[101]

Until the 1990s, the dominant opinion in Marxist historiography was that the societies of the Ancient Near East represented the earliest phase of the slaveholding formation.[102] Slavery was one of the classical topics of Marxist thought and it was intensively studied.[103]

Struve developed the dogma that slavery was the foundation of Ancient Near Eastern economies.[104] In a paper on slaveholding relationships in ancient Mesopotamia, presented at the State Academy for the History of Material Culture in 1933, both Struve's position and his method experienced fundamental changes that were followed by later Marxist historians.[105]

In orthodox Marxist historiography, the Ancient Near East, Classical Greece and Rome are commonly understood to have been slave societies, characterised by a mode of production in which slave labour produces the greatest quantity of surplus value. Slavery need not, according to this concept, be the principal form of labour in respect of numbers of workers or the total amount of production. While peasant farmers may have been responsible for the greater portion of the value produced, slavery will have been the principal means by which the value produced by direct labour was taken by the class of large landowners,

---

98 See Neumann, "Altorientalistik in der DDR," 209–212.

99 Daniel C. Snell, "Slavery in the ancient Near East," in *The Cambridge World History of Slavery, Vol. 1: The Ancient Mediterranean World*, ed. Keith Bradley (Cambridge: CUP, 2010), 4–21.

100 Dandamayev, *Slavery in Babylonia*, 6–29.

101 Snell, Slavery in the ancient Near East, 4–21; Laura Culbertson, ed., *Slaves and Households in the Near East* (Chicago: University of Chicago, 2010).

102 Dandamayev, *Slavery in Babylonia*, 67–102; Diakonoff, *Early Antiquity*; Krikh, Assyriology and Stalinism, 191–209.

103 Snell, Slavery in the ancient Near East, 4–21; Dandamayev, *Slavery in Babylonia*, 30–35.

104 On the Marxist notion of slavery in general see Igor M. Diakonoff, "Slaves, Helots and Serfs in Early Antiquity," *Acta antiqua Academiae Scientarium Hungricae* 22 (1974): 45–78 and Dandamayev, *Slavery in Babylonia*.

105 Krikh, Assyriology and Stalinism, 191–209.

and thus the basis for the leisure and authority of the leading social class.[106] Important data on slavery is available in the cuneiform records.[107]

A considerable body of contributions to the study of the state formations in the Ancient Near East was written by several scholars, among them was the East German scholar Klengel.[108] These contributions are still important today as a part of some concepts of orthodox Marxism like Oriental despotism, etc.[109]

This concept of slaveholding is no longer accepted by specialists and it has been modified. The Marxist scholar M. Dandamayev in his work *Slavery in Babylonia* summarised the issue as follows:

> In Soviet literature on the Ancient Orient the opinion is widespread that the societies of the Ancient Near East constitute the earliest stages of slave society. However, though slaves in the proper sense of the word already existed in Mesopotamia in the third millennium BC, in the second millennium BC, had come to play a significant role in production, nonetheless, slavery never reached in Babylonia such a degree of development that one can speak of slave labor as having the leading role in the economy. Slave labor was only one of several types of forced labor and not always the most significant. That there was no predominance of slave labor in any branch of the Babylonian economy is not the main point; more important is that labor in agriculture was furnished primarily by free farmers and tenants and that free labor also dominated in craft industries.[110]

It is now obvious that the use of slave labour in production was not the driving force of the ancient social formation in the Ancient Near East. It appears that there was neither slaveholding formation in the Ancient Near East nor was there a feudal model in the Near East similar to the European one. [111] It is important to note that the model of the household that is found in the current scholarly works on Mesopotamia is based on a Marxist interpretation of the corpus of cuneiform texts.[112] In Syria-Palestine and Egypt, there is evidence for something resembling the Mesopotamian practice of slavery.[113]

---

106 On slavery in Greek in general see Norbert Brockmeyer, *Antike Sklaverei* (Darmstadt: Wissenschaftliche Buchgesellschaft, 1987), 23–29.
107 Snell, Slavery in the ancient Near East, 4–21.
108 Klengel, "Einige Erwägungen zur Staats-Entstehung in Mesopotamien," 36–55.
109 Neumann, "Altorientalistik in der DDR," 165–268.
110 Dandamayev, Slavery in Babylonia, 660.
111 Neumann, "Altorientalistik in der DDR," 204.
112 See for instance Gregory C. Chirichigno, *Debt-Slavery in Israel and the Ancient Near East* (Sheffield: Sheffield Academic Press, 1993), 30–74.
113 Abd el-Muhsen Bakir, *Slavery in Pharaonic Egypt* (Le Caire: Institut français d'archéologie orientale, 1952).

Contemporary Marxist Perspectives

Apart from the Marxist notions that have been discarded, Marxist approaches have contributed six major elements that are still relevant for the study of the ancient history of the Near East.[114] These include the socio-economic approach, the debate on the origin of the state, studying history from below, a holistic approach to history, evolution and lager-scale economic change as well as Marxist and colonial historiography.

Socio-economic approach: One of the most dominant perspectives for studying Ancient Near Eastern history is the study of the economy and society of the Ancient Near East based on Marxist concepts, analytical tools, and models and methods by scholars who do not themselves identify as Marxists.[115] Among these current topics are social structure, economic structure, and the market, land property, state theories, city communities, etc.[116] Emphasis on the importance of economic and social factors in history was a characteristic not only of Marxist scholars but also the Marxians.[117]

The socio-economic approach to the study the ancient world was already established by Michael Rostovtzeff (1870 – 1952), who never identified himself as a Marxist but nonetheless applied Marxist ideas to ancient history.[118] Scholars used their own understandings of Marxism and were inspired by the materialist notion of history.[119] They concentrated on the statement of Marx in which he asserted that thoughts do not fall from the sky, but reflect more or less accurately objective circumstances, social forces and contradictions beyond the command of men and women and that they exist on the base of the social relations of production or the relationships between social classes.[120] There arose complex legal and political models with diverse cultural, ideological and religious reflections. The materialist notion of history is able to trace this twisting road.[121] There are

---

114 On relevant aspects of Marxist thoughts for ancient history, see the important study achieved by Vlassopoulos, "Marxism and Ancient History," 643 – 669.

115 See Neumann, "Altorientalistik in der DDR," 202 – 205; Liverani, *The Ancient Near East.*

116 Burchard Brentjes, ed., *Das Grundeigentum in Mesopotamien. Jahrbuch für Wirtschaftsgeschichte / Sonderband* (Berlin: Akademie-Verlag 1987); Liverani, *The Ancient Near East.*

117 Hobsbawm, *Marxist Historiography Today,* 182.

118 Michael I. Rostovtzeff, *The Social and Economic History of the Hellenistic World* (Oxford: Clarendon Press, 1941); Heinz Heinen, "Michael Ivanovich Rostovtzeff (1870 – 1952)," in *Klassiker der Geschichtswissenschaft*, vol. 1, ed. Lutz Raphael (Munich; Beck, 2006), 172 – 189.

119 Hobsbawm, *Marxist Historiography Today,* 180 – 187.

120 Topolski, *Methodology of History,* 210 – 212.

121 Klengel, *Kulturgeschichte des alten Vorderasiens.*

currently many fields in which scholars are using Marxist tools. One such example is the study of the Mesopotamian economy.[122] One of the most solid current works on the social and economic history of the Ancient Near East has been produced by the Italian Marxist historian Liverani.[123] Some archaeologists and historians have combined Marxism and structuralism in their studies, while others place the starting point of the debate in the concrete experiences of human existence, with emphasis on the production of the requirements of life.[124]

The origin of the state: One of the most important subjects for Marxist historians is the question of the origin of the state.[125] The question of the beginning of the institution of the state was a central debate which depended on the Marxist studies about the family and the origins of the state that followed Engels, in particular studies produced by East German scholars.[126] Important aspects of this debate are still valid today. In association with the Marxist concept of the Asiatic mode of production, the concept of the state was described in the fashion of the so-called Oriental despotism.[127] Since there are no established and accepted solutions for this matter, the formation and evolution of the early or archaic state continues to remain a big issue of discussion today.[128] Evolutionism is currently an important perspective for some of the former Marxist and Marxist-inspired scholars.[129] In studying the state, the classical Soviet Marxist historians' approach in Russia changed to one of evolution.[130] Marx's theory is an attempt to accept both types of accounts of the Orient and to explain the apparent unity of states often made up of previously independent units which nevertheless cooperated in great communal works such as road building and large-scale irrigation such as in Egypt and Mesopotamia.[131]

---

122 Michael Jursa, ed., *Aspects of the economic history of Babylonia in the first Millennium BC* (Münster: Ugarit Verlag, 2010).

123 Liverani, *The Ancient Near East.*

124 Bryan S. Turner, *Orientalism, postmodernism and globalism* (London: Routledge, 1994), 43.

125 Neumann, "Altorientalistik in der DDR," 202.

126 Klengel, "Einige Erwägungen zur Staats-Entstehung in Mesopotamien," 36–55; Herrmann and Köhn, *Familie, Staat und Gesellschaftsformation.*

127 Anderson, *Lineages of the Absolutist State*, 462–549.

128 Leonid E. Grinin, Robert L. Carneiro, R. L., Dmitri M. Bondarenko, D.M., Nikolay N. Kradin and Andrey V. Korotayev, eds., *The Early State, Its Alter-natives and Analogues* (Saratov: Uchitel Publishing House, 2004); Yoffee, *Myths of the archaic state.*

129 Gill Stein and Mitchell S. Rothman, *Chiefdoms and Early States in the Near East: The Organizational Dynamics of Complexity* (Madison: Prehistory Press, 1994), 1–10.

130 Yoffee, *Myths of the archaic State*; Grinin et al., *The Early State.*

131 Igor M. Diakonoff, "The Rise of the Despotic State in Ancient Mesopotamia," in *Ancient Mesopotamia, Socio-economic History: a Collection of Studies by Soviet Scholars*, ed. Igor M. Dia-

History from below: History from above was for a long time the dominant form of writing history.[132] As an alternative to this, history from below could be described as a response against the conventional historians who are almost exclusively concerned with the society and politics of the ruling classes and religious elites. History from below has been also designated as 'history of everyday life', the 'people's history' and 'history of the common people', etc. The idea of studying history from the bottom or below emerged from Marxist traditions. Although the Marxist historians have heavily influenced the writing of history from below in the twentieth century, there are also others whose writings can be said to have contributed to this trend.

History from below is one of the most significant Marxist ideas which were applied to the study of the ancient history of the Near East and played a key role in extending the concepts of the writing of its history. History from below focuses on *Alltagsgeschichte*, ('history of everyday life') the subaltern social groups such as slaves, peasants, women, minority groups, ethnic groups, nomadic groups and other subaltern groups as well as on prosopography of individuals and groups in addition to oral history. History from below made an attempt to produce wide-ranging history-writing in order to explore the realities of marginalised social units and individuals, to discover original sources and to reconsider the well-known ones. It is a historical viewpoint that rejects the narrative of traditional history. Though the influence of the perspective of history from below has been significant, it has not been able to displace traditional history.[133]

There is no doubt that the notion of history from below represents a challenge for both Marxist historians and other scholars of ancient history in studying how to investigate the subaltern social groups as active performers in history and how to integrate them into historical narrative.[134] Marxist historians have made contributions to the historiography from below as well as to cultural historiography and historiography of the family, slavery, rural communities, noma-

konoff (Moscow: Nauka, 1969), 173–203; Klengel, "Einige Erwägungen zur Staats-Entstehung in Mesopotamien," 36–55.

132 Van de Mieroop, *Cuneiform Texts and the Writing of History*, 85–104.

133 Andrew I. Port, "History from Below, the History of Everyday Life, and Microhistory," in *International Encyclopedia of the Social & Behavioral Sciences*, Vol.11, ed. James D. Wright, ed. (Amsterdam: Elsevier, 2015), 108–113.

134 Jim Sharpe, "History from below," in *New perspectives on historical writing*, ed. Peter Burke (Cambridge: Polity Press, 1991), 24–41.

dic groups, etc. In particular, Marxist historiography has made contributions to the methodology of writing history from below in ancient Mesopotamia.[135]

Marxist historiography from below deals chiefly with the economic development of politically active masses. The role of the individual in history is here an important object of research.[136] The connection of Subaltern Studies with the concept of 'history from below' was popularised by British Marxist historians.[137]

Archaeology from below has also been applied as a method in studying the historical past.[138] This approach is the opposite of the mainstream trend of 'archaeology from above'. One of the most important aspects of archaeology from below is the consideration of the heritage of a social group as an active process of life in the historical past of this group of people. In this case, heritage is regarded as an impressive survival which is developed and altered in the hands of the society to whom it belongs.[139]

Marxist-inspired archaeologists and historians concentrated not just on palaces, castles and fortresses, but also on rural settlements and villages. It actually enriched our knowledge of the past societies by giving attention not only to the high-level issues and developments in society and culture but also to evidence of daily life and the role of the subaltern in society.[140]

Thus, history should be not merely be a representation of rulers' biographies. It should be regarded from below, from the perspective of the men and women who actually did the work in any assumed society, not from that of governors, officials, landowners or other superiors, who have never been more than a small element of human history.

The holistic approach to history: This perspective can be described as an interdisciplinary study covering all domains in the social sciences and humanities and combines it with research achieved by the so-called natural sciences utilising numerous analytical methods and techniques of historic investigation

---

135 Jonathan S. Tenney, *Life at the Bottom of Babylonian Society: Servile Laborers at Nippur in the 14th and 13th Centuries B.C.* (Leiden: Brill, 2011); A. Dornauer, *Assyrische Nutzlandschaft in Obermesopotamien. Natürliche und anthropogene Wirkfaktoren und ihre Auswirkungen* (Munich: Herbert Utz Verlag, 2016).

136 Topolski, *Methodology of History*, 53.

137 Port, History from Below, 108–113.

138 Neil Faulkner, "Archaeology from Below," *Public Archaeology* 1 (2000): 21–33.

139 Benjamin W. Porter, "Near Eastern Archaeology: Imperial Pasts, Postcolonial Presents, and the Possibilities of a Decolonized Future," in *Handbook of Postcolonial Archaeology*, eds. Jane Lydon and Uzma Z. Rizv (London: Routledge, 2010), 51–60.

140 Matt Perry, "History from Below," in *Encyclopedia of Historians and Historical Writing*, 2 vols., ed. Kelly Boyd, (Chicago, Fitzroy Dearborn Publishers, 1999), 543–544.

in these fields. It is an approach that views the world holistically.[141] Marxist historiography insists on such a holistic attitude to analyse human behaviour and to study the history of segments of societies in relation to the whole and individual social groups in terms of wide-ranging networks of relations within the society. Marxist thought emphasised the systemic interdependence of all aspects of social life as a means of assuring the survival of human groups.[142]

The holistic perspective to studying the history of the Ancient Near East as a whole unity is of great importance and gives the possibility for a profound understanding of Ancient Near Eastern culture. Several studies have been written on this topic.[143] In the important study entitled *Early Antiquity*, Russian scholars sought to provide a major universal history of the Near East in ancient times.[144] The holistic approach as a method in studying Mesopotamian history has been employed in some studies which depend on the textual sources.[145] This holistic approach is able to link together economy, society, political institutions and culture and revolution, and to link these with the concept of large-scale historical change, which provides a more comprehensive understanding of the past.[146] The Marxist notions such as the mode of production, infrastructure (base) and superstructure, class, productive forces, productive relations and revolution give the possibility to combine together various processes and are able to reveal long-term changes.[147]

Evolution and large-scale historical changes: An important concept of Marxist historiography, which has been applied to the history of the Ancient Near East, is that of large-scale historical changes such as the Neolithic Revolution in the Marxist tradition that caused sedentarisation followed by urbanisation. Further, large-scale historical change comprises long periods of changes of the historical phases, which caused the development of the different types

---

141 Vlassopoulos, "Marxism and Ancient History," 216–220.

142 Topolski, *Methodology of History*, 179–181.

143 See the study of Richard L. Zettler, "Reconstructing the World of Ancient Mesopotamia: Divided Beginnings and Holistic History," in *Excavating Asian History: Interdisciplinary Studies in Archaeology and History*, eds. Norman Yoffee, Bradley L. Crowell (Tucson: University of Arizona Press, 2006), 113–159.

144 See the important holistic study of John N. Postgate, *Early Mesopotamia: Society and Economy at the Dawn of history* (London: Routledge, 1992) and see also Zettler, *Reconstructing the World of Mesopotamia*, 113–159.

145 Karen Radner and Eleanor Robson, eds., *The Oxford Handbook of Cuneiform Culture* (Oxford: OUP, 2011).

146 Vlassopoulos, "Marxism and Ancient History," 216–220.

147 Topolski, *Methodology of History*, 643–646.

of ancient and archaic as well as modern states.[148] The evolutionary pattern has its Marxist genesis in Engels' *Origin of the Family*. One chief argument of the evolutionary-Marxist notion of history is that any assumed period is genetically and dialectically associated with its predecessors, that is to say, there is a permanent feature to change.

One of the important Marxist approaches, which is still fruitful today, is the evolutionary one: Its purpose is to seek out and identify the development of change in human history through wide-ranging broad standards.[149] The Marxist version of evolutionism has been accepted and given the designation neo-evolutionary perspective.[150] The application of Marxist concepts of social evolution, which involve the comprehensive study of social and political organisation, subsistence systems, trade and settlement patterns, etc. is an important method in dealing with the Ancient Near East.[151] This was a major contribution of Marxist theory to Ancient Near Eastern history and archaeology: an assertion of a degree of cultural continuity through Prehistory up to the emergence of class society in the Bronze Age.[152]

Marxist and colonial historiography: One of the most relevant aspects of Marxist thought is the anti-colonialist attitude. On the notion of colonialism, attention should be given here to two points: how the Marxist historians or Marxist-inspired historians apply the term colonialism in studying the history of the Ancient Near East and secondly the perspectives of colonial history and historiography on the Ancient Near East.[153]

The term colonialism has been applied in studying Mesopotamian history. A good example of this can be seen in the studies of the neo-Marxist, Cuban anthropologist Guillermo Algaze. He studied the progress and spread of civilisation from the Euphrates region to other areas of ancient Mesopotamia. He maintained that colonial expansion initiated in south Iraq radiated northwards and was responsible for the establishment of city-states in northern Iraq and Syria and

---

148 Daniel Little, "Explaining large-scale historical change," *Philosophy of the Social Sciences* 30, no. 1 (2000): 89–112.

149 Childe, *Social Evolution.*

150 Stephen Shennan, "After social evolution: a new archaeological agenda?" in *Archaeological theory: who sets the agenda?*, ed. Norman Yoffee and Andrew Sherratt (Cambridge: CUP, 1997), 53–59.

151 Topolski, *Methodology of History*, 176–181.

152 Childe, *Social Evolution.*

153 Jane Lydon and Uzma Z. Rizv, *Handbook of Postcolonial Archaeology* (London: Routledge, 2010).

south-eastern Asia Minor.[154] Algaze made an analysis of what he called colonialism and imperialism in ancient civilisations, especially the city of Uruk's expansion in ancient Mesopotamia. Uruk seems to have created the world's earliest identified colonial system. It was a well-organised network in order to achieve access to natural resources in Syria, Asia Minor and the Zagros Mountains.[155] Another example of such studies is on the expansion and colonisation of the western Mediterranean by the Phoenicians.[156]

One important aspect of the colonial historiographical approaches to studying the Ancient Near East is that many European scholars considered these countries as their property.[157] It is of significance to study how Western colonial historians have presented these countries in their studies. Recently this topic has been studied by several scholars in the West, among them Marxist historians.[158] Archaeologists, travellers and diplomats not only made journeys in the Middle East, but they also excavated and plundered the treasuries of Egypt and Mesopotamia, etc.[159] Western colonial historians and archaeologists were always heavily influenced by Biblical and colonial ideology and it is important to the study of their historical narratives and how they have presented the indigenous peoples of these countries and their history.[160] It is of interest that postcolonial

---

154 Guillermo Algaze, *Ancient Mesopotamia at the Dawn of Civilization: The Evolution of an Urban Landscape* (Chicago: UCP, 2008), 28–39.

155 Guillermo Algaze, *The Uruk World System: The Dynamics of Expansion of Early Mesopotamian Civilization* (Chicago: UCP, 1993), 8–18.

156 Maria E. Aubet, *Commerce and Colonization in the Ancient Near East* (Cambridge: CUP, 2013).

157 Susan Pollock and Reinhard Bernbeck, eds., *Archaeologies of the Middle East Critical Perspectives* (Oxford: Blackwell, 2005).

158 Mario Liverani, "Imperialism," in *Archaeologies of the Middle East Critical Perspectives*, eds. Susan Pollock and Reinhard Bernbeck (Oxford: Blackwell, 2005), 1999, 223–243; see also Michael Prior, *The Bible and Colonialism: A Moral Critique* (Sheffield: Sheffield Academic Press, 1997).

159 On the plundering of ancient oriental artefacts that filled Western museum such the Louvre, British Museum and Pergamum Museum, Berlin as well as the political role of archaeologist see Charlotte Trümpler, ed., *Das grosse Spiel: Archäologie und Politik zur Zeit des Kolonialismus (1860–1940): Begleitbuch zur Ausstellung, Ruhr Museum Essen, 11. Februar–13. Juni 2010* (Köln: DuMont, 2010); On the approach of Western Archaeologist see the critical study of the Marxist archaeologist Alexander Mongait, *Archäologie und Gegenwart* (Dresden: Verlag der Kunst, 1985).

160 Trigger, "Alternative Archaeologies," 355–370; Nadia Abu el-Haj, *Facts on the Ground: Archaeological Practice and Territorial Self-Fashioning in Israeli Society* (Chicago: UCP, 2002). See also the critical study of the so-called Biblical Archaeology and its colonial goals by Neil A. Silberman, "Promised lands and chosen peoples: the politics and poetics of archaeological narrative," in *Nationalism, politics, and the practice of archaeology*, eds. Philip L. Kohl and Clare Fawcett (Cambridge: CUP, 1996), 249–262.

theory relating to history and archaeology has been inspired by Marxism and the postcolonial scholars are indebted to the theoretical works of Marxist scholarship and the Marxist historical framework.[161] This is sometimes awkwardly interpreted or disavowed.

Conclusion

An overview of the Marxist studies on the Ancient Near East shows that Marxist historians made significant contributions, in particular to the socio-economic structure of the societies of the ancient Near East, to the origins of the state, slavery, etc. Marxist historians and Marx-inspired historians working on the Ancient Near East built an important school after World War II, which continued to the end of the 1980s and presented a challenge for the Western school in studying the Ancient Near East.

This study shows that after the 1990s the Marxist studies have been modified and some of the Marxist historical concepts have been discarded such as class struggle, the six historical stages of human history (instead, eight stages have suggested by Diakonoff) and the idea of a dominant slaveholding formation in the Ancient Near East. Oriental despotism and the Asiatic mode of production are now very doubtful. However, these notions continue to be relevant, but in modified forms.

Furthermore, this paper presented some Marxist perspectives which are still relevant in studying history in general, and those that have been applied in studying the history of the Ancient Near East and are still significant. Among these notions are the socio-economic approaches, theories of the origin of the state, studying history from below, the holistic perspective in studying history, the concept of large-scale historical change and the use of Marxist historiography to analyse colonial historical writings. There are many valid critiques on both Marx's works and the body of Marxist historiography which developed after Marx. However, many of Marx's thoughts are still very useful and might be used to build a framework for the study of the Ancient Near East.

---

161 Patterson, *Marx's Ghost*, 30 – 32.

Amar S. Baadj

Maḥmūd Ismāʿīl and his Historical-Materialist Approach to the History of the Medieval Islamic World

The Egyptian historian Maḥmūd Ismāʿīl ʿAbd al-Rāziq (born 1940) is the founder of a Marxist-inspired historiographical school that has had a great impact on the study of medieval Islamic history in universities across the Arab World from Morocco to Kuwait. Many of his former students are now prominent historians themselves. Together they have revolutionised the study of the social and economic history of North Africa and al-Andalus. Surprisingly, the works of Ismāʿīl and his students have received very little attention from Western specialists in medieval Islamic history. It is the goal of this paper to introduce the work of this important historian to an English-speaking audience and hopefully encourage other scholars to read his books and engage with his ideas.

The first part of this article consists of a brief biographical sketch of Ismāʿīl. This is followed by a discussion of his methodological approaches and his critiques of various Western and Arab scholars. Then we will consider his views on the modes of production, the reasons for the failure of the medieval Islamic World to undergo an 'industrial revolution' and the problem of feudalism. The next part of this article deals with his periodisation of Islamic history and his views on the development of class relations in the Medieval Islamic World. Finally, the last part of this article will give a short overview of the structure of his most important work.

Maḥmūd Ismāʿīl's Career

Maḥmūd Ismāʿīl ʿAbd al-Rāziq was born in 1940 to a family of modest means in a farming village called al-Ṭawīla in the Egyptian governorate of al-Daqahliyya, which is located to the northeast of Cairo. He was a precocious youth who excelled in his studies. He was also exposed to Egyptian politics at an early age through his teachers and relatives. After completing primary and secondary school in Mansura, the provincial capital, he enrolled in the Cairo University Fac-

https://doi.org/10.1515/9783110677744-009

ulty of Arts. Though he initially planned to study journalism or English, he decided to specialise in history, obtaining his BA in 1962.[1]

Ismāʿīl's most influential professors were Muḥammad Anīs (1921–1986), who specialised in modern Egyptian social history and encouraged Ismāʿīl's interest in social history and Marxist historiography, and the medievalist Ḥasan Maḥmūd, who specialised in the history of the Maghrib and had written an important work on the Almoravid dynasty.[2] Ḥasan Maḥmūd directed Ismāʿīl's attention to the medieval Maghrib and under his supervision Ismāʿīl completed an M.A. thesis on the foreign relations of the Aghlabid dynasty in 1967 and a Ph.D. thesis in 1970 on the Kharijites in the Maghrib from the Islamic conquest until the middle of the tenth century AD.[3] Both theses were later published as books and they remain essential works in the field. During the same period that he was preparing his dissertations, Ismāʿīl also played a key role in the newly-founded Center for Contemporary Egyptian History whose first director was his mentor Anīs. Among other duties there, Ismāʿīl headed a commission of historians charged with gathering accounts of the July 1952 Revolution.[4]

In 1971, Ismāʿīl was appointed assistant professor of Islamic history at the ʿAyn Shams University in Cairo. He also began writing regular articles for the famous political magazine *Rose al-Yūsuf*, including an interview with the Palestinian leader Yāsir ʿArafāt. The death of Jamāl ʿAbd al-Nāṣir and accession of Anwār al-Sādāt to the presidency in 1970 brought about major changes in government policies. Socialism fell into official disfavour. Leftist intellectuals and activists were increasingly harassed and persecuted by the security forces while their conservative foes were tacitly encouraged. As an outspoken Marxist heavily involved in the left-wing student movement, Ismāʿīl was frequently detained by the police. A series of articles which Ismāʿīl published on revolutionary ideological movements of the early Islamic period (later published together in one volume as *The Secret Movements in Islam*) provoked an enormous controver-

1 Maḥmūd Ismāʿīl, *Jadal al-Anā wa al-Ākhar: Sīra Dhātiyya* (Cairo: Al-Ruʾya, 2008), 17–32.

2 Ḥasan Aḥmad Maḥmūd, *Qiyām Dawlat al-Murābiṭīn* (Cairo: Dār al-Fikr al-ʿArabī, 1956). On the place of this book within the field of Almoravid studies see ʿIzz al-Dīn Jassūs, "Al-Gharb al-Islāmī bayna al-Baḥth al-Tārīkhī al-ʿArabī wa al-Gharbī," in *Al-Taʾrīkh al-ʿArabī wa Tārīkh al-ʿArab: Kayfa Kutiba wa kayfa Yuktab?Al-Ijābāt al-Mumkina*, ed. Wajīh Kawtharānī (Beirut: Al-Markaz al-ʿArabī li al-Abḥāth wa Dirāsat al-Siyāsāt, 2017), 659–680, esp. 661–667.

3 Maḥmūd Ismāʿīl, *Al-Khawārij fī Bilād al-Maghrib ḥattā Muntaṣaf al-Qarn al-Rābiʿ al-Hijrī*, (Casablanca: Dār al-Thaqāfa, 1976); Idem, *Al-Aghāliba 184 h – 296 h: Sīyāsatuhum al-Khārijiyya* (Cairo: Ein for Human and Social Sciences, 2000).

4 Ismāʿīl, *Jadal*, 34–48.

sy.[5] Islamist leaders accused the author of heresy and Al-Azhar University demanded that the government intervene for the 'protection of Islam'.[6]

One day, Ismāʿīl had a chance meeting with the dean of Fez University from whom he learned that his works on Maghribī history enjoyed immense popularity in Morocco and the neighbouring countries. He was invited to take up a visiting professorship in Fez. Fearing for his professional future in Egypt he readily accepted the offer.[7] Thus began a new and highly fruitful chapter in his career. He remained in Morocco from 1974 to 1984, save for a short return to Cairo in 1979 during which he nearly lost his right to travel outside of Egypt.[8] Though Morocco was an absolute monarchy, Ismāʿīl recounts that he enjoyed a remarkable degree of freedom of speech while he was there and compared the academic environment in Morocco favourably to that of Egypt during the 1970s.[9] Nonetheless, he also assures us that he sought to "avoid creating problems" in his new home.[10] Ismāʿīl was well-integrated into Moroccan cultural life and enjoyed the status of a public intellectual who was famous not only in historical circles but also in the domains of literature and philosophy. While in Fez he published the first volumes of his *magnum opus*, the ten volume *Sociology of Islamic Thought* (*Sūsiyūlūjiyyā al-Fikr al-Islāmī*), as well as a number of important monographs and articles on medieval Maghribī history.[11] He also established a centre for the study of social and economic history in the Fez University Faculty of Letters.[12]

It was during this period that he laid the foundations for a historiographical 'school' which continues to have a great influence on the study of medieval North Africa and al-Andalus in history departments across the Arab World, particularly in Morocco itself. Ismāʿīl trained his students in the discipline of socio-economic history and many of his Moroccan students have continued to work in this area. Among the most prominent of Ismāʿīl's graduate students from this period were Aḥmad al-Ṭāhirī and Ibrāhīm al-Qādirī Būtashīsh. Al-Ṭāhirī wrote his doctoral thesis on "The Common Class in Cordoba during the Caliphate" and he

5 Maḥmūd Ismāʿīl, *Al-Ḥarakāt al-Sirriyya fī al-Islām* (Cairo: Sīnā, 1997).

6 Ismāʿīl, *Jadal*, 52–62.

7 IsmāʿIl, *Jadal*, 63.

8 IsmāʿIl, *Jadal*, 93.

9 I smāʿIl, *Jadal*, 70.

10 Ismāʿīl, *Jadal*, 75.

11 Maḥmūd Ismāʿīl, *Sūsiyūlūjiyyā al-Fikr al-Islāmī*, vols. 1–7 (Cairo: Sīnā li al-Nashr; Beirut: Al-Intishār al-ʿArabī, 2000), vols. 8–10 (Cairo: Miṣr al-Maḥrūsa, 2005).

12 Khālid Ḥuṣayn Maḥmūd and ʿAbd al-ʿAzīz Ramaḍān, eds. *Dirāsāt fī al-Tārīkh wa al-Ḥaḍāra al-Islāmiyya: Buḥūth Muhdā li al-Muʾarrikh wa al-Mufakkir al-Kabīr Maḥmūd Ismāʿīl* (Cairo: Miṣr al-ʿArabiyya, 2009), 22.

has since had a distinguished career as an historian of Islamic Spain.[13] He is currently president of the Hispano-Moroccan Fundación al-Idrisi which is based in Seville and Tetouan and dedicated to research on the history, art and architecture of al-Andalus.[14]

Būtashīsh wrote a thesis entitled "The Influence of Feudalism on the Political History of al-Andalus from 250 A.H. (864 A.D.) to 316 A.H. (928 A.D.)" which we will discuss further in the following section.[15] This was followed by many other publications on the socio-economic history of the western Islamic lands such as two important volumes on society in the Almoravid period and a collection of studies on insurrections and marginalised groups in the medieval Maghrib.[16] He became professor at the Moulay Ismail University in Meknes where he heads a large research group working in the same field.

Būtashīsh has trained a new generation of Moroccan socio-economic historians who have turned their focus to investigating topics such as the history of marginalised groups in medieval society, the effects of plagues and natural disasters and the history of mentalities. Historians from this third generation include ʿAbd al-Hādī al-Bayyāḍ who wrote a work entitled *Natural Disasters and their Influence on Behavior and Mentalities in the Maghrib and al-Andalus from the 12th to 14th centuries*, Ḥamīd Tītāw who wrote about the effects of warfare on late medieval Maghribī society and economy, ʿIzz al-Dīn Jassūs who wrote about the Almoravid concept of government and how it was viewed by the masses in the Maghrib and Al-Andalus and Saʿīd Binḥamāda who has written an important work about Man and Water in al-Andalus.[17] The latter work discusses not only irrigation practices and techniques as one would expect but also the signif-

13 Aḥmad al-Ṭāhirī, *ʿĀmmat Qurṭuba fī ʿĀṣr al-Khilāfa: Dirāsa fī al-Tārīkh al-Ijtimāʿī al-Andalusī* (Rabat: Manshūrāt ʿUkāẓ, 1989).

14 "Fundación al-Idrisi Hispano-Marroquí," accessed June 24, 2018, https://fidrisies.wordpress.com.

15 Ibrāhīm al-Qādirī Būtashīsh, *Athar al-Iqṭāʿ fī Tārīkh al-Andalus al-Sīyāsī min Muntaṣaf al-Qarn al-Thālith al-Hijrī ḥattā Ẓuhūr al-Khilāfa (250 h. – 316 h.)* (Rabat: Manshūrāt ʿUkāẓ, 1992).

16 Ibrāhīm al-Qādirī Būtashīsh, *Mabāḥith fī al-Tārīkh al-Ijtimāʿī li al-Maghrib wa al-Andalus khilāla ʿAṣr al-Murābiṭīn* (Beirut: Dār al-Ṭalīʿa, 1997); Idem, *Al-Maghrib wa al-Andalus fī ʿAṣr al-Murābiṭīn: Al-Mujtamaʿ, al-Dhihnīyāt, al-Awliyyāʾ* (Beirut: Dār al-Ṭalīʿa, 1993); Idem, *Al-Islām al-Sirrī fī al-Maghrib al-ʿArabī* (Cairo: Sīnā li al-Nashr, 1995).

17 ʿAbd al-Hādī al-Bayyāḍ, *Al-Kawārith al-Ṭabīʿiyya wa Atharuhā fī Sulūki wa Dhihniyyāt al-Insān fī al-Maghrib wa al-Andalus: 6–8 h./12–14 m.* (Beirut: Dār al-Ṭalīʿa, 2008); Ḥamīd Tītāw, *Al-Ḥarb wa al-Mujtamaʿ bi al-Maghrib khilāla al-ʿAṣr al-Marīnī: 610–869 h./1212–1465 m.* (Casablanca: Muʾassasat al-Malik ʿAbd al-ʿAzīz, 2010); ʿIzz al-Dīn Jassūs, *Mawqif al-Raʿiyya min al-Sulṭa al-Siyāsiyya fī al-Maghrib wa al-Andalus ʿalā ʿahd al-Murābiṭīn* (Casablanca: Ifrīqiyā al-Sharq, 2014); Saʿīd Binḥamāda, *Al-Māʾ wa al-Insān fī al-Andalus khilāl al-Qarnayn 7–8 h./13–14 m.* (Beirut: Dār al-Ṭalīʿa, 2007).

icance of water in medicine, folk culture and in religion, particularly in relation to Ṣūfī thought.

With the commencement of Ḥusnī Mubārak's presidency in the 1980s, the Egyptian government relaxed its pressure on leftist academics. Maḥmūd Ismāʿīl was able to resume his position at ʿAyn Shams in 1984 as a full professor. Since Egyptian university salaries no longer kept pace with the rising cost of living, it became common for successful academics to seek teaching opportunities in the universities of the Gulf states.[18] Ismāʿīl took a visiting professorship in the University of Kuwait from 1988 to 1995, apart from a hiatus due to the Gulf War from 1990 to 1991. Initially Ismāʿīl faced significant opposition from the Islamist factions in Kuwait but he also had strong support from the considerable liberal and leftist currents there. At a welcoming address which he gave at Kuwait University, an audience member remarked that his lecture "reeked of leftism". Ismāʿīl replied "I am a Marxist in thought and conduct and proud to be so!" to the surprise and delight of the audience.[19]

He soon flourished in the Kuwaiti intellectual scene. He played a major role in the training of a new generation of Kuwaiti historians and helped to established separate faculties of humanities and social sciences at the national university. Ismāʿīl was by now a public intellectual who was well-known from Morocco to the Gulf. He took part in, and often chaired conferences in Kuwait and across the Arab World concerning not only history but also sensitive political, social and religious issues. He appeared in televised lectures and debates, won prizes in literary competitions and regularly contributed to major newspapers.[20]

In the middle of the 1990s Ismāʿīl returned to Egypt for good. He completed the tenth volume of *A Sociology of Islamic Thought* in 2000 and he has recently published works on topics such as historiography and myth, medieval 'popular' literature as an historical source and studies dealing with contemporary political and religious thought.[21] He also continued to supervise many dissertations in medieval Islamic history at ʿAyn Shams University for researchers who have since started promising careers in history departments across the Arabic-speaking world.[22] Khālid Ḥusayn Maḥmūd defended his dissertation on slavery in the Maghrib during the early Islamic period (from the seventh to eleventh centuries)

18 Ismāʿīl, *Jadal*, 121.
19 Ismāʿīl, *Jadal*, 125.
20 Ismāʿīl, *Jadal*, 126–141.
21 The articles on historiography and myth are collected in Maḥmūd Ismāʿīl, *Al-Usṭughrāfiyyā wa al-Mīthūlūjiyyā* (Cairo: Al-Ruʾya, 2009).
22 Ismāʿīl, *Jadal*, 163.

under Ismāʿīl's supervision in 2004.[23] He now teaches at ʿAyn Shams University and is one of the leading Egyptian specialists on the medieval Maghrib, particularly its social and economic aspects. Another of Maḥmūd Ismāʿīl's students after his return to Egypt was the Moroccan historian ʿAbd al-Ilah Binmalīh who wrote his dissertation on slavery in the Maghrib and al-Andalus during the eleventh and twelfth centuries and is now dean of the Faculty of Arts in Fez University.[24]

Ismāʿīl has also influenced the field of historical studies in Algeria. He participated in the doctoral thesis committee of Būba Majānnī, a specialist on the Fatimids who is one of the most prominent medievalists in Algeria and currently teaches at the University of Constantine.[25] In addition he supervised the MA thesis of Fāṭima Bilhuwārī, now a professor of Islamic history in Oran.[26] Over the last two decades Majānnī and Bilhuwārī have trained a large number of younger Algerian historians of the Islamic period who have chosen socio-economic topics for their research. An example of the work produced by this new generation is Dalāl Lawātī's study on the common classes in Aghlabid Qayrawān. While acknowledging the foundational role of the works of Ismāʿīl, al-Ṭāhirī and Būtashīsh for the study of Islamic socio-economic history, she also critiques the historical materialist approach to the history of non-western, pre-capitalist societies and questions the applicability of the Marxist conception of class to medieval Islamic society.[27]

Ismāʿīl's Methodological Justification

The preface to the first volume of Ismāʿīl's *Sociology of Islamic Thought* consists of a lengthy methodological justification. He begins with a defense of historical materialism. According to Ismāʿīl, 'capitalistic' thought in its various forms attacks knowledge under the pretext of its slogans of objectivity and seeks to stop the progress of history.[28] He proceeds to critique alternative theories of

23 Published as *Al-Raqīq wa al-Ḥayāt al-Ijtimāʿiyya bi Bilād al-Maghrib khilāla al-Qurūn al-Arbaʿa al-Ūlā li al-Islām* (Cairo: Miṣr al-ʿArabiyya, 2009).

24 Published as *Al-Riqq fī Bilād al-Maghrib wa al-Andalus* (Beirut: Al-Intishār al-ʿArabī, 2004).

25 Būba Majānnī, *Al-Nuẓum al-Idāriyya fī Bilād al-Maghrib khilāla al-ʿAṣr al-Fāṭimī* (Constantine: Dār Bahāʾ al-Dīn, 2010).

26 Fāṭima Bilhuwārī, *Al-Fāṭimiyyūn wa Ḥarakāt al-Muʿāraḍa fī Bilād al-Maghrib al-Islāmī* (Tlemcen: Dār al-Misk, 2011).

27 Dalāl Lawātī, *ʿĀmmat al-Qayrawān fī ʿAṣr al-Aghāliba* (Cairo: Ruʾya, 2015), 78–89.

28 Ismāʿīl, *Sūsiyūlūjiyyā*, 1:13.

the sociology of knowledge. Emile Durkheim (1858–1917) has substituted "vague collective consciousness for class consciousness." Karl Mannheim (1893–1947) tries to examine thought in isolation from its historical context. Maurice Merleau-Ponty's (1908–1961) phenomenology of perception strips thought of its reality and is an "existentialist narcissism that inflates the self and ignores all human progress."[29] Structuralism ignores theoretical knowledge and employs only empirical knowledge.[30]

Ismāʿīl on Western 'Idealist' Scholarship: The Orientalists

Ismāʿīl then launches into a critique of orientalist scholarship on Islamic civilisation. He observes that orientalism was not motivated solely by the desire for knowledge and was not always objective. According to him, orientalist scholarship was tied to the European colonial project with the aim of providing information to the colonisers and sowing division among the colonised.[31] He characterises the classical orientalist approach as more idealist and descriptive than interpretative. It is a phenomenological view that:

> ...does not advance a construct composed of thought or a general theory, but merely a presentation of its phenomena with the partial and faulty explication of the classical texts which dresses itself in an intellectualism of formalism and technicalism and a non-objective objectivity. This explains the strange contradiction in the explanation of one subject and interpretation of it by the same scholar, not to mention the disagreement between different scholars on various subjects.[32]

Ismāʿīl criticises the orientalists for stressing what he sees as a largely artificial divide between the Maghrib and Mashriq. In this regard he singles out Reinhart Dozy (1820–1883) and Claude Cahen (1909–1991). The latter, according to him, believed that the western Islamic World had a separate culture from that of the East which stood alone, a thesis that Ismāʿīl ascribes to ignorance of the history of the Maghrib. He is also critical of scholars such as Baron De Slane (1801–1878) and Gerlof Van Vloten (1866–1903) for ascribing the achievements of Islamic civilisation to other cultures and of scholars such as De Lacey O'Leary

29 Ismāʿīl, *Sūsiyūlūjiyyā*, 1:14.
30 Ismāʿīl, *Sūsiyūlūjiyyā*, 1:15.
31 Ismāʿīl, *Sūsiyūlūjiyyā* 1:17–18.
32 Ismāʿīl, *Sūsiyūlūjiyyā* 1:19.

(1872–1957), Ignaz Goldziher (1850–1921), David S. Margoliouth (1858–1940) and Ernest Renan (1823–1892) for belittling Arab-Islamic thought and considering it to be mere imitation.[33]

Another error of the orientalists, according to Ismāʿīl, is the separation of political history from cultural history. As an example of this, he cites the famous German Biblical scholar and Arabist Julius Wellhausen's (1844–1918) statement that the political history of Islam has a 'dynamism' of its own separate from cultural history. The orientalists tend to either avoid comprehensive, general explanations or to make generalisations on a purely ideological or theological basis. Thus, the great British orientalist Sir Hamilton Gibb (1895–1971) in one place rejects generalisation on the grounds that it "... distorts and disfigures the detail and complexity of the actual evidence," while elsewhere he argues that religious and ideological factors are key to understanding Islamic social and political history. A consequence of such attitudes is that Orientalism has "... failed to advance a theory that explains and arranges the components of Islamic civilization in a comprehensive unity."[34]

Critique of Idealist Approaches in Modern Arabic Scholarship

Most modern Arabic scholarship on Islamic civilisation has also been idealist in its approach. Ismāʿīl discerns two main trends: the traditionalist trend of 'imitators' (*muqallidūn*), and the 'innovators' (*mujaddidūn*). The traditionalists represent the outlook of the feudal class whose interests were closely tied to those of the colonisers. Ismāʿīl identifies them with the Salafist movement. According to Ismāʿīl, their works are characterised by anti-intellectualism and a complete lack of methodology. They regard the Islamic feudal period as the golden age of mankind and mourn its passing while calling for its revival in the modern world. Their approach towards the medieval Islamic heritage is thus uncritical and apologetic. They argue that Western thought is indebted to the Arab–Islamic World for its achievements. Ismāʿīl notes that scholars of this type often make extravagant claims such as crediting the Arabs with the invention of democracy before the European Enlightenment and boasting that medieval Islamic economic theory is superior to all modern theories including capitalism and socialism.[35]

---

33 Ismāʿīl, *Sūsiyūlūjiyyā*, 1:18–19.
34 Ismāʿīl, *Sūsiyūlūjiyyā*, 1:18–19.
35 Ismāʿīl, *Sūsiyūlūjiyyā*, 1:19–21.

The innovators came from the ranks of the bourgeoisie. Many of them had traditional religious educations in their native countries followed by an extended period of study in the European universities. There they became acquainted with modern ideas and methodologies which they later employed for the first time in their own studies of the Islamic intellectual tradition. "They exposed the nakedness and sterility of the traditional approaches after long hard-won struggles in which they were accused of atheism and heresy."[36] The pioneering works produced by this school include Ṭāhā Ḥusayn's (1889–1973) study on the first Islamic schism (*al-fitna al-kubrā*) and Aḥmad Amīn's (1886–1954) works on the history of Islamic civilisation.[37] These works and others like them drew from various Western methodologies in a haphazard manner but they failed to set forth a "comprehensive vision of interpretation".[38]

For Ismāʿīl, the work of the prominent Syrian poet and intellectual Adūnīs exemplifies the weakness of the idealist, phenomenological approach. In his study *The Permanent and the Changing: A Study in Creativity and Imitation Among the Arabs* (*Al-Thābit wa al-Mutaḥawwil: Baḥth fī al-Ibdāʿ wa al-Itbāʿ ʿinda al-ʿArab*), Adūnīs employs the phenomenological method to comprehend Islamic thought. Adūnīs reaches the conclusion that Arab-Islamic culture was dominated by alternation and conflict between its changing and permanent aspects. The unchanging permanent trend has emerged dominant from this encounter and it influences the entire culture. Ismāʿīl sees this as an extreme generalisation, the result of attempting to study intellectual developments in isolation from their wider social and economic contexts.[39]According to Ismāʿīl, Adūnīs' study merely describes Arab–Islamic thought in its different periods without attempting to understand its context. He writes: "This approach can only yield some observations about the changes and developments in thought itself, without discussing its causes in the social reality."[40] Ismāʿīl notes that Adūnīs admits the necessity of studying the socio-economic structure of the Islamic World but he excuses himself on the grounds that the necessary sources do not exist and he admits that in any case he does not have the training and

---

36 Ismāʿīl, *Sūsiyūlūjiyyā*, 1:21.

37 Ṭāhā Ḥusayn, *Al-Fitna al-Kubrā*, 2 vols. (Cairo: Dār al-Maʿārif, 1959); Aḥmad Amīn, *Fajr Al-Islām*, (Cairo: Lajnat al-Taʾlīf wa al-Tarjama, 1928); Idem, *Ḍuḥā al-Islām*, 3 vols. (Cairo: Lajnat al-Taʾlīf wa al-Tarjama, 1933–1936); Idem, *Ẓuhr al-Islām*, 4 vols. (Cairo: Al-Nahḍa al-Miṣriyya, 1955–1959).

38 Ismāʿīl, *Sūsiyūlūjiyyā*, 1:22.

39 Ismāʿīl, *Sūsiyūlūjiyyā*, 1:23. Adūnīs, *Al-Thābit wa al-Mutaḥawwil: Baḥth fī al-Ibdāʿ wa al-Itbāʿ ʿinda al-ʿArab*, 2 vols. (Beirut: n.p., 1974–1977), vol. 1, referred to in Ismāʿīl, *Sūsiyūlūjiyyā*, 1:23.

40 Ismāʿīl, *Sūsiyūlūjiyyā*, 1:23.

background necessary to undertake such a study! As we will see, Ismāʿīl is convinced that a thorough study of the socio-economic bases of Islamic society is a necessary prerequisite to any survey of Islamic intellectual history. Historical materialism, is, in his view, the only methodology that enables us to understand thought in its wider context.

Historical Materialist Approaches to the Study of Islamic History

After giving an overview of Orientalist and Arab scholarship that approached Islamic history from an 'idealist' perspective, Ismāʿīl discusses the application of historical materialism to the study of Islamic civilisation by scholars in the West and East. He begins by tracing the evolution of Karl Marx's thought on the economic history of the oriental civilisations. In his earliest writings on the subject from 1853, Marx maintained that Oriental societies were static and lacked class consciousness. A despotic central government oversaw the complex irrigation systems necessary in semi-arid regions like the Middle East, and collected the agricultural surplus. This meant that the bourgeoisie was weak or non-existent. Karl Marx and Friedrich Engels also believed, erroneously as we now know, that there was no private property in the Islamic lands and that taxes were collected in kind.[41] After 1881, in part to due to advances in orientalist scholarship which increased his knowledge of non-Western history, Marx revised his views about the static and unchanging nature of Oriental societies. He also recognised that modes of production could develop at different speeds and take different forms according to external circumstances as well as according to the internal structure of the mode of production.[42]

Ismāʿīl says that we cannot uncritically accept the writings of Marx and Engels on the Islamic World because their knowledge of eastern history and cultures was limited, reflecting the state of orientalist scholarship in the nineteenth century as well as the Eurocentric biases of the time. Only a very small part of the corpus of their writings is concerned with oriental societies. He also notes that much of what they wrote about the Orient was general in nature, and actually concerned the Far East more than the Islamic World. Furthermore, Marx and Engels themselves did not believe that their writings were the last word on histor-

---

41 Ismāʿīl, *Sūsiyūlūjiyyā*, 1:25–26.
42 Ismāʿīl, *Sūsiyūlūjiyyā*, 1:26, 31–32.

ical materialism.[43] Ismāʿīl believes that there is much of value even in the little that Marx and Engels wrote concerning non-Western societies, however, he cautions that it is a mistake to consider their statements to be dogma that cannot be further developed and modified in the light of new discoveries and new information.[44]

Another problem is that many of the Marxist scholars are theoreticians rather than historians.[45] Previous attempts to apply historical materialism to the study of Islamic civilisation suffer from the authors' lack of knowledge of the relevant primary source material. "Theoretical contemplation and rational explanation in the absence of the primary information scattered in the Arabic sources is pointless."[46] Theoretical knowledge must be combined with a solid background in Islamic history and a thorough sifting of the Arabic source material for information on socio-economic conditions.[47]

Ismāʿīl says that the French anthropologist Maurice Godelier correctly pointed out the fallacy of a 'return to Marx' that does not take into account the fact that Marx's knowledge reflected the state of European scholarship during his time. However, Godelier's conclusion that "oriental societies form an intermediate stage between primitive society and civilized society" is in his view a theoretical rather than an empirical judgement.[48]

Yves Lacoste, a French Marxist geographer who has written about the medieval Maghrib and its place in history, claimed that the absence of a bourgeoisie in the Islamic World caused slow socio-economic development or prevented such development altogether. He maintained that the Asiatic mode of production held sway in the Mashriq while in the Maghrib and al-Andalus, a system which he calls 'military democracy' existed which resulted in the arrested development of these lands.[49] Ismāʿīl finds no basis for the existence of military democracy in the Islamic West. Furthermore, he rejects the assertion that the western Islamic World followed a radically different path of socio-economic development from the Mashriq.[50]

---

43 Ismāʿīl, *Sūsiyūlūjiyyā*, 1:29.

44 Ismāʿīl, *Sūsiyūlūjiyyā*, 1:24, 26.

45 Ismāʿīl, *Sūsiyūlūjiyyā*, 1:24.

46 Ismāʿīl, *Sūsiyūlūjiyyā*, 1:29.

47 Ismāʿīl, *Sūsiyūlūjiyyā*, 1:29.

48 Ismāʿīl, *Sūsiyūlūjiyyā*, 1:27. Ismāʿīl refers to Jean Chesnaux et al., *Ḥawl al-Namaṭ al-Intāj al-Āsiyāwī* [Sur le mode du production asiatique], trans. Jūrj Ṭarābīshī (Beirut: Dār al-Ḥaqīqa, 1972).

49 Yves Lacoste, *Al-ʿAllāma Ibn Khaldūn* [Ibn Khaldoun: naissance de l'histoire, passé du tiers-monde], trans. Mīshāl Sulaymān (Beirut: Dār Ibn Khaldūn, 1974), 9, referred to in Ismāʿīl, *Sūsiyūlūjiyyā*,1:27–28.

50 Ismāʿīl, *Sūsiyūlūjiyyā*, 1:69.

One of the most famous Western scholars who wrote about the economic development of the Islamic World from a historical-materialist perspective was Maxime Rodinson (1915–2004). Ismāʿīl says that Rodinson failed to give a detailed survey of the socio-economic development of the medieval Islamic World, instead merely selecting a handful of sources from different periods to support his arguments. He finds Rodinson's study to be contradictory and he agrees with the Arabic translator of this work that Rodinson cannot decide whether to build his interpretation of the socio-economic development of the medieval Islamic World on the basis of the Feudal Mode of Production or the Asiatic Mode of Production.[51]

Ismāʿīl says that in the Arab World a number of scholars were influenced by socialist ideas, particularly in the years immediately following independence when there was a general openness to socialist thought.[52] They attempted for the first time to analyse Islamic thought from a sociological perspective. According to Ismāʿīl, these intellectuals suffered from the lack of a comprehensive and reliable survey of the structure of medieval Arab-Islamic society. The few good socio-economic studies that were produced were largely descriptive in approach and they focused only on a single period, thus missing longer-term developments and changes. He mentions the famous Iraqi historian ʿAbd al-ʿAzīz al-Dūrī's (1919–2010) study on the economy of early Abbasid Iraq as a notable example of such a work.[53]

The Use of Modes of Production by Ismāʿīl

Ismāʿīl rejects the notion that the non-Western lands had a distinctive mode of production such as the much debated Asiatic mode of production, which was suggested by Marx in the middle of the nineteenth century, or the uniquely non-Western 'tributary' (*kharāj*) mode of production proposed by the famous Egyptian Marxist economist Samīr Amīn (1931–2018). When Marx and Engels mentioned the Asiatic mode of production in their earlier writings, Western orientalist scholarship was still in its infancy and dominated by Eurocentric and idealist scholars. Hardly any reliable information about Islamic socio-economic development was at hand. Therefore, Marx and Engels' early attempts to compre-

51 Ismāʿīl, *Sūsiyūlūjiyyā*, 1:28; Maxime Rodinson, *Al-Islām wa al-Raʾsmāliyya* [Islam et capitalisme], trans. Nazīf al-Ḥakīm, (Beirut: n.p. 1968), referred to in Ismāʿīl, *Sūsiyūlūjiyyā*, 1:28.
52 Ismāʿīl, *Sūsiyūlūjiyyā*, 1:32.
53 Ismāʿīl, *Sūsiyūlūjiyyā*, 1:33; ʿAbd al-ʿAzīz al-Dūrī, *Tārīkh al-ʿIrāq al-Iqtiṣādī fī al-Qarn al-Rābiʿ al-Hijrī* (Beirut: Markaz Dirāsāt al-Waḥda al-ʿArabiyya, 1995).

hend the economic structure of the Islamic lands were highly tentative, based as they were on limited and inaccurate information, and should not be taken as final statements on the matter.[54]

In Ismāʿīl's vision, the medieval Islamic World was shaped by two competing modes of production: the feudal and 'bourgeois' modes of production. It is clear that Ismāʿīl's bourgeois mode of production is equivalent to the capitalist mode of production but he does not explain his choice of name for this mode. Both modes coexisted but at times one was dominant while the other was present only in a marginal role. The interplay between these two modes of production conditioned the social, political and intellectual development of the medieval Islamic World. In his words:

> This study confirms the veracity of the assertion of the existence of a struggle in Islamic society from its origins until now between two essential forces: Feudalism and the Bourgeoisie. In some periods the bourgeois mode was dominant and in others the feudal mode, but at all times both were present, one as the dominant and the other as the secondary mode of production. This continued for five centuries until the final decisive victory of feudalism and the relegation of the bourgeoisie to a marginal role.[55]

As we can see in the aforementioned quote, a notable feature of Ismāʿīl's thought on the question of modes of production is the idea that more than one mode of production can exist at the same time in a society. The dominant mode exists along with the remnants of previous modes of production. The latter can still exert a modifying influence, albeit weakened, on the current mode of production. Ismāʿīl acknowledges the influence of the ideas of the Hungarian Marxist theoretician and economist Eugen Varga (1879–1964) on his conception of the modes of production. Varga maintained that modes were not absolute and static, but rather always in flux.[56]

An example of how Ismāʿīl applies the concept of dominant and marginal modes of production in coexistence can be seen in his treatment of the intellectual production of the early Abbasid period, or the "first bourgeois awakening" as he calls it. The dominant mode of production at this time was the bourgeois mode. Liberal and rational bourgeois thought was limited by the countercurrent of the remnants of reactionary and obscurantist feudal thought. The struggle be-

---

54 Ismāʿīl, *Sūsiyūlūjiyyā*, 1:29; Idem, "Al-Iqṭāʿ fī al-ʿAlam al-Islāmī, min Muntaṣaf al-Qarn al-Khāmis ilā Awāʾil al-Qarn al-ʿĀshir al-Hijrī: bayn al-Jadal al-Naẓarī wa al-Wāqiʿ al-Tārīkhī," *Ḥawliyyāt Kulliyyat al-Ādāb* 11, (1990): 20.

55 Ismāʿīl, *Sūsiyūlūjiyyā*, 1:30.

56 Ismāʿīl, Sūsiyūlūjiyyā, 1:26; Jean Chesnaux, Maurice Godelier, et al. *Ḥawl al-Namaṭ al-Intāj al-Āsiyāwī*, referred to in Ismāʿīl, *Sūsiyūlūjiyyā*, 1:26.

tween the dominant and secondary modes manifested itself on the intellectual level in the form of thinkers who had to take balancing middle positions between feudal and bourgeois thought and thus could not fully liberate themselves from the influence of the former.[57]

It should be noted that Ismāʿīl does not believe that modes of production inevitably proceed from the primitive to the more advanced. He observes that during the course of Islamic history there have been times when a society in which the bourgeois mode of production had been dominant later reverted to a feudal economy due to complex internal and external factors. Thus, Ismāʿīl's vision of history is not one of inevitable economic progress and development; what has been achieved by a society can be reversed and lost.

Islamic Civilisation and the 'Great Divergence'

Ismāʿīl neither uses the term 'Great Divergence' nor does he refer to the recent Western literature on this problem while in turn his work has not come to the attention of the Western historians involved in the divergence controversy. Nonetheless, his work is of great relevance to the debate since the central question which he seeks to understand in his *Sociology of Islamic Thought* is why the medieval Islamic World, despite its undoubted wealth and sophistication, did not experience an industrial revolution. To him, the answer lies in the weakness of the position of the medieval Islamic bourgeoisie, in comparison to its European counterpart. The precarious position of the bourgeoisie in the Islamic lands prevented it from fully realising its transformative, revolutionary role in society. In the end it was unable to effect the transformation from a feudal to a capitalist system.[58]

Ismāʿīl gives various explanations for the weakness of the Islamic bourgeoisie. He attributes its fragility in part to its "mercantile character", supposing that a bourgeoisie based largely on trade is weaker than a manufacturing bourgeoisie.[59] Furthermore, this mercantile bourgeoisie was relegated to an intermediary

57 Ismāʿīl, *Sūsiyūlūjiyyā*, 1:190–191.

58 Ismāʿīl, *Sūsiyūlūjiyyā*, 2:15–16.

59 Ismāʿīl, *Sūsiyūlūjiyyā*, 2:15. Banaji criticises the strict opposition of commercial capitalism to industrial capitalism which many Marxist historians have made and which in his view has caused them to ignore important developments in the global history of capitalism during the Medieval and Early Modern periods. He also points out that in Europe merchants played an important role in the development of capitalism and of manufacturing. See Jairus Banaji, *Theory as History: Essays on Modes of Production and Exploitation* (Leiden: Brill, 2010), 251–258.

role in international trade in the late Middle Ages when the major maritime routes passed out of the control of the Islamic powers.[60] He also says that the bourgeoisie in the Islamic World lacked homogeneity due to its multi-confessional nature as it encompassed Muslims of various sects as well as large numbers of Jews and Christians.[61]

There were also differences in the relationships of the Islamic and European bourgeoisies to their respective governments and to the feudal classes. The bourgeoisie in the Islamic World was more closely tied to and controlled by the central government which hampered and stifled its growth.[62] Its most important component consisted of merchants involved in long-distance trade. The latter preferred to invest their surplus wealth in the trade of luxury goods or the acquisition of land rather than manufacturing. The prosperity of the mercantile bourgeoisie was closely connected to control of natural resources as well as international trade routes by the state. The Islamic bourgeoisie was not in opposition to the state but rather depended on it and cooperated with it. Thus, unlike in Europe, it did not assume the leadership of the popular rebellions of the lower-classes in order to fully supplant the feudal state. Furthermore, dependence on international trade made the mercantile bourgeoisie particularly vulnerable to external conditions such as foreign wars and nomadic invasions which disrupted their activities. An example of this is when Muslim states lost control of trade routes and ports to European commercial rivals in the late Medieval period.[63]

Geography and climate have also played a part in determining the distinct courses of development in class relations in the medieval Islamic World and medieval Europe. As Ismāʿīl explains:

> The Marxist texts give some brilliant insights into the reasons for the crisis of the bourgeoisie and its weakness and defeat in the medieval Islamic World, most importantly its emergence in an agricultural society surrounded by deserts and the internal and external challenges that this desert environment produced. Internally there were the unique conditions posed by irrigation in a dry environment and the consequent necessity for the authoritarian

60 Ismāʿīl, *Sūsiyūlūjiyyā*, 1:63.

61 Ismāʿīl, *Sūsiyūlūjiyyā*, 2:15–16. An alternative geographical explanation for the 'rise of the West' and inability of the Islamic World to keep pace with it has been proposed by Hodgson. He suggests that Europe's geographical location meant that it escaped the worst effects of the invasions of the Mongols and other Eurasian steppe nomads in addition to being an ideal springboard for maritime travel to the New World. See Marshall G. S. Hodgson, *Rethinking World History*, (Cambridge: Cambridge University Press, 1993), 69.

62 Ismāʿīl, *Sūsiyūlūjiyyā*, 2:15–16.

63 Ismāʿīl, *Sūsiyūlūjiyyā*, 2:200–203.

state which controlled the land and supported feudalism. This put a heavy burden on the bourgeoisie which had to contend with the state in addition to the feudal class, which was protected by the central state. As a result of its failure and weakness, the bourgeoisie was forced to submit to the state and dedicate its energies to serving the state's interests. Thus, members of the bourgeosie focused on commerce in luxury goods and they invested their capital in the purchase of real estate. This caused their interests to coincide with those of the feudal class. Furthermore, the vast bulk of the population were peasants, and peasants are traditionally wary of the bourgeoisie. Therefore, the bourgeoisie could not play its natural role as leader of the urban proletariat to overthrow the feudal class. This explains the failure of the bourgeois revolutionary movements throughout most of Islamic history.[64]

Islamic Feudalism?

A major point of disagreement between Ismāʿīl and some of the Western scholars is over the question of whether or not feudalism existed in the medieval Islamic World. Claude Cahen, a French Marxist scholar who was one of the leading specialists on the economic history of the medieval Islamic World, stressed the distinctiveness of the Islamic *iqṭāʿ* system from European feudalism and he rejected the use of the term feudal to describe Islamic society and institutions in any period.[65] His view was shared by other Western scholars such as Ann Lambton (1912–2008), a prominent historian of medieval Iran.[66] The common objection raised by scholars who do not see parallels between European feudalism and the Islamic iqṭāʿ system is that the iqṭāʿ grants were closely controlled by the central state, in contrast to the medieval European fiefs. They see the iqṭāʿ simply as a method of paying the military. This meant that instead of receiving a direct payment from the treasury, an officer would be paid by the grant of the revenue from a particular estate. Estates could be withdrawn from a grantee and reassigned to others at will. The grantees lived in the cities rather than on their estates, which merely paid their salaries, their estates were often not inheritable,

64 Ismāʿīl, *Sūsiyūlūjiyyā*, 1:30.

65 Iqṭāʿ means a grant of land (often translated into English as fief though the comparison is rejected by many specialists) or of revenue from an estate, however, Ismāʿīl frequently uses the term in another sense as well to refer to the entire system of feudalism, which is usually called *al-iqṭāʿiyya* in modern Arabic. For Cahen's arguments see Claude Cahen, "Ikṭāʿ," *The Encyclopedia of Islam*, 2nd ed. (Leiden: Brill, 1960–2000), 3: 1088–1091.

66 Ismāʿīl, "al-Iqṭāʿ," 18.

and thus the grantees did not develop the close attachments to their lands that the European feudal families had.[67]

Ismāʿīl says that Cahen "... interpreted the term *iqṭāʿ* in a narrow philological sense and failed to see that the context of the term in the Arabic sources suggests the existence of feudalism".[68] He further argues that the orientalists do not fully account for the wide diversity of types of iqṭāʿ that appeared at different times and in different regions of the medieval Islamic World. There were in fact forms of iqṭāʿ that exempted the grantee from paying taxes to the treasury, allowed inheritance of the land in the same family, and which gave the holder full legal rights over the land and its inhabitants without any interference by the state.[69] Būtashīsh mentions a variety of the iqṭāʿ in ninth century al-Andalus in which the holder exercised full administrative, juridical, fiscal and even military authority over his lands so that he was *de facto* independent of the central authority.[70]

Even in Europe, feudalism appeared in various forms in different periods and regions.[71] Therefore, it is not possible to refer to a single ideal type of feudalism as the standard to which all other feudalisms must exactly conform.[72] Ismāʿīl believes that feudalism was certainly present in the medieval Islamic World if we accept the Marxist understanding of the term as describing: "An exploitative relation between the landowner and the peasants subservient to him, so that the surplus which exceeds the most basic needs of the peasants goes to the landlord by force either through direct labour or through rent in kind or specie."[73]

Ismāʿīl maintained that the situation of the peasants who worked the iqṭāʿ lands in the Islamic World was often worse than that of their counterparts

---

67 Cahen, "Ikṭā." It should be noted however that some Western scholars have taken a more nuanced position than that of Cahen on this issue. Irwin draws our attention to iqṭāʿ grants from late 13th century Syria-Palestine in which the Mamluk sultans gave lands as permanent properties to their retainers and the descendants of the latter. Tramontana has shown that in some Ayyubid sources the term iqṭāʿ and its synonym *khubz* (pl. *akhbāz*) have the meaning of places or estates on which the grantee resided, thus they were in some ways similar to the European fiefs. See Robert Irwin, "Iqṭāʿ and the End of the Crusader States," in *The Eastern Mediterranean Lands in the Period of the Crusades*, ed. P.M. Holt (Warminster: Aris and Phillips, 1977), 62–77; Felicita Tramontana, "Khubz as Iqṭāʿ in Four Authors from the Ayyubid and Early Mamluk Periods," *Mamluk Studies Review* 16 (2012): 103–122.

68 Ismāʿīl, *Sūsiyūlūjiyyā*, 2:25.

69 Ismāʿīl, "al-Iqṭāʿ," 18.

70 Būtashīsh, *Athar al-Iqṭāʿ*, 50.

71 Ismāʿīl, *Sūsiyūlūjiyyā*, 2:25.

72 Ismāʿīl, "al-Iqṭāʿ," 18.

73 Ismāʿīl, *Sūsiyūlūjiyyā*, 2:25.

who laboured on the feudal estates of Europe. The condition of the former was akin to slavery in his estimation.[74] As Būtashīsh noted, the relations between the feudal lord and his serfs and their obligations towards one another were stipulated by law while the peasants on iqṭāʿ lands had no formal rights.[75]

The Development of the Class Conflict in Medieval Islamic History

Ismāʿīl describes the society of pre-Islamic Arabia, particularly Mecca on the eve of Islam, as primarily bourgeois with feudal and tribal characteristics.[76] He sees class conflict within Meccan society as an important factor in the rise of Islam.[77] This conflict pitted the great aristocratic merchants against marginalised groups such as the smaller merchants, the indigent and slaves in an environment of limited resources. Muḥammad's message of a "society of brotherhood" had great appeal for the latter and shook the socio-economic foundations of Meccan society. After the death of the Prophet (632) and the adoption of Islam by all parties in the Hijaz, three factions emerged as a result of the unresolved class conflict: the 'old merchant aristocracy', the 'theocratic aristocracy', and the 'revolutionary party' or followers of ʿAlī.[78]

---

74 Ismāʿīl, "al-Iqṭāʿ," 18–19, 21–22.

75 Būtashīsh, *Athar al-Iqṭāʿ*, 49.

76 While Ismāʿīl discusses the socio-economic development of pre-Islamic Arabia, both in the southern and northern ends of the peninsula, at some length, he unfortunately does not devote any space to consideration of the class situation in the wider Near East and the Mediterranean World on the eve of the Arab conquests save for a brief remark in which he asserts that the feudal mode of production was the dominant mode in both the Byzantine and Sassanian empires. Ismāʿīl, *Sūsiyūlūjiyyā*, 1:38–48, 51.

77 It is worth noting that other scholars had previously discussed the importance of changing socio-economic conditions in the Arabian Peninsula and in Mecca in particular for understanding the emergence of Islam. Among them were the Scottish orientalist W.M. Watt (1909–2006), author of the most famous study in English on the Prophet Muḥammad, and the Russian-educated Palestinian historian Bandalī Jawzī (1872–1942), who was the first scholar to apply a Marxist interpretation to the history of Islamic civilisation. See William Montgomery Watt, *Muhammad: Prophet and Statesman* (Oxford: Oxford University Press, 1961), 43–55; Bandalī Jawzī, *Min Tārīkh al-Ḥarakāt al-Fikriyya fī al-Islām* (n.p., Jamʿiyyat al-Ṣadāqa al-Filasṭīniyya al-Sūfiyātiyya, 1981 reprint), 17–53; English translation of the latter work by Tamara Sonn as *Interpreting Islam: Bandali Jawzi's Islamic Intellectual History* (Oxford: Oxford University Press, 1996), 75–91.

78 Ismāʿīl, *Sūsiyūlūjiyyā*, 1:47–49.

The old aristocracy consisted of the great aristocratic merchant families of Mecca who had been the last element in Meccan society to convert to Islam. They naturally wanted to ensure the continuity of their political and economic position in the new Islamic society. Their leaders were the Sufyānids who would later establish the Umayyad caliphate in Damascus.[79]

The revolutionary party was led by ʿAlī and comprised members of the marginalised groups including those among the Prophetic Companions who were of humble or slave origin. This faction was the most committed to the political reforms of Muḥammad and the idea of the 'community of brotherhood'. They were fiercely opposed to attempts by the old aristocracy to reassert its sway.[80]

The theocratic aristocracy consisted of prominent wealthy and aristocratic individuals who had converted to Islam early on when Muḥammad and his followers were still facing severe persecution at the hands of the Meccan aristocracy. As a result they had great prestige in the new Muslim polity. Examples are Abū Bakr, ʿUmar, ʿUthmān, Ṭalḥa and Zubayr. They were the immediate political successors of Muḥammad and they occupied a middle position between the revolutionary faction and the old aristocracy.[81]

According to Ismāʿīl, the factional conflicts of the first Islamic century had their roots in the competition between these three groups. On the surface, the factions justified themselves in ideological and religious terms but their existence was due to deep-seated contradictions in the socio-economic structure of early Islamic society. The second caliph ʿUmar b. al-Khaṭṭāb (634–644), through his fiscal and administrative reforms, was able to curb the power of the old aristocracy and mollify the populist, revolutionary party, thus warding off a major social conflict during his reign.[82] His successor, ʿUthmān (644–656), aligned his interests completely with those of the old aristocrats. He allowed them to carve vast private estates out of the public lands in Iraq and to dispossess the smaller landholders. Accordingly, Ismāʿīl sees ʿUthmān's reign as the beginning of the ascendancy of the feudal mode, which reached full bloom under the Umayyads.[83] These actions aroused the fierce opposition of the populist party under ʿAlī's leadership. The theocratic aristocracy, which had previously represented the middle ground, was unable to survive as a coherent force in the face of the increasing radicalisation on both of its wings. Some

79 Ismāʿīl, *Sūsiyūlūjiyyā*, 1:47–49.

80 Ismāʿīl, *Sūsiyūlūjiyyā*, 1:47–49.

81 Ismāʿīl, *Sūsiyūlūjiyyā*, 1:47–49.

82 Ismāʿīl, *Sūsiyūlūjiyyā*, 1:52–55; Maḥmūd Ismāʿīl and Maḥāsin al-Waqqād, *Tārīkh al-Ḥaḍāra al-ʿArabiyya al-Islāmiyya* (Cairo: n.p., n.d.), 76–78.

83 Ismāʿīl, *Sūsiyūlūjiyyā*, 1:55–56; Idem, *Tārīkh al-Ḥaḍāra*, 78–79.

elements of it joined the populists while others supported the old aristocratic faction.[84]

ʿUthmān was assassinated in 656 and the great *fitna* ('schism') occurred, which Ismāʿīl says was not a civil war, as conventional historiography maintains, but rather a revolution that pitted the populists under ʿAlī against the old Meccan aristocracy whose cause was now taken up by Muʿāwīya b. Abī Sufyān, the governor of Syria. After the inconclusive battle of Ṣiffīn (657), the populist faction split into a 'moderate' opposition party, the Shīʿa, and an 'extreme' one, the Khāwārij, and became weakened by infighting which resulted in the assassination of ʿAlī in 661.

The Umayyad period (661–750) witnessed the preponderance of the feudal mode of production over the bourgeois mode. The Umayyads made no distinction between public and private property according to Ismāʿīl. They and their governors acquired enormous estates at the expense of the small landowners who were under immense pressure to seek the 'protection' of the powerful rich landlords. This was done by either signing over their lands to the latter outright or by giving the great landlords the legal right to pay taxes to the treasury on their behalf. Those small farmers who refused these measures faced crushing taxation and ruthless tax-farmers. Many migrated to the cities.[85]

The rapid expansion of the empire and consequent increased opportunities for trade and demand for worked goods led to a marked growth in the number and size of cities. There the bourgeoisie, consisting of craftsmen, merchants and former peasants, proved to be a fertile recruiting field for the various anti-Umayyad opposition movements whether Shīʿī or Khārijī. Ismāʿīl characterises these as 'bourgeois revolts', the last of which, in his opinion, was the Abbasid Revolution itself.[86] The latter was not a sectarian conflict or an ethnic conflict between Persians and Arabs as some historians suppose. The Sassanian aristocracy intermarried with and was rapidly absorbed into the new Arab-Islamic aristocracy which shared its socio-economic interests while the movements opposed to Umayyad rule included both non-Arab converts to Islam (*mawālī*) and marginalised elements of the Arab population.[87]

The coming to power of the Abbasids in 750 inaugurated the 'first bourgeois awakening' which would last for about one century. The early Abbasid caliphs favoured small private landowners while the large feudal estates were reduced and

84 Ismāʿīl, *Sūsiyūlūjiyyā*, 1:55–57.
85 Ismāʿīl, *Sūsiyūlūjiyyā*, 1:58–68.
86 Ismāʿīl, *Sūsiyūlūjiyyā*, 1:62, 68.
87 Ismāʿīl, *Sūsiyūlūjiyyā*, 1:68.

brought under the close supervision of the bureaucracy.[88] Ideological currents like the Muʿtāzila and the Shīʿī groups were largely urban and bourgeois in nature.[89] They found favour at the court, particularly under the caliph al-Maʾmūn (813–833). The bourgeois ascendancy was reflected on the cultural level by the flowering of liberal, rational thought, helped along by the recent introduction of paper, which was a much cheaper and more convenient writing material than parchment or papyrus, and the vibrant book trade which resulted.[90]

The usurpation of effective power by the caliphs' Turkic guards in the Abbasid Empire in the middle of the ninth century caused a revival of feudalism which lasted until the middle of the tenth century. The military as well as officials and jurists were given land grants in lieu of salaries from the treasury, and often these grants were hereditary.[91] Entire provinces such as Egypt and Khurasan broke off from the empire in all but name. The great agricultural slave revolt known as the revolt of the Zanj rocked southern Mesopotamia in the last years of the ninth century. A similar phenomenon was witnessed in al-Andalus where military commanders established quasi-independent local states while the amirs in Cordoba were nearly powerless.[92] The effects of the socio-economic transformation were also felt in the cultural sphere. The rational Muʿtāzila fell from favour in the East and the caliph al-Mutawakkil (847–861) supported the conservative, literalist trend in Islamic thought represented by Ibn Ḥanbal (780–855). According to Ismāʿīl, the thought produced in a society in which feudalism is the dominant mode of production tends towards obscurantism and stagnation.[93]

The second and most important 'bourgeois awakening' lasted from approximately the middle of the tenth century until the middle of the eleventh century. In Ismāʿīl's view, this was the period of greatest economic expansion and intellectual enlightenment in the history of the medieval Islamic World, when the urban middle class was at the peak of its socio-economic, political and cultural influence. The trend towards political decentralisation and fragmentation was reversed and three great 'bourgeois-influenced states' (the Arabic term used is *mutabarjaza*, meaning literally 'bourgeoisised') arose: the Buwayhids in Iraq and

88 Ismāʿīl, *Sūsiyūlūjiyyā*, 1:74–84; Idem, *Tārīkh al-Ḥaḍāra*, 79–80.

89 Ismāʿīl, *Sūsiyūlūjiyyā*, 1: 123–124. Banaji also notes the connection between the prosperous merchant class and Muʿtazilism, see Jairus Banaji, *Exploring the Economy of Late Antiquity*, (Cambridge: Cambridge Univ. Press, 2016), 221.

90 Ismāʿīl, *Sūsiyūlūjiyyā*, 1:130–131.

91 Ismāʿīl, *Tārīkh al-Ḥaḍāra*, 80.

92 Ismāʿīl, *Sūsiyūlūjiyyā*, 2:31.

93 Ismāʿīl, *Sūsiyūlūjiyyā*, 2:24.

western Iran (945 – 1055), the Fatimids in the Maghrib and later Egypt and Syria (909 – 1171) and the Umayyad Caliphate of Cordoba (929 – 1031). Ismāʿīl uses the term 'bourgeois-influenced' because although the bourgeoisie did not actually assume direct power in any of these states, the bourgeoisie dominated the bureaucracies and institutions of the states and their attitudes influenced the ruling aristocracy.[94] According to Ismāʿīl, in all three states the government moved to confiscate large feudal iqṭāʿ lands and redistribute them in smaller plots. Revolutionary bourgeois ideologies such as Ismāʿīlī Shīʿism (Fatimids) and Zaydism (Buwayhids) were ascendant in this period.[95]

The reversal of the second bourgeois flowering and the resurgence of the feudal mode of production had various causes. One was the migration of warlike pastoral peoples from the peripheries which altered the political and socio-economic structures in the Islamic lands: the Seljuks and other Turkmen in the East, the Arab Banū Hilāl and Banū Sulaym in Ifrīqīya and the Almoravids (al-Murābiṭūn) in the western Maghrib and al-Andalus. Ismāʿīl compares their impact to that of the Germanic tribes on western Europe in the late Roman period. The newcomers were granted estates for their military service which often became hereditary. A form of military feudalism took root in the East beginning with the Seljuks (1037– 1153) and intensifying under the Zengids (1127– 1250), Ayyubids (1171– 1260) and Mamluks (1250 – 1517) while a similar phenomenon appeared in the West under the Almoravids (1040 – 1147), Almohads (1121– 1269) and the successor states of the latter.[96] The crisis of the (largely mercantile) Islamic bourgeoisie was exacerbated due to the loss of control of the international trade routes by the Muslim dynasties first in the Mediterranean to the Italian city states, and later in the Indian Ocean and Red Sea to the Portuguese. Thus, from the late eleventh century onwards feudalism became the dominant mode of production in the Islamic World while the bourgeois mode was relegated to secondary status.[97]

---

94 Ismāʿīl, *Sūsiyūlūjiyyā*, 2:151– 155, 200.

95 Ismāʿīl, *Tārīkh al-Ḥaḍāra*, 80 – 81. Other scholars dispute Ismāʿīl's assertion that the Buwayhids curtailed the spread of the military iqṭāʿ system in Iraq and maintain that iqṭāʿ grants were widespread under their rule. See Būtashīsh, *Athar al-Iqṭāʿ*, 48; Sato Tsugitaka, *State and Rural Society in Medieval Islam*, (Leiden: Brill, 1997), 6.

96 Ismāʿīl, *Tārīkh al-Ḥaḍāra*, 82– 83.

97 Ismāʿīl, "Al-Iqṭāʿ," 25 – 40; for other views on the problem of economic decline in the late medieval Islamic World see Claude Cahen, *Quelques mots sur le déclin commercial du monde musulman à la fin du Moyen Âge*, in *Les peuples musulmans dans l'histoire médiévale*, (Damascus: Presses de l'Ifpo, 1977), 359 – 366; Maya Shatzmiller, "A Misconstrued Link: Europe and the Economic History of Islamic Trade," in *Relazioni economiche tra Europa e mondo Islamico, secc.*

The structure of *A Sociology of Islamic Thought*

Ismāʿīl's largest and most important work consists of ten volumes. It is divided into three parts plus a conclusion. The three parts are 'The Period of Formation', 'The Period of Fluorescence' and 'The Period of Decline'.[98] The first part consists of only volume one. It deals with the period from pre-Islamic Arabia to the middle of the ninth century A.D. when the first 'Bourgeois Awakening' ended, according to Ismāʿīl. The second part consists of volumes two, three, four and five. It is concerned with the period from the middle of the ninth century AD to the middle of the eleventh century AD.This period saw the feudal reaction to the first bourgeois awakening in the late ninth century followed by the second, and more substantial bourgeois awakening of the tenth century and the first half of the eleventh century. The last part consists of volumes six, seven, eight and nine. It covers the period from the middle of the eleventh century until approximately 1500. This was the age of the domination of the feudal mode of production in the Islamic World which Ismāʿīl believes to have lasted until the beginning of the modern period. Though he does not recognise the Ottoman conquest of the Middle East as marking any fundamental socio-economic break with the late medieval Islamic World, Ismāʿīl's survey of Islamic society and culture nevertheless ends with the beginning of the Ottoman period. Volume ten is a conclusion entitled *An Attempt at Theorizing* (*Muḥāwala li al-Tanẓīr*).

For each of the three 'periods' covered in his work, Ismāʿīl begins with a sketch of the socio-economic bases in the Islamic World from east to west. For example, in Volume Two he discusses first the 'Economic Bases' which include land tenure, agriculture, manufacturing and trade. This is followed by a consideration of the 'Social Structure' which discusses the classes whom he divides into aristocracy, bourgeoisie and oppressed classes (peasants, slaves, urban poor). The third section is called 'Sociology of Political History' which gives a sketch of the major political-ideological movements of the period and how the class struggle played out at the level of political history. After sketching the socio-economic conditions and their political ramifications, he delves into a discussion of the superstructure, the cultural and intellectual history of the period. This includes chapters on the natural sciences, the traditional or religious sciences (such as Qur'ān exegesis, traditions of the Prophet, jurisprudence), literature and philology, art and architecture, theology and philosophy, mysticism and fi-

---

XIII–XVIII, proceedings of the 'trentottesima settimana di studi,' 1–5 May 2006, ed. Simonetta Cavaciocchi (Florence: Le Monnier, 2007), 237–415.

98 *Ṭawr al-Takwīn, Ṭawr al-Izdihār,* and *Ṭawr al-Inhiyār.*

nally a detailed discussion of the historical and geographical sciences during the period under study. The intellectual and cultural history is interpreted in the light of the economic and social structures of the period in question. Particular attention is paid to the socio-economic backgrounds of intellectuals and religio-ideological movements are evaluated as expressions of the underlying class situation. This is in line with the author's stated goal in his methodological introduction of writing a comprehensive history of medieval Islamic society which shows the relation of the superstructure to the economic and social bases.

Conclusion

Maḥmūd Ismāʿīl is undoubtedly one of the most influential and creative contemporary Arab historians of the medieval period. In *Sūsiyūlūjiyyā al-Fikr al-Islāmī* he has presented a comprehensive history of medieval Islamic civilisation in its economic, social, political and cultural aspects arranged around a bold, innovative theoretical framework, employing novel terminology and a new system of periodisation. A careful reconstruction of the socio-economic bases in each period covered by the study provides the foundation for understanding first the political history and then the cultural and intellectual production of the period. Perhaps the closest parallel to this book in the Western tradition of Islamic studies is Marshall Hodgson's (1922–1968) *The Venture of Islam*, bearing in mind the important difference that although Ismāʿīl's treatment of the medieval period is more detailed than Hodgson's, Ismāʿīl did not deal with the early modern and modern periods in his book.[99] Both of these highly unique and ambitious works have proven to be fertile sources of inspiration, debate and controversy for succeeding generations of scholars.

Ismāʿīl has also founded an historiographical school, now in its third generation and scattered across universities in several North African and Middle Eastern countries, consisting of scholars who share his interest in the social-economic history of the medieval Islamic World and the historical-materialist approach and who remain critically engaged with the ideas that he set forth in his works.

99 See Marshall G.S. Hodgson, *The Venture of Islam: Conscience and History in a World Civilization*, 3 vols. (Chicago: Chicago University Press, 1974).

Part Three: **Marxism and the Beginnings of Western Capitalism**

Nasser Mohajer and Kaveh Yazdani[1]

Reading Marx in the *Divergence* Debate

Developments in Britain and Europe in Global Perspective

Interest in the 'transition debate' has re-emerged in recent years. At the beginning of the 20th century, classic contributions by Werner Sombart and especially Max Weber were to explain why modern capitalism first appeared in western Europe and not elsewhere, while Franz Borkenau and Henryk Grossman discussed the causes of the emergence of capitalism in Europe (1930s). The works of W.E.B. Dubois, C.L.R. James and most notably Eric Williams on the relationship between slavery and capitalism (1930s and 1940s), as well as the 'Dobb/Sweezy Controversy' (1950s) addressed the underlying factors that triggered the transition from feudalism to capitalism in Europe. A few decades later, other historians took up the issue – a debate which later became known as the 'Brenner Debate' (mid 1970s and early 1980s). Concurrently, scholars like Fernand Braudel, Karl Polanyi, Eric Hobsbawm, Perry Anderson, Tapan Raychaudhuri, Irfan Habib, Immanuel Wallerstein, André Gunder Frank, Samir Amin, Arghiri Emmanuel, Charles Bettelheim and the world-system theory they inspired (1970s and 1980s) inquired into the causes, as well as the effects of 'development and underdevelopment', 'center-periphery relations' and the 'unequal exchange' in global perspective. Around the same time, scholars such as Frederic Lane, William H. McNeill, Douglass North, Angus Maddison, Michael Mann, Robert Fogel, John A. Hall, Jeffrey Williamson, Charles Tilly and Paul Kennedy also worked on issues of the transition to capitalism. The discussion has continued till now as a number of writings on the reasons behind the 'rise of the West' from a global perspective have surfaced. The most widely received were produced at the turn of the twentieth century and rather moved away from the Marxian frameworks that had been prevalent.[2] In contrast to Wallerstein and others

1 We would like to express an abundance of gratitude to Mehrdad Vahabi, Amir Amin, Benjamin Zachariah and Anh-Susann Pham Thi for reading earlier versions of this paper and providing us with valuable comments and suggestions.

2 See, for example, Jared Diamond, *Guns, Germs and Steel: The Fates of Human Societies* (New York: W.W. Norton, 1997); André Gunder Frank, *ReOrient: Global Economy in the Asian Age* (Berkeley: UCP, 1998); David S. Landes, *The Wealth and Poverty of Nations: Why Some are so Rich and*

https://doi.org/10.1515/9783110677744-010

working within the framework of world-system analysis, the 'California School' (Roy Bin Wong, A. G. Frank, Kenneth Pomeranz, Jack Goldstone, etc.) and a number of revisionist academics (Jack Goody, David Washbrook, C. A. Bayly, John M. Hobson, etc.) underlined the polycentricity of the global economy prior to the Industrial Revolution. These writings equally sparked new responses by Marxian scholars.[3] Akin to the Dobb/Sweezy and Brenner debates which juxtaposed 'internalist' versus 'externalist' arguments, the major divide was now between Eurocentrics and anti-Eurocentrics.

While in the first years of the twenty-first century, the debate was rather dominated by non-Eurocentric arguments, in the past decade the pendulum has swung back again in favour of Eurocentric explanations of the 'Great Divide'.[4]

Some so Poor (London: Little, Brown and Co., 1998); Kenneth Pomeranz, *The Great Divergence: China, Europe and the Making of the Modern World* (Princeton: PUP, 2000).

3 See, for example, Eric Mielants, *The Origins of Capitalism and the 'Rise of the West'* (Philadelphia: TUP, 2007); Giovanni Arrighi, *Adam Smith in Beijing: Lineages of the Twenty-first Century* (London: Verso, 2007); Samir Amin, *Global History: A View from the South* (Oxford: Pambazuka Press, 2011); Henry Heller, *The Birth of Capitalism* (London: Pluto Press, 2011); Idem, *A Marxist History of Capitalism* (Abingdon: Routledge, 2019); Alexander Anievas and Kerem Nişancıoğlu, *How the West Came to Rule: The Geopolitical Origins of Capitalism* (London: Pluto Press, 2015); Alain Bihr, *Le premier âge du capitalisme (1415–1763): L'expansion européenne*, 3 Vols. (Lausanne: Syllepse, 2018); Xavier Lafrance and Charles Post (eds.), *Case Studies in the Origins of Capitalism* (Cham: Springer, 2019). See also Jairus Banaji, *Theory as History: Essays on Modes of Production and Exploitation* (Leiden: Brill, 2010); Idem, *A Brief History of Commercial Capitalism* (Chicago: Haymarket Books 2020).

4 See, for example, Walter Scheidel, *Escape from Rome: The Failure of Empire and the Road to Prosperity* (New Jersey: PUP, 2019); Jared Rubin, *Rulers, Religion, and Riches: Why the West Got Rich and the Middle East Did Not* (Cambridge: CUP, 2017); Joel Mokyr, *A Culture of Growth: The Origins of the Modern Economy* (New Jersey: PUP, 2016); Deirdre N. McCloskey, *Bourgeois Equality: How Ideas, Not Capital or Institutions, Enriched the World* (Chicago: UCP, 2016); Steven G. Marks, *The Information Nexus: Global Capitalism from the Renaissance to the Present* (Cambridge: CUP, 2016); Peer Vries, *State, Economy and the Great Divergence. Great Britain and China, 1680s to 1850s* (London: Bloomsbury Publishing, 2015); Idem, *Escaping Poverty: The Origins of Modern Economic Growth* (Vienna: Vandenhoeck & Ruprecht, 2013); Philip T. Hoffman, *Why Did Europe Conquer the World?* (New Jersey: PUP, 2015); Stephen Broadberry et al., *British Economic Growth, 1270–1870* (Cambridge: CUP, 2015); Leonid E. Grinin and Andrey V. Korotayev, *Great Divergence and Great Convergence: A Global Perspective* (Cham: Springer, 2015); Roman Studer, *The Great Divergence Reconsidered. Europe, India and the Rise to Global Economic Power* (Cambridge: CUP, 2015); Rodney Stark, *How the West Won: The Neglected Story of the Triumph of Modernity* (Wilmington: Open Road Media, 2014); Tirthankar Roy, *An Economic History of Early Modern India* (London: Routledge, 2013); Daron Acemoglu and James A. Robinson, *Why Nations Fail: The Origins of Power, Prosperity and Poverty* (London: Crown Publishing Group, 2012); Ricardo Durchesne, *The Uniqueness of Western Civilization* (Leiden: Brill, 2011); Niall Ferguson, *Civilization: The West and the Rest* (London: Penguin, 2011); Timur Kuran, *The Long Di-*

In the meantime, however, some important non-Eurocentric monographs have come into being that continue enriching the debate.[5]

---

vergence: How Islamic Law Held Back the Middle East (New Jersey: PUP, 2010); Toby Huff, *Intellectual Curiosity and the Scientific Revolution: A Global Perspective* (Cambridge: CUP, 2010); J.L. Van Zanden, *The Long Road to the Industrial Revolution: The European Economy in a Global Perspective, 1000–1800* (Leiden: Brill, 2009); Gregory Clark, *A Farewell to Alms: A Brief Economic History of the World* (Princeton: PUP, 2007).

5 See, for example, Jason C. Sharman, *Empires of the Weak: The Real Story of European Expansion and the Creation of the New World Order* (Princeton: PUP, 2019); Priya Satia, *Empire of Guns: The Violent Making of the Industrial Revolution* (New York: Penguin, 2018); Kaveh Yazdani, *India, Modernity and the Great Divergence. Mysore and Gujarat (17th to 18th C.)* (Leiden: Brill, 2017); William J. Ashworth, *The Industrial Revolution: The State, Knowledge and Global Trade* (London: Bloomsbury Publishing, 2017); Arun Bala and Prasenjit Duara, eds., *The Bright Dark Ages: Comparative and Connective Perspectives* (Leiden: Brill, 2016); Tonio Andrade, *The Gunpowder Age: China, Military Innovation, and the Rise of the West in World History* (New Jersey: PUP, 2016); Richard von Glahn, *An Economic History of China: From Antiquity to the Nineteenth Century* (Cambridge: CUP, 2016); Penelope Francks, *Japan and the Great Divergence: A Short Guide* (London: Springer, 2016); Surendra Gopal, *Born to Trade, Indian Business Communities in Medieval and Early Modern Eurasia* (New Delhi: Routledge, 2016); Chhaya Goswami, *Globalization Before its Time: The Gujarati Merchants from Kachchh* (Delhi: Penguin, UK, 2016); Scott Levi, *Caravans: Punjabi Khatri Merchants on the Silk Road* (New Delhi: Penguin, UK, 2015); Sushil Chaudhury, *Companies, Commerce and Merchants: Bengal in the Pre-colonial Era* (New Delhi: Routledge, 2015); Benjamin Elman, *Science In China, 1600–1900: Essays by Benjamin A. Elman* (Singapore: World Century/World Scientific, 2015); Thomas A. Timberg, *The Marwaris: From Jagat Seth to the Birlas* (New Delhi: Vikas, 2014); Sven Beckert, *Empire of Cotton. A Global History* (New York: Knopf Doubleday Publishing Group, 2014); Pedro Machado, *Ocean of Trade: South Asian Merchants, Africa and the Indian Ocean, c.1750–1850* (Cambridge: CUP, 2014); Giorgio Riello, *Cotton: The Fabric that Made the Modern World* (Cambridg: CUP, 2013); Arun Bala, *Asia, Europe, and the Emergence of Modern Science: Knowledge Crossing Boundaries* (New York: Springer, 2012); Radhika Seshan, *Trade and Politics on the Coromandel Coast: Seventeenth and Early Eighteenth Centuries* (New Delhi: Primus Books, 2012); Prasannan Parthasarathi, *Why Europe Grew Rich and Asia Did Not: Global Economic Divergence, 1600–1850* (Cambridge: CUP, 2011); Jean-Laurent Rosenthal and Roy Bin Wong, *Before and Beyond Divergence: The Politics of Economic Change in China and Europe* (Cambridge: CUP, 2011); Nelly Hanna, *Artisan Entrepreneurs in Cairo and Early-Modern Capitalism (1600–1800)* (New York: SUP, 2011); Jonardon Ganeri, *The Lost Age of Reason: Philosophy in Early Modern India 1450–1700*, (New York: OUP, 2011); Jack Goody, *The Eurasian Miracle* (Cambridge: John Wiley & Sons, 2010); Idem, *Renaissances: The One or the Many?* (Cambridge: CUP, 2010); Robert C. Allen, *The British Industrial Revolution in Global Perspective* (Cambridge: CUP, 2009); Victor Lieberman, *Strange Parallels: Southeast Asia in Global Context, c.800–1830*, Vol. 2 (Cambridge: CUP, 2009); Ghulam A. Nadri, *Eighteenth-Century Gujarat: The Dynamics of its Political Economy, 1750–1800* (Leiden: Brill, 2009); René J. Barendse, *Arabian Seas 1700–1763: The Western Indian Ocean in the Eighteenth Century*, 2 vols. (Leiden: Brill, 2009); Jack A. Goldstone, *Why Europe? The Rise of the West in World History, 1500–1800* (Boston: McGraw-Hill Education, 2008); Robert Marks, *The Origins of the Modern World:*

In the wake of the aforementioned research, our quantitative knowledge has been deepened as we have now more information about the GDP levels, demographic evolution, technological progress, immigration, wage differentials, etc. Furthermore, cliometric studies were also developed, including contrafactual hypotheses that help to better understand the reasons behind the Great Divergence. Nonetheless, historians still sharply disagree amongst themselves regarding the origins of capitalism, the Industrial Revolution and the rise of the West. In order to explain these phenomena, most scholars from both the Eurocentric and non-Eurocentric spectrums have put forward rather mono-causal explanations, simply focusing on a few factors that triggered western Europe's great leap forward. Holistic explanations remain intermittent and atypical even though a totalising approach – as proposed by Karl Marx – could help shed light on the complexity of the matter. After twenty years of polemic and polarising controversies between these two opposing camps, a sense of attrition and saturation has emerged that might help overcome the binary terms of the debate.

In the next section, we will elaborate on the so-called original accumulation chapter of *Capital*, Vol. 1 (1867) where Marx furnished an explanation for the genesis of capitalism in England and western Europe. We will also grapple with some of his other writings, especially those on India. Although Marx's primary concern was not the rise of the West and the underlying conditions conducive for the Industrial Revolution in a global perspective, his narrative, in our view, has not lost relevance and continues to be enlightening, particularly when it comes to macro-historical debates pertaining to the subject at hand.[6] Therefore, we are to enquire into the ways in which Marx's account stands up in relation to

---

Fate and Fortune in the Rise of the West (Lanham: Rowman & Littlefield Publishers, 2007); John Darwin, *The Rise & Fall of Global Empires, 1400–2000* (London: Penguin, 2007).

6 Of course not everyone would agree. Marx's conceptualisation of *original accumulation* has not only been contested by liberal scholars but even put into question by some influential Marxist historians. Blaut, for example, argued that *original accumulation* "cannot really be defined with any precision ... the wealth accumulated in the Americas was primitive only in the sense that it was part of a preindustrial-capitalist economy. In other respects, notably in the involvement of labor and value produced by labor, it was regular accumulation." James Blaut, *The Colonizer's Model of the World: Geographical Diffusionism and Eurocentric History* (New York: Guilford Press, 1993), 210 note 20. From a different vantage point, Banaji opines that: "primitive accumulation is no longer the best way to frame the early history of capitalism ... because that remains a *purely teleological perspective* and one that diverts attention from the real lacuna in materialist historiography, which is the study and, one hopes, ultimately a synthesis of the emergence of capitalism, which in the sporadic form that Marx described it as having was certainly in place by the thirteenth century." Banaji, *Theory as History*, 43.

recent scholarship and empirical findings. We shall also explore what it offers to the understanding of the Great Divergence.

The so-called *Original Accumulation*

In the *Grundrisse* (1857–1858) and also in *Value, Price and Profit* (1865) Marx had already grappled with the so-called "original accumulation".[7] In the former, Marx distinguished "original capital accumulation" from other forms of capital accumulation:

> This [original] accumulation, necessary for capital to come into being, which is therefore already included in its concept as presupposition – as a moment – is to be distinguished essentially from the accumulation of capital which has already become capital, where there must already be capitals.[8]

He added that "original accumulation" was part of

> ... antediluvian conditions of capital, belongs to its historic presuppositions, which, precisely as such historic presuppositions, are past and gone, and hence belong to the history of its formation, but in no way to its contemporary history, i.e. not to the real system of the mode of production ruled by it.[9]

It was in Part Eight of *Capital*, Vol. 1, that the issue was examined in detail. As already indicated in the *Grundrisse*, Marx writes that the so-called "original accumulation" (*ursprüngliche Akkumulation*) – which began in the late fifteenth and early sixteenth century – "precedes capitalist accumulation." Accordingly, it is "an accumulation which is not the result of the capitalist mode of production but its point of departure."[10]

---

7 We may assume that for the French edition of *Das Kapital*, Vol. 1, Marx gave his approval to the omission of the adjective so-called from the chapter title and it only occurred once in "Part Seven: The Process of Accumulation of Capital." See, Karl Marx, *Le Capital*, in MEGA: *Zweite Abteilung "Das Kapital" und Vorarbeiten Band 7: Karl Marx. Le Capital. Paris 1872–1875* (Berlin: Dietz, 1989), 494, 631.

8 Karl Marx, *Grundrisse. Foundations of the Critique of Political Economy (Rough Draft)* (London: Penguin, 1993) [1939], 320.

9 Karl Marx, *Grundrisse*, 459.

10 Karl Marx, *Capital*, Vol. 1 (London: Penguin, 1982) [1976], 873. The German adjective *ursprünglich* has been translated into English as "primitive": "We have preferred 'primitive accumulation' to 'original accumulation' as the phrase has become established by now as part of the English language." Marx, *Capital*, Vol. 1, 714 (note). The first English edition of *Capital*, Vol. 1 (1887),

Indeed, the so-called "original accumulation"

> is nothing else than the historical process of divorcing the producer from the means of production. It appears as 'primitive' [original] because it forms the pre-history of capital, – and of the mode of production corresponding to capital.[11]

Marx was of the opinion that the process of proletarianisation and the coercion that accompanied it were the driving force of the so-called *original accumulation:* "The expropriation of the agricultural producer, of the peasant, from the soil is the basis of the whole process."[12] With regard to the brutality and violence that accompanied this process, Marx wanted to distance himself from the prevalent view amongst political economists and offer an alternative to their blissful, glorious and picturesque narrative:

> This primitive [original] accumulation plays approximately the same role in political economy as original sin does in theology. ... Long, long ago there were two sorts of people; one, the diligent, intelligent and above all frugal elite; the other, lazy rascals, spending their substance, and more, in riotous living. ... Such insipid childishness is every day preached to us in the defence of property.[13]

---

translated by Samuel Moore and Edward Aveling and edited by Friedrich Engels also contained the expression "primitive accumulation". We may assume that it had the consent of Engels. Magdoff also pointed out that, "there was a period when 'primitive' had a usage that was similar to 'primary,' but the development of the field of anthropology has changed the use of the term. There is now a clear-cut difference between the connotation of the word 'primitive' and the word 'primary'." Harry Magdoff, "Primitive Accumulation and Imperialism," *Monthly Review* 65, no. 5 (2013) [1972]. Marx's expression is a rough translation and tacit critique of Adam Smith's "idyllic" depiction of a "so-called" previous accumulation. Although Smith never used the term directly in his *Wealth of Nations*, he wrote that: "This accumulation must evidently be previous." Adam Smith, *An Inquiry into the Nature and Causes of the Wealth of Nations*, Vol. 1 (London: Charles Knight and Company, 1793), 408. Marx quoted the following passage of the *Wealth of Nations:* "The accumulation of stock must, in the nature of things, be previous to the division of labour." (873) In the following, we deploy the expression *original accumulation.* The German adjective *ursprünglich* does not exactly mean primitive, rather it signifies 'original' in the sense of previous, prior, initial, primordial, primal, primary or originating.

11 Marx, *Capital,* Vol.1, 875.

12 Marx, *Capital,* Vol.1, 876.

13 Marx, *Capital,* Vol.1, 873. This statement has provoked the critique of liberals, as well as some Marxists. As early as 1885, in his study on Marx, the Austrian politician Groß argued that, "the actual origin of capital" must have been based on "acquired, worked for and self-earned property." Gustav Groß, *Karl Marx: Eine Studie* (Leipzig: Nabu Press 1885), 80. Schumpeter also criticised that: "this children's tale, while far from telling the whole truth, yet tells a good deal of it. Supernormal intelligence and energy account for industrial success and in particular for the founding of industrial positions in nine cases out of ten. And precisely in the initial stages of

The following chapters scrutinise the dynamics that enabled capitalism to become the prevalent mode of production in England and western Europe. These factors include socio-economic developments during the late medieval period, intra- and extra-European processes of commercialisation, the Reformation, the weakening and expropriation of the Catholic Church's landed property, the formation of the bourgeois class, the Glorious Revolution, the role of the state, enclosures, the credit and modern tax system, protectionism, colonialism and slavery which set the context for novel relations of production and new ways of organising the labour process, that is, the eventual subordination of labour and domination of the labour process by capital to emerge. In other words, Marx was explaining socio-economic, technological and institutional dimensions of capitalist development – the latter refers to political, military, cultural, juridical and informal rules.

This process of *original accumulation* also resulted in the formal/legal rights of the "freed" peasants[14] and the establishment of the capital-relation "whereby the social means of subsistence and production are turned into capital, and the

---

capitalism and of every individual industrial career, saving was and is an important element in the process though not quite as explained in classic economics." Joseph A. Schumpeter, *Capitalism, Socialism and Democracy* (London: Routledge, 1976) [1942], 16. In turn, Harvey is of the opinion that Marx's account is "a bit exaggerated" as "Populations were not so much forced off the land as attracted off the land by employment possibilities and the prospects of a better life offered by urbanization and industrialization. The voluntary move to cities from appalling and precarious conditions of rural life, because urban wages were fairly high, has not been uncommon ... The story of primitive accumulation is, therefore, far more nuanced and complicated in its details than the one that Marx tells." David Harvey, *A Companion to Marx's Capital* (London: Verso, Books, 2010), 304. But the complicated and convoluted character of "capital accumulation" in its original stage was nothing that Marx was unaware of as he noted that: "the process in which money or value for-itself originally becomes capital presupposes on the part of the capitalist an accumulation – perhaps by means of savings garnered from products and values created by his own labour etc." Marx, *Grundrisse*, 459. In *Capital*, Vol. 1, he appears to have deliberately exaggerated his case to draw attention to the misconceptions of classical political economy. Concurrently, he admitted that a certain amount of invested capital stemmed from the entrepreneur's labour and inheritance while some artisans and wage-labourers succeeded in becoming "capitalists". Marx, *Capital*, Vol. 1, 728, 914. Furthermore, as Dobb notes: "Reflection creates an immediate doubt as to how such an accumulating process could aid the growth of capitalist production. May it not be, and has it not been at times, an actual obstacle by diverting wealth from productive investment? Is it not the case that gold and silver and objets d'art need to be sold before they can be made the means for investment in means of production – in other words, that their *dis*accumulation rather than their accumulation aids the growth of production?" Maurice Dobb, "Prelude to the Industrial Revolution," *Science & Society* 28, no. 1 (1964): 31–47, 41.

14 Marx, *Capital*, Vol.1, 875.

immediate producers are turned into wage-labourers."[15] Thus *original accumulation* is intimately related to processes of formal and real subsumption of the labour process, primarily through co-operation and other methods which resulted in increasing labour productivity and the socialisation of the labour process itself, the extraction of surplus value, initially as absolute surplus value, followed by extraction of relative surplus value by technical innovations, a hallmark of industrial capital production and modern economic growth.[16]

This chapter also examines how far these aspects are related to current debates on the Great Divergence.

Against Trans-Historicity

Marx did not propose a unilinear understanding of the emergence of capitalism. On the contrary, he was quite sensitive to the spatio-temporal specificities and processes of uneven development:

> The history of this expropriation assumes different aspects in different countries, and runs through its various phases in different orders of succession, and at different historical epochs. Only in England, which we therefore take as our example, has it the classic form.[17]

---

15 Marx, *Capital,* Vol. 1, 874.

16 To put it simply, the formal subsumption of labour under capital and extraction of absolute surplus value were historically determined by the augmentation of the working day (mostly independent small-scale commodity producers), accompanied by an increased rhythm and efficiency of production. Furthermore, merchant capitalists enlarged the degree of control over manufacture, for instance through the putting-out system or surveillance practices, though without transforming the technical conditions of production. On the other hand, real subsumption of labour under capital and the extraction of relative surplus value increase the productivity of labour through revolutionising the means and forces of production by dint of centralisation, intensified division of labour, the introduction of machinery, as well as techno-scientific innovations. Transitional modes of labour subordination and surplus value production may simultaneously combine different forms. The possibility of the coexistence of these different forms – suggested by Marx – illustrates that there is no linear process from less developed to more developed forms of capitalist subsumption and value creation, even though real subsumption and relative surplus value generally presuppose formal subsumption and absolute surplus value. Marx, *Capital,* Vol. 1, 283–672, 1019–1038.

17 Marx, *Capital,* Vol. 1, 876. As Anderson points out, in the revised French edition, Marx changed the last sentence to read: "England is so far the only country where this has been carried through completely ... but all the countries of Western Europe are going through the same development". Similarly, the sentence: "The country that is the more developed industrially only shows, to the less developed, the image of its own future" was rendered into: "The country that is more developed industrially only shows, to those that follow it on the industrial path [*échelle*],

In the French edition of *Capital*, Vol. 1 [18] Marx clarified that his emphasis on England was because it was the first region in the world that underwent a systematic process of *original accumulation*. On the other hand, this development was occurring all over western Europe:

> ... the basis of this whole development is the expropriation of the cultivators. So far, it has been carried out in a radical manner only in England: therefore this country will necessarily play the leading role in our sketch. But all the countries of Western Europe are going through the same development, although in accordance with the particular environment it changes its local color, or confines itself to a narrower sphere, or shows a less pronounced character, or follows a different order of succession.[19]

Again, in 1877, in an unpublished letter to a Russian journal, Marx confirmed that:

> The chapter on primitive [original] accumulation does not pretend to do more than trace the path by which, in Western Europe, the capitalist order of economy emerged from the womb of the feudal order of economy.[20]

In the same letter, similar to earlier statements in the French edition of *Capital*, Vol. 1, Marx mentioned the different trajectories that *original accumulation* could take in changing contexts and distinct world regions. This explains why he distanced himself from sanctifying his

> ... historical sketch of the genesis of capitalism in Western Europe into an historico-philosophical theory of the marche gênerale [general path] imposed by fate upon every people whatever the historical circumstances in which it finds itself.[21]

Most significantly, Marx added that:

> ... *events strikingly analogous* but taking place in *different historical surroundings* led to *totally different results*. By studying each of these forms of evolution separately and then com-

the image of its own future". Kevin B. Anderson, "Marx's Late Writings on Non-Western and Precapitalist Societies and Gender," Rethinking Marxism 14, no. 4 (2002), 84–96, 88, 91; Kevin Anderson, *Marx at the Margins: On Nationalism, Ethnicity, and Non-Western Societies* (Chicago: UCP, 2010), 178.

18 Karl Marx, *Le Capital*, Vol. 1, (Paris: Maurice Lachâtre, 1872)

19 Cited in Anderson, *Marx at the Margins*, 179.

20 Letter of Marx to the editor of *Otetschestwennyje Zapisky* [*Notes on the Fatherland*], end of 1877, in Karl Marx and Frederick Engels, *Selected Correspondence*. 1846–1895, Moscow (n.d.), 353.

21 Letter of Marx to the editor of *Otetschestwennyje Zapisky*, 354.

> paring them one can easily find the clue to this phenomenon, but one will never arrive there by using as one's master key a general historico-philosophical theory, the supreme virtue of which consists in being super-historical.[22] [emphasis ours]

The aforementioned quote clearly illustrates that the development of capitalism unfurls according to different dynamics as it depends on the specific circumstances at hand. In *Capital*, Vol. 3, he once more made plain that, the "entry of capital into agriculture as an independent and leading power does not take place everywhere all at once, but rather gradually and in particular branches of production."[23]

The Middle Ages

As adumbrated before, Marx was of the opinion that the period of 'classical' *original accumulation* pertained to the late fifteenth and especially sixteenth century. At the same time, he was cognizant of incipient capitalist relations of production as early as the late medieval period:

> Although we come across the first sporadic traces of capitalist production as early as the fourteenth or fifteenth centuries in certain towns of the Mediterranean, the capitalistic era dates from the sixteenth century.[24]

Indeed, Marx was aware of the long-term historical processes that engendered capital in both urban (commercialisation) and rural (agrarian capitalism) settings, as well as in the sphere of production. Regarding the latter, he pointed out that:

> ... the modern mode of production in its first period, that of manufacture, developed only where the conditions for it had been created in the Middle Ages. Compare Holland with Portugal, for example.[25]

With respect to the genesis of capitalist financial institutions, Marx emphasised that:

---

22 Letter of Marx to the editor of *Otetschestwennyje Zapisky*, 355.
23 Karl Marx, *Capital*, Vol. 3 (London: International Publishers Company, 1991) [1894], 937.
24 Marx, *Capital*, Vol. 1, 875.
25 Marx, *Capital*, Vol. 3, 450.

> The system of public credit, i.e. of national debts, the origins of which are to be found in Genoa and Venice as early as the Middle Ages, took possession of Europe as a whole during the period of manufacture.[26]

Although Marx could have mentioned a number of other significant financial innovations (see subchapter Financial Capitalism and Mercantilism) his argument about the role of the Italian city-states is well-taken and has been corroborated by recent literature. By the fifteenth century, the city-states of Florence and most notably Genoa and Venice "had developed many of the features that were to be found later on in the Netherlands, England and the United States."[27] To give an example, the bank of San Giorgio, founded in 1407,

> ... was also a predecessor of the Bank of England inasmuch as it invented engraftment, the modern debt-for-equity swap. The three cities [of Genoa, Venice and Florence] had a perpetual debt.[28]

As to the appearance of incipient financial and commercial capitalist practices, Marx noted:

> ... the Middle Ages had handed down two distinct forms of capital, which ripened in the most varied economic formations of society, and which, before the era of the capitalist mode of production, nevertheless functioned as capital – *usurer's capital* and *merchant's capital* (...) *The money capital formed by means of usury and commerce was prevented from turning into industrial capital by the feudal organization of the countryside and the guild organization of the towns. These fetters vanished with the dissolution of the feudal bands of retainers, and the expropriation and partial eviction of the rural population.*[29] [emphasis ours]

It is true that Marx did not take into account developments that took place prior to the fourteenth century. However, Marx seems to have been acquainted with some significant features of western Europe's and particularly England's socio-economic structure during the late Middle Ages. He emphasised that "the urban labour of the Middle Ages already constitutes a great advance and serves as a preparatory school for the capitalist mode of production, as regards

26 Marx, *Capital*, Vol. 1, 919.
27 Michele Fratianni and Franco Spinelli, "Italian City-States and Financial Evolution," *European Review of Economic History* 10, no. 3 (2006), 257–278.
28 Michele Fratianni and Franco Spinelli, "Italian City-States and Financial Evolution," 275.
29 Marx, *Capital*, Vol. 1, 914.

the CONTINUITY and STEADINESS OF LABOUR."[30] He added that "[i]n England, serfdom had disappeared in practice by the last part of the fourteenth century. The immense majority of the population consisted then, and to a still larger extent in the fifteenth century, of free peasant proprietors."[31]

It is a point of contention how far commercial developments contributed to the late fifteenth to eighteenth century processes that Marx referred to. For Marx, the economic structure of Western European capitalism "has grown out of the economic structure of feudal society. The dissolution of the latter set free the elements of the former."[32] However, in Part Eight of *Capital*, Vol. 1, he only covered those factors he deemed to be central to the processes of *original accumulation*. Regarding feudalism, he opined that it was not the expansion of commercialisation as such, but a) the disappearance of serfdom in late medieval England, b) the mid-fourteenth century English labour-statute to extend the working day (see the following section), as well as c) financial and merchant capitalist developments in the aforementioned Italian city states that were essential.

Another aspect of the importance Marx gave to developments taking place during the Middle Ages pertains to his evaluation of technological developments unfolding at the time. Although Marx underscored cumulative processes that helped lay the foundations for technological progress, most of the examples he highlighted only became central after the dissolution of the Roman Empire. To give some examples, Marx underlined the significance of mills and clocks.[33]

---

30 Karl Marx, *"Economic Manuscript of 1861–63 (A Contribution to the Critique of Political Economy),"* in *Marx and Engels Collected Works*, Vol. 33 (New York: International Publishers, 1991), 356. He later specified that the medieval guild system – despite obstructing the transition towards capitalism – was of "crucial importance in Europe for the evolution of both capitalists and free labourers." Marx, *Capital*, Vol. 1, 1029.

31 Marx, *Capital*, Vol. 1, 877.

32 Marx, *Capital*, Vol. 1, 875.

33 Marx highlighted that: "Their development prepares the way for the period of machinery." He added that, "we see in the history of the mill the extraordinarily slow progress in development from Roman times (shortly before Augustus), when the first water mills were introduced from Asia, to the end of the 18th century, when the first steam mills are seen, constructed on a large scale in the United States. Here it is only through an extraordinary accumulation of the experience of generations that there occurs an advance, which is even then only applied sporadically, without overturning the old method of working." Regarding the clock, Marx argued that it "is based on the craftsmanship of artisanal production together with the erudition which characterises the dawn of bourgeois society. It gives the idea of the automatic mechanism and of automatic motion applied to production. The history of the clock goes hand in hand with the history of the theory of uniform motion. What, without the clock, would be a period in which the value of the commodity, and therefore the labour time necessary for its production, are the decisive factor?". He was of the opinion that it is "one of the most remarkable automata"

He also pinpointed three of the four great Chinese inventions even though he might not have been aware of their place of origin:

> *Gunpowder*, the *compass*, and the *printing press* were the 3 great inventions which ushered in bourgeois society. Gunpowder blew up the knightly class, the compass discovered the world market and founded the colonies, and the printing press was the instrument of Protestantism and the regeneration of science in general; the most powerful lever for creating the intellectual prerequisites.[34]

Indeed, along with socio-economic dynamics (especially commerce and relations of production) and new institutions (the state), the role of the means and forces of production were equally pivotal for Marx:

> *The mode of production of material life conditions the general process of social, political and intellectual life … At a certain stage of development, the material productive forces of society come into conflict with the existing relations of production* or – this merely expresses the same thing in legal terms – with the property relations within the framework of which they have operated hitherto. From forms of development of the productive forces these relations turn into their fetters. Then begins an era of social revolution. The changes in the economic foundation lead sooner or later to the transformation of the whole immense superstructure.[35] [emphasis ours]

Amongst Marxists, there has never been a consensus as to England's mode of production during the phase of *original accumulation*. While certain scholars argue it was still feudal, others reason that it belonged to an independent mode of production such as *simple* or *petty commodity production* or already constituted the beginning of a sort of early stage of capitalism. Needless to say, Marx's aforementioned characterisation leaves room for different interpretations.

---

and emphasised "regulation by the stroke of the clock." Marx, *"Economic Manuscript of 1861–63,"* 403, 395, 442, 491. After Marx, a number of renowned scholars have emphasised the importance of the clock for socio-economic development. See, for example, Georg Simmel, *Die Großstädte und das Geistesleben* (Frankfurt am Main: e-artnow, 2006) [1903]; Lewis Mumford, *Technics and Civilization* (Chicago: UCP, 2010) [1934]; Carlo M. Cipolla, *Clocks and Culture, 1300–1700* (London: Norton, 1967); E. P. Thompson, "Time, Work, Discipline and Industrial Capitalism," *Past and Present* 38 (1967), 56–97; David S. Landes, *Revolution in Time. Clocks and the Making of the Modern World* (Cambridge: Viking, 1983).

34 Marx, "Economic Manuscript of 1861–63," 403.

35 Karl Marx, *A Contribution to the Critique of Political Economy* (1859) (Moscow: Progress Publishers, 1977), Preface.

The Transition Period

For Marx, *original accumulation* was intimately connected to the interests of the nobility and aristocracy, the embryonic bourgeoisie and the rise of the proletariat. Regarding the former, Marx argued that "[t]he new nobility was the child of its time, for which money was the power of all powers. Transformation of arable land into sheep-walks was therefore its slogan."[36] Monetisation and commercialisation seem to have been crucial factors in Marx's understanding of the *original accumulation* and the way in which it unfolded. As Marx noted:

> The formation of capital thus does not emerge from landed property (here at most from the tenant [*Pächter*] in so far as he is a dealer in agricultural products); or from the guild (although there is a possibility at the last point); but rather from merchant's and usurer's wealth … It [trade] will subjugate production more and more to exchange value … Dissolves the old relations … However, the dissolving effect depends very much on the nature of the producing communities between which it operates.[37]

In *Capital*, Vol. 3, Marx specified that "[e]ven so, this development, taken by itself, is insufficient to explain the transition from one mode of production to the other."[38] With respect to the bourgeoisie, Marx argued that:

> The industrial capitalists, these new potentates, had on their part not only to displace the guild masters of handicrafts, but also the feudal lords, who were in possession of the sources of wealth.[39]

This line of argumentation has played a significant role in recent writings on the rise of the West and Great Divergence, especially in comparisons of Europe with West Asia and China.[40] Indeed, this process did not occur in any part of Asia in

---

36 Marx, *Capital*, Vol.1, 879.

37 Marx, *Grundrisse*, 505. Similarly, Harvey argues that: "The appropriation of the land was the primary means to dispossess the peasantry, but release of the retainers owed as much to the way in which money power began to be exercised within and over the feudal order (e. g., by merchant capital and usury)." Harvey, *Companion*, 294.

38 Marx, *Capital*, Vol. 3, 444. Cf. Roman Rosdolsky, *The Making of Marx's Capital* (London: Brill, 1977), 275–276.

39 Marx, *Capital*, Vol. 1, 875. See also Christopher Hill, *Reformation to Industrial Revolution* (Harmondsworth:Weidenfeld and Nicolson, 1980) [1967]; Neil Davidson, *How Revolutionary Were the Bourgeois Revolutions?* (Chicago: Haymarket Books, 2012).

40 Mielants, *The Origins of Capitalism*, 47–57; David Graeber, *Debt: The First 5,000 Years* (New York: Penguin, 2011), 271–82; Jürgen Kocka, *Capitalism. A Short History* (Princeton: PUP, 2016), 29–30, 34–35, 51. For the missing political leverage of Chinese merchants vis-à-vis the state,

the seventeenth and eighteenth centuries, not even in the north-western Indian province of Gujarat – one of the only Asian socio-economic 'core regions' – where merchants were strong enough to influence the politics of the state.[41]

The emergence of the modern working-class, the increased number of wage-labourers and the higher degree of commodification of labour-power in western Europe, particularly in Holland, England and their colonies compared to Asia were crucial factors in the Great Divergence between East and West.[42] In the late fifteenth and throughout the sixteenth century, the expropriated rural population was

> ... turned in massive quantities into beggars, robbers and vagabonds, partly from inclination, in most cases under the force of circumstances ... a bloody legislation against vagabondage was enforced throughout Western Europe.[43]

In sixteenth and seventeenth century England, proletarianisation was further accelerated in the wake of the Reformation "and the consequent colossal spoliation of church".[44]

---

see, for example, Fernand Braudel, *Afterthoughts on Material Civilization and Capitalism* (Baltimore: JHUP, 1977), 72–73; Ho-Fung Hung, *The China Boom: Why China Will Not Rule the World* (New York: CUP, 2015), 22–23, 26–28; Matías Vernengo and David Fields, "DisORIENT: Money, Technological Development and the Rise of the West," *Review of Radical Political Economics* 48, no. 4 (2016): 562–568, 566; Taisu Zhang, *The Laws and Economics of Confucianism: Kinship and Property in Preindustrial China and England* (Cambridge: CUP, 2017). See also Patrick O'Brien, "Was the First Industrial Revolution a Conjuncture in the History of the World Economy?," *LSE Economic History Working Papers* 259 (2017): 1–52, 26.

41 Yazdani, *India*, 401–417. For India, see also Kaveh Yazdani, "South Asia in the Great Divergence Debate," in *Oxford Research Encyclopedia of Asian History* (2019), eds. David Ludden et al., https://oxfordre.com/asianhistory/view/10.1093/acrefore/9780190277727.001.0001/acrefore-9780190277727-e-354, accessed April 17, 2020.

42 As Marx pointed out: "The simultaneous employment of a large number of wage-labourers in the same labour process, which is a necessary condition for this change, also forms the starting-point of capitalist production. This starting-point coincides with the birth of capital itself." Karl Marx, *Capital*, Vol. 1, 453. Most recently, Vries has reasserted that Britain, "because of high wages of its proletarians, their permanent availability for and dependency on the labour market and the fact that they also depended on a market for their consumption – [was] a far more likely candidate for innovation in production and for industrialisation than China or any other country in the world." Vries, *Escaping Poverty*, 426.

43 Marx, *Capital*, Vol. 1, 896.

44 Marx, *Capital*, Vol. 1, 881.

Agrarian Capitalism versus Urban Commercialisation

Most importantly, Marx underscored the dispossession of the rural population which, as he thought, provided the urban industry with the necessary labour force:

> The intermittent but constantly renewed expropriation and expulsion of the agricultural population supplied the urban industries, as we have seen, with a mass of proletarians standing entirely outside the corporate guilds and unfettered by them. [45]

However, it is important to note that the earliest regions in England to industrialise were not those that first established agrarian capitalist relations of production.[46]

Furthermore, a considerable quantity of the labour force in the first mechanised factories and incipient industries of the Industrial Revolution in northern England were women and most notably children and young adults from the immediate hinterlands.[47] Before the introduction of the railway we do not have evidence of a substantial degree of labour migration from the south – especially from those areas traditionally associated with the 'agricultural revolution' – to the industrialising regions of England that were connected to sea ports but industrialised despite being economically more backward.[48] Marx and even

45 Marx, *Capital*, Vol. 1, 908.

46 For a recent study, see Joseph E. Inikori, *Africans and the Industrial Revolution in England: A Study in International Trade and Economic Development* (Cambridge: CUP, 2002).

47 Arthur Redford, *Labour Migration in England 1800–1850* (Manchester: MUP 1926); P. Deane and W. A. Cole, *British Economic Growth, 1688–1959* (Cambridge: CUP, 1962). For child labour, see Hugh Cunningham, "The Employment and Unemployment of Children in England, c. 1680–1851," *Past and Present* 126 (1990): 115–150; Clark Nardinelli, *Child Labor and the Industrial Revolution* (Bloomington: IUP, 1990); Carolyn Tuttle, *Hard at Work in Factories and Mines: The Economics of Child Labor During the British Industrial Revolution* (Oxford: Westview Press, 1999); Katrina Honeyman, *Child Workers in England, 1780–1820. Parish Apprentices and the Making of the Early Industrial Labour Force* (Aldershot: Routledge, 2007); Jane Humphries, *Childhood and Child Labour in the British Industrial Revolution* (Cambridge: CUP, 2010).

48 The dominant position in the existing literature is that there was a "relatively modest migration from England's poor agrarian South to the industrializing North". Jeffrey G. Williamson, *Coping with City Growth During the British Industrial Revolution* (Cambridge: CUP, 1990), 131. Most recently, Wallis confirmed that: "Few moved north from rural southern England." Patrick Wallis, "Labour markets and training," in *The Cambridge Economic History of Modern Britain,*

more Friedrich Engels – his long-time colleague and friend – paid attention to the significance of child labour. Marx noted that, "the cotton industry introduced child-slavery into England" and assumed that they were hired from places as far away as London and Birmingham.[49] Although the relevance of migration for the British Industrial Revolution needs to be further explored, Pat Hudson summarises the consensus of the current debate when she highlights that:

> ... the major expansion of proto-industries and urban or centralised manufacturing production occurred outside commercialising agricultural regions which are likely to have been shedding labour. It is thus impossible to explain industrial growth simply in terms of the release of labour from agriculture, particularly from areas that seem to have been increasing their labour productivity most.[50]

For Marx, the incipient agrarian capitalist relations of production not only intensified the exploitation of labourers but also laid the foundations for the rise of a national market:

> Thus the destruction of the subsidiary trades of the countryside, the process whereby manufacture is divorced from agriculture, goes hand in hand with the expropriation of the previously self-supporting peasants and their separation from their own means of production. And only the destruction of rural domestic industry can give the home market of a country that extension and stability which the capitalist mode of production requires.[51]

A number of scholars have endorsed the thesis in one form or the other. Mark Overton, for example, argues that:

> Enclosure facilitated innovation and changes in land use because the constraints imposed by common property rights, the scattering of land, and collective decision making could be

---

Vol. 1: Industrialization, 1700–1860, eds. Roderick Floud et al. (Cambridge: CUP, 2014), 178–210, 197. See also Inikori, *Africans and the Industrial Revolution.*

49 Marx, *Capital*, Vol. 1, 925. To prove his point, Marx quoted John Fielden (*The Curse of the Factory System*, London, 1836), 5–6: "The small and nimble fingers of little children being by very far the most in request, the custom instantly sprang up of procuring apprentices (!) from the different parish workhouses of London, Birmingham, and elsewhere. Many, many thousands of these little, hapless creatures were sent down into the north, being from the age of 7 to the age of 13 or 14 years old." Marx, *Capital*, Vol. 1, 923. For further evidence, see also 924 note 11. For Marx's emphasis on the relevance of child labour in England's industrialisation process, see *Capital*, Vol. 1, 340–416.

50 Pat Hudson, *The Industrial Revolution* (London: Bloomsbury Academic, 1992), 80.

51 Marx, *Capital*, Vol. 1, 911.

overcome. Contemporaries were virtually unanimous that enclosed fields offered more opportunities for making money than did commonfields.[52]

As to the sequence of succession, Robert Allen argues that "[m]ost of the causation, however, ran from expanding world trade, to the growth of urban manufacturing, to rising agricultural productivity, and, finally, to large farms and enclosures."[53]

---

52 Mark Overton, *Agricultural Revolution in England: The Transformation of the Agrarian Economy 1500–1850* (Cambridge: CUP, 1996), 165. See also John Saville, "Primitive Accumulation and Early Industrialization in Britain," *Socialist Register* 6 (1969): 247–271; Robert Brenner, "Agrarian Class Structure and Economic Development in Pre-industrial Europe," in *The Brenner Debate: Agrarian Class Structure and Economic Development in Pre-Industrial Europe*, eds. T. H. Aston and C. H. E. Philpin (Cambridge: CUP, 1985), 10–63; Ellen Meiksins Wood, *The Origins of Capitalism: A Longer View* (London: Verso, 2002); N. F. R. Crafts and C. K. Harley, "Precocious British Industrialisation: a general-equilibrium perspective," in *Exceptionalism and Industrialisation: Britain and its European Rivals, 1688–1815*, ed. L. Prados de la Escosura (Cambridge: CUP, 2004), 86–107; Spencer Dimmock, *The Origin of Capitalism in England, 1400–1600* (Leiden: Brill, 2014). Most recently, Hodgson has emphasised that "enclosures made land saleable and usable as collateral." Geoffrey M. Hodgson, "1688 and all that: property rights, the Glorious Revolution and the rise of British capitalism," *Journal of Institutional Economics* 13, no. 1 (2017): 79–107, 9 note 8. As to those who contest the importance of enclosure acts as the driving force of capitalism, see Deirdre N. McCloskey, "The Economics of Enclosure: A Market Analysis," in *European Peasants and Their Markets: Essays in Agrarian Economic History*, eds. E. L. Jones and William Parker (Princeton: PUP, 1975), 123–160. Recently, McCloskey, one of the most renowned liberal scholars in the field of economic history, reiterated that Marx "instanced enclosure in England during the sixteenth century (which has been overturned by historical findings that such enclosure was economically minor) and in the eighteenth (which has been overturned by findings that the labor driven off the land by enclosure was a tiny source of the industrial proletariat, and enclosure happened then mainly in the south and east where in fact little of the new sort of industrialization was going on, and where agricultural employment in newly enclosed villages in fact increased)." Deirdre N. McCloskey, *Bourgeois Dignity: Why Economics can't Explain the Modern World* (Chicago: UCP, 2010), 154.

53 Allen, *British Industrial Revolution*, 58. For the importance of the demand-side in spurring agricultural growth, see Stephan R. Epstein, "Rodney Hilton, Marxism and the Transition from Feudalism to Capitalism," in *Rodney Hilton's Middle Ages*, eds. C. Dyer, P.R. Coss and C. Wickham (Oxford: Oxford Journals, 2007), 248–269, 264; E.A. Wrigley, *Energy and the English Industrial Revolution* (Cambridge: CUP, 2010), 34; Shami Ghosh, "Rural Economies and Transitions to Capitalism: Germany and England Compared (c.1200–c.1800)," *Journal of Agrarian Change* 16,2 (2016): 255–290, 283, 273–274; Joseph E. Inikori, "The development of capitalism in the Atlantic world: England, the Americas, and West Africa, 1400–1900," *Labor History* 58, no. 2 (2017): 138–153, 149. See also Joel Mokyr, "The Industrial Revolution and the New Economic History," in *The Economics of the Industrial Revolution*, ed. J. Mokyr (London: Avalon Publishing, 1985), 21. For an overview of works emphasising the role of cities in stimulating agricultural growth, see Leif van Neuss, "Why Did the Industrial Revolution Start in Britain?" (2015), 23; retrieved from: http://

Yet, Marx made the significant point that land productivity and surplus production equally increased despite diminishing numbers of agriculturalists:

> In spite of the smaller number of its cultivators, the soil brought forth as much produce as before, or even more, because *the revolution in property relations on the land was accompanied by improved methods of cultivation, greater co-operation, a higher concentration of the means of production* and so on, and because the *agricultural wage-labourers were made to work at a higher level of intensity,* and the field of production on which they worked for themselves shrank more and more.[54] [emphasis ours]

Moreover, in the preceding remarks, Marx is explicit in depicting how capital – through converting the character of the means of production by socialising it, and contemporaneously by organising labour through co-operations and the intensification of the labour activities – increased the level of productivity. A historically new mode of production was taking hold:

> Capitalist production only really begins ... when each individual capital simultaneously employs a comparatively large number of workers, and when, as a result, the labour-process is carried on on an extensive scale, and yields relatively large quantities of products. A large number of workers working together, at the same time, in one place ... in order to produce the same sort of commodity under the command of the same capitalist, constitutes the starting-point of capitalist production. This is true both historically and conceptually. With regard to the mode of production itself, manufacture [*Manufaktur*] can hardly be distinguished, in its earliest stages, from the handicraft trades [*Handwerksindustrie*] of the guilds, except by the greater number of workers simultaneously employed by the same individual capital.[55]

Current scholarship has corroborated the substantial seventeenth century shift of the English labour force from agriculture to manufacture and services. This pivotal transformation seems to have been unparalleled in other parts of the world. Overton confirms that labour productivity in English agriculture doubled between 1700 and 1850.[56] E. A. Wrigley adds that, the English population "more

---

ssrn.com/abstract=2696076, accessed 17/04/2020. For an overview of demand-side arguments in the making of the Industrial Revolution, see van Neuss, "Why Did the Industrial Revolution Start in Britain?" 28 – 32.

54 Marx, *Capital*, Vol. 1, 908.

55 Marx, *Capital*, Vol. 1, 439.

56 Overton, *Agricultural*, 131; Stephen Broadberry et al., *British Economic Growth, 1270 – 1870* (Cambridge: CUP, 2015). See also Deane and Cole, *British Economic Growth*, 62 – 75; N. F. R. Crafts, *British Economic Growth during the Industrial Revolution* (Oxford: Government Institutes, 1985), 44. Needless to say, increased agricultural productivity was crucial in the growth of urbanization. Between 1600 and 1850 the English population living in towns with 5,000 or more inhab-

than quintupled between 1550 and 1850, and until the last quarter-century, it continued to obtain almost all of its food from local produce, apart from tropical products such as sugar."[57] Indeed, net imports in 1791 merely accounted for two percent of total consumption and only slightly rose to five percent in 1801.[58] However, from the 1790s onwards, England was transitioning to a net importer of grain.[59] It remains a matter of debate whether industrial development could have been sustained without the importation of foodstuffs, especially from Ireland, which only became part of the United Kingdom in 1801. From the turn of the nineteenth century "imports increasingly became important in meeting the demand for food, so that by mid-century they were accounting for over one sixth of [English] consumption," that is, twelve percent in 1831 and sixteen percent in 1851.[60] It is interesting to note that by the early decades of the nineteenth century "some 70 per cent of English food imports were from Ireland."[61] What remains to be resolved is the question whether southern England – the region traditionally associated with the agricultural revolution – supplied foodstuffs to the industrial regions of the north as hard statistical evidence on this matter seems to be missing. In fact, it is questionable whether large amounts of grain were transported in long-distance trade before the introduction of the railway.[62]

itants increased from 3.2% to 43.5%. L Shaw-Taylor and E. A. Wrigley, "Occupational structure and population change," in *The Cambridge Economic History of Modern Britain, Volume 1: 1700–1870*, eds. R. Floud et al. (Cambridge: CUP, 2014), 53–88, 76.

57 E. A. Wrigley, "Reconsidering the Industrial Revolution: England and Wales," *Journal of Interdisciplinary History* 49, no. 1 (2018): 9–42, 19.

58 Overton, *Agricultural*, 75 (Table 3.5).

59 B. R. Mitchell, *British Historical Statistics* (Cambridge: CUP, 1988), 221.

60 Overton, *Agricultural*, 89, 75. See also E. A. Wrigley, *The Path to Sustained Growth. England's Transition from an Organic Economy to an Industrial Revolution* (Cambridge: CUP, 2016), 46 (note 1), 57–60. Between the 1780s and the 1850s, imported foodstuffs amounted to 35–40% of total imports by value. But foodstuffs such as grain, meat, butter and cheese accounted for only a tenth of the overall total until the 1840s. Wrigley, *The Path to Sustained Growth*, 58.

61 Overton, *Agricultural*, 88. Meredith and Oxley point out that this process had already begun by the mid-18th century when Scotland, Wales and especially Ireland were key suppliers of English foodstuffs: "as early as the 1750s and 1760s, beef imports from Ireland trebled, and there were big increases in butter and pork." David Meredith and Deborah Oxley, "Food and fodder: feeding England, 1700–1900," *Past and Present* 222, no. 1 (2014): 163; Overton, *Agricultural* 214, 172. See also Brinley Thomas, *The Industrial Revolution and the Atlantic Economy: Selected Essays* (London: Routledge, 1993), 81; Overton, *Agricultural*, 99.

62 In a personal correspondence regarding the question about the movement of food surplus from the "agricultural" counties to the parts of northern England in which there was rapid population growth associated with growth in the secondary sector, Wrigley opined that it was of minor importance, but direct quantitative evidence is lacking. It seems to us that Wrigley underlines the following points: The first is that as long as goods transport over land was chiefly by

But it cannot be ruled out that southern England might have played a role in the industrialisation of the north through the transfer of money, know-how and the diffusion of innovations. Be that as it may, increased agricultural productivity enabled a larger part of the population to engage in the secondary and tertiary sectors – fifty-six percent of the labour force by the end of the seventeenth century.[63] According to Wrigley, the latest estimates

> ... suggest that 62.9 percent of the male labor force was employed in agriculture in 1601 and 38.2 percent in 1801, implying that the male labor force at these two dates totaled 686,000

---

horse and cart it was feasible to move grain only over relatively short distances. Von Thunen in his remarkable analysis of land use, *The Isolated State* (1826), described how moving grain from his estate of Tellow to Rostock meant that the horses consumed 150 lbs of the 2,400 lbs which they were transporting. Long distance movement by land (by water was very different) made no sense over long distances. Grain-producing counties in East Anglia and other southern counties had a very large local market to serve because London was a big city. In any case the normal diet in much of the north included oats-based food such as porridge. And the potato was grown from a very early date in Lancashire. It was probably the first county in which the potato became an important food source in the 18th century. Regarding water transport, almost all canal construction was related to the movement of coal. Moreover, canal construction only became important in the later 18th century. However, the quantity of grains transported along the English coastline remains unknown. E. A. Wrigley, personal correspondence, 30.6. and 12.10.2018. In a personal correspondence, Dan Bogart corroborated that grain could not be shipped competitively from the south to the north of England by road. He questioned that it could even be shipped competitively by canal. On the basis of a new database of coastal sailings c.1830, he did not identify a high number of ships going from southern ports to the industrial northwest of England. Dan Bogart, personal correspondence, 20. and 28.10.2018. See also Dan Bogart et al., "Canal carriers and creative destruction in English transport," *Explorations in Economic History* (forthcoming); Dan Bogart et al., "Speedier delivery: coastal shipping times and speeds during the age of sail," *Working Paper* (2018); Patrick K. O'Brien, "Agriculture and the home market for English industry 1660–1820," *English Historical Review* 100 (1985): 773–800; Roger Scola, *Feeding the Victorian City: The Food Supply of Manchester, 1770–1870* (Manchester: MUP, 1992), 7, 36.

63 Wrigley, "Reconsidering the Industrial Revolution," 23; Wrigley, *The Path to Sustained Growth*. This was a much larger proportion of what Marx had thought. The sources he consulted acted on the assumption that, "even in the last third of the 17th century, four-fifths of the English people were agriculturalists." Marx, *Capital*, Vol. 1, 877 note 1. According to Allen, the percentage of the population in agriculture dropped from 75% in 1500 to 35% in 1800. Allen, *British Industrial Revolution*, 17–8. Most recently, Wallis et al. have calculated that there was "a decline in the share of the male workforce in agriculture in England from around 68 percent in 1600, to around 48 percent in the early eighteenth century." Peter Wallis et al., "Structural change and economic growth in the British economy before the Industrial Revolution, 1500–1800," *Journal of Economic History* 78, no. 3 (2018): 862–903. See also Shaw-Taylor and Wrigley, "Occupational structure and population change".

and 824,000, respectively—an increase of 20 percent over a period during which the population increased by 108 percent.[64]

Besides the aforementioned factors, it is important to add the role of technological progress, the effects of population growth in the enhancement of agricultural and industrial productivity, climate recovery from the Little Ice Age in the eighteenth century, as well as the importance of the productivity of open fields (compared to large-scale farms).[65]

Marx called attention to the unintended consequences of agrarian developments in the sphere of industrial production:

> The new manufactures were established at sea-ports, or at points in the countryside which were beyond the control of the old municipalities and their guilds. Hence, in England, the bitter struggle of the corporate towns against these new seed-beds of industry.[66]

Indeed, the countryside was penetrated by merchant capital's deepening grip on and the increased monopolisation of production (for example, of textiles). This development, also described as putting-out or 'proto-industrialisation,' was conducive to capital accumulation and the strengthening of merchant capitalists. As a result, increased control over production provided greater possibilities of exploitation while individual producers and the state lost opportunities and sources of income.[67] This development made possible processes of commodification and the production of exchange values which could be sold on the market:

> ... the events that transformed the small peasants into wage-labourers, and their means of subsistence and of labour into material [*sachliche*] elements of capital, created, at the same time, a home market for capital. Formerly, the peasant family produced means of subsis-

---

64 Wrigley, "Reconsidering the Industrial Revolution," 22.

65 Regarding the significance of demographic factors, Marx emphasised that: "The constant generation of a relative surplus population keeps the law of the supply and demand of labour, and therefore wages, within narrow limits which correspond to capital's valorization requirements." Marx, *Capital*, Vol. 1, 899. For the role of technological progress between the 17th and 19th century, see James B. Ang et al., "Innovation and Productivity Advances in British Agriculture: 1620 – 1850," *Southern Economic Journal* 80, no. 1 (2013): 162 – 186; For climate change, see José L. Martínes-González, "Did climate change influence English agricultural development? (1645 – 1740)," *EHES Working Paper* 75 (2015), retrieved from: http://www.ehes.org/EHES_75.pdf accessed April 17, 2020. For the productivity of open fields, see Allen, *British Industrial Revolution*, 57 – 79.

66 Marx, *Capital*, Vol. 1, 915.

67 Marx, *Capital*, Vol. 1, 909.

> tence and raw materials, which they themselves for the most part consumed. These raw materials and means of subsistence have now become commodities.[68]

Marx was fully aware that the predominance of agrarian capitalist relations of production in England was not to be accomplished before the Industrial Revolution:

> Still, the manufacturing period, properly so called, does not succeed in carrying out this transformation radically and completely. It will be remembered that manufacture conquers the domain of national production only very partially, and always rests on the handicrafts of the towns and the domestic subsidiary industries of the rural districts, which stand in the background as its basis ... A consistent foundation for capitalist agriculture could only be provided by large-scale industry, in the form of machinery; it is large-scale industry which radically expropriates the vast majority of the agricultural population and completes the divorce between agriculture and rural domestic industry, tearing up the latter's roots, which are spinning and weaving. It therefore also conquers the entire home market for industrial capital for the first time.[69]

In this context, Marx also relativised his polemical tone vis-à-vis classical political economy and conceded that:

> Doubtless many small guild-masters, and a still greater number of independent small artisans, or even wage-labourers, transformed themselves into small capitalists, and, by gradually extending their exploitation of wage-labour and the corresponding accumulation, into 'capitalists' without qualification.[70]

The State

Marx emphasised the crucial role played by the state, especially the English state, in the establishment of capitalism. He had the intention to write a book and systematic account on the state but passed away before he could fulfil this task.[71] In the *Communist Manifesto* (1848), Marx and Engels argued that, in the final analysis, "[t]he power of the modern state is merely a device for ad-

68 Marx, *Capital*, Vol. 1, 910.
69 Marx, *Capital*, Vol. 1, 911–913.
70 Marx, *Capital*, Vol. 1, 914.
71 Marx, *Grundrisse*, 53–54, 108–109.

ministering the common affairs of the whole bourgeois class."[72] In *Capital*, Vol. 1, the genealogy of this historical process and the coming into power of the bourgeoisie was traced. It is worth noting that Marx highlighted the importance of long-term processes in empowering the state and subjugating wage-labourers:

> Legislation on wage-labour, which aimed from the first at the exploitation of the worker and, as it progressed, remained equally hostile to him, begins in England with the Statute of Labourers issued by Edward III in 1349. The Ordinance of 1350 in France, issued in the name of King John, corresponds to it. The English and French laws run parallel and are identical in content. Where these labour-statutes aim at a *compulsory extension of the working day … Workers' combinations are treated as heinous crimes from the fourteenth century until 1825,* the year of the repeal of the laws against combinations. The spirit of the Statute of Labourers of 1349 and its offshoots shines out clearly in the fact that *while the state certainly dictates a maximum of wages, it on no account fixes a minimum.*[73] [emphasis ours]

As Marx argued, the dissolution of feudal relations of production and the establishment of modern private property in estates was stimulated in the wake of the restoration of the English monarchy during the Stuart period (1660–1688). But it was the Glorious Revolution of 1688 that brought into power a class alliance between

> … the landed and capitalist profit-grubbers. They inaugurated the new era by practising on a colossal scale the thefts of state lands which had hitherto been managed more modestly … The bourgeois capitalists favoured the operation, with the intention, among other things, of converting the land into a merely commercial commodity, extending the area of large-scale agricultural production, and increasing the supply of free and rightless proletarians driven from their land. Apart from this, the new landed aristocracy was the natural ally of the new bankocracy, of newly hatched high finance, and of the large manufacturers, at that time dependent on protective duties.[74]

---

72 Karl Marx and Friedrich Engels, "Manifesto of the Communist Party (1848)," translated from the first edition by Terrell Carver (1996), in *The Cambridge Companion to The Communist Manifesto*, eds. Terrel Carver and James Farr (New York: CUP, 2015), 239.

73 Marx, *Capital*, Vol. 1, 900.

74 Marx, *Capital*, Vol. 1, 884. For recent works, stressing the significance of the 'Glorious Revolution' in the genesis of industrial capitalism, see Daron Acemoğlu and James A. Robinson, *Why Nations Fail: The Origins of Power, Prosperity and Poverty* (London: S. Fischer, 2012); Neil Davidson, *How Revolutionary Were the Bourgeois Revolutions?* (Chicago: Haymarket Books, 2012); G. W. Cox, "Was the Glorious Revolution a Constitutional Watershed?," *Journal of Economic History* 72, no. 3 (2012): 567–600; Hodgson, "1688 and all that"; Kara Dimitruk, ""I Intend Therefore to Prorogue": the effects of political conflict and the Glorious Revolution in parliament, 1660–1702," *European Review of Economic History* 22, no. 3 (2018), 1–37.

Marx also highlighted the advancements particular to the eighteenth century. This was a period when "the law itself" became "the instrument by which the people's land is stolen, although the big farmers made use of their little independent methods as well."[75] He described those "Bills for Inclosure of Commons" as a "Parliamentary form of the robbery … ." In other words,

> … decrees by which the landowners grant themselves the people's land as private property, decrees of expropriation of the people … While the place of the independent yeoman was taken by tenants at will, small farmers on yearly leases, a servile rabble dependent on the arbitrary will of the landlords, the systematic theft of communal property was of great assistance, alongside the theft of the state domains, in swelling those large farms … and in 'setting free' the agricultural population as a proletariat for the needs of industry.[76]

The following statement makes unambiguously clear what a pivotal role Marx attributed to the state:

> The rising bourgeoisie needs the power of the state, and uses it to 'regulate' wages, i.e. to force them [the workers] into the limits suitable for making a profit, to lengthen the working day, and to keep the worker himself at his normal level of dependence. This is an essential aspect of so-called primitive [original] accumulation. [77]

Marx's emphasis on the crucial role the state played in giving birth to capitalism has been confirmed by some of the most authoritative historians of the twentieth

75 Marx, *Capital*, Vol. 1, 885.

76 Marx, *Capital*, Vol. 1, 885 f. Whether Parliamentary Enclosures were directly responsible for the dispossession of the peasantry is a controversial issue. For classical Marxian approaches, see J.L. and Barbara Hammond's *The Village Labourer, 1760–1832* and E.P. Thompson, *The Making of the English Working Class*. For a different view, see Chambers and Mingay's *The Agricultural Revolution, 1750–1880*. Interestingly, Lavrovsky points out that: "By the 1780's we see in Brampton a well-defined land monopoly of the big landowners (gentry, nobility, tithe impropriators) and the expropriation of the peasantry who retained only 5.7 per cent of the total land subjected to parliamentary enclosure." V. M. Lavrovsky, "Expropriation of the English Peasantry in the Eighteenth Century", *The Economic History Review* 9, no. 2 (1956): 271–282, 280. Neeson's recent work equally supports Marx's position, arguing that "in most of the villages studied here parliamentary enclosure destroyed the old peasant economy. It did this not only by more than decimating small occupiers and landlords and by reducing their total acreage, but also by more completely separating the agricultural practice of small and large farmers, by pushing the smaller occupiers into the market more thoroughly than before, and by expropriating from the landless the commons on which much of the economy depended." J. M. Neeson, *Commoners: Common Right, Enclosure and Social Change in England, 1700–1820* (Cambridge: CUP, 1993), 223.

77 Marx, *Capital*, Vol. 1, 899.

and twenty-first century writing on the reasons behind the Industrial Revolution, the rise of the West, British supremacy and the Great Divergence.[78] As Fernand Braudel famously wrote: "Capitalism only triumphs when it becomes identified with the state, when it is the state."[79] Patrick O'Brien expounds upon this assessment by pointing out the fact that the broad thrust of the British government's

> ... fiscal and financial policies combined with naval mercantilism can be represented as effective support for the endeavors of private capitalist enterprise carrying the economy through a process of Smithian growth into a transition for the technological breakthroughs for a first industrial revolution.[80]

In an ironic summary of some of his arguments, Marx substantiated that:

> The spoliation of the Church's property, the fraudulent alienation of the state domains, the theft of the common lands, the usurpation of feudal and clan property and its transformation into modern private property under circumstances of ruthless terrorism, all these things were just so many idyllic methods of primitive [original] accumulation. They conquered the field for capitalist agriculture, incorporated the soil into capital, and created for the urban industries the necessary supplies of free and rightless proletarians.[81]

Financial Capitalism and Mercantilism

One of the most relevant and topical factors that Marx thought to be instrumental in the process of *original accumulation* was the credit system via banks and the stock exchange. Remarkably, he anticipated a trait that was to become a characteristic feature of capitalism from then on. In fact, he highlighted that the national debt

> ... marked the capitalist era with its stamp. The only part of the so-called national wealth that actually enters into the collective possession of a modern nation is – the national debt ... the modern doctrine [is] that a nation becomes the richer the more deeply it is in debt ...

---

78 See, for example, Pomeranz, *The Great Divergence*; John M. Hobson, *The Eastern Origins of Western Civilisation* (Cambridge: CUP, 2004); Jack Goldstone, *Why Europe? The Rise of the West in World History, 1500–1850* (New York: McGraw-Hill Education, 2008).

79 Braudel, *Material Civilization and Capitalism*, 64.

80 Patrick Karl O'Brien, "The formation of states and transitions to modern economies: England, Europe, and Asia compared," in *The Cambridge History of Capitalism: Volume I, The Rise of Capitalism: From Ancient Origins to 1848*, eds. Larry Neal and Jeffrey G. Williamson (New York: CUP, 2014), 357–402, 373.

81 Marx, *Capital*, Vol. 1, 895.

> The public debt becomes one of the most powerful levers of primitive [original] accumulation.[82]

Accordingly, the full development of this process is intimately related to the establishment of the Bank of England in 1694.[83]

Marx was describing a phenomenon some 150 years ago that we still encounter today although in different forms and postures. The emphasis Marx put on the importance of the Bank of England, central banking, credit and the national debt has been shared by authoritative publications throughout the twentieth and twenty-first century.[84] As Jürgen Kocka reiterates, the Bank of England "made an important contribution to state formation and to the further development of capitalism," while Matias Vernengo and David Fields underline that, "it is in the ability to finance the state, and the role that monetary and financial markets played in funding the military apparatus, that the West might ultimately have had the edge."[85] It is important to note that, in China, no large-scale bank came into existence prior to the late nineteenth century while it was only in the twentieth century (1921) that the legal grounds for the stock

82 Marx, *Capital*, Vol. 1, 919.

83 "It was not long before this credit-money, created by the bank itself, became the coin in which the latter made its loans to the state, and paid, on behalf of the state, the interest on the public debt. It was not enough that the bank gave with one hand and took back more with the other; it remained, even while receiving money, the eternal creditor of the nation down to the last farthing advanced" (920).

84 Joseph A. Schumpeter, *Business Cycles: a Theoretical, Historical, and Statistical Analysis of the Capitalist Process* (New York: McGraw-Hill Book Company, 1939); John Brewer, *The Sinews of Power: War, Money and the English State, 1688–1783* (London: Routledge, 1989); Geoffrey Ingham, *Capitalism: With a New Postscript on the Financial Crisis and Its Aftermath* (Cambridge: John Wiley & Sons 2008); Jens Beckert, *Imagined Futures: Fictional Expectations and Capitalist Dynamics* (Cambridge: HUP, 2016).

85 Kocka, *Capitalism. A Short History*, 65; Vernengo and Fields, *DisORIENT*, 564. See also Wolfgang Reinhard, *Die Unterwerfung der Welt. Globalgeschichte der europäischen Expansion 1415–2015* (München: C.H.Beck 2016), 22. For the correlation between public debt and the acceleration of the British Industrial Revolution, see Jaume Ventura and Hans-Joachim Voth, "Debt into Growth: How Sovereign Debt Accelerated the First Industrial Revolution," *NBER Working Paper* 21280 (2015): 1–29. Whereas research has long considered the rise of debt in eighteenth century Britain as either detrimental, or as neutral for economic growth, Ventura and Voth have recently argued that Britain's borrowing explosion contributed to the British Industrial Revolution, thus, confirming Marx's emphasis on debt (though without mentioning him by name). For recent publications on the importance of debt and credit in Europe, see Mark Dincecco, *Political transformations and public finances. Europe, 1650–1913* (Cambridge: CUP, 2011); David Stasavage, *States of Credit. Size, Power and the Development of European Polities* (Princeton: PUP, 2011).

exchange were established.[86] Marx had already called attention to the correlation between the national debt and the rise of joint-stock companies, "the modern bankocracy," higher investments and increased taxes.[87] The absence of similar state policies and financial instruments in China has only recently entered the Great Divergence debate. Compared to Europe and India, China stood in a very different geo-political context. It was a relatively pacified empire that had not been subjected to the same degree of inter-state and international competition, as well as severe military and economic pressures caused by the exigencies of continuous warfare. As Peer Vries points out:

> Taking into consideration differences in population, the revenue that Great Britain's central government collected was many times larger than that of its Chinese counterpart. The same applies to its expenditures. In (Great) Britain these were so high that government incurred huge debts that it, however, always managed to honour. In China government until halfway into the nineteenth century never spent more than it received.[88]

Last but not least, Marx also emphasised the significance of protectionism:

> The system of protection was an artificial means of manufacturing manufacturers, or expropriating independent workers, of capitalizing the national means of production and subsistence, and of forcibly cutting short the transition from a mode of production that was out of date to the modern mode of production. The European states tore each other to pieces to gain the patent of this invention, and, once they had entered into the service of the profit-mongers, they did not restrict themselves to plundering their own people, indirectly through protective duties, directly through export premiums, in the pursuit of this purpose. They also forcibly uprooted all industries in the neighbouring dependent countries, as for example England did with the Irish woollen manufacture.[89]

By contrast, in the Ottoman domains, "Imports were encouraged as they added to the availability of goods. As a result, the Ottomans never used protectionism

---

86 Wing-kin Puk, *The Rise and Fall of a Public Debt Market in 16th-Century China. The Story of the Ming Salt Certificate* (Leiden: Brill, 2016), 168–169.
87 Marx, *Capital*, Vol. 1, 919, 921.
88 Peer Vries, *State*, 427–428. See also Geoffrey Ingham, "'The Great Divergence': Max Weber and China's 'missing links'," *Max Weber Studies* 15, no. 2 (2015): 160–191. For an emphasis on the lack of deficit financing and borrowing in Song China in contrast to their Southern European counterparts through the late Middle Ages and Renaissance, see William N. Goetzmann, *Money Changes Everything. How Finance Made Civilization Possible* (New Jersey: PUP, 2016), 199.
89 Marx, *Capital*, Vol. 1, 921.

as an economic policy … exports were tolerated only after the requirements of the domestic economy were met."[90]

In late eighteenth century Asia, the South Indian sultanate of Mysore under the reign of Tipu Sultan (1761–1799) was probably the only region where a systematic attempt of mercantilist and protectionist policies had been pursued.[91]

It is striking to note that, Marx's aforementioned observations – the significance of the Italian city states' and especially Holland's and England's establishment of a national debt and national bank which, in turn, opened up previously unknown opportunities of investment and also required the introduction of a modern tax system – have only recently entered the Great Divergence debate. For over forty years, influential academics such as Douglass North and Robert Thomas, Eric Jones, John Hall, Ernest Gellner, William McNeill, David Landes, Alan Macfarlane, John Nye, Joel Mokyr, Deirdre McCloskey and Niall Ferguson – to differing degrees – have argued that factors such as *laissez-faire*, the invisible hand, lack of state interference, expanding markets and secure property rights laid the foundation for Europe's global economic supremacy.[92] In the past fifteen years, however, scholars are increasingly beginning to examine in more detail what a fundamental role the English state, its protectionist and mercantilist policies, as well as the national debt, central banks and comparatively high tariffs have played in making possible Britain's supremacy vis-à-vis their most powerful European, Asian and African counterparts. For one, Patrick O'Brien has illustrated that the Industrial Revolution and its consolidation depended to a considerable extent on Britain's successful mercantilist policies and victorious wars.[93]

90 Şevket Pamuk, "Institutional Change and Economic Development in the Middle East, 700–1800," in *The Cambridge History of Capitalism*, Vol. 1, eds. Larry Neal and Jeffrey G Williamson, (Cambridge: CUP, 2014), 214.

91 Yazdani, *India*, 170–184.

92 For a short overview of arguments, see Vries, *State*, 9–14. He points out that: "What is lacking so far in most analyses by institutionalist economists are explicit, systematic thoughts on any potential positive effects on economic life of proactive, interventionist government policies that are not focusing on 'getting the prices right'." Vries, *State*, 14.

93 Patrick K. O'Brien, "Contributions of Warfare with Revolutionary and Napoleonic France to the Consolidation and Progress of the British Industrial Revolution," *LSE Economic History Working Papers* 264 (2017): 1–78. See also Parthasarathi, *Why Europe Grew Rich*; Sophus A. Reinert, *Translating Empire. Emulation and the Origins of Political Economy* (Cambridge: HUP, 2011); Victoria Bateman, *Markets and Growth in Early Modern Europe* (London: Routledge, 2012); Joe Studwell, *How Asia Works. Success and Failure in the World's most Dynamic Region* (London: Open Road, 2013); Philip T. Hoffman, *Why Did Europe Conquer the World?* (Princeton: PUP, 2015); Jerry Hough and Robin Grier, *The Long Process of Development. Building Markets and States in Pre-Industrial England, Spain and their Colonies* (Cambridge: CUP, 2015); For an overview, see Vries, *State*, 19–21; Idem, "States: a Subject in Global History," in *Explorations in History and*

William Ashworth too, highlights protection of the incipient domestic industries and the excise, lowly taxed or untaxed British commodities (cotton, iron and porcelain), profits from the exploitation of African slave labour, British trading monopolies and its successful fiscal-military state, as well as increasing tax revenues as important causes for the Industrial Revolution.[94] Most recently, Geoffrey Hodgson underlined that:

> The need to protect and maintain a growing trading empire pressured the British state to reform its finances, gather more taxes, and purchase industrial, agricultural, and service outputs destined for its army and navy. The development of the financial system created new incentives and later possibilities for the use of landed property as collateral to finance investments infrastructure and industry.[95]

Furthermore, it is worth noting that recent scholarship has stressed the western European states' higher collection of tax revenue and expenditures when compared to their Asian counterparts.[96] In the particular case of Britain, O'Brien reiterates that:

> Between 1670 and 1815 total revenues from taxes rose by a factor of around 17, while national income increased by a multiplier of 3. The bulk of these formally sanctioned appropriations by Parliaments of 'notables' were allocated by central government to service a national debt, incurred to fund no less than eleven wars against other European powers and economic rivals ... From a nominal capital of less than £2 million in the reign of James II, Britain's national debt grew to reach the astronomical sum of £854 million, or 2.7 times the national income for 1819. The shares of taxes devoted to servicing, what ap-

Globalization, eds. Catía Antunes and Karwan Fatah-Black (Abingdon: Routledge, 2016), 155–176.

94 William J. Ashworth, *Customs and Excise: Trade, Production and Consumption in England, 1640–1845* (Oxford: OUP, 2003); Idem, *The Industrial Revolution: The State, Knowledge and Global Trade* (London: Bloomsbury Publishing, 2017).

95 Hodgson, "1688 and all that," 2.

96 See Bartolomé Yun-Casalilla and Patrick K. O'Brien, eds., *The Rise of Fiscal States: A Global History*, 1500–1914 (Cambridge: CUP, 2012); K. Kivanç Karaman and Şevket Pamuk, "Ottoman State Finances in European Perspective, 1500–1914," *The Journal of Economic History* 70, no. 3 (2010): 593–629; Idem, "Different Paths to the Modern State in Europe: The Interaction Between Warfare, Economic Structure, and Political Regime," *American Political Science Review* 107, no. 3 (2013): 603–626; Vries, *State*; Debin Ma, "State capacity *and* great divergence, *the* case *of* Qing China *(*1644–1911*),*" *Eurasian Geography* and *Economics* 54, no. 5–6 (2014): 484–499; Tirthankar Roy, *An Economic History of Early Modern India* (London: Routledge, 2013); Yazdani, *India*.

peared to a majority of taxpayers as an incubus of royal-cum-public debt, jumped from modal ratios of 2–3% before the Glorious Revolution to 60% after the Napoleonic War.[97]

Extra-European Stimuli to the Accumulation Process

Marx argued that the expropriation of the peasants from their land – as the major precondition for the emergence of the capital-relation – constituted the most important moment of *original accumulation.* At the same time, he also put great emphasis on long-standing trans-regional and inter-continental linkages. For him, the process of *original accumulation* in its classic form, was impossible without long-term developments starting in Italy and Spain and, most importantly, England's entanglement with both its European neighbours and colonies. Marx alluded to the incipient but premature conditions of capitalism in Italy:

> In Italy, where capitalist production developed earliest, the dissolution of serfdom also took place earlier than elsewhere. There the serf was emancipated before he had acquired any prescriptive right to the soil.[98]

More significantly, Marx underscored the importance of Venice's credit system and southern Europe's impetus to the *original accumulation* process which laid the basis for future developments in western Europe:

> Along with the national debt there arose an international credit system, which often conceals one of the sources of primitive [original] accumulation in this or that people. Thus the villainies of the Venetian system of robbery formed one of the secret foundations of Holland's wealth in capital, for Venice in her years of decadence lent large sums of money to Holland ... The different moments of primitive [original] accumulation can be assigned in particular to Spain, Portugal, Holland, France and England, in more or less chronological order. These different moments are systematically combined together at the end of the seventeenth century in England ... The discovery of gold and silver in America, the extirpation, enslavement and entombment in mines of the indigenous population of that continent, the

---

97 O'Brien, "Industrial Revolution," 27. As O'Brien underscores, throughout the period 1688–1815, 60% of the total expenditures were allocated to Britain's armed forces. In turn, "Government borrowing to wage war also promoted the development of financial intermediation in London and moves towards integration of a national capital market across the kingdom (linked to European money markets) which raised both the elasticity of the money supply and improved the allocation of investible funds." O'Brien, "Industrial Revolution," 31, 39.

98 Marx, *Capital*, Vol. 1, 876.

> beginnings of the conquest and plunder of India, and the conversion of Africa into a preserve for the commercial hunting of blackskins, are all things which characterize the dawn of the era of capitalist production. These idyllic proceedings are the *chief moments* of primitive [original] accumulation. Hard on their heels follows the commercial war of the European nations, which has the globe as its battlefield. It begins with the revolt of the Netherlands from Spain, assumes gigantic dimensions in England's Anti-Jacobin War, and is still going on in the shape of the Opium Wars against China, etc.[99] [emphasis ours]

In England, the expropriation of the peasantry and usurpation of the common lands was an immediate response to developments in the Low Countries.[100] A similar line of argumentation has recently been put forward by Alexander Anievas and Kerem Nişancıoğlu in the context of the Great Divergence debate. They argue that the spread of the Black Death to Europe from the East was facilitated by the unification of the Eurasian land mass accomplished by the Mongols. Accordingly, the Black Death facilitated the transition process from feudalism to capitalism in England.[101]

---

99 Marx, *Capital*, Vol. 1, 920 and 915. We may assume that Marx gave his approval to the omission of the following sentence from the French edition: "These idyllic proceedings are the chief moments of primitive [original] accumulation." Anderson asks: "Was this an example of what Engels had protested, the removal of dialectical language from the French edition for reasons of popularisation? Perhaps. It is also possible, however, that Marx removed this sentence for more substantive reasons, to avoid merging India and the Americas—and China as well—into a single totality in which all societies could be seen as necessarily following the same pathway." Anderson, *Marx at the Margins*, 188. Or did Marx think that such a formulation would distract from the violent divorce of the western European and especially English and Scottish cultivators from their land? In any case, the concession to Engels' hypothesis becomes less plausible if we take into account that a similar formulation reappeared in *Capital*, Vol. 3 (450): "There can be no doubt ... that the great revolutions that took place in trade in the sixteenth and seventeenth centuries, along with the geographical discoveries of that epoch, and which rapidly advanced the development of commercial capital, were a *major moment* in promoting the transition from the feudal to the capitalist mode of production. The sudden expansion of the world market, the multiplication of commodities in circulation, the competition among the European nations for the seizure of Asiatic products and American treasures, the colonial system, all made a fundamental contribution towards shattering the feudal barriers to production."

100 "The rapid expansion of wool manufacture in Flanders and the corresponding rise in the price of wool in England provided the direct impulse for these evictions," 878–879.

101 Anievas and Nişancıoğlu, *How the West Came to Rule*, 66. See also 77–87. Indeed, the Black Death caused a sharp population decrease, a rise of wages and tax revenues. As a result, the plague is said to have stimulated technological innovation. See, for example, Sevket Pamuk, "The Black Death and the origins of the Great Divergence across Europe, 1300–1600," *European Review of Economic History* 11, no. 3 (2007): 289–317; Allen, *Industrial Revolution*; Nico Voigtländer and Hans-Joachim Voth, "The Three Horsemen of Riches: Plague, War and Urbanization in Early Modern Europe," *Review of Economic Studies* 80, no. 2 (2013): 774–811; Gregory Clark,

Holland was "the model capitalist nation of the seventeenth century," as Marx puts it. When the economic centre shifted from the Dutch Republic to England, the former played a crucial role in the development of capitalism in the latter through "the lending out of enormous amounts of capital" from 1701 to 1776.[102] The importance of Dutch lending for the success of the British Empire and the development of English capitalism has been widely confirmed by research conducted in the second half of the twentieth century.[103] Dutch foreign inflows of capital financed the account deficit, "allowing investment to be greater than national saving. Therefore, foreign flows of capital as well as domestic private saving paved the way for the industrial revolution."[104] Most recently, Pepijn Brandon has also highlighted that, "the Amsterdam capital-market became

"Microbes and Markets: Was the Black Death an Economic Revolution?," *Journal of Demographic Economics* 82, no. 2 (2016): 139 – 165.

102 Marx, *Capital*, Vol. 1, 920.

103 As Riley summarises the existing literature, in the late 1770s, when the funded debt in Britain totalled between £131 and 144 million, Dutch holdings alone accounted for one-sixth to one-eighth (12.5 to 16.5 percent). He adds that: "Dutch assets would have equaled some £21 million (about f. 240 million at current rates) and all foreign holdings something in excess of that. Unless there was significant (and unobserved) disinvestment in the interim, foreign holdings in 1762 probably did not exceed £25 million./Estimates of Dutch holdings in the public debt in the late 1770s indicate that the Republic was the dominant source of foreign investment." In 1750 "Dutch assets accounted for 77.8 percent of that share, 20 or some 11.7 percent of the total. That ratio was maintained and expanded (to between 12.5 and 16.5 percent of the total) while the funded debt increased from £71.8 million at the end of 1749 to £144.1 million at the end of 1779./ During the Seven Years' War (when £57.3 million was added to the funded debt) Dutch investment appears to have equaled some 7 percent of net expenditures totaling £122 million ... During the early stages of the War of the American Revolution previous Dutch investment levels were maintained but the gap between Britain's ordinary revenues and expenditures did not widen as rapidly as it had in the previous conflict. Between the end of 1775 and the end of 1779 £19.8 million was added to the funded debt. Thereafter the deficit increased and the funded debt rose at a sharply higher rate than did new investments from abroad." James C. Riley, *International Government Finance and the Amsterdam Capital Market, 1740 – 1815* (Cambridge: CUP, 1980), 123 – 124.

104 Elise S. Brezis, "Foreign capital flows in the century of Britain's industrial revolution: new estimates, controlled conjectures," *The Economic History Review* 48, No 1 (1995): 46 – 67, 59 – 60. See also Charles Wilson, *Anglo-Dutch Commerce & Finance in the Eighteenth Century* (Cambridge: CUP, 1966) [1944]; P. G. M. Dickson, *The Financial Revolution in England: A Study in the Development of Public Credit, 1688 – 1756* (London: Routledge, 1967); Larry Neal, *The Rise of Financial Capitalism: International Capital Markets in the Age of Reason* (Cambridge: CUP, 1990); Lisa Jardine, *Going Dutch: How England Plundered Holland's Glory* (London: Harper Collins, 2008).

a major source of money-capital underpinning the British state-debt and private investment … feeding into the British industrial revolution."[105]

Holland and its colonies likewise played a vital role in the development of financial innovations: "The colonial system, with its maritime trade and its commercial wars, served as a forcing-house for the credit system. Thus it first took root in Holland."[106]

Marx equally underlined the importance of the colonisation of India for the process of *original accumulation*. Even before writing *Das Kapital*, he had indicated that cotton textiles produced in Great Britain constituted one-eighth of the total export of the country in 1850 of which one-fourth was shipped to India. Accordingly one-eighth of the population was involved in the cotton industry contributing to one-twelfth of the national income.[107] In turn, Marx emphasised that on the subcontinent, the lion's share of the net revenue the British acquired and spent stemmed from Indian resources: "nearly three-fifths of the whole net revenue are derived from the *land*, about one-seventh from *opium*, and upward of one-ninth from *salt*. These resources together yield 85 per cent, of the whole receipts."[108] Even so, the British hardly spent money in infrastructure – out of British gross revenue of £19.8 million in 1851–1852, only £166,300 was "expended on roads, canals, bridges and other works of public necessity".[109] But, India was not only looted through tax revenues but also by dint of theft and an exclusive monopoly of the East India Company (EIC) on the tea and Chinese trade, salt, opium, betel, etc.. Hence, "the Company and its officials obtained £6,000,000 between 1757 and 1766 from the Indians in the form of gifts. Between 1769 and 1770, the English created a famine by buying up all the rice and refusing to sell it again, except at fabulous prices."[110]

---

105 Pepijn Brandon, "Marxism and the 'Dutch Miracle': The Dutch Republic and the Transition-Debate," *Historical Materialism* 19, no. 3 (2011): 106–146, 139.

106 Marx, *Capital*, Vol. 1, 919.

107 Karl Marx, "The East India Company – Its History and Results," *New-York Daily Tribune*, July 11, 1853, in, *Collected Works* (*MECW*), Vol. 12 (1856–1858), Karl Marx and Frederick Engels, n.d., 154. On the same page he adds: "On the same rate at which the cotton manufactures became of vital interest for the whole social frame of Great Britain, East India became of vital interest for the British cotton manufacture."

108 Karl Marx, "The War Question – Doings of Parliament – India," July 19, 1853, in *MECW*, Vol. 12, 213.

109 Karl Marx, "The Russian Humbug – Gladstone's Failure – Sir Charles Wood's East India Reforms," *New-York Daily Tribune*, June 7, 1853, in *MECW*, Vol. 15 (1856–1858), n.d., 124.

110 Marx, *Capital*, Vol. 1, 917. In the footnote, Marx added that: "In the year 1866 more than a million Hindus died of hunger in the province of Orissa alone. Nevertheless, an attempt was

To summarise, Marx did not leave any doubt about the centrality of colonialism for the economic growth of Europe. Nowhere did he make it as clear as in the following paragraph:

> The colonial system ripened trade and navigation as in a hothouse. The 'companies called Monopolia' (Luther) were powerful levers for the concentration of capital. The colonies provided a market for the budding manufactures, and a vast increase in accumulation which was guaranteed by the mother country's monopoly of the market. The treasures captured outside Europe by undisguised looting, enslavement and murder flowed back to the mother-country and were turned into capital there.[111]

It was obvious to him that the rise of the first industrial regions of England were intimately connected to the Atlantic Slave Trade: "Liverpool grew fat on the basis of the slave trade. This was its method of primitive [original] accumulation."[112] Furthermore, Liverpool "occasioned vast employment for shipping and sailors, and greatly augmented the demand for the manufactures of the country."[113]

Marx's following remark anticipated and influenced approaches ranging from dependency theory (late 1940s to 1970s), world-system theory (1970s and 1980s) to contemporary forms of world-system analysis, as well as world and global history: "In fact the veiled slavery of the wage-labourers in Europe needed the unqualified slavery of the New World as its pedestal."[114]

Marx also gave an evident reason for the importance of commerce and colonisation:

> Today, industrial supremacy brings with it commercial supremacy. In the period of manufacture it is the reverse: commercial supremacy produces industrial predominance. Hence the preponderant role played by the colonial system at that time.[115]

Marx did not leave any doubt about the capitalist nature of European slavery in the Atlantic world. As early as 1847, he underscored that:

> Direct slavery is just as much the pivot of bourgeois industry as machinery, credit, &c. Without slavery you have no cotton; without cotton you cannot have modern industry. It is slavery which has given their value to the colonies; it is the colonies which have created the

---

made to enrich the Indian treasury by the price at which the means of subsistence were sold to the starving people" (917).

111 Marx, *Capital*, Vol. 1, 918.
112 Marx, *Capital*, Vol. 1, 924.
113 Marx, *Capital*, Vol. 1, 925.
114 Marx, *Capital*, Vol. 1, 925.
115 Marx, *Capital*, Vol. 1, 918.

> commerce of the world, it is the commerce of the world which is the condition of the great industry. Thus slavery is an economic category of the highest importance.[116]

Twenty years later, Marx stipulated that the cotton producing slaves in the southern states of the American Union – similar to the *corvée* in the Danubian Principalities – were producing "surplus value itself".[117] He also made it clear, in contrast to adherents of the "New History of Capitalism," revisionist Marxists and a variety of non-Eurocentric scholars, including segments of the field of *Global Labour History*, that, "slavery is then possible there only because it does not exist at other points; and appears as an anomaly opposite the bourgeois system itself."[118]

Throughout the twentieth century, Marx's emphasis on the importance of slavery for Western Europe's socio-economic development inspired a considerable number of historians, most notably Eric Williams. Although the latter overstated the effects of the Atlantic Slave Trade on the British Industrial Revolution, ever since the publication of his *Capitalism and Slavery*, the "Williams Thesis" has become indispensable for understanding modern slavery.[119] Williams highlighted the triangular trade's "triple stimulus to British industry": 1) Slaves were bought with British manufactures, 2) they produced goods (for example, sugar, cotton, indigo, molasses) that stimulated the emergence of new industries

116 Karl Marx, *The Poverty of Philosophy* (New York: Cosimo, 2008) [1847], 121; Idem, *Misère de la philosophie: réponse à la Philosophie de la misère de M. Proudhon* (Paris: Bruxelles, 1847), 102.
117 Marx, *Capital*, Vol. 1, 345. Cf. to *Capital*, Vol. 3, 940 where he writes that on the American plantations, "the capitalist conception prevails."
118 Marx, *Grundrisse*, 464. In other words, "*Negro slavery* – a purely industrial slavery – which is, besides, incompatible with the development of bourgeois society and disappears with it, *presupposes* wage labour, and if other, free states with wage labour did not exist alongside it, if, instead, the Negro states were isolated, then all social conditions there would immediately turn into pre-civilized forms." Marx, *Grundrisse*, 224.
119 Eric E. Williams, *Capitalism and Slavery* (Chapel Hill: Capricorn Books, 1944). For a recent endorsement of the Williams's thesis, see Barbara L. Solow, *The Economic Consequences of the Atlantic Slave Trade* (Lanham: Lexington Books, 2014). For critiques, see Stanley L. Engerman, "The Slave Trade and British Capital Formation in the Eighteenth Century: A Comment on the Williams Thesis," *Business History Review* 46, no. 4 (1972): 430–443; Patrick K. O'Brien, "European Economic Development: The Contribution of the periphery," *Economic History Review* 35, no. 1 (1982): 1–18; David Eltis and Stanley L. Engerman, "The Importance of Slavery and the Slave Trade to Industrializing Britain," *The Journal of Economic History* 60, no. 1 (2000), 123–144. Interestingly, Crouzet concluded that: "The capital which made possible the creation of large-scale 'factory' industries in Britain came, then, mainly from industry itself." François Crouzet, *Britain Ascendant: Comparative Studies in Franco-British Economic History* (Cambridge: CUP, 1990) [1985], 179.

in Britain and 3) the New World plantations provided a market for British commodities.[120]

Research conducted in the past ten years has reinforced the assertion that the vitality of seventeenth to nineteenth century international commerce, Europe's and especially England's overseas expansion and colonial subjugation of the Americas, parts of Asia and Africa fed Britain's industrialisation process.[121] Recent literature has also underpinned the crucial role that the European Companies, especially the English East India Company and the state's support of colonisation and the exploitation of slave labour played in enhancing British industrial transformations.[122] The New World silver stimulated the domestic manufactures of north-western Europe, permitted the Europeans to be way more competitive in Asian and African markets and boosted the 'industrious revolution' and industrialisation at home through new products and import substitution. Profits derived from the Atlantic slave trade enhanced the bourgeoisie vis-à-vis the aristocracy and also stimulated investment in new industries, including the contribution of export markets and profits from slave labour to those industries that pioneered the use of industrial methods (textile, mining, metal) and financial institutions (marine insurance, the development of banking, especially regarding the national debt). As John Lord has argued "[i]t was with money gained from the West India trade that capital was eventually found to finance Watt."[123] Most significantly, the New World – apart from being a British popula-

---

120 Williams, *Capitalism and Slavery* , 52.

121 Javier Cuenca Esteban, "The rising share of British industrial exports in industrial output, 1700 – 1851," *Journal of Economic History* 57 (1997): 879 – 906; Juan-Carlos Cordoba, "Malthus to Romer: On the Colonial Origins of the Industrial Revolution," *MPRA Paper* 4466 (2007): 1 – 41; Ronald Findlay and Kevin H. O'Rourke, *Power and Plenty: Trade, War, and the World Economy in the Second Millennium* (Princeton: PUP, 2009); Allen, *Industrial Revolution*; Idem, "Why the industrial revolution was British: commerce, induced invention, and the scientific revolution," *The Economic History Review* 65, no. 2 (2011): 357 – 384; Peter M. Solar, "Opening to the east: Shipping between Europe and Asia, 1770 – 1830," *The Journal of Economic History* 73, no. 3 (2013): 625 – 661; Gregory Clark et al., "The growing dependence of Britain on trade during the Industrial Revolution," *Scandinavian Economic History Review* 62, no. 2 (2014), 109 – 136; Nuala Zahedieh, "Overseas Trade and Empire," in, *The Cambridge Economic History of Modern Britain: Volume 1: 1700 – 1870*, eds. Roderick Floud et al. (Cambridge: CUP, 2014), 392 – 420; Nuno Palma, "Sailing away from Malthus: intercontinental trade and European economic growth, 1500 – 1800," *Cliometrica* 10, no. 2 (2016), 129 – 149; P.C. Ferreira et al., "Globalization and the Industrial revolution," *Macroeconomic Dynamics* 20,3 (2016): 643 – 666. For an overview of arguments, see Neuss, "Why Did the Industrial Revolution Start in Britain?," 32 – 37.

122 Pomeranz, *The Great Divergence*.

123 Robin Blackburn, *The Making of New World Slavery. From the Baroque to the Modern, 1492 – 1800* (London: Verso, 1997), 520 – 532, 542 – 554, 563 and 572. Lord quotation 551. Inikori, *Africans*

tion outlet – along with Africa and Asia provided an important market for finished goods. As O'Brien has recently reaffirmed:

> at least half of the increment to industrial production which came on stream over a long 18th century (1688–1815) was sold overseas ... Already by the close of the Seven Years War, something like half of the nation's workforce (de-linked from agriculture) depended directly and indirectly on markets overseas for its livelihood.[124]

In addition, New World crops (for example, potatoes and maize), guano, timber, meat and sugar, American, Indian and Egyptian cotton, African palm oil, cocoa, gold and rubber, Eastern resources like tea and coffee and Australian wool became indispensable in the rise of caloric intake and factory-employment, stimulating population growth and urbanisation in Europe. Indeed, land-saving products from the Americas such as cheap guano, cotton, sugar, wood, etc. relieved Europe's eco-system and stimulated further specialisation in manufactures.[125] Other regions of the world did not have the same amount of land at their disposal. In addition, the enormous amount of cotton imports from the colonies enhanced the technical refinements of the all-important textile industry and in its part helped in sustaining the Industrial Revolution.[126] Maxine Berg highlights the geographical extension of the frontiers through colonies, especially Britain's eighteenth century empire, which provided a crucial connection be-

---

and the Industrial Revolution, 81–88 and 475–482; Daron Acemoğlu et al., "The Rise of Europe: Atlantic Trade, Institutional Change, and Economic Growth," *The American Economic Review* 95, no. 3 (2005): 546–579, 572.

124 Patrick O'Brien, "Provincializing the First Industrial Revolution," *Working Papers of the Global Economic History Network (GEHN)* 17/06 (2006), 1–40, 14 retrieved from: http://www.lse.ac.uk/Economic-History/Assets/Documents/Research/GEHN/GEHNConferences/conf2/WorkingPaper17-POB.pdf accessed April 17, 2020. Most recently, O'Brien even went as far as arguing that the "British Industrial Revolution is not separable from the global, historical, geographical and geopolitical contexts in which it took place." O'Brien, " Industrial Revolution," 52. For a different view, see Peer Vries, *Escaping Poverty: The Origins of Modern Economic Growth* (Vienna: Vandenhoeck & Ruprecht, 2013), 104–109, 234–262 and 419–422.

125 Sidney Mintz, *Sweetness and Power. The Place of Sugar in Modern History* (New York: Penguin, 1985); Pomeranz, *The Great Divergence*; John Richards, *The Unending Frontier. An Environmental History of the Early Modern World* (Berkeley: UCP, 2003); Nathan Nunn and Nancy Qian, "The Potato's Contribution to Population and Urbanization: Evidence from an Historical Experiment," *The Quarterly Journal of Economics* 126 (2011): 593–650; Jonathan Hersh and Joachim Voth, "Sweet Diversity: Colonial Goods and the Rise of European Living Standards after 1492," *Economics Working Papers* 1163, Department of Economics and Business, Universitat Pompeu Fabra (2011); Edward Barbier, *Scarcity and Frontiers. How Economies have Developed through Natural Resource Exploitation* (Cambridge: CUP, 2011).

126 Pomeranz, *The Great Divergence.*

tween consumption and production, resulting in a British consumer industry.[127] Christopher Alan Bayly further attests that wealth generated in the wider-world (for example, slave and sugar trade, activities of the EIC) added to Britain's capital stock for investment, while African consumers' demands and tastes helped to sustain the British Industrial Revolution.[128] Moreover, as Marx has demonstrated, the rise of Britain seems to have been more extensively connected to the exploitation of India than has often been supposed in the past.[129]

Beyond Marx – Contributions and Confines

Although chance certainly played an important role in the genesis of capitalism and the Great Divergence, some influential scholars have overemphasised the significance of contingency and fortuitous factors (such as Moishe Postone, Robert Brenner, Kenneth Pomeranz and Prasannan Parthasarathi) at the expense of structural causations and the effects of agency. Marx, on the other hand, did not seem to take into account the possible results of contingent encounters. However, a careful reading of the *original accumulation* chapter suggests that the different moments of the conjuncture examined by Marx, bear elements of contingency; though only implicitly.[130] Indeed, for Marx, the emergence of the capital-

127 Maxine Berg, "In Pursuit of Luxury: Global History and British Consumer Goods in the Eighteenth Century," *P&P* 182, no. 1 (2004): 85–142.
128 Christopher Alan Bayly, *The Birth of the Modern World, 1780–1914: Global Connections and Comparisons* (Oxford: OUP, 2004), 174, 471.
129 Yazdani, *India*, 565–570.
130 Marx's implicit notion of contingency may be demonstrated as follows: "The knights of industry, however, only succeeded in supplanting the knights of the sword by making use of events in which they had played no part whatsoever" (875). Althusser and Balibar also point out that, "the elements combined by the capitalist structure have different and independent origins. It is not one and the same movement which makes free labourers and transferable wealth. On the contrary, in the examples analysed by Marx, the formation of free labourers appears mainly in the form of transformations of agrarian structures, while the constitution of wealth is the result of merchant's capital and finance capital." Louis Althusser and Étienne Balibar, *Reading Capital (Part 1)* (Paris: Verso, 1968) 282. Similarly, Read notes that, "the laws and acts that turned common lands into pasture and forced the peasantry off the land did not have as their goal the creation of the proletariat as a propertyless working class; rather, this was an unintended effect that was later seized by other agents and actors ... It is not the same subject that dissolves the old mode of production and produces the new one." Jason Read, *The Micro-Politics of Capital Marx and the Prehistory of the Present* (Albany: Suny Press, 2003), 24–25. As Roberts underscores, in the sphere of agrarian relations, "Marx argues that landlords amassed land through enclosure and expropriation, thereby creating also the modern

relation in the wake of the different phases of *original accumulation* was neither the intended product of conspiratorial elites, nor the preordained outcome of some historical processes. At the same time, it was a historical conjuncture founded on specific causes and an effect of both long-term continuities and more or less sudden ruptures with the past.

In explaining the processes of *original accumulation*, Marx also touched upon aspects that are relevant to our understanding of the rise of the West and British industrial transformation. As he was not to delve into that subject and was primarily concerned with the genesis of capitalism, he did not go into detail about those aspects. This task can be achieved with less effort today as we have much more access to data to compare living standards and wages, and observe the effects of inter-state competition, disease and warfare on the social structure and patterns of production than was available to Marx 150 years ago.[131] We have a greater quantity of facts and figures about socio-economic, political and techno-scientific developments which puts us in a much better situation to grasp the possible reasons behind technological innovation and modern economic growth than Marx had at his disposal.

In the context of western Europe, there are a number of factors that need to be added in order to better comprehend the transition towards industrial capitalism. Especially in the seventeenth and eighteenth century, parts of western Europe experienced a consumer revolution that increased incentives for inventions

---

class of wage labourers; the capitalists then rose up between these two classes, coming to dominate both by exploiting the newly available resource of unattached labour-power. The process of primitive accumulation 'incorporated the soil into capital' (Marx, 1976: 895), but not by making the capitalists the owners of the soil. Instead, the owners of the soil, the landlords, became dependent, for the cultivation of their land, upon the capitalists' mediation... . The capitalists' power does not grow from conquest and plunder. The capitalists' power comes from being neither the conquerors nor the plundered." William Clare Roberts, "What was Primitive Accumulation? Reconstructing the Origin of a Critical Concept," *European Journal of Political Theory* (2017): 1–21, 10 https://journals.sagepub.com/doi/10.1177/1474885117735961 accessed April 18, 2020.

131 Nonetheless, it is interesting to note that, Marx compared the wages of English and Indian labourers. To give an example, he thought that Indian wages were low, "partly because of the HINDOOS' limited needs and partly because of the fertility of the soil, WHENCE LOW PRICE OF RICE, etc.". Marx, "Economic Manuscript of 1861–63," 348. Pradella also points out that Marx "compared wage levels in various countries like, for example, Britain and India (MEGA^2 IV/6: 79)." Lucia Pradella, *Globalisation and the Critique of Political Economy. New Insights from Marx's Writings* (Abingdon: Routledge, 2015), 85. Regarding inter-state rivalries, Marx emphasised the importance of "the commercial war of the European nations, which has the globe as its battlefield. It begins with the revolt of the Netherlands from Spain, assumes gigantic dimensions in England's Anti-Jacobin War, and is still going on in the shape of the Opium Wars against China, etc." (915)

as well as innovations in production and finance. The consumer revolution also enlarged internal markets compared to other parts of the world.[132] As Irfan Habib rightly points out, one of the main differences between India and Europe "lie in the nature of the market for urban craft-producers: in India, it was confined to the aristocracy and its dependents, while in Europe it included the rural gentry as well as the emerging middle classes."[133]

Given Marx's chronological framework, the exclusion of long-term factors, most notably the contributions of Asia and North Africa to the rise of the West, is obvious but understandable as they only constitute secondary causes in explaining the *original accumulation* in western Europe.

While a number of Marxists prefer 'internalist' (such as Maurice Dobb, Robert Brenner, Ellen Meiksins Wood and other adherents of 'political Marxism') or 'externalist' (such as Arghiri Emmanuel and Immanuel Wallerstein) rather than inter-connected approaches, we do not think that this can be applied to Marx as such. As Harry Magdoff already pointed out in 1972, "the debate over whether the key development was the home or the export market in England is irrelevant. It is neither one nor the other, but a combination of the two. One simply takes precedence in one period and the other takes precedence in another period."[134]

---

132 Vries, *Escaping Poverty*, 231–234, 418–419; Vernengo and Fields, *DisORIENT.* See also John Brewer and Roy Porter, eds., *Consumption and the World of Goods* (London: Routledge, 2007); Jan de Vries, *The Industrious Revolution: Consumer Behavior and the Household Economy, 1650 to the Present* (Cambridge: CUP, 2008); Ina Baghdiantz McCabe, *A History of Global Consumption: 1500–1800* (Abingdon: Routledge, 2014); Maxine Berg, ed., *Goods from the East, 1600–1800. Trading Eurasia* (London: Springer, 2015); Anne Gerritsen and Giorgio Riello, eds., *The Global Lives of Things. The Material Culture of Connections in the Early Modern World* (Abingdon: Routledge, 2015); Frank Trentmann, *Empire of Things: How We Became a World of Consumers, from the Fifteenth to the Twenty-first* (London: Penguin, 2016). As Humphries and Weisdorf point out, in England, there was a "post-1600 continuous increase in the length of the working year and the intensification of this growth in the run-up to industrialization". However, whether "the English increase in labour input was voluntary, as workers gave up leisure for material goods, or imposed as a consequence of structural changes in employment, or the erosion of alternatives to wage labour, or shifts in bargaining power, remains to be examined." Jane Humphries and Jacob Weisdorf, "Unreal Wages? Real Income and Economic Growth in England, 1260–1850," *EHES Working Papers in Economic History* 121 (2017): 1–62, 30.

133 Irfan Habib, "Introduction: Marx's Perception of India," in *Karl Marx on India*, ed. Iqbal Husain (New Delhi: Tulika Books 2006), xxx. For a similar view, see also Christopher Alan Bayly, "South Asia and the 'Great Divergence'," *Itinerario* 24 (2000): 89–103, 95. In the context of British rule, Marx himself pointed out that the exploitation of the British in India made "the expansion of production more or less impossible" and reduced "the direct producers to the physical minimum of means of subsistence". Marx, *Capital*, Vol. 3, 922. Cf. Yazdani, *India*, 357–358.

134 Magdoff, "Primitive Accumulation," https://monthlyreview.org/2013/10/01/primitive-accumulation-and-imperialism/

It is true that the middle Marx of the early 1850s had a tint of a Eurocentric bent, but, between the late 1850s and early 1880s, the shadow of Marx's Eurocentrism was gradually fading.[135] Nevertheless, Marx did not take into account how the economic, technological and scientific practices and achievements in East, South and West Asia, as well as North Africa, enhanced merchant capitalist developments and techno-scientific progress in the Italian city-states and western Europe throughout the medieval period, Renaissance, Scientific Revolution and Enlightenment up to the Industrial Revolution. Indeed, the socio-economic (agricultural innovations, production of commodities and intercontinental trade networks), techno-scientific (mathematics, chemistry, metallurgy, medicine, empirical methods, paper, the compass, gunpowder and firearms) and institutional contributions (financial practices, credit institutions and the examination system) of the tenth to eighteenth century Asia (especially West Asia, China and India) and their diffusion in Europe have been neglected. That is, if perceived from the retrospective view of what we now know due to new research.

Although Marx was fully aware of the centrality of protectionism, mercantilism, the Atlantic Slave Trade and colonialism, as well as the high quality of Indian textiles, he dispensed with some key micro-historical and international dimensions of the *original accumulation* process. Concurrently – something which has escaped the attention of many Marxologists – he did not confine the genesis of incipient capitalist elements to western and southern Europe alone but explicitly highlighted that Istanbul (Constantinople) was part of this development as one of several hubs of inter-continental trade:

> The original historic forms in which capital appears at first sporadically or locally, alongside the old modes of production, while exploding them little by little everywhere, is on one side manufacture proper (not yet the factory); this [manufacture] springs up where mass quantities are produced for export, for the external market – i.e. on the basis of large-scale overland and maritime commerce, in its emporiums like the Italian cities, *Con-*

---

135 Labelling Marx as Eurocentric emerged in the 1960s, but did not become a currency prior to the late 1970s and especially in the 1990s after the writings of Edward Said, Gyan Prakash, André Gunder Frank and numerous post-colonial critiques were published. For a recent critique – inspired by postcolonial theory – that exaggerates Marx's Eurocentrism, see Kolja Lindner, "Marx's Eurocentrism: Postcolonial Studies and Marx Scholarship," *Radical Philosophy* 161 (2010), 27–41. Some Marxists too, have accused Marx of Eurocentrism. Anderson, for instance, argues that, in 1853, some of Marx's statements contained "strong Eurocentric overtones". Anderson, *Marx at the Margins*, 22. However, we agree with Ahmad that Anderson "concedes too much on questions of Marx's 'Eurocentricity'." Aijaz Ahmad, "Karl Marx, "Global Theorist,"" *Dialect Anthropol* 39 (2015): 199–209, 203.

> *stantinople*, in the Flemish, Dutch cities, a few Spanish ones, such as Barcelona etc.[136] [emphasis ours]

Up to the mid-nineteenth century, Asian manufactured goods such as textiles and ceramics were the most competitive commodities in the world market. One of the factors for England's protectionist policies was uneven development in the sphere of production which, in turn, led to higher degrees of geographical mobility to purchase foreign commodities and, more importantly, measures of import substitution.[137] Why did Marx dispense with these important details of *original accumulation?* The following remark illustrates that he was aware of certain underlying reasons behind import substitution:

> The sudden expansion of the world market, the multiplication of commodities in circulation, *the competition among the European nations for the seizure of Asiatic products* and American treasures, the colonial system, all made a fundamental contribution towards shattering the feudal barriers to production.[138] [emphasis ours]

Marx seems to have endorsed the then well-established opinion that Indian cotton textiles were unrivalled before the sale of mechanised British cloth gathered momentum. At the same time, he did not attach too much importance to the superior quality of Indian commodities as its methods and techniques of production belonged to a pre-capitalist socio-economic formation.[139] In other words: "It is not what is made but how, and by what instruments of labour, that distinguishes different economic epochs."[140]

---

136 Marx, *Grundrisse*, 510 – 11.

137 For details on Asio-African socio-economic, techno-scientific and intellectual contributions to the rise of the West, see Kaveh Yazdani and Dilip Menon, "Introduction," in *Capitalisms: Towards a Global History*, ed. idem (Oxford: OUP, 2020); Yazdani, *India*, Introduction.

138 Marx, *Capital*, Vol. 3, 450.

139 To this effect, he quoted Murray et al., *Historical and Descriptive Account of British India…, Vol. 2* (Edinburgh: J. & J. Harper, 1832) 449 – 450: "The muslins of Dacca in fineness, the calicoes and other piece goods of Coromandel in brilliant and durable colours, have never been surpassed. Yet they are produced without capital, machinery, division of labour, or any of those means which give such facilities to the manufacturing interest of Europe. The weaver is merely a detached individual, working a web when ordered of a customer, and with a loom of the rudest construction, consisting sometimes of a few branches or bars of wood, put roughly together. There is even no expedient for rolling up the warp; the loom must therefore be kept stretched to its full length, and becomes so inconveniently large that it cannot be contained within the hut of the manufacturer, who is therefore compelled to ply his trade in the open air, where it is interrupted by every vicissitude of the weather." Marx, *Capital*, Vol. 3, 459.

140 Marx, *Capital*, Vol. 1, 286.

Marx gave precedence to macro-historical dynamics in the explanation of the *original accumulation.* He concentrated on the trajectories of western Europe, particularly England, and identified the extra-European factors that constituted the chief moments of the whole process or totality. He only mentioned those factors that he thought were absolutely crucial ("epoch-making"). Moreover, the middle Marx was not as pessimistic of colonialist policies to enhance capitalist development in the East as the late Marx. In the following section we will briefly delve into this topic on the basis of some of his writings on India.

In the 1850s, Marx wrote a number of pieces for the *New York Tribune* where he grappled with Asia and the Indian question in particular. Amongst many, he wrote two brilliant articles titled "The British Rule in India" and "The Future Results of British Rule in India," both in 1853; where he tackled British colonisation and the socio-economic structure of the subcontinent.[141] In spite of their distinct brevity, these articles remain unsurpassed in their observance and reflection on the British colonisation of India and the way in which it undermined the socio-economic structure of the subcontinent. A close reading of the two articles leaves no doubt that Marx had studied the subject intensely and read a significant portion of the available English, French and German material (writings by Bernier, Wilks, Campbell, Raffles, etc.).[142] In addition he was well-acquainted with Hegel's writings on India.[143] Hegel was of the opinion that: "The spread of Indian

141 Karl Marx, "The British Rule in India," *New-York Daily Tribune* 10.6.1853, "Future Results," New-York Daily Tribune 22.7.1853; both in *MECW*, Vol. 12, n.d.

142 For a list of Marx's main sources on Oriental societies, see Lutfi Sunar, *Marx and Weber on Oriental Societies. In the Shadow of Western Modernity* (Farnham: Routledge, 2014), 41. What needs to be added to Sunar's list are the numerous works cited in Marx's notes on Kovalevskij's *Obscinnoe zemlevladenie* (*Communal Landownership*), published in 1879, where he quoted Anquetil-Duperron and remarked that he was the first to understand that in India the Great Moghul was not the only proprietor of the soil (via Mill, *History of British India*, 1840). He also cites John Dowson's *The History of India, as told by its own historians. The Muhammedan period*...(1867) where he learned about some Indo-Persian chronicles. These excerpts were edited by Hans-Peter Harstick, ed., *Karl Marx über Formen vorkapitalistischer Produktion. Vergleichende Studien zur Geschichte des Grundeigentums 1879–80* (Frankfurt: Campus Verlag, 1977), 39–93. Furthermore, Sunar also misses to mention Marx's *Notes on Indian History (664–1858)*, taken in 1879–80 and published in 1960 (Moscow), as well as the "volumes and parliamentary debates and reports, especially those preceding the Charter Act of 1853." Habib, "Introduction: Marx's Perception of India," xxii.

143 Hegel's account of India, had been written a few decades before Marx. Hegel had portrayed India as being "stationary and fixed" (*statarisch und fest geblieben*) and indifferent to "all political revolutions" for the common Hindu's "lot is unchanged." Georg Wilhelm Friedrich Hegel, *Vorlesungen über die Geschichte der Philosophie*, Vol. 3 (Frankfurt am Main: Reclam 1986) [1837], 174, 194; Idem, *The Philosophy of History*, trans. J. Sibree, (Kitchener: Courier Corporation,

culture is pre-historical, for History is limited to that which makes an essential epoch in the development of Spirit" and that "it is the necessary fate of Asiatic Empires to be subjected to Europeans."[144]While Hegel thought that India's stagnation had to do with her oppressive belief system, leading to a lack of self-consciousness and reflection[145], Marx identified a variety of factors, including the specificities of India's political configuration, socio-economic structure (village communities), the "many independent and conflicting states" and the lack of transport facilities, etc. without disregarding the anti-emancipatory elements of the Hindu religion and caste system.[146] This let him to conclude that:

> Hindostan is an Italy of Asiatic dimensions . . Just as Italy has, from time to time, been compressed by the conqueror's sword into different national masses, so do we find Hindostan ... [Yet,] in a social point of view, Hindostan is not the Italy, but the Ireland of the East. And this strange combination of Italy and of Ireland, of a world of voluptuousness and of a world of woes, is anticipated in the ancient traditions of the religion of Hindostan.[147]

2001), 156, 172. This publication is based on notes of Hegel's lectures given between 1822 and 1831. Even before Hegel expressed these views, India's supposed "unchangeability" was a common trope amongst early nineteenth century British observers. See, for example, James Mill, *The History of British India*, Vol. 1 (London: Baldwin, Cradock, and Joy, 1817), 100 – 101.

144 Hegel, *Philosophy of History*, 159–-160. A few pages later, he argued that: "What we call historical truth and veracity – intelligent, thoughtful comprehension of events, and fidelity in representing them – nothing of this sort can be looked for among the Hindoos." (180) See also 181–182.

145 Hegel held that: "The Hindoo is incapable of holding fast an object in his mind by means of rational predicates assigned to it, for this requires reflection." Hegel, *Philosophy of History*, 175. See also 156 – 158. Elsewhere, Hegel wrote that, in India, "things" were "stripped of rationality, of finite consistent stability of cause and effect." Hegel, *Philosophy of History*, 159. He added that, in the Orient, "internal subjectivity is not yet recognized as independent" (164) and that, in India, "morality and human dignity are unknown." (165)

146 Regarding the village community, Marx quoted a long passage from the *The Fifth Report from the Select Committee on the Affairs of the East India Company* (1812), including the following description: "Under this simple form of municipal government, the inhabitants of the country have lived from time immemorial. The boundaries of the villages ... have been but seldom altered; and though the villages themselves have been sometimes injured, and even desolated by war, famine or disease, the same name, the same limits, the same interests, and even the same families have continued for ages. The inhabitants gave themselves no trouble about the breaking up and divisions of kingdoms; while the village remains entire, they care not to what power it is transferred, or to what sovereign it devolves; its internal economy remains unchanged." Marx, "British Rule," 131. Cf. Irfan Habib, *Essays in Indian History: Towards a Marxist Perception* (London: Anthem Press 2002) [1995], 19; Anderson, *Marx at the Margins*, 15.

147 Karl Marx, "British Rule," 125.

His remark on India's history aroused the disavowal of a number of commentators:

> Indian society has no history at all, at least no known history. What we call its history, is but the history of the successive intruders who founded their empires on the passive basis of that unresisting and unchanging society.[148]

In the wake of this statement, Marx has often been accused of depriving Indians of history altogether. However, these critiques overlook that just prior to the aforementioned remark, Marx made the following observation: "the whole of her [India's] past history, if it be anything, is the history of the successive conquests she has undergone." Hence Marx was not of the opinion that India lacked history. What he seemed to be alluding to is that what was known as India – which was not a united entity and a nation-state in the modern sense of the word till the mid-nineteenth century, and as such, lacked a national history – cannot be understood without taking into account the numerous invasions, fragmentation and "dismemberment in the political configuration."[149] Indeed, India's history was intimately connected to almost unremitting conquest and occupation. Thereby, Marx gave important insights that still help us to better understand post-Mughal India in the wake of the British EIC's intrusion. He pointed out that India was

> A country not only divided between Mahommedan and Hindoo, but between tribe and tribe, between caste and caste; a society whose framework was based on a sort of equilibrium, resulting from a general repulsion and constitutional exclusiveness between all its members. Such a country and such a society, were they not the predestined prey of conquest?[150]

Importantly, Marx argued that "[t]he political unity of India, more consolidated, and extending farther than it ever did under the Great Moguls, was the first condition of its regeneration."[151]

---

148 Marx, "Future Results," 217–218.
149 Marx, "British Rule in India," 125. In the European context, historians such as Greenfeld *(Spirit of Capitalism)*, Landes *(The Wealth and Poverty)*, Magnusson *(Nation, State and the Industrial Revolution)*, Moe *(Governance, Growth and Leadership)* and Sen *(Military Origin of Industrialization)* have recently confirmed that nationalism or national consciousness and identity enhanced economic development and growth. For an overview, see Vries, *Escaping Poverty*, 56.
150 Marx, "Future Results," 217. See also Deepak Lal, *The Hindu Equilibrium: India c. 1500 B.C.–2000 A.D.* (Oxford: OUP, 2005). Lal's arguments contain a sort of vulgarised version of Marx's equilibrium-thesis, however without giving Marx the due credit.
151 Marx, "Future Results," 218.

On the other hand, Marx alluded to India's rudimentary and inadequate means of transportation:

> It is notorious that the productive powers of India are paralyzed by the utter want of means for conveying and exchanging its various produce. Nowhere, more than in India, do we meet with social destitution in the midst of natural plenty, for want of the means of exchange.[152]

Interestingly enough, this is one of the main arguments of a recently published book on India and the Great Divergence even though the author does not refer to Marx in this context.[153]

Marx pointed out India's dismembered polities throughout history apart from a few exceptional periods when centralisation was more pronounced, as under the Mughals. He was cognizant of the fact that, at least in a number of districts in India, public works and the productivity of agriculture were dependent on the "interference of the centralizing power of Government."[154]

Marx stipulated that the British colonial intrusions had wreaked immense damage and destruction on India. Significantly, he laid bare the EIC's policies that substantially decreased agricultural productivity and destroyed Indian manufactures. He also emphasised that Indians were able to "throw off the English yoke altogether" after the British had violently introduced capitalism in South Asia.[155] And this, despite the fact that

> ... the misery inflicted by the British on Hindostan is of an essentially different and infinitely more intensive kind than all Hindostan had to suffer before ... England has broken down the entire framework of Indian society, without any symptoms of reconstitution yet appearing. This loss of his old world, with no gain of a new one ... separates Hindustan, ruled by Britain, from all its ancient traditions, and from the whole of its past history.[156]

---

152 Marx, "Future Results," 219.

153 Roman Studer, *The Great Divergence Reconsidered. Europe, India, and the Rise to Global Economic Power* (Cambridge: CUP, 2015). Needless to say, this argument goes back to thinkers such as Bodin, Montesquieu, etc.

154 Marx, "British Rule," 125, 127. Karl A. Wittfogel was inspired by Marx when he published his influential *Oriental Despotism: A Comparative Study of Total Power* (New Haven: YUP, 1957).

155 Marx, "Future Results," 221.

156 Marx, "British Rule," 126. He later reiterated this point in quoting William Howitt (*Colonisation and Christianity* 1838, 9): "The barbarities and desperate outrages of the so-called Christian race, throughout every region of the world, and upon every people they have been able to subdue, are not to be paralleled by those of any other race, however fierce, however untaught, and however reckless of mercy and of shame, in any age of the earth." Marx, *Capital*, Vol. 1, 916.

Nevertheless, he argued that British colonisation had unintended consequences in Asia by bringing about "the only *social* revolution ever heard of in Asia."[157] Marx also penned the following famous lines:

> England has to fulfill a double mission in India: one destructive, the other regenerating – the annihilation of old Asiatic society, and the laying the material foundations of Western society in Asia.[158]

For Marx "the annihilation of the old Asiatic society" with its entrenched caste system and deep-rooted superstition could not have occurred without the emergence of a new Asiatic society.[159] The unintended consequences of British rule consisted of the following elements:

> The political unity of India ... was the first condition of its regeneration strengthened ... and perpetuated by the electric telegraph. The native army, organized and trained by the British drill-sergeant, was the sine qua non of Indian self-emancipation ... The free press ....[160]

Apart from railways and steamships that would enable regular and rapid communication, Marx also emphasised the prospects of the rise of a new Indian bourgeoisie:

> From the Indian natives, reluctantly and sparingly educated at Calcutta, under English superintendence, a fresh class is springing up, endowed with the requirements for government and imbued with European science.[161]

---

157 Marx, "British Rule in India," 131–133. For Marx's argument on the EIC's responsibility for the decline of agriculture, see 127–128.
158 Marx, "Future Results," 217–218. Marx and Engels seem to have made a similar argument regarding the British Opium War against China in the *Communist Manifesto*. Karl Marx and Friedrich Engels, *The Communist Manifesto* (London: Routledge, 2008) [1848; 1888], 39. As for the progressive role of colonialism, Ahmad points out that: "Marx was far less sanguine about such a role than not only British liberals of the nineteenth century but also the whole range of Indian modern intelligentsia of the same period... Marx's fundamental positions on some of the key issues were in fact more advanced than those held by luminaries of India's own Independence Movement [including Gandhi] even in the first half of the 20th century." Furthermore, he rightly emphasises that: "even in his writings on India in 1853, denunciations of the bad side of colonialism far outweigh any hope that it might also have a good side, and even this is subjected to an unconditional affirmation of India's right to liberation from colonialism." Ahmad, 'Karl Marx,' 203, 207, 209.
159 Marx, "British Rule," 132.
160 Marx, "Future Results," 218.
161 Marx, "Future Results," 218.

What is relevant in the context of the Great Divergence debate is that Marx was not of the opinion that Indians needed any prolonged phase of colonial supervision and tutelage. As soon as the obstructive traditions of Indian society were shattered and the sprouts of industrial development were implanted, Indians were perfectly able to independently acquire the necessary skill and knowledge of steam machinery as illustrated by the native engineers of the Calcutta mint and Burdwan coal districts.[162]

With the inception of the anti-colonial Indian revolt in 1857, Marx wrote a number of articles for the *New York Tribune* which vividly depict his genuine concern and empathy for the plight of the Indian people. As in his writings of 1853, Marx reiterated the main causes of British supremacy in India:

> The Roman *Divide et impera* [divide and rule] was the great rule by which Great Britain, for about one hundred and fifty years, contrived to retain the tenure of her Indian empire. The antagonism of the various races, tribes, castes, creeds and sovereignties, the aggregate of which forms the geographical unity of what is called India, continued to be the vital principle of British supremacy.[163]

When Marx was writing on the 'Indian Rebellion' of 1857, and then again drafted what later became *Capital*, Vols. 1 and 3, it was already evident to him that British rule in India could hardly lay "the material foundations of Western society in Asia." By contrast, he underscored that India was being degraded to an English supplier of primary products (*Capital*, Vol. 1, 579). He added that:

> More than that of any other nation, the history of English economic management in India is a history of futile and actually stupid (in practice, infamous) economic experiments. In Bengal they created a caricature of English large-scale landed property; in the south-east they created a caricature of peasant smallholdings. In the north-west they did all they could to transform the Indian economic community with common property in the soil into a caricature of itself.[164]

---

162 Marx, "Future Results," 220. To this effect, Marx approvingly quoted G. Campbell (*Modern India: a Sketch of the System of Civil Government*, 59 – 60): "that the great mass of the Indian people possesses a great industrial energy, is well fitted to accumulate capital, and remarkable for a mathematical clearness of head, and talent for figures and exact sciences ... Their intellects ... are excellent."

163 Karl Marx, "The Revolt in the Indian Army," 15.7.1857, in *MECW*, Vol. 15 (1856 – 1858), n.d., 297.

164 Marx, *Capital*, Vol. 3, 451 note 50. In similar vein, Marx also described English colonial policies in Ireland: "Every time Ireland was about to develop industrially, she was CRUSHED and reconverted into a purely AGRICULTURAL LAND." Karl Marx, "Outline of a Report on the Irish Question to the Communist Educational Association of German Workers in London"

In the third and last draft of his letter to Vera Zasulich (1881), the Russian writer and revolutionary, Marx conceded that, in India, "the suppression of communal land ownership was nothing but an act of English vandalism pushing the natives not forward but backward."[165] He added that the English "only accomplished to ruin indigenous agriculture and to augment the number and intensity of famines."[166] In that very letter, he argued that Russia could appropriate the "positive achievements developed by the capitalist system without having to pass through its humiliating yoke (*fourches caudines*). It could gradually supplant parcellised cultivation by dint of combined and machine assisted agriculture."[167] This may have been one of Leon Trotsky's main sources of inspiration in developing and coining the concept of "uneven" and "combined" development. Be that as it may, Marx did not seem to have changed his opinion regarding India's potentialities for capitalist development between the 1850s and 1870s. In *Capital*, Vol. 1, he accurately depicted the "unchanging market" of large areas of rural India.[168] He argued that:

(1867), in *Marx-Engels Collected Works, Vol. 21 – Marx and Engels: 1867–1870*, Moscow (n.d.), 200.

165 Karl Marx, "Entwürfe einer Antwort auf den Brief von V. I. Sassulitsch," in *Karl Marx/Friedrich Engels – Werke* (*MEW*), Vol. 19 Berlin 1973 [1962], 384–406, 402; Roger Dangeville, "Lettres de Marx à Véra Zassoulitch," *L'Homme et la société* 5 (1967): 165–179, 176. The translation is ours. The original letter was written in French.

166 Marx, "Entwürfe einer Antwort," 405; Dangeville, "Lettres de Marx," 178. In the same year, Marx made clear that: "What the English take from them [Indians] annually in the form of rent, dividends for railways useless to the Hindus; pensions for military and civil service men, for Afghanistan and other wars, etc., etc. – what they take from them *without any equivalent* and quite apart from what they appropriate to themselves annually *within* India, speaking only of the *value of the commodities* the Indians have gratuitously and annually to *send over* to England – it amounts to *more than the total sum of income of the sixty millions of agricultural and industrial labourers of India!* This is a bleeding process, with a vengeance!" Letter of Marx to Danielson, February 19, 1881, in Karl Marx and Frederick Engels, *Selected Correspondence*. 1843–1895, Moscow (n.d.), 383.

167 Marx, "Entwürfe einer Antwort," 405; Dangeville, "Lettres de Marx," 178. Earlier, in the preface to the first edition of *Capital*, Vol. 1, he had already indicated that: "One nation can and should learn from others. Even when a society has begun to track down the natural laws of its movement – and it is the ultimate aim of this work to reveal the economic law of motion of modern society – it can neither leap over the natural phases of its development nor remove them by decree. But it can shorten and lessen the birth-pangs" (92). Similarly, Ernst Bloch's theory of "non-simultaneity" also appears to have been inspired by Marx's concept of "the unequal rate of development." See Frederic J. Schwartz, "Ernst Bloch and Wilhelm Pinder: Out of Sync," *Grey Room* 3 (2001): 54–89.

168 Marx, *Capital*, Vol. 1, 478.

> Those small and extremely ancient Indian communities, for example, some of which continue to exist to this day, are based on the possession of the land in common, on the blending of agriculture and handicrafts and on an unalterable division of labour ... Most of the products are destined for direct use by the community itself, and are not commodities ... It is the surplus alone that becomes a commodity, and a part of that surplus cannot become a commodity until it has reached the hands of the state, because from time immemorial a certain quantity of the community's production has found its way to the state as rent in kind ... The simplicity of the productive organism in these self-sufficing communities ... supplies the key to the riddle of the unchangeability of Asiatic societies.[169]

In *Capital*, Vol. 3, he added that:

> Usury has a revolutionary effect on pre-capitalist modes of production only in so far as it destroys and dissolves the forms of ownership which provide a firm basis for the articulation of political life and whose constant reproduction in the same form is a necessity for that life. In Asiatic forms, usury can persist for a long while without leading to anything more than economic decay and political corruption. It is only where and when the other conditions for the capitalist mode of production are present that usury appears as one of the means of formation of this new mode of production, by ruining the feudal lords and petty production on the one hand, and by centralizing the conditions of labour on the other.[170]

Marx was aware of the British EIC's export of huge sums of American bullion to India.[171] Nevertheless, he held that money, including American metals, were mainly hoarded.[172] Furthermore, he argued that in India, "we have not yet reached the stage of the formal subsumption of labour under capital" as capital did not penetrate production.[173] Marx's insights have sparked plenty of research and controversies throughout the twentieth and twenty-first centuries. His analyses have remained a forceful explanation for the different socio-economic trajectories of western Europe and South Asia.

However, research conducted in the past fifty years has demonstrated that the image of self-sufficient Indian village communities needs to be somewhat qualified.[174] Although the degree to which villages were self-sufficient remains

169 Marx, *Capital*, Vol. 1, 477–479.

170 Marx, *Capital*, Vol. 1, 732.

171 Marx mentioned "the circulation of American silver from the West to the East; the metallic band between America and Europe on one side, with Asia on the other side, since the beginning of the modern epoch." Marx, *Grundrisse*, 227.

172 Marx, *Capital*, Vol. 1, 228, 232.

173 Marx, *Capital*, Vol. 1, 1023.

174 Yazdani, *India*, 121–124; Habib, "Introduction: Marx's Perception," xxxii, xxxiii. Habib notes: "The contrast that Marx drew, between an exchange economy based on the disposal of

a matter of debate, there is little doubt that pre-colonial Indian society "was clearly a developed class society, with a ruling class of surplus appropriators and a division of labour based on exchange outside the village community."[175] Moreover, in advanced regions of seventeenth and eighteenth century India (for example, Mysore and Gujarat), the degree of urbanisation was on the rise. The level of urban, as well as rural monetisation was considerable while remuneration in money and tax collection in cash, as well as commodity exchange in both cities and the countryside were of substance. Apart from that, in some regions of Mysore and Gujarat, capital was encroaching upon the sphere of production while *absolute surplus value* was being created in some sectors of manufacture such as textile, shipbuilding and paper production. In Mysore, a few artisans had become merchants, a number of well-off weavers employed servants and some owners of iron forges siphoned the lion's share of output.[176] In turn, Gujarat was the most commercialised and urbanised region in South Asia. It underwent processes of *Smithian* growth, witnessed the emergence of a 'middle class' and harboured powerful merchant communities. Segments of the latter possessed considerable political leverage. They belonged to the world's wealthiest merchants of the seventeenth and eighteenth centuries and reinvested substantial portions of their money capital.[177]

---

the surplus and the 'natural economy' within the village serving for its basis, must still stand, though the intrusion of commodity production and differentiation within the village might yet have been more extensive than Marx allowed for. In his view, the urban economy was largely parasitical; and here we have an important suggestion as to why the potentialities of capitalistic development in the Indian economy remained thwarted." Habib, "Introduction: Marx's Perception," xxxv.

175 Habib, "Introduction: Marx's Perception," xxxi.

176 This is important, as Marx argued that, "the really revolutionising way" is when the producer becomes "a merchant and capitalist, in contrast to the natural agricultural economy and the guild-bound handicraft of medieval urban industry." Marx, *Capital*, Vol. 3, 452.

177 Yazdani, *India*, 116–129, 170–183, 184–211, 363–379, 401–475. In India, a high degree of monetisation was already visible from the 13th century onwards. In Mughal India, payments in cash predominated and as much as 70.9% of Mughal India's economy might have been monetised by the late sixteenth century. Habib, *Essays*, 262; Haider, "South Asian Economy," 16; Moosvi, "The Silver Influx, Money Supply, Prices and Revenue-Extraction in Mughal India," *JESHO* 30, no. 1 (1987): 47–94; John F. Richards, ed., *The monetary system of the Mughal Empire* (New Delhi: OUP, 1987). In 1880, Marx himself remarked that Akbar's taxes amounted to one-third of the produce and that to "settle the equivalent of this amount in money, regular statements of prices were taken over all the country for 19 years, and the average was the amount demanded in coin." Karl Marx, *Notes on Indian History (664–1858)*, Moscow n.d., 36.

In brief, Marx (and Engels) cogently pointed out that European feudalism differed from what he termed the "Asiatic Mode of Production" (AMP).[178] Between 1879 and 1882, Marx once again returned to intensive research on India.[179] In *Capital*, Vol. 3, Marx had argued that, in Asia, "there is no private landed property, though there is both private and communal possession and usufruct of the land."[180] However, from the late 1870s onwards, he drew attention to the fact that there existed pockets of private landed property in Asia.[181] Concurrently, Marx argued that Maxim Kovalevskij (1851–1916) – Russian sociologist and historian – wrongly identified a western European style of Indian feudalism as a) benefices and the giving away of offices on lease was also practiced in Rome and therefore not a feudal practice, b) there was no serfdom (*Leibeigen-*

178 It was in the preface to the *Critique of Political Economy* (1859) that Marx first made use of the concept of the AMP. But as early as 1853, Marx seems to have identified significant differences between the modes of production in Europe and Asia. See "Marx an Engels in Manchester [London] 2.6.1853," in *MEW*, Vol. 28, Berlin 1963, 254; Marx, "British Rule," 127. In the latter article, he somewhat overstated the unchangeability of socio-economic conditions in Asia, when he argued that India's "social condition has remained unaltered since its remotest antiquity, until the first decennium of the 19th century." Marx, "British Rule," 128.

179 As to India, see the three following notebooks written in 1879–82: Harstick, ed., *Marx über Formen*; Lawrence Krader, ed., *The Ethnologial Notebooks of Karl Marx* (Assen: van Gorcum & Comp. 1974); Karl Marx, *Notes on Indian History*. In the latter notebook, Marx remarked that Akbar "made Delhi into the greatest and finest city then existing in the world." Marx, *Notes on Indian History*, 36.

180 Marx, *Capital*, Vol. 1, 927. In a letter to Engels from June 2, 1853 – after having come across some of Bernier's writings – Marx wrote of the absence of private property in land in the East. But in a subsequent letter to Engels (June 14) he noted that: "As to the *question* of *property*, this is a very *controversial* one among the English writers on India. In the broken hill-country south of Krishna, property in land does seem to have existed." Karl Marx and Frederick Engels, *Selected Correspondence*. 1843–1895, Moscow (n.d.), 99, 104. Marx further learnt about different forms of private landed property through reading Kovalevskij's *Obscinnoe zemlevladenie. Priciny, khod i posledstvija ego razlozenija* (*Communal Landownership: The Causes, Processes, and Consequences of Its Disintegration*), published in 1879 (Moscow). As already indicated, Marx's notes were edited by Harstick and published as *Karl Marx über Formen vorkapitalistischer Produktion*, 39–93.

181 In his 1879 excerpts of Kovalevskij's work on landownership, he noted that since the time of the Delhi Sultanate in the 13th century, the "iktadar" had acquired "mulk or milk," that is full property (*volles Eigenthum*). Most significantly, he explained that when barren land was handed over to persons who would cultivate it, the respective tiller(s) obtained irrevocable (*unwiderruflich*) and hereditary landed property rights ("milk" or "mulk"). Harstick, ed., *Marx über Formen*, 68–69, 73. It was after the time of Firuz Shah Tughlaq (1351–1388) that an *iqta'* would often pass from father to his son. Iqtidar Alam Khan, ed., *Historical Dictionary of Medieval India* (Lanham: Scarecrow Press, 2008) 78–79. Marx was well aware that it was especially from the reign of Firuz Shah Tughlaq onwards that the *iqta'* started to become hereditary. Harstick, ed., *Marx über Formen*, 70–71.

schaft) in India, c) no similar form of protection of both free and unfree peasants except for *vaqfs* (pious endowments), d) the land was nowhere noble in the sense of being, for example, inalienable (*unveräußerlich*) to *roturiers* (non-nobles), e) no patrimonial jurisdiction regarding civil law and f) different forms of inheritance between Europe and India ("according to Indian law, the ruling power is not subject to division among the sons; thus a great source of European feudalism is blocked [*verstopft*].")[182] Furthermore, in *The Ethnological Notebooks*, compiled during the period 1880–1882, Marx reiterated that: "This jackass [*Esel*] Phear calls the constitution of the village *feudal*."[183] As the late Lawrence Krader rightly noted:

> The application of the category of feudalism to the oriental community by cultural and social historians, ethnologists, Marxists, so-called Marxists, etc., is a simplistic periodisation and a simplistic typology without reference to a chronology implicit in the periodisation of oriental society, feudalism, etc. It is an abstraction from history and an ethnocentrism, whether performed by Europeans or not, casting the history of the world in the European mold.[184]

Indeed, in theorising this concept, Marx's lasting contribution is to have recognised that there were significant differences between the socio-economic formations in Europe and Asia.[185]

---

182 Harstick, ed., *Marx über Formen*, 76, 69. Marx did not see many similarities between the feudalisms of post-Mughal India and western Europe. This was different in the case of Japan. In *Capital*, Vol. 1, he noted that: "Japan, with its purely feudal organization of landed property and its developed small-scale agriculture, gives a much truer picture of the European Middle Ages than all our history books, dictated as these are, for the most part, by bourgeois prejudices" (878 note 3).

183 Krader, ed., *Ethnological Notebooks*, 256. Through reading Phear, Marx even might have recognised pre-colonial Indian forms of class formation, social differentiation, monetisation and wage-labour. Krader, ed., *Ethnological Notebooks*, 247, 249–250, 253, 256, 258, 262–263, 267–271, 277. But as Treide rightly points out, it is not always clear which of the phenomena described by Phear and excerpted by Marx were considered to be the outcome of pre-colonial dynamics or colonial rule. Dietrich Treide, "Karl Marx' Kowalewski- und Phear-Exzerpte und die koloniale Frage," *Marx-Engels-Forschungsberichte* 6 (1990), 5–36, 19–20.

184 Treide, "Karl Marx' Kowalewski- und Phear-Exzerpte und die koloniale Frage," 33. For a similar assessment, see also Hans-Peter Harstick, "Einleitung," in idem, ed., *Marx über Formen*.

185 We agree with Shanin that in employing the concept of AMP, Marx attempted to propose an "alternative to unilinear explanations" of historical development. Teodor Shanin, "Late Marx: gods and craftsmen," in *Late Marx and the Russian Road: Marx and the Peripheries of Capitalism*, T.Shanin ed. (New York: NYUP, 1983), 5. As Habib points out: "The reserve apparently entertained by Marx in his later years in respect of the Asiatic category did not imply that he was willing to overlook the specific features of Indian society and economy. This is clear from his objec-

As already mentioned, the so-called *original accumulation* chapter of *Capital*, Vol. 1, examined the preconditions of the emergence of the capitalist mode of production in western Europe. Therefore, Marx did not need to delve into the causes of the Industrial Revolution and the reasons behind the Great Divergence. Only some significant factors that paved the way to Britain's global supremacy in the nineteenth century needed to be underlined and integrated in the narrative. We shall call attention to an array of further facts: similar to Japan and rather dissimilar to China and India – Britain benefitted from fortuitous geo-climatic circumstances that happened to be conducive to an industrial breakthrough. The land was relatively small, densely populated and relatively urbanised. England had plenty of navigable rivers and canals which facilitated the transportation of commodities, including coal. This contributed to the emergence of an integrated market, as well as industrial production. Britain was protected from disease, devoid of regular natural calamities and more difficult to conquer due to its geographical location as an island. The latter also allowed for the construction of a viable navy without the necessity of a large amount of ground forces.[186] Environmental conditions made possible exceptionally large populations of animals,[187] high agricultural yields and were well suited for domestic, as well as international transport and communication. In contrast to China, England's coal reserves happened to be near the industrial centres and Britain's cold weather stimulated its utilisation as a source of fuel.[188] As O'Brien summarised the existing literature on that matter:

---

tion to any designation of the Indian communities as 'feudal'. It is also best to remember that his thesis of the union of agriculture and craft, on the one hand, and an immutable division of labour, on the other, as the twin pillars of the Indian village economy remains of lasting value." Habib, "Introduction: Marx's Perception of India," xxiv–xxxv. In the words of Jameson: "The problem with removing this particular mode of production from the active list is that in that case you are left with nothing but feudalism as far as the eye can see." Fredric R. Jameson, "Ancient Society and the New Politics: From Kant to Modes of Production," *Criticism* 58, no. 2 (2016): 327–339, 333.

186 By 1688, Britain possessed the largest merchant marine fleet in Europe. It had augmented from 2 million tonnes in 1660 to 3.4 million in 1686. Frank O'Gorman, *The Long Eighteenth Century: British Political and Social History 1688–1832* (London: Bloomsbury Publishing, 2016) [1997], 28.

187 As O'Brien points out, "animals provided the high value raw materials (wool, leather and bones), food in the form of meat and dairy produce, extra supplies of energy and flows of organic fertiliser that had carried the productivity of English agriculture towards the head of European league tables." O'Brien, "Industrial Revolution," 12.

188 Cf. Pomeranz, *The Great Divergence*; Vries, *Escaping Poverty*, 414; Vries, *State, Economy and the Great Divergence*, 55. For scholars who try to explain the *Great Divergence* by geographical factors, see also Eric Jones, *The European Miracle: Environments, Economies and Geopolitics in*

> Britain's coal output for 1815 implies that 15 million acres (equivalent to 88% of its arable area) had counterfactually by then been released from forestry to grow grains, vegetables, industrial raw materials and to sustain even more livestock and to facilitate urbanization.[189]

In turn, the pumping technology that was needed for coal mines stimulated iron casting and knowledge of the vacuum, which was crucial for the development of steam engines.[190] Parthasarathi rightly points out that, in India, "the abundance of wood meant that there was no need to experiment with coal and the exploi-

---

the History of Europe and Asia (Cambridge: CUP, 2003) [1981]; Ian Morris, *Why the West Rules – for Now: The Patterns of History and what they Reveal about the Future* (London: Farrar, Straus and Giroux 2010). For the significance of coal as a source of energy during severe British winters, see Adam Smith, *An Inquiry Into the Nature and Causes of the Wealth of Nations*, Vol. 2 (London: Oliphant, Waugh & Innes, 1778), 490; John D. Post, *Food Shortage, Climatic Variability, and Epidemic Disease in Preindustrial Europe: The Mortality Peak in the Early 1740s* (Ithaca: Cornell University Press, 1985), 61; John F. Richards, *The Unending Frontier: An Environmental History of the Early Modern World* (Berkeley: UCP, 2003), 235.

189 O'Brien, "Industrial Revolution," 20. He further adds that: "Heat-intensive industrial processes in metallurgy, glass making, brewing, refining sugar and salt, chemistry, in baking food and bricks etc., could all be conducted more cheaply with coal. The feedbacks and technological spin-offs from these industries to metallurgy and to the making of kiln's, pots, vats and containers became important for industrial development. While lower cost bricks and metals for the construction of houses in cities, towns and industrial villages, saved capital which could be invested in social overhead facilities and/or manufacturing industry." O'Brien, "Industrial Revolution," 20–21.

190 For the importance of coal in the making of the British Industrial Revolution, see J. H. Clapham, *An Economic History of Modern Britain, Vol. 1: The Early Railway Age, 1820–1850* (Cambridge: CUP, 1926); J. U. Nef, *The Rise of the British Coal Industry*, Vols. 1 & 2 (London: Routledge, 1932); T. S. Ashton, *The Industrial Revolution* (Oxford: OUP, 1948); Phyllis Deane, *The First Industrial Revolution* (Cambridge: CUP, 1965); Fernand Braudel, *The Structures of Everyday Life* (New York: Collins, 1981); Roy Church, *The History of the British Coal Industry*, Vol. 3. 1830–1913 (Oxford: Clarendon Press, 1986); E. A. Wrigley, *Continuity, Chance and Change* (Cambridge: CUP, 1988); Pomeranz, *The Great Divergence*; Rolf Peter Sieferle, *The Subterranean Forest: Energy Systems and the Industrial Revolution* (Cambridge: CUP, 2001); Parthasarathi, *Why Europe Grew Rich*. For arguments questioning the vitality of coal and steam in the Industrial Revolution, see Gregory Clark and David Jacks, "Coal and the Industrial Revolution," *European Review of Economic History* 11 (2007), 39–72; Joel Mokyr, *The Enlightened Economy: An Economic History of Britain 1700–1850* (New Haven: YUP, 2010), 101–102; Alexander Tepper and Karol J. Borowiecki, "Accounting for Breakout in Britain: The Industrial Revolution through a Malthusian Lens," *Journal of Macroeconomics* 44 (2015): 219–233. For an overview of arguments, see Neuss, "Industrial Revolution," 11–12. Regarding the importance of energy for economic development, see Vaclav Smil, *Energy in World History* (Boulder: Routledge, 1994); Paolo Malanima et al., *Power to the People. Energy in Europe over the Last Five Centuries* (Princeton: PUP, 2013).

tation of its sizable deposits would await the nineteenth century."[191] However, we should not underestimate the fact that, in England, wood scarcity alone does not explain the application of fossil energy. Paul Warde highlights this important fact: "By the early 18th century, over half of the energy consumed in England was supplied by coal."[192] And as Vries emphasises: "Britain was already experimenting with new ways of producing energy when population pressure still was quite low. Wood scarcity was often a problem because demand was so high, not because supply was so low."[193]

Of England's greatest strengths during the seventeenth and eighteenth centuries, what is often overlooked is the combination of a relatively free home market, secure property rights for the elite, social mobility, as well as a degree of civil rights and liberties for the bourgeoisie on the one hand and militaristic, interventionist and exploitive policies vis-à-vis the rest of the world and domestic labour force on the other hand.[194] These factors – in conjunction with the processes of *original accumulation* described by Marx, efficient institutions (joint-stock companies, a central bank, the stock exchange and national debt, the Parliament, universities), a distinct British "engine culture" and the "industrial enlightenment," the effects of inter-state and global competition, the adoption of American and Afro-Asian knowledge (techno-scientific advancements) and resources (for example, bullion and cotton), as well as the results of unintended conjunctures and the corollaries of uneven development amongst other factors – gave Britain an edge; ushering in the emergence of industrial capitalism.

---

191 Parthasarathi, *Why Europe Grew Rich*, 11. This argument had already been put forward by Qaisar, *Indian Response*, 81–82.

192 Paul Warde, "Energy and Natural Resource Dependency in Europe, 1600–1900," *BWPI Working Paper* 77 (2009): 9.

193 Peer Vries, "Challenges, (Non-)Responses, and Politics: A Review of Prasannan Parthasarathi, Why Europe Grew Rich and Asia Did Not: Global Economic Divergence, 1600–1850," *JWH* 23, no. 3 (2012): 649.

194 At one end of the extreme, the benefits of a European culture of growth, knowledge, innovation and liberalism is being emphasised. See, for example, Joel Mokyr, *Culture of Growth*. At the other end, the illiberalism of British policies is being highlighted. See, for example, Sven Beckert, *Empire of Cotton*. For a rare exception, underlining both aspects, see the writings of Peer Vries.

Original Accumulation – Precondition or Ongoing Process?

Marx and Engels were both prominent and path-breaking historians in their own right. What follows are the contemporary implications of Marx's historical work and analyses. Right at the beginning of Chapter Eight of *Capital*, Vol. 1, Marx makes clear what an important role force and violence played in this whole process and how it has been construed by classical political economy:

> In actual history, it is a notorious fact that conquest, enslavement, robbery, murder, in short, force, play the greatest part. In the tender annals of political economy, the idyllic reigns from time immemorial.[195]

In other words, the history of the expropriation of the producers "is written in the annals of mankind in letters of blood and fire."[196] Elsewhere, Marx reiterated that "[f]orce is the midwife of every old society which is pregnant with a new one ... capital comes dripping from head to toe, from every pore, with blood and dirt."[197] In this regard, Marx explicitly underlined the combination of force and the power of the state, as well as its jurisdiction:

> Thus were the agricultural folk first forcibly expropriated from the soil, driven from their homes, turned into vagabonds, and then whipped, branded and tortured by grotesquely terroristic laws into accepting the discipline necessary for the system of wage-labour.[198]

Marx's emphasis on force and violence influenced some of the twentieth century luminaries of political economy such as Thorstein Veblen, Rosa Luxemburg and Ernest Mandel. Veblen, for instance, argued that: "The pursuit of industry requires an *accumulation of wealth*, and, barring force, fraud, and inheritance."[199] But it is only since the turn of the century that the preoccupation with processes

---

195 Marx, *Capital*, Vol. 1, 874. See also Friedrich Engels, "The Role of Force in History" (1887/1888) in *MECW*, Vol. 26, New York 1990. For the ways in which some classical political economists (Hume, Smith and Mill) understood the role of war and violence, see Yukihiro Ikeda and Annalisa Rosselli, eds., *War in the History of Economic Thought: Economists and the Question of War* (Abingdon: Routledge, 2018), Part 1.

196 Marx, *Capital*, Vol. 1, 875.

197 Marx, *Capital*, Vol. 1, 916; 926.

198 Marx, *Capital*, Vol. 1, 899.

199 Thorstein Veblen," On the Nature of Capital," *The Quarterly Journal of Economics* 22, no. 4 (1908), 517–542, 534.

of *original accumulation* has gained increased scholarly attention. As Massimo de Angelis points out, between the 1950s and 1980s, scholars generally accepted that *original accumulation* constituted the pre-history of capitalism.[200]

Some scholars have recently emphasised the defining role of force and violence in the emergence and consolidation of capitalism.[201] Following Luxemburg's emphasis on violence and imperialism as vital pillars of capital accumulation, others have tried to apply Marx's notion of the so-called *original accumulation* to describe phenomena within capitalism itself, even employing it to depict processes that are happening in the present.[202] What most of these scholars have in common is that they disagree with Marx's relegation of the *original accumulation* to the pre-history of capitalism. A prominent representative of this view is David Harvey who prefers the expression "accumulation by dispossession". He has recently argued that, there is "a real problem with the idea that primitive accumulation occurred once upon a time, and that once over, it ceased to be of real significance ... we need to take the continuity of primitive accumu-

---

200 Massimo De Angelis, "Marx and primitive accumulation: The continuous character of capital's 'enclosures'," *The Commoner* 2 (2001), 4.

201 See e. g. Mehrdad Vahabi, *The Political Economy of Destructive Power* (Cheltenham: Edward Elgar Publishing 2004); Ronald Findlay and Kevin H. O'Rourke, *Power and Plenty. Trade, War, and the World Economy in the Second Millennium* (Princeton: PUP, 2007); N. A. M. Rodger, "War as an economic activity in the "long" eighteenth century," *International Journal of Maritime History* 22, no. 2 (2010): 1–18; Anievas and Nisanciogu, *How the West Came to Rule* and especially Sven Beckert, *Empire of Cotton. A Global History* (New York: Knopf Doubleday Publishing Group 2014); Heide Gerstenberger, *Markt und Gewalt. Die Funktionsweise des historischen Kapitalismus* (Münster: Westfälisches Dampfboot, 2017); Rafael Torres-Sánchez, Pepijn Brandon and Marjolein 't Hart, "War and economy. Rediscovering the eighteenth-century military entrepreneur," *Business History* 60, no. 1 (2018): 4–22.

202 Rosa Luxemburg, *Die Akkumulation des Kapitals. Ein Beitrag zur ökonomischen Erklärung des Imperialismus* (Berlin: Buchhandlung Vorwärts Paul Singer, 1913), Section 3; Peter Kropotkin, "Western Europe" [1924], in *The Conquest of Bread and Other Writings*, ed. Mashall S. Shatz (Cambridge: CUP, 1995), 221; Ernest Mandel, *Late Capitalism* (London: NLB, 1975) [1972], 46–47; Samir Amin, *Accumulation on a World Scale: A Critique of the Theory of Underdevelopment* (New York: Monthly Review Press 1974), 3; David Harvey, The New Imperialism (Oxford: OUP, 2003); Silvia Federici, *The Caliban and the Witch: Women, the Body, and Primitive Accumulation* (New York: Autonomedia 2004), 12; Michael Hardt and Antonio Negri, *Commonwealth* (Cambridge: CUP, 2009), 86, 93, 138; Paresh Chattopadhyay, *Marx's Associated Mode of Production. A Critique of Marxism* (New York: Springer, 2016), 186; Nancy Fraser, "Expropriation and Exploitation in Racialized Capitalism: A Reply to Michael Dawson," *Critical Historical Studies* 3 (2016), 163–178. For a critique of some of these approaches, see Tom Brass, "Unfree labour as primitive accumulation?," *Capital & Class* 35, no. 1 (2010): 23–38; Alex Callinicos, *Deciphering Capital. Marx's Capital and its Destiny* (London: Bookmarks Publications 2014), 199–200; Michael Hardt and Toni Negri, *Assembly* (New York: Campus Verlag, 2017), 179–180.

lation throughout the historical geography of capitalism seriously."[203] He refers to the violent exploitation of natural resources in Africa; the dispossession, expulsion and extermination of rural populations in South America, South and East Asia; colonial and imperialist rule; the use of state powers to reallocate resources and assets to a capitalist class; criminal machinations of financial institutions; slavery and human trafficking. He rightly points out that, since the neoliberal turn of the 1970s, the credit system, the enclosure of the commons and privatisation of water, education, healthcare, state lands and assets has proliferated, especially in the past few decades.[204] Indeed, it is hard to dismiss that force, violence and dispossession pervade the history of capitalism. Moreover, it is difficult imagining a British industrial breakthrough and the perpetuation of industrialisation and modern economic growth without the combined effects of chattel slavery, colonial resources, an aggressive naval mercantilism, protectionism, colonial and imperialist exploitation, as well as unequal exchange.[205]

---

203 David Harvey, *A Companion to Marx's Capital* (London: Verso, 2010), 305. He adds that: "none of the predatory practices that Marx identified have gone away, and in some instances they have even flourished to a degree unimaginable in Marx's own times ... in our times, the techniques for enriching the ruling classes and diminishing the standard of living of labor through something akin to primitive accumulation have proliferated and multiplied ... I think Marx was in error in confining these forms of struggle to the prehistory of capitalism ... The idea that the politics of primitive accumulation and by extension accumulation by dispossession belong exclusively to the prehistory of capitalism is surely wrong." Harvey, *Companion*, 309, 313.
204 Harvey, *Companion*, 306–312. For important economic writings on these issues, see Yoram Barzel, *A Theory of the State: Economic Rights, Legal Rights, and the Scope of the State* (Cambridge: CUP, 2002); Mehrdad Vahabi, *The Political Economy of Predation: Manhunting and the Economics of Escape* (Cambridge: CUP, 2016). We would also like to point out that there are some Marxists who minimise the role of force or violence in the development of imperialism. See, for example, Leo Panitch, *The Making of Global Capitalism: The Political Economy of American Empire* (London: Verso, 2013). Furthermore, the anarchist perspective equally needs to be taken into account. See especially James Scott, *The Moral Economy of the Peasant: Rebellion and Subsistence in Southeast Asia* (New Haven: YUP, 1976); Idem, *Domination and the Arts of Resistance* (New Haven: YUP, 1990); Idem, *The Art of Not Being Governed, An Anarchist History of Upland Southeast Asia* (New Haven:YUP 2009).
205 Robin Blackburn, *The Making of New World Slavery: From the Baroque to the Modern*, 1492–1800 (London: Verso, 1997); André Gunder Frank, *ReOrient: Global Economy in the Asian Age* (Berkeley: UCP, 1998); Pomeranz, *Great Divergence*; Inikori, *Africans and the Industrial*; Hobson, *Eastern Origins*; Acemoğlu et al., "The Rise of Europe," 546–579; Patrick Karl O'Brien, "The Formation of States and Transitions to Modern Economies: England, Europe, and Asia Compared," in *The Cambridge History of Capitalism*, Vol. 1, eds. Neal and Williamson 357–402; Yazdani, *India*. On unequal exchange, see Arghiri Emmanuel, *Unequal Exchange: A Study of the Imperialism of Trade* (London: Monthly review Press 1972) [1969] with additional comments by Charles Bettelheim. It is interesting to note that we can already see some notion of what later became

As in some other previous writings (such as in *Communist Manifesto*), Marx pointed out that exploitation was a phenomenon characteristic of the capitalist mode of production but also formed part of other socio-economic formations. Nonetheless, for him, capitalist exploitation was different in form.[206] It is true that the enforcement of the capital-relation, which took off in the period of *original accumulation*, developed after capitalism had become the prevalent socio-economic system:

> It is in fact this divorce between the conditions of labour on the one hand and the producers on the other that forms the concept of capital, as this arises with primitive [original] accumulation, subsequently appearing as a constant process in the accumulation and concentration of capital, before it is finally expressed here as the centralization of capitals already existing in a few hands, and the decapitalization of many.[207]

Concurrently, Marx underpinned that, at least in the industrialised world, the "silent compulsion of economic relations set the seal on the domination of the capitalist over the worker. Direct extra-economic force is still of course used, but only in exceptional cases."[208] Marx may have overestimated the "silent compulsion" at the expense of "extra-economic force". Indeed, as a number of scholars since Luxemburg have underlined, violence and force remained an integral part of expanded reproduction. This might partly have been the result of the fact that Marx neglected to examine the vital role of institutions and, above all, the state in enabling and perpetuating processes of capital accumulation. He put forward the thesis that "as soon as capital has become capital as such,

known as the "unequal exchange debate" in Marx's economic thought: "The relationship between labour days of different countries may be similar to that existing between skilled, complex labour and unskilled, simple labour within a country. In this case the richer country exploits the poorer one, even where the latter gains by the exchange." Karl Marx, *Theories of Surplus-Value. Volume IV of Capital PART III* (Moscow: Progress Publishers 1971), 105–106. See also Marx, *Capital*, Vol. 1, 580.

206 Marx, *Capital*, Vol. 1, 875.

207 Marx, *Capital*, Vol. 3, 354–355.

208 Marx, *Capital*, Vol. 1, 899. As Roberts points out, "Marx was an outlier among 19th-century socialists." Figures like William Thompson, Bronterre O'Brien, Karl Heinzen, Eugen Dühring and Pierre-Joseph Proudhon "echoed the theory of the Saint-Simonians, according to which the accumulation of capital, and the attendant exploitation of the workers, are the direct consequence of the conquest of the land and the extortion this allowed the landed to exact from the poor producer" and regularly employ physical force. Roberts, "What was primitive accumulation?," 6–7; Idem, *Marx's Inferno: The Political Theory of Capital* (Princeton: PUP, 2017), Chapter 4.

it creates its own presuppositions."[209] However, in relegating *original accumulation* to the "pre-history of capital," Marx elucidated that the logic and mechanisms of capitalist "creative destruction" (Schumpeter) are fundamentally different from the rationale and consequences of pre-capitalist destructive power. This applies to neoliberal policies beginning in the 1970s, as well as the neo-colonial and imperialist wars and interventions in Afghanistan, Iraq, Syria, Libya and Mali. Indeed, as Paul Zarembka points out, "'accumulation of capital' proper, without need for an adjective 'primitive,' includes force and violence in achieving capitalist aims of separation of laborers from their means of production; there is no need to invoke 'primitive' to recognise this fact."[210] On the same note, Mehrdad Vahabi stipulates that,

> Contrary to Potlach, strategic destruction or destructive entrepreneurship in a capitalist economy is not anti-economic, it is conducted with the intention of breeding new market opportunities. In this sense, it is part of the process of market creation ... In this process, the introduction of *new* products *precedes* the destruction of *old* ones. In war destruction, the Schumpeterian process of creative destruction is inverted, since the destruction of *old* products *precedes* the reconstruction of new ones ... While creative entrepreneurship promotes the market through *creative destruction*, destructive entrepreneurship promotes the market outlets through *destructive creation*. In a capitalist economy, destructive creation may lead to war economies in which waging wars may be more important than winning them.[211]

We can conclude that, as Marx emphasised the dull compulsion of economic relations, he did not pay due attention to continuous extra-economic accumulation within advanced reproduction itself. Thus, Marx's conflation of capitalist accumulation with economic exploitation and expropriation (competition and monopolisation) created the prerequisites to interpreting extra-economic accumulation as *original accumulation*. At the same time, the dull compulsion of economic relations may be regarded as an abstract 'ideal type' that may become 'hegemonic' in the Gramscian meaning of the term.

As a matter of fact, not only private property, relatively well-functioning markets, complex forms of division of labour and some degree of commodification,

---

209 Marx, *Grundrisse*, 460. He added that: "It no longer proceeds from presuppositions in order to become, but rather it is itself presupposed, and proceeds from itself to create the conditions of its maintenance and growth." Marx, Grundrisse, 460.

210 Thus, "we can utilize Luxemburg's understanding of 'accumulation of capital' proper as separation, with all the blood, sweat and tears it entails! We don't have to give up 'primitive accumulation' as being historical in order to confront the reality of separation/dispossession." Paul Zarembka, "Primitive Accumulation in Marxism, Historical or Trans-historical Separation from Means of Production?," *The Commoner* (March 2002): 1, 3.

211 Vahabi, *Political Economy*, 186.

but also the exploitation of labourers by coercion and violence have already existed before the prevalence of capitalism.[212] The question whether a rudimentary form of 'capitalism' existed before the advent of industrial capitalism is one of the controversial issues that started prior to Marx's time and persist until now. Marx was reluctant to use the term capitalism. He only used it twice in the three volumes of *Das Kapital* and preferred the expression "capitalist mode of production." He did not seem to think that before the advent of industrial capitalism in the nineteenth century, any country deserved to be called capitalist per se. By contrast, Max Weber in his late writings (1920) employed the expression political or booty capitalism in the ancient Roman Empire, as well as in eastern empires. This type of capitalist exploitation was based on the use of brutal force. Braudel also refers to capitalism of long-distance trade going back to antiquity.[213]

In deploying the concept of *original accumulation*, Marx intended to analyse the pre-history that enabled the emergence of the capitalist mode of production in England and western Europe. He portrayed a complex encounter of different processes concurring and colliding in the course of several centuries heralding an interim phase that was neither pre-capitalist nor capitalist.[214] Historically speaking, the process of *original accumulation* belongs to a period when capitalism had not yet become the dominant mode of production. It preceded and made possible the prevalence of the capital-relation. After a particular country successfully undergoes this process, the conjuncture of *original accumulation* henceforth belongs to the past and therefore cannot repeat itself provided that socio-economic development is not vaulted to a pre-capitalist state – for example, through natural disasters or warfare.[215] But in other countries and regions, where this

---

212 Cf. Geoffrey M. Hodgson, *Conceptualizing Capitalism. Institutions, Evolution, Future* (Chicago: UCP, 2015), 251, 253; Marcel Van der Linden, *Workers of the World. Essays toward a Global Labor History* (Leiden: Brill, 2008), 261; Geoffrey Ingham, *Capitalism* (Cambridge: CUP, 2013) [2008], 53; Steven G. Marks, *The Information Nexus: Global Capitalism from the Renaissance to the Present* (Cambridge: CUP, 2016), 78 and chapter 3; Werner Plumpe, "Der Kapitalismus als Problem der Geschichtsschreibung," *Journal of Modern European History* 15, no. 4 (2017): 457–469, 459. See also Wood, *Origins of Capitalism*.

213 On "political capitalism," see Nasser Mohajer and Mehrdad Vahabi (forthcoming). On the conceptual history and definitions of capital, capitalist and capitalism, including Marx's use of these terms, see Kaveh Yazdani, "Capitalism – Begriffsgeschichte and Definition of a Concept" (forthcoming).

214 For the argument that the epoch of original accumulation was a period of passage from feudal to capitalist socio-economic formations, see also Althusser and Balibar, *Reading Capital*, 279; Read, *Micro-Politics*, 26.

215 For a different and idiosyncratic interpretation, see Roberts who argues that: "Marx does not confine primitive accumulation to the past, or to the frontiers of capitalism. He argues,

process did not take place between the late fifteenth and eighteenth centuries, *original accumulation* occurred in the nineteenth or twentieth centuries (for example, in Germany, Japan, Egypt and Persia), illustrating the often staggering, uneven emergence of this historic phenomenon. However, after England's *Sattelzeit* or transition period (1760–1830) ushering in industrial capitalism, all the following regions went through processes of catching-up and combined development. The realisation of the capitalist mode of production outside Britain – be it in other parts of Europe, the US, Japan or China – were based on a different bundle and set of moments than those depicted by Marx in Part 8 of *Capital*, Vol. 1. In a number of regions of the world, the penetration of western capital and the effects of colonialism even acted as a break on capitalist development or at least postponed the transition throughout most parts of the nineteenth and early twentieth century (such as in India). As Marx pointed out,

> By ruining handicraft production of finished articles in other countries, machinery forcibly converts them into fields for the production of its raw material. Thus India was compelled to produce cotton, wool, hemp, jute and indigo for Great Britain.[216]

He added that colonised lands were

> ... converted into settlements for growing the raw material of the mother country ... A new and international division of labour springs up, one suited to the requirements of the main industrial countries, and it converts one part of the globe into a chiefly agricultural field of production for supplying the other part, which remains a pre-eminently industrial field.[217]

Whether enclosures, dispossessions and other conjunctures are part of processes of *original accumulation* or not can only be determined in hindsight and depends on the realisation of the capital-relation in the course of expropriation. The passage from pre-capitalist socio-economic formations to capitalism may be characterised by the Hegelian concept of *Aufhebung* (sublation) that also inspired Marx. The German term has three meanings: to preserve, dissolve/abolish and elevate.

---

rather, that primitive accumulation is an ongoing necessity internal to capitalism, but always anterior to the specific operations of capital. Capital cannot carry out primitive accumulation, even though it needs primitive accumulation in order to create the conditions in which alone it can operate. Hence, capital cannot be the only agent of capitalism; some other agency has to do the dirty work. In the case of England, the original agents of primitive accumulation were the lords of the land. In general, however, the primary agent of primitive accumulation has been and continues to be the state." Roberts, "What was primitive accumulation?," 15.

216 Marx, *Capital*, Vol. 1, 579.

217 Marx, *Capital*, Vol. 1, 579–580.

It can be harnessed to delineate the transitional dynamics: some pre-capitalist elements are being preserved, others dissolve while the development of capitalism may rise to new heights through reproducing "the separation and the independent existence of material wealth as against labour on an ever increasing scale."[218] In effect, the transition period of *original accumulation* is either simultaneously or successively being conserved, removed and/or transformed into capitalist accumulation, thereby creating forms and conditions that can be reproduced on expanded or contracted magnitudes. In the words of Marx: "Accumulation merely presents as a *continuous process* what in *primitive* [original] *accumulation* appears as a distinct historical process, as the process of the emergence of capital and as a transition from one mode of production to another."[219]

Conclusion

It is worth pointing out that Karl Marx's multi-dimensional, complex and dialectical narrative in the so-called *original accumulation* chapter of his magnum opus *Das Kapital* remains an exceptional masterpiece of scholarship that students of the Great Divergence debate would greatly profit from reading, studying, enquiring into and grappling with in detail. One of the reasons why we can still learn immensely from Marx's writings is that he had a very lucid knowledge of the historical epoch in which he was living and an in-depth understanding of the genesis of capitalism. In his own words, "a correct grasp of the present, then also offer the key to the understanding of the past."[220] Furthermore, he was a student of social science in the true sense of the term as he constantly reassessed the empirical and historical bases of his analyses.

What caused the Great Divergence was a combination of convoluted factors, a *global dialectical conjuncture* based on a concatenation of intra-European, extra-European and entangled, long-term, short-term, continuous and contingent factors. Marx gives a glimpse of this, when he argues that the combination of the different moments of *original accumulation*

> ... embraces the colonies, the national debt, the modern tax system, and the system of protection. These methods depend in part on brute force, for instance the colonial system. But they all employ the power of the state, the concentrated and organized force of society, to

---

218 Marx, *Theories of Surplus-Value*, 315.
219 Marx, *Theories of Surplus-Value*, 272.
220 Marx, *Grundrisse*, 461.

> hasten, in a hothouse, the process of transformation of the feudal mode of production into the capitalist mode, and to shorten the transition.[221]

In our view, the lack of holistic approaches or what Marx – under the influence of Hegel – termed totality, is the greatest shortcoming in current debates on the Great Divergence. Deirdre McCloskey, for example, excludes all factors except for liberal ideas and "bourgeois virtues," whereas Sven Beckert argues that "the Great Divergence can largely be explained not by an emphasis on cultural factors, resource endowments, climate, or geography, but by the capacities of states."[222] By contrast, we would like to underscore that, in order to understand the causes of the Great Divergence, a multiplicity of factors must be taken into consideration: 1) geo-climatic conditions, 2) the dynamics of uneven development, agency as well as responses to historical necessities, 3) the level of market integration, wages, living standards and 'human capital' formation, 4) the spread and circulation of information, as well as 'useful knowledge', 5) patterns of both supply and demand, 6) the causes and effects of techno-scientific innovations in comparative perspective, 7) global contexts (e. g. competition in the world market), 8) world-wide exchange and global entanglements (e. g. diffusion of knowledge), 9) the role of the state, institutions and policies 10) the level of production and manufacture, as well as the relationship between productive and unproductive labour, 11) the emergence of capitalism, 12) coercion in its different shades (force, violence, compulsion, etc.) and warfare, 13) culture, 14) the role of chance and accident, etc. These factors need to be incorporated, combined and synthesised into an overarching narrative to do justice to the intricacies at hand. What can be learned from Marx in this context is to distinguish between more or less relevant factors in the making of these processes and better understand how they were interconnected and *articulated*.

Needless to say, Marx was not aware of all the relevant factors behind the rise of the West, the genesis of capitalism, the Industrial Revolution and the

---

221 Marx, *Capital*, Vol. 1, 915. Some pages later he writes: "Colonial system, public debts, heavy taxes, protection, commercial wars, etc., these offshoots of the period of manufacture swell to gigantic proportions during the period of infancy of large-scale industry." Marx, *Capital*, Vol. 1, 922.
222 McCloskey, *Bourgeois Dignity*; Sven Beckert, "The New History of Capitalism," in *Capitalism. The Reemergence of a Historical Concept*, eds. Jürgen Kocka and Marcel van der Linden (London: Bloomsbury Publishing, 2016), 243. One can only recall Marx's emphasis on the importance of cultural and ideological factors. Suffice it to say, he was of the opinion that the "advance of capitalist production develops a working class which by education, tradition and habit looks upon the requirements of that mode of production as self-evident natural laws." Marx, *Capital*, Vol. 1, 899.

Great Divergence, not least because what he tried to unmask in the first place were the underlying causes for the emergence of capitalism in western Europe. Nonetheless, his multi-dimensional and dialectic approach helps in bridging the gap between Eurocentrics and reverse-Orientalists. Chapter Eight of *Capital,* Vol. 1, could serve as a significant source of analysis to break through the polarising and simplistic propositions that have dominated the debate in the past twenty years and bring forward a different reading and understanding of the 'West and the rest' question.

Jorge Grespan

The Renewal of Marxist Historiography through the Study of Enslavement

The Case of Brazil

The pattern of Karl Marx's general criticism on the capitalist system, even more than what he actually wrote about modern slavery, greatly influenced the research on slavery undertaken by a large branch of historiography in the three places in which enslavement of African populations was more extensive and lasting in the American continent, Brazil, the United States and the Caribbean. The fact that in these three areas slavery persisted and even spread out during the nineteenth century, when it was disappearing from other parts of the Atlantic zone, is a paradox that made some historians and social scientists recently return to Marxian dialectics in search of a convincing explanation[1]. Indeed, the contradictory character of capital as defined by Marx explains its tendency to create structures out of opposing parts, like the Atlantic market in the sixteenth century, which then transforms the general structure. This contradictory movement involved both European mother countries and American colonies in an ever-changing whole. Since the twentieth century historians from Brazil, the United States and the Caribbean are therefore engaged in researches that have Marxism as a paradigm. In this chapter, I will concentrate on Brazilian historiography,[2] one of the most productive in regard to the subject of enslavement, and I will refer to the other two historiographical traditions only when necessary for its better understanding.

---

1 I refer here to the perspective inaugurated by the work of Robin Blackburn, *The Making of New World Slavery: From the Baroque to the Modern, 1492–1800* (London: Verso, 1997) and followed by the work of Dale Tomich, *Through the Prism of Slavery: Labor, Capital, and World Economy* (New York: Rowman & Littlefield, 2004). Their idea is that a "Second Slavery" was created in the nineteenth century corresponding to the new industrial capitalism and determining the above mentioned paradox of the renewal of slavery in Brazil, Cuba and the United States. The explanation given by Marx of the Industrial Revolution as a consequence of the establishment of capitalism between the sixteenth and the eighteenth centuries is crucial for Blackburn and Tomich, because it permits determining the continuities and ruptures of the "second" and the "first" slavery. Traditional historians, however, don't see any paradox in the recrudescence of slavery and keep explaining it as a persistence of the old patterns already existant in the three previous centuries.

2 In the footnotes and bibliography, books and articles will be quoted in English when there is an available translation or, if not, in the original edition in Portuguese.

https://doi.org/10.1515/9783110677744-011

My aim here is to show how Brazilian research on slavery can be considered as the unfolding of various analytical possibilities encompassed in Marx's project of a 'critique of political economy'. Each phase of this movement – or rather, each one of the paths it tracked – discloses an aspect already present in Marx's work. The following four sections will explain this development, beginning with the first debates on slavery between Marxist authors and those belonging to what can be called traditional historiography, as well as between Marxists themselves. The second section presents the new forms taken by the debates in university research of the 1960s and 1970s. The third section goes on to explain how criticism of this research in the 1980s and 1990s was partly based on aspects of Marxism rather than on a completely different perspective. If formerly the main purpose of Marxist historians was to describe the connection of slavery with the broader capitalist world system, their later intention was to produce a kind of microhistory that emphasised class struggle and the many features of slave resistance and negotiation between slaves and masters. The fourth and last section analyses the questions and themes propounded by contemporary historians in the twenty-first century in order to show that, even if their research succeeds in deepening and multiplying the fields of knowledge on slavery, it actually performs a synthesis of former trends. Their work executes a permanent move from the macrohistory of the first periods of historiography, centred on the determinations of slavery by the Atlantic trade and by the relationship between the American colonies and the European centres, to the microhistory of slave's daily life in towns or single farms, focused by the mentioned criticism of the 1980s and 1990s.

In summary, the course of Brazilian historiography on enslavement reveals a peculiar and interesting quality of Marxism itself, namely its ability to appear in a variety of forms, and to stir research whose political motivations are either immediate or mediated by academic inquisitiveness. In any case, here again the ideas of Marx proved to constitute a most fertile matrix for explaining the intricate phenomena of modern slavery and its contemporary manifestations.

Slavery as a World System or Mode of Production

Historians inspired by Marxist ideas in Brazil first became involved in the debate on slavery soon after the Russian Revolution of 1917 and the foundation of the Brazilian Communist Party (PCB) in 1922. The essays written initially by members of the PCB, however, were merely attempts to interpret the political and social situation of Brazil according to the canon defined for it by the Third International in Moscow (1919–1943), which adopted an interpretation of world history necessarily passing by the successive stages of slavery, feudalism, capitalism and socialism. According to this view, countries whose mode of production was slavery had to experience feudalism before coming to capitalism and socialism. No original idea was then actually produced by Marxists until 1933, when Caio Prado Jr. (1907–1990) published *A evolução política do Brasil*.[3] In 1942, he developed his central arguments in *Formação do Brasil contemporâneo*.[4] In these two books, slavery was not only dealt with but considered as "what first and foremost characterized Brazilian society at the beginning of nineteenth century", because "wherever this institution has existed, its influence on social life has been unequalled and the role it played in all sectors has been a major one".[5]

With these words, Caio Prado Jr. dismissed decades of traditional historiography in Brazil that minimised the importance of slavery or its oppressive nature and which, even favouring its abolition, had an undeniably racist character.[6] The Marxist view of Caio Prado Jr. led him to put the abolition question not in terms of a conflict between humanitarian principles and pragmatic interests, but rather as a struggle between two different economic and political projects of the nineteenth century: one proposing to keep slaves as the cheapest labourers for export agriculture; the other maintaining that slaves were not the most profitable kind of labour power for export agriculture or for the other productive branches of a growing and modernising economy. The Marxist view led Caio Prado Jr. to see slavery as a whole way of life rather than a mere economic device, secondary among other social institutions.

However, a note must be introduced here on another book published in 1933 by a historian who, together with Caio Prado Jr., revolutionised the conventional approach to the question of slavery in Brazil. Its author, Gilberto Freyre (1900–1987), studied anthropology with Franz Boas at Columbia University, New York,

---

3 Caio Prado Jr., *A evolução política do Brasil* (São Paulo: Revista dos Tribunais, 1933).

4 Caio Prado Jr., *The Colonial Background of Modern Brazil* (Los Angeles: University of California Press, 1967).

5 Caio Prado Jr., *The Colonial Background of Modern Brazil* (Los Angeles: University of California Press, 1967), 313.

6 The debate on the necessity either of abolishing or of maintaining slavery began by the middle of the nineteenth century in Brazil, producing as its most important works: *A escravidão no Brasil* (1866) by Perdigão Malheiro (1824–1881), and *Abolicionismo* (1883) by Joaquim Nabuco (1849–1910). The greatest historian of the next generation, Capistrano de Abreu (1853–1927), although very much sympathetic to the indigenous population of Brazil, scarcely mentions African slaves in his celebrated book, *Capítulos de história colonial*, published in 1907. Historians contemporary of Caio Prado Jr. were either openly conservative, as Pedro Calmon (1902–1985), in *História da Civilização Brasileira* (1932), or openly racist, as Oliveira Viana (1883–1951) in *Evolução do Povo Brasileiro* (1923).

in the 1920s and wrote *Casa Grande e Senzala*[7] with the aim of underlining the patriarchal character of Brazilian society, in which African slavery was a significant feature. Half of his book is dedicated to the study of "the negro slave in the sexual and family life of the Brazilian", representing a positive image of integration of Africans through interracial crossing and the possibility of individual manumission given to former slaves. Freyre thus contrasted the open and flexible model of Iberian slavery with the rigid Anglo-Saxon model, which barred miscegenation and social contact between white and black people.[8]

This contrast of the two models presented the risk of creating an attenuated image of slavery in Brazil that did not recognise the ruthless exploitation intrinsic to it. Although not criticising Freyre directly, Caio Prado Jr. stressed the brutal side of slavery present in the 'sexual and family life' of the big patriarchal landowners. Masters often subjected enslaved women to sexual abuses, preventing a true racial or cultural integration of the African within the Brazilian 'family'.[9] Instead of being a positive sign of the inclusion of Africans in the population of Brazil, interracial crossing was realised through violent abuse. This specifically targeted slave women, but also served to terrorise slaves in general and keep them fearful. It was a crucial component of a mode of production based on brutality towards the worker.

Unlike other historians of his time, Caio Prado Jr. conceived the colonisation of the Americas and of Brazil in particular as essential to the European mercantile expansion inaugurated by Portugal in the fifteenth century. Inserted in the 'commercial enterprise', slavery was decisive in providing the necessary labour power for production of tropical commodities sold in Europe at a very high price, first by the Portuguese and later by the Spanish, Dutch, French and British. In this way, the original people of America, mistakenly called 'Indians' by the arriving Europeans, were the first to be enslaved. But as soon as the Portuguese grasped the enormous profits they could obtain from the slave trade, they began to buy slaves on the African coast and sell them to settlers of the At-

---

7 Gilberto Freyre, *The Masters and the Slaves. A study in the development of Brazilian Civilization* (New York: Alfred Knopf, 1946).

8 In his 1946 book *Slave and Citizen*, the historian Frank Tannenbaum (1893–1967) took from Freyre this idea of an Anglo-Saxon closed system of slavery opposed to an open Iberian model.

9 "The other function of the slave, or rather of the female slave, that mere instrument for the satisfaction of her lord and master's sexual needs ... did not go beyond the crude and purely animal level of sexual contact" and, as a result, "Contrary to what is now usually affirmed, the formation of Brazil was not based on the family unit, save in the limited and ... sadly deficient case of the upper class Big House". Caio Prado Jr., *The Colonial Background of Modern Brazil*, 401–409.

lantic islands and later, Brazil. Caio Prado Jr. described how the export of products like sugarcane, tobacco and cotton to Europe involved millions of slaves in the Americas. He explained that it was not by chance that the slave trade became the main commercial branch during colonial times and afterwards,[10] until it ended in 1850.

It was precisely these commercial bonds between Portugal, Brazil and Africa that determined the general structure of the colonial system, according to Caio Prado Jr., in spite of his rich description of the conditions of work and life of the slaves within the colony. The mode of immediate production, the forms of labour inside the colony, should only be understood through their insertion in the major framework of the Atlantic trade.[11] This point of view would lead Caio Prado Jr. to an inevitable conflict with the official interpretation of the Communist Party. It is necessary here to examine this question in more detail.

The industrialisation of Brazil, starting at the time of World War I and accelerating after the end of World War II, gave a renewed meaning and relevance to the concept of *mode of production*. The transition from one mode of production to another was a strategic question in Marxist debates all over the world.[12] In Brazil, it defined the tactic of the PCB to establish alliances with other political parties favourable to industrialisation, in order to foster capitalist modernisation as a necessary precondition for a socialist revolution. For many Marxist historians close to the PCB, slavery should then be considered as a mode of production that would eventually be surpassed by feudalism and capitalism. That was especially the case of Nelson Werneck Sodré (1911–1999), whose books *Panorama do Segundo Império* and *Formação Histórica do Brasil*, published respectively in

---

10 "The most important branch of the import trade was, however, the traffic in slaves brought to Brazil from the African coast… . Slaves made up more than a quarter of the colony's imports. This figure confirms what has been said about the nature of the Brazilian economy: the Negro slave means sugar, cotton, gold – export commodities". Caio Prado Jr., *The Colonial Background of Modern Brazil*, 270.

11 "The analysis of a country's commercial structure always reveals, more clearly than any individual analysis of particular sectors of production, the essential character and organization of an economy. It provides a synthesis which both summarizes and explains this economy"; in the case of Brazil, "The direction of trade is clearly evident: outgoing tropical staples, gold and diamonds, are destined via the mother country for international commerce. This is the axis of colonial activities around which all the other elements rotate". Caio Prado Jr., *The Colonial Background of Modern Brazil*, 265, 274.

12 The eventual transition from capitalism to socialism triggered in the 1950s the famous debate of the transition from feudalism to capitalism, with articles written to the review *Science & Society* by eminent Marxists like Maurice Dobb (1900–1976), Paul Sweezy (1910–2004) and Christopher Hill (1912–2003). The global character of the issue was evident by the participation in the debate of the Japanese Marxist Kohashiro Takahashi (1912–1982).

1939 and 1960,[13] have as their central concept slavery as a mode of production from which the other features of the colonial system, like colonial trade and slave trade, must be deduced. Werneck Sodré was in tune with the issues of that time, and with the international debates on the capitalist transition. For him, the mode of production based on slavery was supplanted in Brazil around the end of the nineteenth century by a feudal mode of production, which should in turn be succeeded by a capitalist one.

For Caio Prado Jr., on the contrary, the form of labour adopted in Brazil was not decisive to determine the mode of production. The fact that slaves were employed for such a long time did not mean that they ought to be replaced by feudal serfs or by wage labourers as a necessary step on the way to socialism. As a part of the Atlantic commercial system, Brazil would have always been a capitalist economy, even when slaves or compulsory workers of other kinds were employed.

In the 1960s, above all after the military *coup d'état* of 1964,[14] the ideas of Werneck Sodré and Caio Prado Jr. were debated from the perspective of how their possible misinterpretations prevented an effective political reaction to the coup. The debate resulted in the publication of *A revolução brasileira* (1966) by Caio Prado Jr., as a response to Werneck Sodré's book *Formação Histórica do Brasil*.[15] But by that time, another element had appeared in the intellectual Marxist milieu, completely changing the perspective of research on slavery – university studies.

The Beginning of Academic Research on Slavery

As remarked in the aforementioned section, after World War II the industrialisation of Brazil and other Latin American countries, such as Argentina and Mexico, greatly modified the issues at stake for their historians and sociologists. A

13 Nelson Werneck Sodré, *Panorama do Segundo Império* (São Paulo: Companhia editora nacional, 1939). Nelson Werneck Sodré, *Formação histórica do Brasil* (São Paulo: Brasiliense, 1960).
14 Immediately after the coup d'état of 1964 the new military government did not take intense actions against Marxist intellectuals. In the following years, however, especially after the University Reform of 1969, academics who criticized the government were considered politically dangerous by the military and were fired from their chairs in public universities all over Brazil. That was the case of Emília Viotti da Costa, Florestan Fernandes, Paul Singer, Otávio Ianni, Fernando Henrique Cardoso, José Arthur Giannotti and many others. Marxist inspired research on slavery was then clearly jeopardised but not completely hindered.
15 Caio Prado Jr, *A revolução brasileira* (São Paulo: Brasiliense, 1966).

new trend of opinion and policy making emerged, whose main idea was that Latin America was now able to recover from centuries of underdevelopment and catch up with the richest countries of the world. This trend was soon called 'developmentalism'[16] and had its central agency in the UN Economic Commission for Latin America and the Caribbean (CEPAL). Almost immediately, a criticism of this optimistic view also emerged, expounding what would be known as the 'dependency theory'.[17] For its supporters, close to the standpoint of Caio Prado Jr., capitalism must be understood as a world system in which each part had a function determined mainly by the whole and not by itself. It would then be an impossible task for Latin America to simply catch up with the most advanced capitalist countries; history could never be conceived as a marathon in which countries and people individually run towards the goal of development as if they were unrelated to each other.

The debate between these two contrary positions continued in the 1950s and 1960s, impacting research about modes of production and slavery. The question for followers both of 'developmentalism' and 'dependency theory' was: Could the predominance of slavery for such a long time in the past prevent modernisation in the present? Not only individual investigators but also political parties and research institutes[18] took part in the debate. It acquired a particular feature in universities. Brazilian universities were adapting their structures of teaching and research to the requirements of industrialisation, and in the field of social sciences and history this meant a reorientation towards diversifying theoretical references and adopting empirical methods. Instead of long and comprehensive attempts to understand Brazilian history as a whole, typical of the former literature, academic research began to focus on the peculiar, that is regional, local and temporal differences.

In this new moment, the University of São Paulo played the most significant role. From the end of the 1950s to the 1970s, a circle of researchers gathered around professor Florestan Fernandes (1920 – 1995) in order to investigate slavery and its consequences for twentieth century Brazilian society. Fernandes himself had started with an ethnological study of the culture of native Brazilians. He pro-

---

16 Free translation from "desenvolvimentismo" in Portuguese, or "desarrollismo" in Spanish.

17 Among the most renowned supporters of this theory are Brazilian authors like Ruy Mauro Marini (1932 – 1997), Theotônio dos Santos (1936 – 2018) and Vânia Bambirra (1940 – 2015); the non-Brazilian André Gunder Frank (1929 – 2005) must also be mentioned here.

18 The most important research institute of the time was the IBESP (Instituto Brasileiro de Economia, Sociologia e Política) attached to the Ministry of Education and Culture and transformed in 1955 to ISEB (Instituto Superior de Estudos Brasileiros). ISEB lasted until 1964, when the military dictatorship established in that year obliged it to close.

duced this under the supervision of Roger Bastide (1898–1974), who had come to the University of São Paulo in 1938 with a group of young French professors that included Claude Lévi-Strauss (1908–2009) and Fernand Braudel (1902–1985). While still under the influence of Bastide, who held the chair of sociology at the University of São Paulo until 1954, Fernandes turned to an analysis of how and to what extent the descendants of enslaved Africans were integrated in a society that saw itself as predominantly white. His object was not exactly slavery itself but the period subsequent to its abolition and the struggle of emancipated slaves and their children to be accepted as free workers in the first half of the twentieth century.

As a result of these studies, Fernandes published *A integração do negro na sociedade de classes*[19] in 1964 and *O negro no mundo dos brancos* in 1972.[20] Both books analysed ethnic and class aspects in close connection, without confusing the correspondent sociological categories. Empirical research about the city of São Paulo allowed Fernandes to derive important conclusions about the persistence of slavery – not only in the economic and juridical realms but also in the mentality of employers, who, for instance, refused to give black workers the jobs given to white workers, or, when they did so, refused to pay black workers the same wages as those paid to the whites. Ethnic and social class categories had to be crossed in order to grasp their dynamics.[21] If Afro-Brazilians were considered inferior because their ancestors had been enslaved, that situation should have disappeared with the official abolition of slavery in 1888. However, economic changes occurred faster than sociocultural and psychosocial adjustments. These analytical results were possible even within the general framework of Marxism, but of a Marxism decided to overcome the theorem of base and superstructure, according to the so called Western Marxism[22] that was soon going to make its entrance in Brazilian intellectual scenario.

The concept of different rhythms for economic and socio-psychologic events was also central in one of Fernandes' former books, *Mudanças sociais no Brasil*,

19 Florestan Fernandes, *The Negro in Brazilian Society* (New York: Columbia University Press, 1969).

20 Florestan Fernandes, *O negro no mundo dos brancos* (São Paulo: Difusão europeia do livro, 1972).

21 "In the sphere of race relations, the class society is becoming an open social system, but the patterns of racial domination inherited from the past are not being updated". Fernandes, *The Negro in Brazilian Society*, 380.

22 For the definition of "Western Marxism," see Perry Anderson, *Considerations on Western Marxism* (London: New Left Books, 1976).

published in 1960.[23] Here slavery was dealt with directly, with Fernandes arguing that it was crucial for understanding the modernisation and industrialisation of Brazil. The developmentalist thesis was confronted with evidence of how policies and mentalities reluctant to accept new social conditions can impede the construction of a competitive capitalist economy. Although this reasoning is apparently grounded on the mentioned Marxist difference between base and superstructure, it operates in a complex way, for which the essential point is the diversity of spheres and their temporalities, rather than ideological phenomena being simply caused by socioeconomic conditions. To establish this point, Fernandes avoided holding on strictly to Marxism and integrated elements of other sociological traditions, especially that of Max Weber but also Karl Mannheim and Émile Durkheim, in order to complement his analysis of social groups with a psychosocial and cultural approach.[24] The integrated elements must be, however, comprised within the framework of social class and class conflict, which ultimately defines the field of emerging contradictions and the resulting differentiation of phenomena in time and space.

Difference in rhythms constitutes an important insight in Fernandes' research programme, developed in subsequent years by himself and by the circle of his assistant professors at the University of São Paulo. While Fernandes was concentrating on the analysis of ethnic and social groups in the state of São Paulo, Octavio Ianni (1926–2004) and Fernando Henrique Cardoso (born 1931) were focusing on the analysis of slavery and ethnic relations in the South of Brazil. Regional diversity is crucial in these case studies, in which particular forms of economic life and colonisation determine particular patterns of social and ethnic relations as much as the dynamics of their change.[25]

---

23 Florestan Fernandes, *Mudanças sociais no Brasil: aspectos do desenvolvimento da sociedade brasileira* (São Paulo: Difusão Europeia do Livro, 1960).

24 Fernandes, *Mudanças sociais no Brasil* (São Paulo, DIFEL: 1960). It must be observed here that in specifically analysing Brazilian society of the colonial era and the nineteenth century, Fernandes denies the possibility of applying the concept of social "class" to it, instead reserving the term for the capitalist society that was just emerging in Brazil at that time. For him and his followers, the most adequate concept for grasping the condition of slaves and masters is "status", reassuming and applying the definition of "Stand" by Max Weber. The difficult condition of black people in twentieth-century Brazil is then caused by the transition from a status to a class position.

25 Octavio Ianni and Fernando Henrique Cardoso, *Cor e mobilidade social em Florianópolis* (São Paulo: Companhia Editora Nacional, 1960). Octavio Ianni, *Raças e classes sociais no Brasil* (Rio de Janeiro: Civilização Brasileira, 1966). Fernando Henrique Cardoso, *Capitalismo e escravidão no Brasil Meridional* (São Paulo: DIFEL, 1962). Fernando Henrique Cardoso later turned to the study of "dependency theory" and wrote with the Chilean sociologist Enzo Falleto (1935–

Another branch of this programme investigated the social condition of the class composed by poor freemen who were neither slaves nor slave owners. The question was also rooted in the writings of Fernandes, and was the subject of Maria Sylvia de Carvalho Franco's book *Homens livres na ordem escravocrata*, published in 1969 and dedicated to her supervisor Fernandes.[26] There she analyses how the social position of free poor people in the nineteenth century and beginning of the twentieth century was negatively defined by slavery as if this position rested on non-belonging to a binary world. Social disarray was just another manifestation of the discrepancy already observed by Fernandes in the rhythms, spaces and life spheres of a society that, like the Brazilian, had been for such a long time grounded in slavery.

But even more so than social scientists, historians of the University of São Paulo also inspired by Marxism produced at that time important works for understanding slavery and its consequences to Brazil. One of them was Fernando Novais (born 1933), who reassumed the argument of Caio Prado Jr. about the role of colonial Atlantic trade in determining slavery in general, and proposed that the slave trade must be considered the crucial element of this economic system. In his book *Portugal e Brasil na crise do antigo sistema colonial*, published in 1979 after long research, Novais stated that the decision to enslave Africans rather than the original inhabitants of Brazil was determined by the interests of European merchants. The key element here was the high profits rendered by the slave trade between the coasts of Africa and Brazil as early as the sixteenth century. The original inhabitants met by the Portuguese in their South American colony were also enslaved, but their price was lower than that of enslaved Africans because the price of the latter incorporated the costs and risks of the long and dangerous journey across the South Atlantic Ocean. Hence, only the poorest parts of the colony employed enslaved 'Indians'; for the richest colonists, on the contrary, the choice was always for enslaved Africans who were also considered to be better workers. Novais proposes that the crucial role of the slave trade reveals the capitalist character of modern slavery insofar as the enslaved was a commodity, and concludes, "paradoxically, slave trade explains and determines African slavery, not the converse".[27]

Novais thus made an important contribution to the debate on modes of production, defending the thesis that the specific forms of labour adopted in Brazil

---

2003), the book *Dependency and Development in Latin America* (Los Angeles: University of California Press, 1979).

26 Maria Sylvia de C. Franco, *Homens livres na ordem escravocrata* (São Paulo: IEB/USP, 1969).

27 Fernando Novais, *Portugal e Brasil na crise do antigo sistema colonial* (São Paulo: Hucitec, 1979), 105. My translation.

were determined not by internal conditions alone but mainly by the insertion of the country within the broader system of Atlantic trade. He synthesised the ideas of Caio Prado Jr., Braudel (who had come with French colleagues to the University of São Paulo in 1937, as mentioned in the aforementioned section) and the Caribbean historian Eric Williams (1911–1981), whose influential work[28] Novais helped introduce in Brazil. More than just a synthesis, however, Novais added his proposition about slave trade to the perspective of the former authors, emphasising the point of view they all have in common.

To all the works produced in this first period of academic historiography, Marxism furnished categories and questions. Notwithstanding the different answers given to these questions, every historical description of slavery conceived it as a social structure pervaded by contradictions within itself and in its relationship to the broader capitalism system. Particularly important was to respond to the question of how compulsory labour could have existed and been functional to capitalism in Europe, a place in which labour power was increasingly turning to wage labour. In the context of Brazil, this question should generate several other questions: Was this contradiction between capitalism and slavery a determining factor in the demise of slavery? Does it mean that Brazilian society would also develop a purely class organisation, modernise its institutions and become an industrialised country? What, then, would be the position of Afro-descendants within this new order? To all these questions university research could give more and more specific answers, leading academics to gradually give up any hope of a unified solution. The next period would reinforce this tendency, creating fresh perspectives.

From Economic to Social History

In Brazil, a strong criticism of the previous Marxist historiography on slavery prevailed chiefly in the 1980s and 1990s, but the shift in focus from external determinations to internal conditions had actually begun earlier, with two books that, published in the late 1960s, kept a relative distance from the traditional debate on the modes of production. Writing at a similar time on a similar subject, Emília Viotti da Costa (1928–2017) and Paula Beiguelman (1926–2009) addressed the conditions that led to the abolition of slavery in Brazil.

---

28 Eric Williams, *Capitalism and Slavery* (Chapel Hill: University of North Carolina Press, 1944). The influence especially of this book on Brazilian historiography testifies to the mutual connections, mentioned above, between historians from Brazil, the Caribbean and the United States.

Emília Viotti da Costa restored the argument advanced by Caio Prado Jr. and Williams about the incompatibility of the development of industrial capitalism in England with slavery in the Americas in order to explain the long and persistent opposition of the British to the slave trade – opposition that finally led to the effective eradication by the Brazilian government of this 'infamous trade' in 1850. In a book published in 1966, *Da Senzala à Colônia*, Viotti da Costa says: "Not only the legitimacy but also the productivity of slave labour power begun to be put into question".[29] This statement was completed in another book *Da monarquia à república*, published in 1977,[30] in which Viotti da Costa refers to the British public opinion of the time:

> To some, the existence of millions of slaves in colonial areas seemed to contradict their fundamental liberal ideas – a moral outrage. To others, it seemed an obstacle to the expansion of the markets for manufactured products. From this point on slavery, as a system, was doomed.[31]

It was a new statement of the relevance of economic elements over humanitarian ones for the emancipation of slaves. Viotti da Costa proceeds to a detailed exposition of the political and economic circumstances of the end of slavery after the slave trade was abolished. She focuses on the contrast between the two richest plantation areas of that time in Brazil, namely the Vale do Paraíba – a valley situated between São Paulo and Rio de Janeiro, where coffee plantations were older and used masses of slaves – and the 'New West' in the interior of the state of São Paulo – where coffee plantations were recent and the transition from using slaves to employing wage labour had begun. The contrast between these two places was accentuated when the end of the slave trade raised the prices of African slaves so much that plantations newly established in the west of São Paulo could no longer afford to buy them and had to experiment with other forms of labour power. This economic divergence created a political opposition according to which representatives of the New West in the Brazilian Parliament of the time tended to be liberal, favouring the abolition of the slave trade and slavery in general. Indeed, they formed a political tendency acting on the domestic front in the

29 Emília Viotti da Costa, *Da Senzala à Colônia* (São Paulo: Difusão Europeia do Livro, 1966), 30.

30 Emília Viotti da Costa, *Da monarquia à república* (São Paulo: Grijalbo, 1977). English translation: *The Brazilian Empire, Myths and Histories* (Chicago: The University of Chicago Press, 1985).

31 Emília Viotti da Costa, *The Brazilian Empire, Myths and Histories* (Chicago: The University of Chicago Press, 1985), 125.

same direction as Britain on the external front. More than merely reinforcing British external pressure, however, internal politics proved to be decisive, states Viotti da Costa.

This argument was also advanced by Paula Beiguelman in her book *A formação do povo no complexo cafeeiro: aspectos politicos*, published in 1968.[32] At the very outset she proposes a refinement of Viotti da Costa's thesis about the political constitution of the New West' of São Paulo, and then makes an important objection to the idea that the development of industrial capitalism in England was incompatible with modern slavery in the Americas. Beiguelman traces an initial distinction between older and newer areas inside the New West, dealt with as homogeneous by Viotti da Costa. She is, therefore, able to explain more accurately the political attitudes and positions of the representatives of each area in the Parliament. For the older areas, the suppression of the slave trade meant valorisation of the slaves already in their possession and the possibility of selling them at a higher price to farmers of the newer areas. Consequently, their deputies in the national Parliament pressed for the approval of laws that would only step by step abolish slavery. Once they succeeded, however, political conditions changed completely.

Beiguelman begins the second proposition by recalling the definition of a 'slave' as more than a compulsory worker: a slave is a commodity that can be bought and sold. When the abolition of the African slave trade in 1850 removed the possibility of buying and selling slaves, at least on the Atlantic market, there was no longer a difference between slaves and other kinds of compulsory workers, rendering it a matter of indifference whether the colonial system continued to operate with this form of cheap labour. External British pressure abruptly diminished and Beiguelman could explain the gradual abolition of slavery that took place in Brazil between 1850 and 1888 as a result of the internal politics described in the aforementioned section. Therefore, for Beiguelman, it was not slavery itself but the slave trade that was incompatible with the development of capitalism in the mother countries of Europe.

This shift from the external to the internal scenario of Brazil was completed in the 1980s by another shift, the one from economic to social history. Viotti da Costa and Beiguelman had already changed the focus from economic to political conditions. However, new trends in world historiography were emphasising social and anthropological aspects of daily life more than the political ones strictly related to state institutions. At the beginning of the 1980s, with the decline of military dictatorship in Brazil, historians were feeling the full impact of the

32 Paula Beiguelman, *A formação do povo no complexo cafeeiro* (São Paulo: Pioneira, 1968).

so-called third generation of the French Annales School and of the Italian microhistory best represented by the work of Carlo Ginzburg (born 1939). A new perspective on slavery was then formulated in Brazil, but Marxism again furnished important concepts for this innovative research. Under the influence of the British New Left, especially Edward P. Thompson (1924–1993), and also of the Frankfurt School, above all Walter Benjamin (1892–1940) and his *On the Concept of History*, relevant works were written on slavery in the last two decades of the twentieth century in Brazil. As will be seen in the following section, they argued that the abolition of slavery was neither a demand and a need of world capitalism nor an interest of Brazilian landowners, but a consequence of the struggle for freedom of the enslaved themselves.

A last but not unimportant shift that must be indicated in this new phase of academic research in Brazil is its dissemination beyond São Paulo to other places like the universities of Rio de Janeiro, Minas Gerais, Campinas and Bahia. One of the first and most representative works of this period was *Slave Rebellion in Brazil: the African Muslim Uprising in Bahia in 1835*, written by João José Reis (born 1952) as a PhD thesis for the University of Minnesota in 1982 and published by him as professor of the University of Bahia in 1986.[33] The book describes the most important urban slave upheaval that took place on the American continent. In 1835 the so-called 'Malês' – African Muslims enslaved in Benin and brought to Bahia – rebelled in the city of Salvador, prompting a sharp and definitive change in governmental procedures towards slaves in Brazil. Reis reconstitutes facts from testimony given by the rebels themselves when they were later put on trial; he then inserts their testimony within the social and economic context of the time, constantly going from the general level of structures to the particular level of slaves' narratives.[34] It is an effort to make the enslaved speak, clearly spurred by Benjamin's proposition of "brushing history against the grain", thus inverting the traditional "process of transmission" of his-

---

33 João José Reis, *Slave Rebellion in Brazil: The African Muslim Uprising in Bahia in 1835* (Baltimore: John Hopkins University Press, 1993). The Thesis was later published in Brazil as: *Rebelião escrava no Brasil, a história do Levante dos Malês* (São Paulo: Brasiliense, 1986).

34 From this author, see also: João José Reis, *Liberdade por um fio. História dos Quilombos no Brasil* (São Paulo: Companhia das Letras, 1996); João José Reis, *Death is a festival: Funeral rites and rebellion in nineteenth century Brazil* (Chapel Hill: North Carolina University Press, 2003). And together with other two authors: João José Reis, Flávio Gomes and Marcus Carvalho, *O Alufá Ruffino. Tráfico, escravidão e liberdade no Atlântico Negro – 1822–1853* (São Paulo: Companhia das Letras, 2010).

tory, that is to say, instead of "empathizing with the victor", "materialist historians" must empathise with the defeated.[35]

Another good representative of this fresh trend of investigation on slavery was a new book by Emília Viotti da Costa. After the abovementioned book of 1966,[36] she was dismissed by the military dictatorship from her chair at the University of São Paulo and had to go into exile. She became a professor at Yale University in the United States, and there she wrote *Crowns of Glory, Tears of Blood: The Demerara Slave Rebellion of 1823.*[37] This work, published in 1994, took as its subject a slave rebellion in British Guiana that exposed the deep conflict between masters and slaves. What she offered here was not long-term analysis but a narrative of individual events and actions that exposed the profound contradictions of a society in which real people lived and acted. The general name of the first two chapters is, precisely, "contradictory worlds",[38] showing the large scope and expressive potential of the Marxist concept, since the "contradiction" of the first "world" and chapter concerns "planters and missionaries" while that of the second "world" and chapter concerns "masters and slaves". This last contradiction corresponds to the Marxist concepts of social class and class struggle, and constitutes for Viotti da Costa the fundamental cleavage from which the first one can be established. Yet, it would be impossible to explain the events in Demerara without the "contradiction between planters and missionaries". The word is given again to the actors of the real drama, especially to the "defeated" rebel slaves whose testimony in the trials that followed the events of 1823 is carefully analysed. Once again, as in the book by Reis, one can find here a concept of history that must, in the words of Benjamin, "appropriate a memory as it flashes up in a moment of danger", namely "the danger of becoming a tool of the ruling classes".[39] This is clearly proposed by Viotti da Costa when she asserts that "crises are moments of truth".[40]

---

35 Walter Benjamin, "On the Concept of History," *Selected Writings*, vol. 4 (Cambridge, MA: Harvard University Press), 391–392.

36 Emília Viotti da Costa, *Da senzala à colônia*. São Paulo: Difusão Europeia do Livro, 1966.

37 Emília Viotti da Costa, *Crowns of Glory, Tears of Blood: The Demerara Slave Rebellion of 1823* (Oxford: Oxford University Press, 1994).

38 The full title of the first chapter is "Contradictory Worlds: Planters and Missionaries," and the full title of the second chapter is "Contradictory Worlds: Masters and Slaves".

39 Benjamin, "On the Concept of History," 391. Although neither Viotti da Costa nor Reis quotes Benjamin directly, their approach is evidently inspired by Benjamin's concepts of "materialism" and "class struggle, which for an historian schooled in Marx is always in evidence" (Benjamin, "On the Concept of History," 390).

40 Viotti da Costa, *Crowns of Glory, Tears of Blood*, xiii (introduction). The text continues: "They [crises] bring to light the conflicts that in daily life are buried beneath the rules and routines of

In a slightly different perspective, other works were written by that time, inspired by the British historian E. P. Thompson and his *Making of English Working Class* of 1963. Instead of the industrial workers in their daily life and culture, Brazilian historians focused on the routines and rituals of slaves in their ordinary working day. This was a special feature of the book *Campos da violência*, published in 1988 by Silvia Hunold Lara (born 1955), professor at the University of Campinas. Slavery is studied here through the punishment by which the enslaved was normally compelled to work; but not punishment as an arbitrary practice, rather as a rule instituted by laws and enforced by justice courts. Hunold Lara concentrated her analysis on the sugar plantations of Rio de Janeiro's rural areas between 1750 and 1808, but derived from it general conclusions about the 'contradictory' policy of violence and paternalism of Brazilian masters, and of the resistance and accommodations by enslaved Africans.[41] The Marxist concept of class struggle once more underlies this characterisation, but from a quite original standpoint that stresses the dialectics by which the extremes of terror and profit calculation could be balanced in the daily discipline of domination and labour. Through it, the system of production obviously attempted to avoid slave revolts. But a distinctive aspect of Hunold Lara's study was "scrutinizing practices, customs, fights, resistances, accommodations, and solidarities present in the daily life of those men and women"[42] as a way to describe how the system actually worked.

Other works were inspired by the same motive. Sidney Chalhoub (born 1957), professor at the University of Campinas, published *Visões da liberdade* in 1990. Like his colleagues, he quoted Thompson in his introduction in order to defend an anti-economist Marxism, open to the cultural and anthropological dimensions of class struggle.[43] Chalhoub also focuses on a particular case, namely the city of Rio de Janeiro in the decades before the abolition of slavery and the different status of free poor people, recently emancipated slaves and the enslaved that were fighting for their freedom. This issue was also pursued by Hebe Mattos de Castro in her 1995 book *As cores do silêncio*. She investigates here "the meanings of freedom" in the plantations of the Brazilian Southeast during the nineteenth century with the aim of revealing the multiplicity of significances

---

social protocol, behind the gestures that people make automatically, without thinking of their meanings and purposes. In such moments the contradictions that lay behind the rhetoric of social harmony, consensus, hegemony, or control are exposed," xiii–xiv.

41 Silvia Hunold Lara, *Campos da violência* (São Paulo: Paz e Terra, 1988), 115–123.

42 Hunold Lara, *Campos da violência*, 341.

43 Sidney Chalhoub, *Visões da liberdade* (São Paulo: Companhia das Letras, 1990), 23.

the word freedom could have for different social groups of slaves or poor white people.[44]

Many other examples could be given to characterise the trend followed by Brazilian historians after 1980 in their research on enslavement.[45] For all of them, emancipation is a result of the struggle of the enslaved and not a concession due to the indulgence of the powerful. More than general schemes, individual stories were brought to light to show how in real life a balance between compromise and conflict was precariously established, only to be broken in moments of crisis. Marxism was still a model and theoretical context for many historians of that time, but it was a Marxism much closer to the New Left and Frankfurt School paradigms of social history than to the older one attached to the political and economic questions of national modernisation and bourgeois revolution. In a certain sense, this new approach was irreversible.

Contemporary Tendencies

Historical research in the twenty-first century retains many traits of the preceding period. Narrative and a concern for individual situations still predominate in the work mostly produced in universities, whose goal is making documents known to the general public as much as providing future academics with more information for their own investigations. Some historians mentioned in the previous section are still pursuing their original lines of research: for example, Silvia Hunold Lara, João Reis and Sidney Chalhoub.[46] Others associated with them in researching slavery include Gustavo Pacheco,[47] Flávio Gomes and Marcus Carvalho,[48] and Gladys Ribeiro and Martha Abreu.[49]

44 Hebe Mattos de Castro, *As cores do silêncio* (Rio de Janeiro: Arquivo Nacional, 1995).

45 Some authors that must also be mentioned are: Beatriz Mamigonian, *Africanos livres. A abolição do tráfico de escravos no Brasil* (São Paulo: Companhia das Letras, 2017); Flávio dos Santos Gomes, *Histórias de quilombolas: mocambos e comunidades de senzalas no Rio de Janeiro, século XIX* (Rio de Janeiro: Arquivo Nacional, 1995) and Luiz Geraldo Silva, "Esperança de liberdade. Interpretações populares da abolição ilustrada (1773–1774)," *Revista de História* 144 (2001): 107.

46 Apart from the many articles these three historians have written for specialized journals, they have also published new books. Hunold Lara, *Fragmentos setecentistas: escravidão, cultura e poder na América portuguesa* (São Paulo: Companhia das Letras, 2007). Sidney Chalhoub, *A força da escravidão: ilegalidade e costume no Brasil setecentista* (São Paulo: Companhia das Letras, 2012). And For João José Reis see footnote 26.

47 Hunold Lara and Gustavo Pacheco, *Memória do jongo* (Rio de Janeiro: Folha Seca, 2007).

48 Flàvio Gomes and Marcus Carvalho, "África e Brasil entre margens: aventuras e desventuras do africano Rufino José Maria, c. 1822–1853," *Estudos Afro-asiáticos* 26 (2004): 257–303.

The work of historians at the University of Rio de Janeiro has also been very important, in particular that of João Fragoso (born 1958) and Manolo Florentino (born 1958), who since the 1990s have contested traditional views about slavery and colonial Brazil. In 1993, Florentino and Fragoso published a significant book together, *O arcaísmo como projeto*, which was followed in 1998 by Fragoso's *Homens de grossa Aventura*.[50] They refute mainly Caio Prado Jr. for the emphasis he placed on external trade to explain the meaning of colonisation. Instead, Fragoso and Florentino note how the accumulation of capital in colonial Brazil had internal causes and how part of the capital generated by slave labour remained within the colony. Their current work intensifies this line of criticism, as can be observed from the two chapters they wrote in 2011 for *The Cambridge World History of Slavery*, edited by David Eltis and Stanley Engerman. Together with Ana Rios, Fragoso describes the important role slaves played in the political game of Brazilian elites in the colonial era, occasionally even serving their masters as warriors in the struggle for regional power. In another chapter of the book, Florentino and Márcia Amantino reveal how slaves resisted the system by running away from plantations and founding communities of freemen in the Brazilian hinterland – the 'quilombos'. In both texts a sort of political turn is discernible as they depict enslavement more as a power relationship than an economic bond between masters and compulsory workers.[51] Yet this shift cannot be discerned in the work of another historian of Rio de Janeiro, Marcelo Badaró Mattos (born 1966). For example, his book *Escravizados e livres*, published in 2008, also takes account of individual stories of slaves and workers, but never loses sight of the fundamental economic basis of the system of slavery in which violence is but a means of keeping workers submissive and productive.[52]

Against the backdrop of these lines of inquiry, a new field emerged with the book *O trato dos viventes*, published in 2000 by Luiz Felipe de Alencastro (born

---

49 Gladys Ribeiro and Martha Abreu, *Escravidão e cultura afro-brasileira* (Campinas: Ed. Unicamp, 2016).

50 João Fragoso and Manolo Florentino, *O arcaísmo como projeto* (Rio de Janeiro: Civilização Brasileira, 1993). João Fragoso, *Homens de grossa aventura* (Rio de Janeiro: Civilização Brasileira, 1998).

51 João Fragoso and Ana Rios, "Slavery and Politics in Colonial Portuguese America: The Sixteenth to the Eighteenth Centuries," in *The Cambridge World History of Slavery*, eds. David Eltis and Stanley Engerman (Cambridge: Cambridge University Press, 2011), 350 – 377. Manolo Florentino and Márcia Amantino, "Runaways and *quilombolas* in the Americas," in *The Cambridge World History of Slavery*, eds. David Eltis and Stanley Engerman (Cambridge: Cambridge University Press, 2011), 708 – 739.

52 Marcelo Badaró Mattos, *Escravizados e livres: experiências comuns na formação da classe trabalhadora carioca* (Rio de Janeiro: Bom Texto, 2008).

1946).[53] Brazilian historiography of the last two decades had fallen into a localism[54] that could be explained by the attachment to primary sources, but that led to the separation between the studies about slavery in Brazil and those made in and about the other countries of the American continent. Alencastro's book returns to the Atlantic market as the fundamental element to understand slavery and colonial exploitation in Brazil while including a rich description of daily life that concerns nourishment, education of children and religious customs. In this sense, his work can be seen as a synthesis of the Marxism of Caio Prado Jr. and Novais with the Marxism of Viotti da Costa and Hunold Lara. But he goes a step further, comprising a careful study of the conditions of enslavement in Africa by the Portuguese and of the social forms slave trade created there, in order to compound the picture of an authentic triangular system embracing Portugal (Europe), Brazil (America) and Angola (Africa). This broader point of view allows Alencastro to give new answers to questions that formerly were dealt with separately by each particular tendency of historiography cited in the abovementioned section. Questions concerning the preference for the enslavement of Africans instead of the original population of Brazil after the seventeenth century; or the reasons for ending the slave trade in 1850 and not at the time of its official prohibition in 1831, are now answered based on life conditions in Africa and on the changing profitability of the Atlantic slave trade. For instance, Alencastro carefully analyses how, after the wars successfully led by the Portuguese in West Africa, the prices of the enslaved brought to Brazil could be high enough to compensate the costs of transport from Africa, making this trade more profitable than fighting the original population of Brazil. But even more important than these explanatory advantages is the fact that Alencastro's broader point of view relates his work to the recent North-American historiography on Atlantic history and to the work of Immanuel Wallerstein (1930–2019) and Giovanni Arrighi (1937–2009) on world systems.

---

53 Luiz Alencastro, *The Trade in the Living* (New York: Sunny Press, 2018). See also: Alencastro, "The African Slave Trade and the Construction of the Iberian Atlantic," in *The Global South Atlantic*, eds. K. Bystrom and Joseph Slaughter (New York: Fordham University Press, 2017), 192–209.

54 I think here on a tendency that can be found in some of the authors mentioned in the third section, above, as Silvia Lara, Sidney Chalhoub or Hebe Mattos. In their works the field of analysis is focused on specific areas in Brazil. To the works already quoted the following can be added: Maria Cristina Wissenbach, *Sonhos africanos, vivências ladinas. Escravos e forros em São Paulo – 1850–1880* (São Paulo: Hucitec, 1998); Mariza Soares, *Devotos da cor. Identidade étnica, religiosidade e escravidão no Rio de Janeiro, século XVIII* (Rio de Janeiro: Civilização Brasileira, 2000).

Alencastro thus opened the road for new investigations that try to link up micro with macro levels of analysis, pursuing their complementarity together with their differences in what can be called a dialectical approach. Atlantic and world-system studies imply a joint consideration of slavery in Brazil, in the United States and in the Caribbean. More than that, however, the ideas developed by Marx on the specificity of capitalism and industrial revolution inspired the already mentioned North-American historians Dale Tomich (born 1946) and Robin Blackburn (born 1940) to differentiate two or three moments in modern slavery, indicating the originality of nineteenth century slavery.[55]

Following in these steps, Rafael Marquese (born 1972) took Brazil and Cuba as the theme of his book *Feitores do corpo, missionários da mente*, published in 2004, and more recently of *Slavery and Politics*, written with Tâmis Perron and Márcia Berbel and published in English in 2016.[56] This last book compares the "refoundation of the Brazilian slave order by the Imperial Constitution of 1824" with a similar Cuban "rearrangement, which permitted the emergence of the contraband slave trade to the Hispanic Caribbean"[57] after the crisis of the slave systems existent from the sixteenth to the eighteenth centuries. In the nineteenth century a new rationality, inspired by industrial science and determined by capitalist profit, gradually would have replaced the Christian one prevalent until then. Capitalist calculation penetrated the forms of production performed by slaves, making the survival of slavery possible for a while, adapted to the needs of the new economic system.

A very important aspect of *Slavery and Politics* is the role of political decisions within Brazil and Cuba to reshape the "slave order" to an industrial world. One of its authors, Tâmis Parron, had already detailed this point in his book *A política da escravidão no Império do Brasil*, published in 2011.[58] There he unfolds the investigations of Paula Beiguelman, but focusing on the period prior to that studied by her, with the purpose of explaining the political reasons leading to the reinforcement of slave smuggling from Africa after the abolition of the official trade in 1831. Yet Parron doesn't neglect the weight of slave revolts in pressing deputies in parliament to compromise, mentioning the rebellion of the

55 For indication of their books and a short summary of their ideas, see footnote 2.

56 Rafael Marquese, *Feitores do corpo, missionários da mente* (São Paulo: Companhia das Letras, 2004). Rafael Marquese, Tâmis Parron, and Márcia Berbel, *Slavery and Politics: Brazil and Cuba, 1790–1850* (Albuquerque: New Mexico University Press, 2016).

57 Marquese, Perron, and Berbel, *Slavery and Politics*, 129 and 143 respectively.

58 Tâmis Parron, *A política da escravidão no Império do Brasil, 1826–1865* (Rio de Janeiro: Civilização Brasileira, 2011).

Malês in 1835 and of Carrancas in 1833 as the most influential, but not the only ones.[59] Thus, he joins the group of historians of the last two decades of the twentieth century that, as already examined, pointed up forms of slave resistance as the crucial element of analysis.

This is perhaps the common trait of recent historiography on slavery, namely, its ability to recognise the relevance of old subjects of research and to reintegrate them in the current framework. It can thus be viewed as a synthesis of the many elements Marxism shaped in the research trends of the past, combining class conflict, the capitalist world system and the forms of slave resistance.

Final Considerations

From the moment Marx's ideas began to be known in Brazil, many historians and social scientists understood how fertile these ideas were for a critical analysis of a country shaped since colonial times by African slavery. While the first interpretations felt strictly committed to Marxism, part of the later university research did not, but nonetheless had to refer to those first interpretations as a background of questions and categories from which every further debate could progress. Even when subsequent investigations criticised former Marxist explanations of slavery, they did so by developing other analytical possibilities in Marx's theory, such as the concepts of class struggle, revolution and cultural resistance.

Current historical research continues in this path; Marxism remains directly or indirectly an important reference point for comprehending the complex social situations of the past and their persistence in the present, as well as a means of changing them. For instance, when Caio Prado Jr. stated that racial miscegenation resulted from the brutal practice of sexual abuse of enslaved women and not from a positive lack of prejudice of Portuguese men, he was effectively assuming a political attitude. When Florestan Fernandes proposed to understand the condition of the Afro-descendant in twentieth century Brazil through class struggle, showing the interface between economic status and racism as the main reason for the permanence of social obstacles to the integration of the successors of the enslaved in capitalist society, he was also passing from theory to political practice. More recently, that was the case of Luiz Alencastro's testimony

59 Parron, *A política da escravidão*, 93–94. Marquese, Perron, and Berbel, *Slavery and Politics*, 138–139.

to Brazil's Supreme Court in 2014 on the racial quotas in universities.[60] He declared that the State of Brazil connived at slavery in the nineteenth century, and that it later imposed on emancipated slaves a kind of labour akin to slavery; it should therefore assume the responsibility for the situation of Brazilian Afro-descendants and recognise their right to study at public universities as compensation for past and present losses.

The debates condensed in this paper deal with these themes and have a direct influence on practical issues also in recent times. The present research on slavery is very much concerned with the origin of social inequality that always damaged more the Afro-descendant population than other groups, and that is dramatically increasing with the neoliberal policies put into practice in the last years by Brazilian governments. It is not by chance that problems like unemployment and low wages make the Afro-descendants more vulnerable and condemn them to live in the periphery of big cities, where they are target of police harassment for being considered potential criminals. It is not by chance that many traditional forms of cultural and political resistance of the Afro-descendant, for instance in music and in religion, are being attacked today by conservantism combined with neoliberalism. These and similar situations are echoes of a past of slavery and social exclusion of which historians are aware and by which they guide their research. Those inspired by Marx understand the major capitalist structure in which slavery was inserted, and that this structure should be transformed in order to eradicate the consequences of slavery. They show how structural transformation was the work of the oppressed and enslaved themselves, and that it is already present in every current act of resistance. In moments of crisis – whether the crisis is economic or political – in moments threatened by regression to old racial and social prejudices and to old methods of economic exploitation, radical forms of knowledge are always welcome.

60 Luís Alencastro, "As cotas raciais na UNB: um parecer apresentado ao STF contra a ADPF 186," in *Políticas da Raça – Experiências e legados da Abolição e da pós-emancipação no Brasil*, eds. Flávio Gomes and Petrônio Domingues (São Paulo: Selo Negro, 2014), 403–411.

Part Four: Marxism and the Study of the Contemporary World

Lutz Raphael

Farewell to Class?

Languages of Class, Industrial Relations and Class Structures in Western Europe since the 1970s

"The history of all hitherto existing society is the history of class struggles."[1] This statement from the *Communist Manifesto* of 1848 was the source of inspiration for Marxist social history, whose narrative continuity was based on labour disputes and political conflicts between labour and capital. In critical contrast to the political history of powerful states and the biographical narratives of great statesmen, it developed as a history of strikes and 'labour politics' presented as central events in history. Its aim was to expose both fundamental conflicts in society and structural changes in capitalism. While this tradition of a 'heroic' and activist understanding of history was and still is found in left-wing movements, political parties and trade unions worldwide, in the social sciences and historical research its significance and standing have suffered a substantial decline. This is particularly the case in Europe and North America, the traditional centres of (industrial) capitalism. Here the languages of social class, whether they were social-democratic, communist, left-wing socialist or left-wing liberal academic, all became entangled in the downward spiral of de-industrialisation, the promise of a new individualised labour world of digital services, the rise of new social movements and the collapse of the socialist regimes in central and eastern Europe. Admittedly, the parallel global expansion of industrial capitalism over the past fifty years has resulted in a considerable broadening and internationalising of the history of labour in capitalism.[2] However, this led at best to a local and regional delay in the demise of the traditional master narrative of the labour movement but not ultimately to its prevention. The critics of the old narrative of class struggle had good cause: it was Eurocentric, male-dominated, blind to the effects of religion, culture and language, fixated on socio-economic processes, hyper-collectivist and had a teleological faith in progress – a never-ending list of objections. So what can today's critical historical research learn from Karl Marx's legacy when addressing the issues of labour conditions, labour

1 Karl Marx and Friedrich Engels, *The Manifesto of the Communist Party*, English translation (Chicago: Charles H. Kerr & Company, 1888).
2 Jan Lucassen, ed., *Global Labour History. A State of the Art* (Bern: Lang, 2006); Marissa Brookes and Jamie K. McCallum, "The New Global Labour studies: A Critical Review," *Global Labour Journal* 8 (2017): 201–217.

https://doi.org/10.1515/9783110677744-012

relations, social protest, labour conflicts and social and economic inequality? Do we need a new approach to explain the wider connection between social conflict and the formation of social factions and groups – one whose Archimedean point is still the contrast between capital and labour?

Fruitful Revisions in Class Theory

> The classic questions of Marx and Thompson remain highly relevant: can a category of people be made to enter production with nothing to offer but labor power? What kinds of mechanisms translate the purchase of workers' time into the production of commodities and surplus value? What possibilities exist in different structures of production and reproduction that workers can seize to make themselves into something more than anonymous sellers of labour power? How do such dynamics alter relations between men and women, among neighbours, among people claiming different forms of affiliation with each other, between patrons and clients, and among citizens?[3]

Coming from the perspective of African labour history, the questions Fred Cooper formulates here are crucial to critical historical research in the field of capitalist forms of labour. He makes the case for continuing to use the analytical potential of Marx's questions but discarding the constraints of Marxist tradition in the field of labour history. In the following, I will be endorsing Cooper's approach and arguing that Marx's concept of class can be heuristically productive for a social history of labour. I would, therefore, answer the questions posed by Cooper in the aforementioned section in the affirmative, but only on condition that fundamental positions that would have been non-negotiable for Marx (and Friedrich Engels) should be reviewed and revised. Of these, three main revisions are:

- First, the impact of theory, that is, its power to define social positions and to position collective actors in a social space, to mobilise them and represent them. The images and mental maps of class vary largely worldwide and their impact is not adequately covered by the traditional Marxist concepts of class ideology and class consciousness. I will argue that languages of class and categories of society in general are central for the paths from class relations to class structures.
- This is directly linked to the second revision of the classic approach of Marxist scholarship when it comes to the working class. Instead of defining this class solely through the conflict between labour and capital, social history

3 Frederick Cooper, "African Labor history," in *Global Labour History. A State of the Art*, ed. Jan Lucassen (Bern: Lang, 2006), 91–116, 116.

has to start from the representations of class in society, from languages or ideologies of class, nation and citizenship circulating in a given society. It can then reconstruct the way new forms of capitalist production alter these representations, giving way to new interpersonal relations and changing affiliations among individuals and groups.
- Third, an analytical differentiation of Marx's concept of class in two dimensions: class relations and class structures. Both aspects are often seen as closely interrelated but social historians frequently encounter situations in which the development of social affiliations and groupings in society are not determined by relations between capital and labour in the capitalist production. Differentiating between class relations and class structures in its analysis liberates social history from linear master narratives and theoretical dead ends.

Before addressing the above-mentioned points in detail, I'll shortly comment on the need for a clear methodological and theoretical line to be drawn between a politico-economic concept of class (antagonism of capital and labour) and a sociohistorical concept of class. This implies a clear distinction between two different dimensions of the Marxist concept of class: 'class relations' and the 'structuring of class'.[4]

In the words of Thomas Welskopp, 'class relations' means the following:

> ... the central structural principle of social relations of production in industrial capitalist societies that divides the owners and controllers of the means of production (i.e. the strategic management) antagonistically from those who offer their labour or qualifications and who tend to be without ownership, but at the same time ties them to each other in mutual productive dependency and interrelatedness of the expansive or at least intrinsically dynamic process of the exploitation of capital.[5]

Thus on the macro level of societies and markets, whether internationally or nationally regulated, we find an all-embracing structural principle that divides industrial capitalism from other forms of society. It also allows a more precise determination of the historical dynamic of modern capitalism proceeding from the tensions between capital and labour, and therefore enables this theoretical basis to be used to differentiate between different types and varieties of capitalism.

---

4 Thomas Welskopp, "Ein modernes Klassenkonzept für die vergleichende Geschichte industrialisierender und industrieller Gesellschaften," in *Mikropolitik im Unternehmen: Arbeitsbeziehungen und Machtstrukturen in industriellen Großbetrieben des 20. Jahrhunderts*, ed. Karl Lauschke (Essen: Klartext, 1994): 48–106.

5 Welskopp, "Ein modernes Klassenkonzept," 74.

In analytical terms, this concept of class relations has to be separated from the dimension of class structures. Social history traditionally followed sociological tradition and linked these two dimensions using the notion of social class. Cooper's questions reminds us that there never was a direct and simple link from work relations to affiliations with colleagues, neighbours and citizens. Again, we may follow here Welskopp who, drawing on Anthony Giddens and Max Weber, defines "class structures as an extremely variable process of the development and reproduction of class relations found in the workplace and the labour market".[6] It also comprises the level of the formation of social, political and cultural structures as they interact with class relations. Thus 'classes' from this perspective are historically extremely fluid social configurations. At this point we encounter the notion from the social sciences of 'classes on paper'.[7] Here, theoretical models and plausible typologies of this interaction between class relations and the structuring of class are constructed and placed in various social containers – usually nation state entities – thus mapping out these social spaces. Such models are then deployed in the political and ideological struggle to interpret and define the social world. Historians, unlike sociologists, are less involved in these struggles over the political and moral framing of today's social reality but they do have to study their effects on the class relations and the structuring of class in the past. The historians' primary political role seems to be to confirm or question the social existence of classes that did exist or still do exist as mobilised and represented social categories in the past. It comes as no surprise then that questions of the 'formation of class' have always had a particular appeal for historians.[8]

The discussion that follows of the key Marxist concepts of class is mainly a rethinking of empirical research on the social history of industrial labour in Western Europe (France, Britain and West Germany) during the period of de-industrialisation after the 1970s.[9] The following arguments do not, therefore, attempt a systematic (re-)construction of the theoretical debates on Marx's concept of class but plead in favour of a heuristic use of it to better understand the historical findings about recent changes in contemporary capitalist society.

6 Welskopp, "Ein modernes Klassenkonzept," 74.

7 Pierre Bourdieu, "The Social Space and the Genesis of Social Groups," *Theory and Society* 14, no. 6 (1985): 723–744.

8 Welskopp, "Klassenkonzept."

9 Lutz Raphael, *Jenseits von Kohle und Stahl. Eine Gesellschaftsgeschichte Europas nach dem Boom* (Berlin: Suhrkamp, 2019).

The Impact of Theory: The Working Class as a Concept and as an Interpretive Model

The question of how to categorise the 'working class' (*Arbeiterklasse, classe ouvrière*) as a collective subject in an academic context cannot be separated from the conflict over the classification of the social world and the observable impact of theory on it. There is no way round Pierre Bourdieu's most clearly formulated conclusion that Marx's theory of class has itself become part of the 'objective' reality of class, and that, as with every other theory of the formation of social structures in modern capitalism, it is always situated on two levels. One is academic dispute over the adequate presentation of empirical findings and social data and the other is the political and ideological dispute over the legitimate classification of the social world. This effect is found outside the conscious ambition to change society cherished by Marx, Engels and other Marxist class theorists. It is also beyond the scope of classical inner-Marxist debates on 'class in itself' and 'class for itself' and on class consciousness and trade unionism. As soon as the concept of class or any of its counter concepts become part of social communication, they generate a view of the world of work which causes this world to change. This means that any history of knowledge applied to the Marxist classification of 'class' occurs on at least four different levels:

- controversies among academics about the concept of class and its place in the categories of social analysis;
- the role that states and international organisations attribute to socio-economic 'classes' when dealing with official categories, such as in statistics or social and labour law;
- the significance of the semantics of 'class' for common belief (*doxa*) propagated in the media and amongst the general political public, when referring to social conditions and affiliations to social collectives or the identities of these collectives;[10]
- the (sense of) social orientation of social actors who are either only partial or passive participants in the three academic fields mentioned above (political economy, sociology and history): as a rule, this is the majority of those who might be considered possible vehicles of 'class identities' and 'class consciousness'.

---

10 Pierre Bourdieu, *Outline of a Theory of Practice* (Cambridge: CUP, 1977).

I would like to briefly discuss these different uses of the concept of class in the political language of Britain, France and the Federal Republic of Germany and how it changed radically during the 1980s and 1990s.[11] In Britain, on one hand industrialisation had provided concrete material for an effective model of the interpretation of industrial revolution, liberal capitalism and class struggle and, as a result, had influenced important political concepts in other languages. However, it is also clear that on the other hand the emerging British 'working class' developed its own political idiom to refer to the peculiarities of its own country.[12] In the development of the British labour movement, electoral reform, trade union recognition and free collective bargaining can be regarded as significant milestones, but they have also become significant points of reference in political language across the spectrum in Britain. Even liberals and conservatives accepted, though by no means gladly, that there was organised class struggle in their country and tried to win support and votes from the increasing number of industrial workers who were trade union members. This liberal model of Britain as a nation which saw its political community as a society determined by class affiliation and class origin was consolidated in the twentieth century by the national mobilisation of industrial workers in two successful world wars. As a result, even in the Thatcher era of de-industrialisation (1979–1992), 'class' remained a natural though ambiguous point of reference in all areas of political language, whether official statistics, sociological analyses or everyday speech.[13]

In West Germany, after the end of World War II, political and social language and official categories were anxious to neutralise class differences and class conflicts as far as possible.[14] The linguistic strategies of euphemism and harmonisation were reactions against the ideological charge and linguistic radicalisation of the industrial clash of interests during the German Kaiserreich (1871–1918) and the Weimar Republic (1919–1933). They had turned the Reich into a battleground for conflicting interpretations of the social order and semi-religious ideologies, whereby a key role was attributed to the industrial workforce with regard to the fate of the country's political and social order. Considering the strength of a labour movement whose language was orthodox Marxist, the labour question

11 Raphael, *Jenseits von Kohle und Stahl*, 102–129.

12 Edward P. Thompson, *The Making of the English Working Class* (New edition. London: Penguin Books, 2013). Gareth Stedman Jones, *Languages of Class: Studies in English Working Class History, 1832–1982* (Reprint. Cambridge: CUP, 1996).

13 Arthur Marwick, *Class: Image and Reality in Britain, France and the USA Since 1930.* (London: Macmillan, 1990); David Cannadine, *Class in Britain* (New Haven: YUP, 1998).

14 Paul Nolte, *Die Ordnung der deutschen Gesellschaft: Selbstentwurf und Selbstbeschreibung im 20. Jahrhundert* (München: Verlag C. H. Beck, 2000).

in the German Reich was much more than a socio-political problem – rather it was closely connected to the legitimacy of class struggle and class conflict within the political order. This underlying tension was not relieved by defeat in World War I, in spite of the 'social-patriotic' integration of the Social Democratic Party (SPD) and the trade unions. On the contrary, the ensuing decades saw its renewal through ideological radicalisation. The National Socialist movement and dictatorship were also a radical response to this ideological conflict. The *völkisch* re-interpretation of the concept of *Volksgemeinschaft* ('community of all German citizens') invoked in the Weimar Republic massively enhanced the symbolic value of the labour force while effectively excluding them from political power.[15] This enforced integration on a national political level was inherited by the two German states after 1945, and they strove to ensure that the conflict between (working) class and nation state was not revived. In West Germany, the ideological confrontation of the Cold War severely restricted the use of any rhetoric to do with class conflict or socialism and was a considerable force behind the fact that the many nationalist and socially conservative interpretative models of the industrial world were de-radicalised. In the official statistics of the Federal Republic of Germany, the three categories fundamental to the German social state since the German Empire were retained. For national or social insurance purposes they differentiated only between manual workers, 'white collar workers/employees and state or public employees of any kind' (*Arbeiter/Angestellte/Beamte*) and, unlike official British or French statistics, did not distinguish between different income categories, types of work or positions in the hierarchy of labour organisation. As a result, there was no such thing as 'class' 'on paper' and West German sociologists conceived the image of a society 'beyond class and rank' correspondingly early on.[16] With its Godesberg programme in 1959, German social democracy broke away from its traditional store of Marxist ideology relatively soon in comparison with its international partners. It was then able to pave the way for a social-liberal interpretation of economic and social conflicts of interest. This meant that the conflict of interest between capital and labour was firmly anchored in West German democracy but was organised and legally confined. From then on, the place that had been occupied in the political imagination by the class-aware industrial worker until 1945 was gradually supplanted by the figure of the self-confident industrial citizen. For strategic rea-

15 Rüdiger Hachtmann, *Industriearbeit Im "Dritten Reich": Untersuchungen zu den Lohn- und Arbeitsbedingungen in Deutschland 1933–1945* (Göttingen: Vandenhoeck & Ruprecht, 1989); Dietmar Süß, *'Ein Volk, Ein Reich, Ein Führer': Die Deutsche Gesellschaft im Dritten Reich* (München: C.H. Beck, 2017).
16 Nolte, *Ordnung*, 351–361.

sons, the German Trade Union Confederation (DGB) chose the generic juridical term *Arbeitnehmer* to replace the current notions of *Arbeiter, Angestellter* and *Beamter* and to organise all three categories in its unions.[17]

In France, the socio-political patterns of interpretation developed less according to the social realities of the new industrial society than within the context of the political and social conflicts created by the French Revolution. The fact that there was both a broad class of rural land-owners and a preponderance of trades with non-industrial or small-scale industrial structures until well into the twentieth century meant that in spite of a strong socialist tradition it was not until the inter-war period that the industrial workforce and their class conflict became a key point of reference in political speech. Much more attention was paid to ordinary radical and republican-minded people, the *peuple*, than to the workers, the *ouvriers.*[18] The *classes populaires* ('popular classes') was the dominant concept for more than 100 years and is still useful for various different political interpretive models today. Changes in the interpretive model of the industrial labour world, which then lasted for more than three decades, were triggered by the 'popular front' (*front populaire)* which came to power in 1936, then the defeat of Republican France and the establishment of the authoritarian Vichy regime in 1940 followed by liberation in 1944. Only then did the labour movement's talk of class struggle strike a chord and the social problems in industry, which was still regionally dominated, lodge themselves more firmly in the political consciousness. As a result, the industrial workforce became an integral part of the vision of France as a democratic nation. This rapidly expanding new section of society had been hitherto neglected and its socio-political and symbolic integration became a central reference point for the many programmes of reform required to provide the democratic republic with a new social foundation. After World War II this vision of the new social order was occupied by Gaullists, Christian Democrats, Socialists and Communists in a variety of interpretive models. It led to a shaky compromise between the explicit language of class struggle on the left and the more socially harmonious language of the 'bourgeois' parties promoting ideas closer to the middle ground.[19]

The tradition of fundamental countercultural opposition to the hegemony of 'bourgeois' interpretive models of the social world, which was embedded in all

---

17 Stefan Wannenwetsch, "'Es gibt noch Arbeiter in Deutschland.' Zur Transformation der Kategorie Arbeiter in der westdeutschen Arbeitnehmergesellschaft" (PhD. thesis Tübingen, 2019).
18 Pierre Rosanvallon, *Le peuple introuvable: histoire de la représentation démocratique en France* (Paris: Gallimard, 1998).
19 Louis Chauvel and Franz Schultheis: "Le sens d'une dénégation: L'oubli des classes sociales en Allemagne et en France," *Mouvements* 26 (2003): 17–26.

three labour movements from the start, was upheld until the 1970s. In their long political struggle to become politically and socially visible and accepted, the political representatives of the industrial workforce had learnt to mobilise various resources, typically the experience that although they were not able to find support for their views and standpoints in the mainstream media, they could rely on their grassroots, that is, their own supporters and supporters of their own social class or relevant social and moral milieu. This experience was reflected in the various different types of class language used by British, French and West German trade unionists, Communists, Socialists and left-wing Catholics to assert themselves in the battle of conflicting interpretations of social reality. There was a revival of this class language in the 1960s and 1970s as a result of the favourable conditions for industrial workers in the labour conflict and supported by the new political consciousness and insurgencies amongst (middle class) thinkers. This meant that a type of militant language was in circulation which enjoyed far greater popularity with certain sections of the labour force but also with the younger generation of middle-class party members with a university education than its liberal or conservative equivalents. Significantly it also allowed the expression of positions that were in critical opposition to the socially harmonious interpretations of the existing social order. These were then adopted by established left-wing actors in the political field and translated into political criticism and political goals. It is characteristic of this unstable de-industrialisation period that the knowledge and experience inherent in this discourse of mobilisation lost its validity and significance remarkably quickly. This was particularly true for Britain and France, since there the traditions of the labour movement had been maintained to a far greater extent than in West Germany and were deliberately reactivated for the purpose of mobilisation.

Interestingly, up until the middle of the 1980s the two largest left-wing parties in France used Marxist and socialist *topoi* ('themes') and stereotypes of class conflict in their language as a means of mobilising their voters.[20] The change in mobilisation strategies and communication routines in the Socialist Party (PS) after 1984, when it became the strongest political party on the left, must have seemed all the more drastic. Instead of its previous left-wing Keynesian programme, the PS increasingly adopted the social-democratic language of its sister parties in the north and east. It began to propagate the virtues of technocratic pragmatism and economic efficiency and point out the practical constraints of

20 Anne-Marie Hetzel and Claire Bernard, *Le syndicalisme à mots découverts: Dictionnaire des fréquences (1971–1990)* (Paris: Syllepse, 1998); Henri Rey, *La gauche et les classes populaires: histoire et actualité d'une mésentente* (Paris: la Découverte, 2004).

the new policy of austerity. In effect, in the same way as its sister parties in West Germany and Britain in the 1990s, it aligned itself with successful mainstream interpretive models found in science and the media. An initial finding is that in all the three countries the language that had previously lent the various different occupational groups within the industrial labour force a collective identity as a represented class lost its force and eventually became barely audible.

One reason for this was that left-wing social scientists and actors in the cultural sector gradually disassociated themselves from established interpretive models and from their own criticism of existing social and political conditions on behalf of a supposedly underprivileged working class. As a result, it became more difficult for average workers to make their voice heard as a group in the political process and in public discussion in the media about social problems and cases of unfairness and inequality. Instead they became the object of cultural criticism and satire and so to a certain extent replaced the 'petit bourgeois' figure in the imaginary world of those in the cultural sector.[21] This change of perspective took place rapidly in the 1980s and 1990s and brought to an end the brief flourishing of close contact between social historians and social scientists and topics related to labour and labour history. In historiography, more than in any other research area, the proliferation of new and old left wingers following the 1968 protest movement led to an increase in research on industrial labour and labourers by scholars with a Marxist leaning or an affinity and proximity to labour movements. This trend reached its peak in the 1980s and early 1990s and coincided with a dramatic collapse of the established socialist, social-democratic and communist traditions of labour policy in western Europe. The collapse of the socialist dictatorships in eastern Europe after 1989 had a similar effect. Those artists and intellectuals whose chosen topics had given them a home in (what was for most of them) an alien, 'chosen' and imagined class identity in their own countries now entered a new phase of strident reorientation and renewed searching for objects to identify with and to be the focus of their political morals. Their endeavours to act as advocates through art, culture and science were now deliberately concentrated on other groups and new areas of social discrimination and inequality were taken up by the 'artistic and social critique'.[22] In all the three countries, belated censure of racism and xenophobia, feminist critique of ongoing sexual discrimination and imbalance of power, and the fight for the right to freedom for sexual minorities became principle themes of critical cul-

---

21 Owen Jones, *The Demonization of the Working Class* (London, New York: Verso, 2012).
22 Luc Boltanski and Ève Chiapello, *The New Spirit of Capitalism* (London, New York: Verso, 2005).

tural output and intellectual interventions. The move in academic preferences towards other social groups and historical categories is also an indication that for social scientists and social historians in western metropoles there had been a shift in the balance within the symbolic and socio-structural parameters of expertise. At the critical end of these disciplines with their ambition to be the critics of society and of power, the narrow nation-centric perspective of labour movement research with its criticism of capitalism was considered 'old-fashioned'. Any historian who wanted to combine academic work with a politically and morally highly-regarded role as an advocate or spokesperson for legitimate interests or a champion of neglected victim groups could earn much greater plausibility and expect much more public attention and academic recognition by focussing on almost any topic and social group other than the aged heroes of the old narratives of class struggle. This shift was particularly dramatic in the United States, Britain and France, (reflecting the social and political upheaval in their ambient societies). It took place shortly afterwards in other countries in western Europe, influenced by more moderate social democracy. In a global perspective, postcolonialism, gender and race have become political reference points in today's academic world, and they cannot be ignored if any intellectual study of industrial labour is not to appear merely antiquated and nationally blinkered. However, it is important not to overlook the wider political context of this artistic and intellectual critique. It is a symptom of a less common critical awareness of 'identity politics'. It recognises other demarcations which are independent of economics and largely oriented to cultural, linguistic or religious differences, and emphasises them, makes them socially visible and politicises them. In the face of global migration and an ever more closely inter-connected global economy, diversity has become the chief guiding principle in the formation of groups and processes of politicisation. In this intellectual environment a return to Marx's analysis of class has sufficient potential to return the focus of attention to work processes and labour relations. It can also address the fundamental problems of social inequality and the social distribution of labour and knowledge that threaten to be obscured by naturalised, apparently elemental affiliations such as race, ethnicity and religion. All this ultimately supports the argument in favour of articulating and organising structurally 'weak interests' in capitalism within the socio-political debate.

Class Struggle Without Class: The Erosion of Political Representation and the Power of Mobilisation

It is striking that in all these countries (Britain, France and Germany) these shifts resulted in the disintegration of representative structures that had, in their specific national form, given workers a place in the political arena. This loss of representation corresponded to a growing sense of distance on the part of people belonging to these socio-economic categories from those organisations that professed to speak in their name. This was true for trade unions and political parties, regardless of their political agenda. For France Louis Chauvel has spoken of the *classes populaires* ('popular classes') undergoing an 'experience of atomisation' as a class-specific variant of the process of subjectivisation observed in society as a whole.[23] Chauvel's colleagues Stéphane Beaud and Michel Pialoux speak of the 'disappearance' and the 'end' of the *classe ouvrière* ('working class'). By this they mean the end of that concrete historical collectivity that had emerged from political representation, a sense of specific group identity and shared experiences and values.[24] As a class it had also disassociated itself clearly and often with some degree of self-confidence from 'bourgeois' interpretive models and representatives of the established order. The French *classe ouvrière* was 'class' in the same sense as the English working class, whose emergence was described by Edward P. Thompson.[25] It disappeared in the twin processes of change in political and cultural representation and socio-economic change. Although the conditions of representation in West Germany also shifted towards less presence and increasing distance, there was one crucial difference. In the 1930s, long before 1989, West German workers had lost this kind of compact class existence. After 1945, the languages of class disappeared and were replaced by quite different kinds of political and trade union representation, until after 1975, when recessions, crises in industry and the so-called third industrial revolution upset their social structure and socio-economic situation once again. Whereas links between working people and the major parties, especially the SPD, began to weaken, just as they did in France, the level of organisation in

23 Louis Chauvel, "La déstabilisation du système des positions sociales." in *L'épreuve des inégalités*, ed. Hugues Lagrange (Paris: Presses universitaires de France, 2006), 91–112.
24 Stéphane Beaud and Michel Pialoux, *Retour sur la condition ouvrière: enquête aux usines Peugeot de Sochaux-Montbéliard* (Paris: Fayard, 1999), 14–16.
25 Thompson, *Making.*

trade unions remained extremely high and the collective representation of interests at company level even intensified, as we will see in the following section. The situation in Britain is somewhere between that of France and West Germany. De-industrialisation hit parts of the working classes with material force and led to the break-up of regional centres of traditional working class culture. This erosion was exacerbated by the political crisis of the Labour Party and the trade unions in the 1980s and early 1990s, with the effect that the strength of the political representation of the working classes in Britain also declined or disappeared completely.

Overall the coordinates of the socio-political categories used in public debate changed. The aura of the collective singular 'class', *classe* or *Klasse* (though in West Germany '*Arbeiterschaft*' – 'workforce' was more common) that had always accompanied the mobilising language of social protests was dispelled. At the same time, organisations such as trade unions that required strict group cohesion were disapproved of and considered to be an outdated remnant from a bygone age by a growing number of conservatives, liberals and even unpolitical sceptics.

In this historical constellation, the phrase that Thompson proposed for conflicts in eighteenth century British society – 'class struggle without class'– regains significance.[26] It can be seen that after 1980 in the three western European countries considered here, industrial workers were increasingly less visible as a 'mobilised' class. They drew attention to themselves by means of spectacular defensive actions such as strikes, take-overs and rallies but after the 1990s they were noticeably less likely to act as a collective when articulating their interests towards representatives of capital. Above all, industrial workers lost their ability to set an example of political mobilisation or trade union organisation to adjacent categories of workers, particularly in the new and old service sectors, or to function as their allies in this field. For a combination of practical and cultural reasons the charisma of 'class struggle' (referring in Britain, France and Germany to very different understandings of mobilisation and legitimisation) was considerably eroded. For growing numbers of low-status workers who were employed in industry or the service industries in these three countries, whether skilled or unskilled, men or women, the likelihood of collective representation of their interests at their place of work receded. What is important to me in this context is simply that the concept of 'class struggle without class' allows us to uphold a critical politico-economic perspective without imagining the existence of mobi-

26 Edward P. Thompson, "Eighteeenth-century English Society: Class Struggle without Class?" *Social History* 3 (1978): 133–185.

lised or represented classes. In a global historical perspective this brings the experiences of western European countries over the past three decades closer to parallel situations in other regions of the world and their production regimes of global 'digital finance capitalism'. 'Class struggle without class' also seems to me to be a useful formula for highlighting the way in which the political representation of class interests, and situation-specific interests and affiliations changes its form, as can be observed in western European democracies during the late twentieth century. As class language in politics diminished or disappeared and represented classes were thus no longer competing in the national political parties, different priorities for the representation of 'weak' interests emerged. In France and Britain and later in the Federal Republic of Germany, the notions of 'exclusion' and 'precarity' – closely connected to the figure of the long-term unemployed and the underclass or ghetto – led to the emergence of 'new' social 'problem' groups.[27] In the political sphere particular attention was now paid to the appropriate representation of other social groups such as 'migrants' and even more markedly 'women' as specific groups within the electorate.

The Transformation of Industrial Class Relations: Western Europe in the Late Twentieth Century

If this holds true, a social history of class conflicts has to admit that there is no direct connection from antagonistic work relations to the making of social classes and the politics of class. In the light of historical analysis, the existence of an all-embracing, more-or-less unchanging working class frequently turns out to be merely a theoretical hypothesis or a figment of imagination in the traditional narrative of Marxist labour (movement) history. For this reason the theoretical distinction between class relation and class structure should be used when studying the transformations in West European societies in the late twentieth century.

Class relations are situated in the relationship between management and workforce and are manifest in the microcosm of a company or business. The macro level of the regimes of accumulation and production cannot be reached empirically without examining the company level. Here there were significant changes in the mode and organisation of production in the period after the

27 Sarah K. Haßdenteufel, *Neue Armut, Exklusion, Prekarität. Debatten um Armut in Frankreich und der Bundesrepublik Deutschland, 1970–1990* (Berlin/Boston: De Gruyter, 2019).

first oil crisis in 1973–1974, and they led again to significant re-adjustments in industrial relations between capital and labour. During this transition period key ideas included a third industrial revolution based on new computer and information technologies and new management policies such as lean management and human resource management. Although the results of sociological research on industry at this time are very diverse, they do agree in one aspect, namely that the main characteristics which had shaped the 'Fordist' (industrial) production regime since at least the 1930s were becoming less dominant in the late twentieth century. The most important changes were the introduction of competition and market principles within companies; the creation of company and production networks; and the use of new information technology to restructure internal information, communication and control systems, resulting in more responsibility being delegated but also in tighter controls. The results of my comparative study of the three western European countries (Britain, France and Germany) found both a re-distribution of responsibilities and participation rights among groups of employees, with a variety of consequences for company hierarchies, and also a re-appraisal of the value of knowledge and experience involved in specialist technical and production skills.[28] Teamwork and job enrichment grew but there was no agreed pattern to their organisation and implementation. The level of participation and autonomy of production teams varied hugely; neo-Taylorist solutions and cooperative-autonomous solutions could be found side by side on the shop floor. However, for the purposes of the socio-historical debate, it is important to note that in the 1980s and 1990s a major part of internal company (social) relations were involved in a kind of experimental re-structuring which affected horizontal labour relations in those concrete work units (workshops, production units, departments, etc.) with hierarchies and communication structures. These changes had no single direction and no uniform consequences but the evidence suggests that there may be some general tendencies applicable to certain countries and branches of industry. In West German companies, especially those involved with exports, one model seems to have won through more easily. This was one in which qualified production teams made up of engineers, technicians and skilled workers gained wide-ranging rights to participate in the organisation of production and to a lesser extent in its management.[29] This model played a much more minor role in France and Britain, where in

28 Raphael, *Jenseits von Kohle und Stahl*, 276–285, 383–418.

29 Klaus Dörre, "Gibt es ein nachfordistisches Produktionsmodell? Managementprinzipien, Firmenorganisation und Arbeitsbeziehungen im flexiblen Kapitalismus," in *Ein neuer Kapitalismus? Akkumulationsregime – Shareholder Society: Neoliberalismus und neue Sozialdemokratie*, eds. Mario Candeias and Frank Deppe (Hamburg: VSA 2001), 83–107.

the same period forms of neo-Taylorist labour relations developed more markedly than in West Germany. This happened mainly in the various branches of the consumer goods industry such as food, furniture, electric and electronic goods, and the automobile industry.[30]

Two points relevant to research on class relations seem to emerge from this. The first can be described as a shift towards the company or factory as the centre of focus. At a time when the industrial labour world and its production units were having to respond to crisis by re-structuring, at the same time industrial labour markets were deteriorating; the general tendency towards marketisation led not only to an increase in discipline amongst employees but also to an increase in their focus on the company or factory and their willingness to cooperate within it. Similarly, as external equity owners increased pressure on management (via financial market control, new company targets and changing sales markets), the parameters in the relationship between 'capital' and labour' also shifted. What essentially emerged was an element of technical cooperation in terms of the product and its production. In Marxist terms, this orientation towards the use value of production and the labour process paved the way to cooperation between management and workers. Contrary to Marx's expectation and prognosis, it gained in significance through the modification of production processes in the third industrial revolution. This led to institutional agreements and shifts in power structures, whereby management conceded various degrees of participation to employees, right up to the point of co-management. On closer inspection, however, it can be seen that such changes are determined by two particular factors on the macro level which relate to the level of political and legal institutions, namely the institutional safeguarding of the professional or employment status of workers and the legal safeguarding of the employees' right to participation, also by means of collective bargaining.[31]

The second point relevant to research on class relations is that the upheaval experienced in this period posed a challenge to the legal basis of the wage labourer in a company. In western Europe standards, social legislation and wage policies were based on the idea of industrial citizenship, negotiated by the workforce through their collective representatives, shop stewards, trade union delegates and members of works councils. The breakdown of rigid company hierarchies and the advent of new forms of cooperation between management and

30 Thomas Amossé and Thomas Coutrot, "Socio-Productive Models in France: An Empirical Dynamic Overview, 1992–2004," *Industrial and Labour Relations Review* 64 (2011): 786–817; Thomas Coutrot, *L'entreprise néo-libérale, nouvelle utopie capitaliste? Enquête sur les modes d'organisation du travail* (Paris: la Découverte, 1998).

31 Raphael, *Jenseits von Kohle und Stahl*, 213–225.

workers cast doubt on the principle of collective representation by trade unions attached to one specific trade or company. With or without collective representation, the question of more flexible labour relations became the key feature distinguishing the many different types of industrial relations emerging at the company level during this time. They grew rapidly and in various forms, regardless of national boundaries or specific branches of industry. These changes were accompanied by a number of other phenomena, including a recourse to autocratic rule by management based on power and law and combined with the most up-to-date forms of computer-controlled production and labour. Further elements were cooperation within a company (with trade unions and in the case of West Germany, works councils), the delegation of decision-making powers and the dismantling of hierarchies.[32]

Regulation Theory: A possible Framework for Micro Studies of Class Relations

How can these empirical findings on the micro level be incorporated in a broader perspective on change in industrial capitalism? A framework of this kind can be found in numerous studies of the French School of Regulation.[33] They took Marx's ideas on class relations as a starting point and applied them to changes in Western capitalism, which had been primarily industry-based prior to 1980. Both their theoretical and empirical studies rely on the definition of specific Regimes of Accumulation within the overall capitalist mode of production. Robert Boyer makes a systematic distinction between five different elements that determine Regimes of Accumulation as institutional parameters. First, the monetary system, which regulates the relation of exchange between the various market actors but especially the relations between the domestic and foreign markets. Second, the status of 'wage labour' (*statut salarial*) not only comprises legal aspects of employment in its narrowest sense, such as its regulation and forms of payment, but also any direct or indirect social benefits and entitlements to do with the employment contract and any processes set up by the state to safeguard this employment. Further distinct elements identified by regulation theory are, thirdly, the concrete regulation of competition; and fourthly, the different ways

32 Raphael, *Jenseits von Kohle und Stahl*, 376–383.

33 Robert Boyer, *Regulation Theory: The State of the Art* (London: Routledge, 2001); Robert Boyer, *Économie politique des capitalismes: théorie de la régulation et des crises* (Paris: La Découverte, 2015).

in which each national economy is embedded in international competition. As a fifth element, it introduces the policies implemented by the state to deal with expenditure, investment and debt. In a macro-economic model such as this, the key question is: what basic principles of the structuring of class positions emerge from these institutional parameters? When different solutions to these five elements are combined or matched robustly, they will result in different Regimes of Accumulation historically, regionally but also sector-wide. The Regulation School initially concentrated its empirical research on the crisis-induced changes experienced by the global Fordist production regime within the international automobile industry. They then went on to examine the effects of the emergence of international financial market capitalism on the further development and transformation of various production systems in the industrial and service sectors. It is the explicit aim of their typologies and models to provide a more precise description of historical change within capitalism since the nineteenth century. They do not, however, find a clear relationship between these elements structuring the relationship between capital and labour and the existence of concrete social classes based on socio-economic situations or active representation in the political or cultural sphere. Even the popular model of stages within production regimes and Regimes of Accumulation, such as the recent stage of Fordist to post-Fordist, is regarded with scepticism and criticism by the Regulation School. This is why this politico-economic approach is so useful for social historians. In social history, its aim is to obtain an adequately realistic picture. It also acknowledges that different conflicting production regimes may co-exist within one particular national economy or economic region or branch of industry. Advocates of Regulation theory have rightly pointed out that the diversity of capitalist economic orders cannot be satisfactorily explained by the antithesis of liberal and coordinated market capitalism, as is generally attempted by the 'varieties of capitalism' approach. Nor has international financial market capitalism become a new global model. This is particularly evident in the case of industrial production, which in the face of crisis developed quite different ways of cooperating with the main actors of state, society and business, all of which had to react to changing markets. As the Regulation School also recognises the significance of historically developed institutions and attitudes, its approach is the most compatible with the socio-historical perspective argued for here.

A politico-economic perspective such as this recognises the underlying tension between capital and labour and certainly provides a more promising framework for studies of social conflict in the world of work than vague sociological theories of globalisation. The Regulation School has developed typologies of regulation specific to individual nations, which take into account the different developments in labour relations in Latin America, Asia and Africa during the expansion of financial market capitalism.[34] It also provides points of reference and comparison in the field of global labour history for current discussions on the role of unfree labour on the one hand and the informal job sector on the other. How were these modes of labour integrated into the various capitalist Regimes of Accumulation? Where did these new Regimes of Accumulation develop niches and gaps? How were they connected to the decline of the formal labour market and, in concrete terms, to those legal and socio-political institutions that guaranteed status, social rights and social benefits to wage labourers beyond the terms of their labour contracts? It is important to ask these broad questions because of their relevance to the informalisation of the labour market – a process which can be observed with varying intensity and social implications in Africa, Asia and Latin America as well as in the capitalist centres of Europe and North America. Paradoxically, a kind of methodological nationalism seems to have become embedded in Marxist-oriented labour (movement) history and this politico-economic dimension is an extremely useful way of overcoming it.

Class, Gender and Race: Dimensions of the Social Fabric of *classes populaires*

What about the dynamics of class structures under the impact of new political languages and changing class relations in Western Europe in the late twentieth century?

Class structures as defined in the aforementioned sections cannot be conceived outside the triangular relationship of class, gender and race or ethnicity. Although, in theory all three categories have long been recognised as equally important and interconnected and have become an integral part of the critical Marxist tradition,[35] it is often much more difficult to do justice to the relevance of all three dimensions of social inequality in empirical studies. Empirical research on the situation in western Europe at the end of the twentieth century raises several points which are of theoretical relevance here.

A social history of western European industrial workers is not complete without the question of migration and therefore the significance of ethnic divides.

---

34 Boyer, *Economie politique.*

35 Stuart Hall, *The Fateful Triangle. Race, Ethnicity, Nation* (Cambridge MA: Harvard UP, 2017); Fiona Devine et al., eds., *Rethinking Class: Culture, Identities and Lifestyles* (Houndmills, New York: Palgrave Macmillan, 2005); Beverley Skeggs, *Class, Self, Culture* (London: Routledge, 2004).

Race is a notion that cuts across class relations and class positions and has left its mark on the industrial world of work. After World War II, the industrial workforce in West Germany, France, and to a much lesser extent Britain, experienced a huge influx of migrant workers, who increasingly took over poorly-paid unskilled and semi-skilled jobs. In the last two decades of the twentieth century, it was these migrant workers and their children who were harder hit by unemployment than other sections of the workforce. Ethnic discrimination and racism were evident within the workforces of France, Britain and Germany. Yet, it cannot be said for any of these three countries that ethnic or racial divides led to obvious rifts in the social space of the working classes. What they did, led to an increase in the number of workers whose socio-economic (class) position in the social space of their host country was ambivalent. Many of them continued to live in a kind of transitional social space between two countries and two cultures. This kind of social structuring has been termed 'double absence' by the French sociologist Abdelmalek Sayad.[36] Yet the shared experience of work and gaining professional qualifications helped workers from different backgrounds in these three countries to build bridges that connected them to their neighbours and fellow workers and brought them closer. The example of Germany shows that industrial work proved to be the most effective form of inclusion of migrants, even though this was linked to their clear relegation to the world of the *classes populaires.*[37] Where the (industrial) labour market was particularly segmented and access to the labour market was blocked to certain categories (youth unemployment, long-term unemployment among older and unskilled workers), certain areas and economies began to favour certain ethnic groups.

In all the three countries industrial work was a man's world. The percentage of female workers never rose above twenty per cent. When the western European textile industry went into decline it was mainly women's jobs that were lost. As with other unskilled industrial jobs, they moved to new industrial locations in Asia, Latin America and, after 1990, eastern Europe. After 1970, industry was still dominated by male workers and trade unions were dominated by men representing male values. This is nothing new for social historians.

Things are different if we turn to the changes that were taking place within households whose members were industrial workers – male or female. The focus on family in the workforce, which has been noted for the 1950s and 1960s, was a trend that continued, but there was a notable change in the social profile of the

36 Abdelmalek Sayad, *La double absence: des illusions de l'émigré aux souffrances de l'immigré.* (Paris: Seuil, 2003).

37 Olivier Schwartz, "Peut-on parler des classes populaires? La vie des idées," 13 September 2011, accessed 25–2–2020, http://www.Laviedesidees.Fr/Peut-on-Parler-Des-Classes.html.

working class. Increasing numbers of working-class women started working in old and new areas of the service sector. After having children, more and more married women returned to the jobs they were trained for, but they also moved into other jobs, often on a part-time basis. The short-lived ideal of the sole male breadwinner disappeared in working households in these three countries after 1970. As jobs in the industrial sector became less secure, women frequently became the temporary or permanent breadwinners in traditional working-class households, mostly in the non-industrial sector. This led to what the social historians perceive as a shift in the balance of power between the sexes. The next question then concerns the affect this shift had on gender images and gender roles. These questions are yet to be answered and require empirical studies, since contemporary surveys and studies remain inconclusive.

At the same time, these changes cast doubt on the validity of the good old sociological habit of constructing 'classes on paper' on the basis of the data relating to the occupation and the income of the heads of households, who were generally men. This principle was followed much too often and unquestioned in critical studies. In contrast, households as places where differing trajectories of men and women intersect and as intergenerational nodes of upward and downward mobility with their own separate economic and social strategies and cultural practices are suitable objects of research in the quest to discover the dynamics of the *classes populaires.*

This perspective calls into question the customary differentiation between workers and low-wage employees. The changes in the labour market, especially with respect to low-wage jobs in the expanding private service sector, make it necessary to reconsider the relationship between gender and class in western European social space. In future social history should take care not to lose sight of gender and class.

Local Effects: Socio-spatial and Cultural Dimensions of Class Structuring

Even by the end of the 1990s, the radical shifts in political language and ideas of social order conveyed by the media had had remarkably little effect on the social orientation *(sens social)* of workers and low-wage employees. The majority of them in all three countries in the study were still convinced that social inequality stemmed from inequality in traditional social structures, in spite of the claims of common belief propagated by the media that it was the result of a kaleidoscope of fine distinctions. Respondents in self-placement studies in these countries used the standard binary 'them and us' as well as the established pattern of a tripartite social space. Even in Germany where, as we have seen, the perception of social inequality was neither clear nor determined by any official position, low income groups saw themselves as members of a separate section of society, distinct from 'them up there' as well as from middle to higher level employees or the alien world of public servants with a secure employment status.[38] If we take these findings seriously, there is a strong argument for not denying the existence of a large socio-economic group of 'workers' and for concentrating our attention on regional and local social environments, where there were broad and persistent expressions of solidarity, mostly with trade unions. In this case the existence of 'workers' or 'workforce' as a tangible and operative group would be found mainly in those social spaces where such continuity in representation and mobilisation efforts played a significant role. Even during the industrialisation phase, the workforce was an assemblage of different groups of regional or small-scale character, and owed its collective existence largely to political representation on the part of social democratic or socialist parties. In this respect, a social history of the late twentieth century should be able to draw on that of the nineteenth century, but with the major difference that it is dealing with a process of decline, in which a significant role is played by forms of political representation and language. Such sociological research findings raise the question of which concepts or theories can adequately describe not only processes of social group formation, socio-spatial proximity and neighbourhood but also distance and opposition, all of which are part of the process of 'class struggle without class'. It seems to me that the concept proposed by the French ethnologist Olivier Schwartz – *classes populaires* ('popular classes') – is eminently suitable here. In his study of the private lives and cultural practices of workers and employees in France, Schwartz uses the term *classes populaires*[39] to bring together two dimensions that are frequently separated and analysed from completely different perspectives and using very different categories, namely socio-economic inequality and cultural distance or difference. What links these two categories in his view is the relationship between the 'dominating and the dominated' (*dominants-dominés)*. It is only through this relationship, Schwartz maintains, that both socio-economic and cultural differences acquire social relevance and meaning. Com-

---

38 Rainer Geißler and Sonja Weber-Menges, "'Natürlich gibt es heute noch Schichten!' Bilder der modernen Sozialstruktur in den Köpfen der Menschen" in *Soziale Milieus und Wandel der Sozialstruktur. Die gesellschaftlichen Herausforderungen und die Strategien sozialer Gruppen*, eds. Helmut Bremer and Andrea Lange-Vester (Wiesbaden: Westdeutscher Verlag 2006). 102–127.
39 Schwartz, "Classes populaires"; Olivier Schwartz, *Le monde privé des ouvriers: hommes et femmes du Nord.* (Paris: Presses Universitaires de France, 1990).

bining a perspective on inequality that was originally sociological with one that is culturalist seems a particularly suitable approach to analysis of the changes observed in the three countries during the period under investigation. *Classes populaires* is a term that permits us to link the formation of classes or social status groups based on economic status with cultural dynamics and new considerations of cultural capital. It also permits us to recognise the deficits of traditional class analysis, which is unable to capture the logic of both cultural and socio-economic influences. For my purpose of writing a comparative social history there are numerous benefits of using the term *classes populaires*, (which incidentally cannot be adequately translated into German). First, it enables the disparate national traditions of class formation to be seen as variations of a basic constellation. Second, it helps to account for cultural and economic factors in equal measure. Third, it makes it possible to conceptualise the social and cultural convergence of previously separate occupational groups and social status groups.

It is clear then that the term *classes populaires* meets the conditions set out at the beginning of this chapter, namely that the impact of theory and the cultural dimensions of class structuring be taken seriously. Finally, to illustrate the value of this approach, I will use an example of changes that affected workers and low-wage employees in the social space of the three western European countries studied. My focus will be on processes which are extraneous to the world of work within a company but are closely connected to the process of de-industrialisation and to changes in regimes of capitalist accumulation in western Europe. I will concentrate on transformations in the social geography of labour and living.[40]

First, the social spaces of industrial working and living environments withdrew to the peripheries. This peripheralisation was caused by large-scale industry moving out of the urban centres and new industries moving back to more rural or small-town sites. It meant that workers themselves relocated to the edges of cities or straight to small and medium-sized towns or even to villages. While this was the case for the traditional industrial areas hit by spectacular structural and social crises (northern England, parts of Scotland and Wales, former East Germany, parts of the Ruhr and the north German coastal towns, northern and eastern France), it was also true for those areas where there was a rise in new (industrial) jobs, such as in many rural regions of France and in south and south-west Germany. This shift towards the periphery also contributed to all three societies becoming service economies, whose centres lay in the core metropolitan areas. They in turn were boosted culturally and economically by gentri-

40 More details in Raphael, *Jenseits von Kohle und Stahl*, 419–466.

fication and urbanist image enhancement, such as by means of tourist attractions and buildings designed by signature architects – a development evident in all three countries since the 1990s. This shift of industrial normality to the urban periphery or into the provinces follows seamlessly from the ordering of social space in the bourgeois nineteenth century and its symbolic and cultural evaluation of social space producing what Bourdieu calls 'site effects'[41]. At the same time a serious social crisis developed in the large estates and high-rise blocks in industrial areas and urban peripheries due to inadequate funding, selective privatisation and an almost complete halt in the construction of social housing. Dilapidated public buildings and the withdrawal of state authority from the *zones urbaines sensibles* (the French planners' politically correct term) were only the most media-effective aspects of a much wider socio-spatial process.[42]

Second, during the de-industrialisation phase growing numbers in the *classes populaires* advanced to become home and property owners. This was increasingly the case for those skilled industrial workers who were at the core of the declining industrial firms but also for those families and households with more than one source of income. It was boosted in particular by the increase of job opportunities for women in the new service sector. Many of these households financed their properties with cheap credit and ended up heavily in debt. The resulting 'lower middle-class' residential areas (as they were called in Germany), or those of the *classes populaires,* well-documented for France, provided social anchorage[43] for the shift of the labour markets over to the various service sectors. In its absence, there arose a state of socio-spatial neglect all too visible to all social policy makers and the wider public in the form of deprived areas on the urban fringe and the ruins of mono-industrial cities (of which there were in fact very few). Contrary to the predictions of progressive social democrat programmes during the expansion phase, society did not become increasingly fluid within an increasing socio-spatial mix. Most workers were unable to change their circumstances or accommodation and were kept in their place in the lower

---

41 Pierre Bourdieu, *The Weight of the World. Social Suffering in Contemporary Society* (London: Polity Press 1999), 123–129.

42 Nicole Tabard, "Des quartiers pauvres aux banlieues aisées: une représentation sociale du territoire," *Economie et statistique* 270, 1 (1993): 5–22 https://doi.org/10.3406/estat.1993.5822, accessed 25–2–2020, Edmond Préteceille, "La ségrégation contre la cohésion sociale: la métropole Parisienne." in *L'épreuve des inégalités,* ed. Hugues Lagrange (Paris: Presses universitaires de France, 2006), 195–246.

43 Marie Cartier, *La France des "petits-moyens": Enquête sur la banlieue pavillonnaire* (Paris: La Découverte, 2008).

half of the social space of these three countries. It is also important to note that these were the areas where the majority of migrant workers made their homes if they had left their original transit locations. From a socio-spatial perspective, these zones remained relatively stable during the period of this study. Another reason why they could provide social anchorage was that there was a steady increase in the number of workers commuting daily or weekly from their homes to their places of work. The trend was similar in all three countries: from the 1970s until 2000 and later, there was a steady increase both in the number of commuters and in the distances they were commuting.[44]

Third, apart from very few exceptions, in all these countries the large-scale industrial conurbations disappeared. In the heyday of industrialisation between 1889 and 1970, they had made it possible to establish very close links between the industrial production space and industrially determined social space. Two examples of these compact industrial labour worlds are the coal and steel producing regions and the large automobile manufacturers. The industrial districts of the digital age are completely different and resemble far more the type of spatial order that has always been characteristic for rural and small-scale businesses. These are settlement structures influenced by small towns with a mixed economy and where different socio-economic status groups are closely interconnected.

Peripheralisation also amounts to a symbolic downgrading and those concerned were indeed sensitive to it as a form of exclusion. The *classes populaires* partly saw themselves once again pushed to the periphery where they were made more or less invisible and deprived of their social recognition by the socio-spatial consequences of de-industrialisation. This perspective on socio-spatial changes provides a sociohistorical foundation for the thesis advanced by cultural and political historians that there was a crisis of representation and that the appreciation of problems and experiences of industrial workers was disappearing.

What emerges from these findings is paradoxical. Whereas on the national level (of social statistics, political and media representation and mobilisation) the existence of the working classes has become doubted and doubtful, as a category of analysis and description *classes populaires* still remains a valid concept. It exposes a variety of different milieus which by no means present a homogenous picture. This concerns the social milieus of the old industrial centres with heritage status but also to a much greater extent those milieus

---

44 Raphael Emanuel Dorn, *Alle in Bewegung. Räumliche Mobilität in der Bundesrepublik Deutschland 1980–2010* (Göttingen: Vandenhoek & Ruprecht, 2018).

still based on industrial production, often located outside the large-scale industrial hubs. For all the three countries, the geography of existing sociological and ethnographic studies is extremely complex and the resulting image is of small-scale areas of high density. This is a pattern already well known to social historians from the nineteenth and early twentieth centuries. Social historians of the working class in the nineteenth century also used this kind of local case study to paint an overall picture of the working class on a national level, and found it divided into diverse local social and occupational milieus but united by common forms of organisation and representation. In this history of success and emancipation, diversity had its place as part of a whole. Diversity at the end of the twentieth century is the result of a process of political and cultural erosion, but also of socio-spatial resilience, renewal and progress. Where these milieus are strongest, there is evidence that migrant workers and other new arrivals are integrated into these contexts and patterns of meaning. This regional concentration has been and still is mainly described as a consequence of traditional job orientation, the reproduction of social status and habitus, which found its way into the dynamically changing class relations in companies that adapted to the new worlds of industrial capitalism emerging in the last decades of the twentieth century in western Europe. As Cooper said, at this level we may find workers who seize the opportunity "to make themselves into something more than anonymous sellers of labor power" and arrange new "relations between men and women, among neighbors, among ordinary people ...and among citizens".[45]

45 Cooper, "Labor History," 116.

Matthias Middell

Marx and Today's Global History

There was an astonishing growth of interest in Marx around 2018, but we do not know for how long after the 200th anniversary of his birth that we will see articles reflecting upon the many Marx – Marx the economist,[1] Marx the philosopher[2] and Marx the analyst of capitalism.[3] Historians count him among the classics in their field, but his distance from professional national history writing was too evident to make him a true part of the discipline. This has changed with the renewal of global history that has been developing since the early 1990s. Karl Marx now seems to have a permanent seat even in large overviews of the history of historiography.[4] This is somehow paradoxical since Marxism had lost a lot of its creditability due to the many crises international communism and state socialism had gone through – be it Joseph Stalin's terror in the 1930s and the temporary pact with Adolf Hitler in 1939, the suppression of the revolts in East Central Europe between 1953 and 1956 as well as in 1968 by Soviet troops, or the slow decline of the attractiveness of the state socialist model during the second half of the Cold War. At the end of the 1980s, there was very little popular support for the regimes in East Central Europe. The collapse of the Soviet Union followed in 1991, and the communist parties in Western Europe collapsed as well while liberal triumphalism unmistakably declared Marxism dead forever. But it was exactly at that moment of decline and delegitimisation that one of the first synthesis of the new global history was published by an author who declared himself Marxist and looked back with some chagrin at the 'short 20th cen-

---

1 Henrik Müller, "Der Kapitalismus geht zugrunde. Was kann uns Karl Marx heute noch sagen?" Spiegel online, accessed April 29, 2018, http://www.spiegel.de/wirtschaft/soziales/karl-marx-und-das-ende-des-kapitalismus-kolumne-a-1205335.html.

2 Volker Gerhardt, "Die Asche des Marxismus: Über das Verhältnis von Marxismus und Philosophie," in *Marxismus: Versuch einer Bilanz*, ed. Volker Gerhardt (Magdeburg. Scriptum, 2001), 339–376.

3 Jürgen Neffe, Kontrollverlust: Der Mensch ist zum Objekt seiner wichtigsten Schöpfung geworden – des Kapitalismus. Karl Marx war dessen hellsichtigster Analytiker. Selbst unsere digitale Gegenwart lässt sich noch in "seinen Begriffen fassen", *Die ZEIT*, April 26, 2018, 22–23.

4 Daniel Woolf, *Global History of History* (Cambridge: CUP, 2011), somehow surrenders to the "complex and prolific" character of the way Marx and Engels wrote history (384). There are large subchapters on Marx and Marxism in *Weltgeschichte der Historiografie von 1750 bis heute*, ed. Georg Iggers, Edward Wang and Supriya Mukherjee (Göttingen: V&R, 2013), 120–123, 248–252. See also Matthias Middell, 'Karl Marx', in *Klassiker der Geschichtswissenschaft*, ed. Lutz Raphael (Munich: Beck, 2006), vol. 1, 123–141.

https://doi.org/10.1515/9783110677744-013

tury'. In Eric Hobsbawm's interpretation this short century was one where the Soviet Union had saved liberal democracy in the West several times from self-destruction by overcoming militarily Hitler's *Wehrmacht* and by driving the West into a decades-long competition for the better welfare system.[5] An even broader stream that poured into the ambitions of new historiography comprised new explanations of global developments through the emergence of one or more world-system(s). Immanuel Wallerstein had made the idea popular that the dominance of the West has long roots – reaching back at least to the fifteenth century – and became stabilised in a way that it reproduces systematically global inequality – and became between what he called the core and the peripheries of the world-system. When reading the first two volumes of Wallerstein's great synthesis,[6] one cannot overlook the inspiration from Marx and his twenty-third and twenty-fourth chapter of *Capital*; furthermore, Wallerstein critically engages with this predecessor by considering dependency theory, which developed in the 1960s and 1970s.

Interestingly enough, within the world-system school at least two fundamental questions related to each other were already being raised: how novel and how Western really was the world-system described by Wallerstein? Although André Gunder Frank and Barry K. Gills accepted Wallerstein's analysis of the modern world-system, they asked if the world-system has a history of 500 or 5,000 years, during which many processes could be observed from the Mesopotamian times and are not that new.[7] This argument was first a strategic one and targeted Eurocentrism as a strong weapon of Western intellectual – and political – dominance. But only a few years later, Frank, in his book *ReOrient*, turned it into an empirical one: China in particular and East Asia in general were only for a relatively short period of time peripherised by Western powers and economies; however, they were able to recover, as indicated by the most recent economic

5 E. J. Hobsbawm, *Age of extremes: The short twentieth century, 1914–1991* (London, New York: Michael Joseph, 1994). While the shortness of the past century, opening with World War I and ending with the disappearance of the Soviet Union, was at the heart of Hobwsbawm's book, Giovanni Arrighi insisted on a much longer perspective of about 700 years to understand the recalibration between capital accumulation and state formation: Giovanni Arrighi, *The Long Twentieth Century: Money, Power and the Origins of our Times* (London: Verso, 1994).
6 Immanuel Wallerstein, *The Modern World-System I: Capitalist Agriculture and the Origins of the European World-Economy in the Sixteenth Century* (New York, London: Academic Press, 1974); Immanuel Wallerstein, *The Modern World-System II: Mercantilism and the Consolidation of the European World-Economy, 1600–1750* (New York et. al.: Academic Press, 1980).
7 Andre Gunder Frank, Barry K. Gills, eds., *The World System: Five Hundred Years or Five Thousand?* (London, New York: Routledge, 1993).

performance.[8] Some of these debates continued previous discussions among Marxist and non-Marxist historians about the great transformation from feudalism to capitalism,[9] but none of them were completely detached from the problems already discovered or made popular by Marx in the midst of the nineteenth century.

Larger parts of global history, however, moved from these debates centred around problems of socioeconomic interpretations to new ones about the circulation of cultural patterns[10] or of geopolitics.[11] This may also have to do with new alliances built between global history and area studies,[12] under the impact of the cultural and the spatial turn.[13] This, however, does not mean that Marxian perspectives have become lost completely. On the contrary, while some criticise the Eurocentrism in the analysis of Marx devoted to the development of capitalism in England and France and especially his remarks on India (which depended mainly on secondary literature of his time),[14] the old questions of global inequality, the specific dynamics characteristic of the capitalist mode of production, or the various forms of labour and the resulting formats of resistance to exploitation remain at the centre of large parts of global history.

This renewed interest in questions formulated by Marx has resulted in a situation where the primary query is no longer if Marx was right or wrong and if he could be mobilised as a powerful ally in historico-political internal fights. Today, rather, he receives attention due to his capacity as a highly intelligent contemporary observer of the moment when the global condition slowly emerged and produced an increasingly interconnected and interdependent world. Marx was already able to historicise this particular moment, not as an absolute point of

---

8 Andre Gunder Frank, *ReOrient: Global economy in the Asian Age* (Berkeley: UCP, 1998).

9 S. H. Rigby, *Marxism and History: A Critical Introduction* (Manchester, New York: MUP, 1998).

10 Jerry H. Bentley, *Old World Encounters: Cross-cultural Contacts and Exchanges in Pre-modern Times* (New York: OUP,1993).

11 Paul M. Kennedy, *The Rise and Fall of Great Powers: Economic Change and Military Conflict from 1500 to 2000* (Lexington, MA: Knopf Doubleday Publishing Group, 1987).

12 Dominic Sachsenmaier, *Global Perspectives on Global History: Theories and Approaches in a Connected World* (Cambridge, New York: CUP, 2011).

13 As an overview to the diversity of approaches among global historians, see Sven Beckert, Dominic Sachsenmaier, eds., *Global History, Globally: Research and Practice around the World* (London: Bloomsbury Publishing, 2018); Matthias Middell, ed., *The Practise of Global History: European Perspectives* (London: Bloomsbury Publishing 2019).

14 For an analysis of the recent debate about Marx and the colonial question, see Kolja Lindner, "Globale Herausforderungen: Marxismus und Pluralismus im 21. Jahrhundert," in *Kommunismus jenseits des Eurozentrismus*, eds. Ulrich Mählert et. al. (Berlin: Metropol Verlag, 2019), 255–271.

departure but as a main station on the road from archaic to modern globalisation.

Without any doubt, the many dimensions of the relationship between Marx and current global history can be approached from different angles. There is a strand within global historiography that describes itself overtly as Marxist. But even among these Marxists there is a difference and sometimes a dispute to which tradition of references to Marx one should refer. The work of Marx is obviously heterogeneous enough to feed a variety of approaches, and the many social, political and intellectual constellations have multiplied these tendencies across the world since his death in 1883. There is obviously not the one Marxism everyone can agree to – for both political and conceptual reasons. While there is an abundant literature with which (often orthodox) authors defend their version of Marxism against others and denounce them for not belonging to the 'church', there is no satisfying overview of the many Marxisms that have been (and still are) propagated. There is a painful history of disqualifying intellectuals as revisionists within a Marxist rhetoric fuelled by the confusion between the exchange of arguments and decisions about politics. Whereas in research revisionism is, in general, seen as a positive characteristic of productive engagement with the already known, in the politicised discourse of socialist and communist movements revisionism has remained for a long time a negative sign of disloyalty. Global history, as it emerged in the 1980s and 1990s, is overtly revisionist in many respects: it is to the one or the other degree critical towards the universalistic, Eurocentric and Western-biased narratives of old-fashioned world and universal history.[15] This fundamentally pluralistic character of the new global history, which has so far avoided some of the major risks of orthodoxy,[16] makes it even more difficult to identify Marxist substreams in a broad river. Mainstream global history would therefore rather subscribe to the idea that Marx has been and might still continue to be a strong inspiration given his status as an intelligent contemporary observer of the emerging global condition. His analysis of capitalism as resulting in new forms of global inequality and his interest in the transformation of the pre-industrial world to a slowly industrialising one is echoed by current global history. This connection can also be observed in his involvement in the

---

15 Patrick Manning, *Navigating World History: Historians Create a Global Past* (New York: Springer, 2003) based upon a strong link to the area studies as well as to subaltern studies and postcolonial studies. See for the latter: Dipesh Chakrabarty, *Provincializing Europe: Postcolonial Thought and Historical Difference* (Princeton: PUP 2000).

16 For an interesting debate about this feature of recent global history, see the debate between Jürgen Osterhammel and Pierre-Yves Saunier in eds. Marek Tamm, Peter Burke, *Debating New Approaches to History* (London, New York: Bloomsbury Publishing 2018), 21–48.

formulation of global ideologies such as socialism and liberalism. The slogan "Workers of the world, unite!" contains a complex agenda for social and cultural as well as political history that tries to go beyond the limitations of methodological nationalism. It took, however, quite some time to place this slogan in new ways at the centre of scholarly attention. Accordingly, through the perspective of new global labour history, the question, for example, was asked how to construct solidarity across the many facets of labour and how to deal with the fact that free wage labour, the ideal type also placed by Marx at the centre of investigation, was rather the exception than the rule during the nineteenth and larger parts of the twentieth centuries.[17] Or, there was a critical examination of how the internationalism of the working class, to which Marx contributed himself a lot, transformed into the legitimate basis for state socialism as in Joseph Stalin's Soviet Union.[18]

"Historiography beyond the sole focus on the nation-state", as the phrase by Jürgen Osterhammel goes,[19] has developed an ambivalent relationship to the texts written by Marx during the second third of the nineteenth century. Similar to some postcolonial theorists, they are shocked by the easiness with which Marx uses container-like units of analysis, such as Britain, France and India, in a manner that is seemingly not very sensitive to today's concern for the constructedness of social, economic and political spaces. However, they must recognise that Marx also applies his strong sense for the historicity of almost everything to fragile spatial configurations, such as Germany, Spain, Italy and Russia, which had been at the time of his writing on the way to becoming sovereign states instead of already being ones. The story of the great transformation from empire to nation-state, which is at the centre of many narratives about the nineteenth century European history, turns out to be more complex than it was told in the past. What is evident for the British Empire – already from its name – also holds true for France or the USA: they went, starting with revolution in the late eighteenth century, through a process of democratisation, constitu-

---

17 Marcel van der Linden, *Workers of the World: Essays Toward a Global Labour History* (Leiden, Boston: Brill, 2008).

18 For a nuanced report on the different faces of red globalization, see James Mark and Tobias Rupprecht, "The Socialist World in Global History. From Absentee to Victim to Co-Producer," in *European Perspectives on Global History*, ed. Matthias Middell, (London: Bloomsbury, 2019), as well as James Mark, Péter Apor, "Socialism Goes Global: Decolonization and the Making of a New Culture of Internationalism in Socialist Hungary, 1956–1989," *Journal of Modern History* 87 (2015), 852–891; Oscar Sanchez-Sibony, Red Globalization, *The Political Economy of the Soviet Cold War from Stalin to Khrushchev* (New York: CUP, 2014).

19 Jürgen Osterhammel, *Geschichtswissenschaft jenseits des Nationalstaats. Studien zu Beziehungsgeschichte und Zivilisationsvergleich* (Göttingen: V&R, 2001).

tionalism and nationalisation when it comes to their metropolitan territories. But, and that is important to note, these processes went hand in hand with the colonisation of other territories – in the American West as well as around Algeria and other parts of the Maghreb, later on in Indochina for France and in the Philippines or Puerto Rico in the case of the USA. The same is to be observed for the continuous efforts by the Spanish or the Portuguese as well as the Russian crown to bring liberal reforms together with imperial features.[20] What we can conclude from these examples – followed during the late nineteenth and the early twnetieth century by more states combining nationalisation and colonisation to form a hybrid new spatial format that we may call nation-state-cum-empire[21] – is that it was not nation-states that emerged out of the Atlantic revolutions. Instead, it was a central intellectual operation run by the emerging social sciences at the turn from the nineteenth to the twentieth century that tended to hide the imperial component of the dominant spatial format and consequently brought the then reigning methodological nationalism to the fore.[22]

Such methodological nationalism was, as we can conclude from this timeline, not of the highest relevance for Marx, although it became so for future global historians after 1900 when the nation-state had become the leading category in the study of societies subordinating other spatial formats, such as places, or cities or international entanglements of all kinds, to the logic of a teleology of the nation-(state). Marx, on the contrary, was confronted with a mix of nation-states in statu nascendi, nation-states with large (and further growing) imperial extensions, and emerging world international organisations. The consequence of this observation is obvious and has been drawn as often as it had been neglected by others: we have to historicise Marx and put him into the world he was able to observe. To expect that Marx had answers to our questions at the beginning of the twenty-first century would, on the one hand, at least not be very Marxian. On the other hand, we would not be interested in him – despite the occasion of his 200th birthday – if there was not anything that speaks to current challenges as well.

---

20 See, for example, the interesting comparative study by Josep M. Fradera, *The Imperial Nation: Citizens and Subjects in the British, French, Spanish, and American Empires* (Princeton, Oxford: PUP, 2018.

21 Matthias Middell, "The Category of Spatial Formats: To What End?," in *Re-spatializations under the Global Condition: Towards a Typology of Spatial Formats*, eds. Matthias Middell, Steffi Marung (Berlin: de Gruyter, 2019), 15–47.

22 Jeremy Adelman, ed., *Empire and the Social Sciences. Global Histories of Knowledge* (London, New York: Bloomington, 2019).

In order to read Marx along his own logics and intentions, we have to take his own intellectual programme seriously and keep in mind *first* his point of departure in the critique of religion from a Hegelian perspective and *second* put *Capital* into his larger plan of a multivolume history of the relationship between economy and statehood. We should not forget that Marx, in contrast to Friedrich Engels, who learned about nineteenth-century capitalism in Manchester, started writing against the social background of the rather pre-modern situation of peasantry in the Mosel region and the strong tradition of artisanal work long before structures of mass production and consumption were established in this region. His main concern in the first years of publishing was to enlighten people about the causes, features and consequences of misrepresenting social relationships of misery – arguing that the reason for the miserable situation of the many poor is to be found on earth and not in heaven. The famous 'opium of the people' characteristics of religion is connected to the question of why such a misrepresentation works. The answer is to be found in the stability of this social world, in the complete lack of dynamics that would allow a substantial differentiation of social chances and of wealth. While the social background of Marx's early writings is the pre- and proto-industrial[23] economy of his region of origin, the intellectual background is the intense reading of the history of the French Revolution.[24] All the details taken from the forty volumes of sources and narratives published by Buchez and Roux[25] made Marx familiar with the opposition of an economy of

23 Since the early discussions of an industrialisation before the industrial epoch (Peter Kriedte, Hans Medick and Jürgen Schlumbohm, *Industrialisierung vor der Industrialisierung: gewerbliche Warenproduktion auf dem Land in der Formationsperiode des Kapitalismus* (Göttingen: Vandenhoeck und Ruprecht, 1977)), there has been a broad historiographical tradition investigating the various features of proto-industries and their relationship with coal-based industry during the nineteenth century. It has inspired a series of central debates not only in global history but also in developmental studies. The recent discussion about the Anthropocene and the unlikeliness of the possibility to repeat 19th-century emission-intensive industrialization in other parts of the world have given the debate a new push. See David Christian, *Big History: The Big Band, Life on Earth, and the Rise of Humanity* (Chantilly: Carl Hanser Verlag, 2008); Christophe Bonneuil and Jean-Baptiste Fressoz, *The Shock of the Anthropocene: The Earth, History and Us* (London: Verso, 2016).

24 The remaining authority on this is the precise reconstruction by *Hans-Peter Jaeck, Die französische bürgerliche Revolution von 1789 im Frühwerk von Karl Marx* (Berlin: Topos, 1979).

25 Histoire parlementaire de la révolution française, ou, Journal des Assemblées nationales depuis 1789 jusqu'en 1815, la narration des événements; les débats des assemblées; les discussions des principales sociétés populaires, et particulièrement de la société des jacobins: les procès- verbaux de la Commune de Paris, les séances du tribunal révolutionnaire le compte-rendu des principaux procés politiques; le détail des budgets annuels; le tableau du mouvement moral, extrait des journaux de chaque époque, etc.; précédée d'une introduction sur l'histoire de

land concentration in the hands of rich planters, grand farmers and the bourgeois industrialists, investing profit into land and office, on the one hand, and the egalitarian communitarianism that, set aside a part of the land for the needs of social welfare and profited from the redistribution of (church and emigrés') land during the revolution, on the other hand. He learned about alternative ways to deal with the situation of mature proto-industrialisation, either by following the English model of concentration of wealth and expropriation of the former landholders he described later in *Capital* as a sort of ideal type or by defending the (partly shared) property rights as well as the political power of the village community. The latter became the basis, which Marx was convinced of, for the programme of (Jacobin) radical democracy that developed the necessary thrust to overcome a cruel Ancien Régime and to hinder its reconstruction definitively. At the same time, Marx indicates that this egalitarian approach was among the sources of modern communism but it was not communist at all.[26] From Jacques Roux to Théophile Leclerc and finally to François Noel Babeuf, he drew a line of tradition; it also becomes clear that the world of the radical left during the French Revolution did not yet have very much to do with the capitalism he was confronted with in the mid-nineteenth century (at least confronted with as an intellectual challenge but not necessarily as a social reality in his home region). Capitalism in late eighteenth century France and capitalism in the 1840s in the Midlands of England and some parts of Belgium were quite different things. Technology had advanced decisively towards the use of steam engines and mechanised weaving mills based upon progress with the production of steel. But industrialisation was at its beginning and projections into the future were not to be confused with descriptions of the reality. Social consequences, such as the ones proclaimed in the *Communist Manifesto* of the poor being about to transform quickly and completely into a property-free proletariat, were convincing to some readers already at the time – and many more later – as a clear-sighted prognosis. However, these consequences were not necessarily related directly to the few examples of the new machinery but rather to a more complex social puzzle that had its origins in the reconfiguration of agriculture,

France jusqu'à la convocation des Etats-Généraux par Philippe-Joseph-Benjamin Buchez et Prosper-Charle Roux-Lavergne, Paris 1834–38.

26 For a detailed interpretation of how Jacques Roux, as the representative of the Enragés, the perhaps most radical group within the egalitarian spectrum, made it into the early writings of Marx, such as *The Holy Family* by Marx where he gives a sort of genealogy of the modern communist movement he dreamed of, see Walter Markov, *Jacques Roux und Karl Marx* (Berlin: Akademie Verlag 1965).

handiwork, trade and welfare.[27] Marx observed the first elements of a very complex process and read into them two general societal trends, which have not proven to be completely wrong but, nevertheless, turned out to be less deterministic than he would have wished for. One was the dynamics inherent in the combination of technological progress and profit orientation in capitalism. Marx was convinced that these two elements became drivers for each other, so that productivity would increase and would be unable to be stopped. The other trend would be a necessary consequence of the first – a growing number of people forced to work in the capitalist business and to sell their workforce. From his study of radical interventions by the poor and subaltern into the history of the French Revolution, Marx concluded that their growing number would make their success more likely while, at the same, the increasing productivity of capitalism would make the victory of communist concepts possible. In contrast to the failure of Babeuf and his fellow conspirators in 1796, when they remained a small minority of idealists not able to convince larger audiences of their utopian dream, Marx expected in his dialectical way of thinking a sort of determined success for future communist movements since they alone would be able to overcome the contradictory character of modern capitalism. As a consequence he devoted the decades after the defeat of 1848/49 in both France and Germany to a new intellectual adventure, now focusing much more on the most advanced economy of his time.

The Global Condition – When Did Present Time Start?

Fed by his friend Engels with cigars and statistics from the English midlands and soon moving to the reading room of the British Library, Marx developed a fascinating painting of the emerging industrial capitalism. Of course, he remained

---

27 It was the Soviet historian Anatolij Ado who not only brought research on alternative ways to capitalism together in his great monograph on peasants and their upheavals during the French Revolution, but also reminded the scholarly community of the many traces these realities had left in Marx' early writings. Anatoli Ado, *Paysans en Révolution: Terre, pouvoir et jacquerie 1789–1794* (Paris: Société des études robespierristes, 1996). (The first edition of his work was published in Russian already in 1971 and made known by a short summary in French written by Albert Soboul in 1976, the second Russian edition from 1987 became then translated into German in 1996, and finally from there into French. If it needs proof for the sometimes complicated and delayed perceptions between the various sorts of Marxist interpretations across borders of countries, blocs, and academic schools, then we have here an excellent one.)

critical towards exploitation, but what he saw first and foremost was the dual potential of new mass production, with machines to replace the old social hierarchies by new ones based upon modern-class building processes and to lead society beyond the limitations of this class division. Steam ships and railways, textile fabrication based on a world market of cotton, as well as the exportation of wheat from the black soil areas across the planet became the signature of the world Marx was now dealing with – a sharp contrast to the small wine farmers at the Mosel. The picture Marx drew has become the central point of reference in modern global history writing. The mid-nineteenth century sits at the core of larger synthesis[28] and is a subject of specialised monographs. There is an emerging consensus that something like the global condition emerged around that time.[29] Some call it modern globalisation in contrast to an archaic one;[30] others describe it as the first appearance of world markets worthy of the name.[31] The web of networks across boundaries of continents, regions and empires grew rapidly in density and functionality as the much faster communication proves.[32] It is among many others also Marx who profited from the new possibilities in the communication system as the professional and globally oriented journalist[33]

---

28 Christopher A. Bayly, *The Birth of the Modern World, 1780–1914. Global Connections and Comparisons* (Malden, MA: Wiley, 2004); Jürgen Osterhammel, *Die Verwandlung der Welt. Eine Geschichte des 19. Jahrhunderts* (Munich: C.H.Beck, 2009).

29 Charles Bright and Michael Geyer, "Benchmarks of Globalization: The Global Condition 1850–2010," in *A Companion to World History*, ed. Douglas Northrop (Malden, MA, Oxford and Chichester: John Wiley & Sons 2012), 285–302.

30 Christopher A. Bayly, "'Archaic' and 'Modern' Globalization in the Eurasian and African Arena, c. 1750–1850," in *Globalization in World History*, ed. Anthony G. Hopkins (London: Random House, 2002), 47–73.

31 Kevin H. O'Rourke and Jeffrey G. Williamson, "When Did Globalisation Begin?," *European Review of Economic History* 6 (2002): 23–50; Christof Dejung and Niels P. Petersson, eds., *The Foundations of Worldwide Economic Integration: Power, Institutions, and Global Markets, 1850–1930* (New York: CUP, 2013).

32 Roland Wenzlhuemer, *Connecting the Nineteenth-century World: The Telegraph and Globalization* (Cambridge, New York: CUP, 2013); Deep Kanta Lahiri Choudhury, *Telegraphic Imperialism: Crisis and Panic in the Indian Empire, c.1830–1920* (New York: Springer, 2010); Simone M. Müller, *Wiring the World: The Social and Cultural Creation of Global Telegraph Networks* (New York: Columbia UP, 2016).

33 Jürgen Herres, "Karl Marx als politischer Journalist im 19. Jahrhundert," in *Beiträge zur Marx-Engels-Forschung. Neue Folge 2005*, Berlin (2005), 7–28; Giesela Neuhaus and Manfred Neuhaus, "Karl Marx und Friedrich Engels als Auslandskorrespondenten der einflußreichsten progressiven bürgerlichen Zeitung am Vorabend des nordamerikanischen Bürgerkrieges: Zur Geschichte der Mitarbeit der Klassiker des Marxismus an der "New York Tribune"". In *Marx-Engels-Forschungsberichte*, H. 1, Leipzig (1981), 12–62.

he became in the 1850s, who assembled incoming news for his analytical overviews published in American as well as British newspapers.

This intensification of worldwide connections has inspired global historians to echo the definition of globalisation proposed by their colleagues from the social sciences and in particular from economics: globalisation is the result of the increasing mobilities of goods, people, capital and cultural patterns across the borders of economies, societies and states. The advantage of such a definition is that it can be relatively easy operationalised in form of charts showing the volume in trade or migration, foreign direct investments and so on. Marx would have agreed to this definition, at least in part. He highlights the all-encompassing, planetary character of capitalism, its capacity to ignore and overcome borders and to create world markets. This is part of his analysis in *Capital*. But the study of modern capitalism comes together with the many other texts on political affairs – for instance, from the series written between August and December 1854[34] and then in 1856[35] for the *New-York Daily Tribune* on Spanish revolutions since the early nineteenth century to the reportages on the American Civil War in the early 1860s,[36] and from the study of Bonapartism in France[37] to the first interest in Russian affairs in the correspondence with Vera Zasulich in 1881,[38] not to forget the texts on India under British colonial rule.[39] With the exception of a few parts of the world, Marx brought together knowledge about a globalising world under construction, and he contributed to this cosmopolitan view as the journalist and historian he was. Two problems are at the centre of his attention: the first is the conflictual character of the transition to modern capitalism. In stark contrast to the idea that a somehow anonymous essence of capitalism frees the productive forces from the bonds of traditional social relations (respectively they free themselves), this process goes hand in hand with wars, revolutions, quasi-permanent political crises, civil wars and coup d'états. Marx takes the high degree of violence that accompanied this process, which in some passages of *Capital* appears as a civilising mission exercised by capital, as an invitation to rethink the transition happening. As a political theorist, he thinks in alternative ways to react to the challenge of modern capitalism. People are not

---

34 Karl Marx and Friedrich Engels, *Werke* (in the following *MEW*) vol. 10 (Berlin: Dietz, 1961) 433–485.

35 *MEW* vol. 12, 43–48.

36 For example *MEW* vol. 15, 486–495.

37 Marx, "Der achtzehnte Brumaire des Louis Bonaparte," in *MEW* vol. 8, 111–207

38 Teodor Shanin, "1881 Letters of Vera Zasulich and Karl Marx," *The Journal of Peasant Studies* 45, no. 7 (2018): 1183–1202.

39 *MEW* 9, 127–133.

simply exposed to an ever more powerful mechanism of increasing entanglements, they also try to bring this mechanism under control. The means of control can be traditional ones or very innovative ones.

This leads Marx to the second problem he was working on: the weight of traditional structures in developing appropriate tools for gaining control again over the global flows. His main interest is the transition to modern capitalism, but he consequently historicises it, for example, this is demonstrated in the largest chapter in volume I of *Capital* on primitive accumulation. Here, he comes back to the tension between his own social background in a (roughly speaking) preindustrial region and the modern industry he recognises as the feature of the future. This inspired an entire debate among Marxist and non-Marxist historians, starting with the Dobb-Sweezy controversy in the late 1940s, about the role of the early modern transformation for later success in the breakthrough to modern industry. In the context of modernisation theory, the political interest in these debates mainly focused on the relevance for Third World societies catching up with the West – or not and why not. This has its offshoots even today in the Great Divergence debate.[40]

What distinguished the period up to 1800 or 1820 from the subsequent period is the relatively little weight of transregional connectedness in contrast to intraregional resources of mainly agrarian societies. Undoubtedly, there were contacts and there was a relevant flow of ideas across oceans, and there was the pattern of the plantation economy in the Caribbean that brought manpower, capital, and the fertility of soil from different world regions together. Nevertheless, Braudel had already insisted on the fact that different *économies-mondes* remained relatively separate from each other and followed primarily their own logics. Arguably, Marx, as many of his followers, were wrong in calculating correctly the economic contribution that was made by the colonies until 1800 to European superiority in world economy. This does not exclude massive social effects of high profits from colonial trade at some hotspots of maritime Europe.[41]

The situation changed dramatically in the mid-nineteenth century, when further competitive economic development of societies became increasingly dependent on its integration into an entangled world of increasing specialisation and division of labour. Marx, who was fascinated with the potential of the

---

40 Roy Bin Wong and Jean-Laurent Rosenthal, *Before and Beyond Divergence: The Politics of Economic Change in China and Europe* (Cambridge, Mass: CUP, 2011).

41 On this controversy, see, especially, the contributions by Patrick O'Brien, who estimates the colonial resources at 3 to 6 per cent of the European GDP. Patrick K. O'Brien, "Colonies in a Globalizing Economy 1815–1948," in *Globalization and Global History,* eds. Barry Gills and William Thompson (London: Routledge, 2004) (GEHN WP 08/04).

new technologies in the growth of productivity was convinced of the prognosis that this will lead in the long run to a borderless world. On the other hand, he was well aware that against all internationalist and cosmopolitan tendencies (which he openly welcomed in India, for example, as a means to overcome traditional parochialism, largely ignoring the unfair, protectionist and illiberal practices of the British authorities[42]), his time was a time of national bordering and the completion of the process of territorialisation.[43] These dialectics of increasing flows and growing as well as renewed control over such flows by means of territorialisation constitute the core problem Marx has addressed but not completely solved in his work. This is due to the unfinished character of not only *Capital* but also of the completely missing volumes on the state and the political organisation of societies. True, parts of his ideas are developed in other studies, for example the one on class struggle in France[44] or the article series mentioned in the aforementioned section on Spain in the 1850s or North America in the 1860s. But his focus on the economic analysis of modern capitalism strengthens the impression that he presents first and foremost a universal theory to explain a capitalist mode of production. Only when digging deeper, both in *Capital* and his other works, do we realise that he describes the pathways to modern capitalism as well as the variants of that capitalism in the plural, and is far away from a universalistic narrative. In terms of today's global history, there is not one globalisation as a quasi-natural process but many globalisations happening at the same time, being entangled together as we compete with each other.[45] I would even go a step further and not speak of different globalisations but of globalisation projects, insisting with this term on the political character of reactions to global flows and on the intentionality of these reactions.

Marx, who started his intellectual journey with an interest in France, and compared French developments to his unfulfilled dreams of German political modernity, went then to London not only for the better working conditions there but also in order to analyse the emerging industrial capitalism at its core. That has led to an image of Marx being interested in the triangle France–Britain–Germany, which only became among European historians and Europeanists outside the continent the canon of historical variants to be studied. But the empirical basis for Marx was

42 Prasannan Parthasarathi, *Why Europe Grew Rich and Asia Did Not. Global Economic Divergence, 1600–1850* (Cambridge, New York: CUP, 2011).
43 Charles S. Maier, *Once within Borders: Territories of Power, Wealth, and Belonging since 1500* (Cambridge, MA: CUP, 2016).
44 *MEW* vol. 28, 503–509.
45 Jürgen Osterhammel, *Die Flughöhe der Adler: Historische Essays zur globalen Gegenwart* (Munich: C.H.Beck, 2017) 12–41.

much broader, and especially his work on Spain is much more than a regional variation of the already well known. He put the particular way Spanish middle classes started their globalisation project by colonising the Iberian Peninsula in the fifteenth century in order to expand to South and Central America afterwards, in contrast to the belayed industrialisation of the country and its continued failure in the interimperial competition. The series of long articles is explicitly not limited to socioeconomic considerations, albeit written while Marx intensively took notes for *Capital*. And the same holds true for the series on the British–Indian conflict in the late 1850s or on the US Civil War.

In conclusion, we can state that Marx was in search of a general explanation of modern capitalism but this was only (an important) part of his interest in the complexity of the political affairs of his time, which he analysed as reactions to the emerging global condition and rather as different globalisation projects than as an economically determined trend towards a world society. The empirical basis was much broader than the classical triangle Britain–France–Germany, but, of course, not as broad as today's global history. All three elements – the study of the global condition as dialectics of global or transregional flows and (at the time primarily territorialising) control; the interest in globalisation projects and its diverse actors, including the working class; and the large empirical basis – make Marx interesting for different strands of global history nowadays.

A Global History Without Revolution?

There is, however, the topic of revolution, which was so central to Marx and has been so much left aside by current global historians (at least until very recently) that it raises the question for possible explanations of this difference. Marx had the history of the French Revolution in his intellectual luggage when analysing societies for their revolutionary potential, such as in 1848. He called revolutions "locomotives of world history"[46] and the term is omnipresent in his work, albeit not without different meanings and a lot of ambiguities. He makes a series of arguments as why the nineteenth century was later seen as an age of revolutions (Hobsbawm). In contrast, current global history is concerned with many dimensions of global entanglements and conflicts although it does not seem specifically interested in the role of revolutions, which are identified with unnecessary societal rupture (to be avoided by timely reform) and the outbreak of violence.

46 Karl Marx, "Die Klassenkämpfe in Frankreich 1848 bis 1850," in: Karl Marx and Friedrich Engels, *Werke*, Bd. 7 (Berlin: Dietz Verlag, 1960), 85.

Even neologisms such as peaceful or velvet revolution for the events in the German Democratic Republic or Czechoslovakia in 1989 have not helped to give the revolution a better image.

There are two trends for the time being. The first follows the global traces of formerly national revolutions. People like Bailey Stone, who already in 1992 developed an explanation of the French Revolution out of the interimperial competition between France and England, or Lynn Hunt, who emphasises the role of international finance (at the time concentrated in Geneva and not at Wall Street) in the outbreak of the revolutionary crisis, meet with those scholars who have completely reworked the relationship between Saint-Domingue and the metropolitan Hexagone. Revolutions, we learn, are never isolated events but are rather part of a larger global crisis and reactions to the globalising strategies of the elites in the country as well as internationally.

The second trend is less interested in the potential of revolutions to build new societal fundaments, instead taking them as indicators (parallel to war and civil war, political crisis and unconstitutional changes of government) for the failure of globalisation projects and their highly conflictual character.[47] It can also be interpreted as forms of protest by certain social groups against the disciplining and territorialising character of globalisation projects as demonstrated by Peter Linebaugh and Marcus Rediker.[48]

But one has to confess that these impulses come rather from specialised fields of historiography, where the history of revolutions remained traditionally strong, such as the transatlantic entanglements of upheaval and protest between 1770 and 1830[49] or the series of revolutions at the beginning of the twentieth century.[50]

What we have gained through these efforts is a more globalised picture of certain revolutionary complexes. The revolutionary Atlantic discovered by Robert

47 Charles Bright and Michael Geyer, "Globalgeschichte und die Einheit der Welt: Weltgeschichte als Globalgeschichte – Überlegungen zur einer Geschichte des 20. Jahrhundert," *Comparativ: Leipziger Beiträge zur Universalgeschichte und vergleichenden Gesellschaftsforschung* 4, no. 5 (1994): 13–46.

48 Peter Linebaugh and Marcus Rediker, *The Many-Headed Hydra: Sailors, Slaves, Commoners and the Hidden History of the Revolutionary Atlantic* (Boston: Verso, 2001).

49 For the rediscovery by global historians of a topic that was dealt with in other historiographies for more than half a century, see David Armitage and Sanjay Subrahmanyam, eds., *The Age of Revolutions in Global Context, c. 1760–1840* (Houndmills et al.: Macmillan International Higher Education, 2010).

50 As one example from the huge production of the commemorative industries in 2017: *1917 and its Aftermath from a Global Perspective*, eds. Stefan Rinke and Michael Wildt (Frankfurt: Campus Verlag, 2017).

Palmer and Jacques Godechot in 1955 expands not only into the Maghreb and sub-Saharan Africa but also into the Indian Ocean and has its echoes even in the Pacific. In similar ways is the Russian Revolution of 1917, no longer placed only in relationship to what happened in Central Europe, becoming more and more part of a worldwide theatre of discontent and reorganisation of control over the global flows between the 1890s and the 1920s.[51] Other examples chosen for the study of synchronous upheaval are 1956, 1968 and 1989.

This has inspired thoughts about global moments, defined as (1) short time spans within which turmoil and upheaval happens in very different places in the world; (2) moments that are collectively and transregionally remembered as important for the development of humankind; and (3) a series of events that can be narrated as an important rupture in the global spatial order.[52]

But this cannot hide the fact that the Marxian challenge to define what role revolutions have within a global history of modern capitalism has been largely ignored by global historians for quite some time. Books by Theda Skocpol[53], Manfred Kossok[54], Charles Tilly[55], or Jack Goldstone[56] – most of them rather historical sociologists than global historians – have become classics without successors. It is not the place here to speculate about the reasons for this. I would rather insist on a double challenge similar to the one Marx lived through. It may inspire thoughts about revolution again. First, we are just about to enter a period of completely new technologies changing the character of capitalism dramatically, for instance digitalisation. Second, we are confronted with a similar process of politicisation of globalisation projects as observed by Marx in the later nineteenth century. The belief that the technologically induced process

51 Charles S. Maier, "Leviathan 2.0. Die Erfindung moderner Staatlichkeit," in *Geschichte der Welt 1870–1945: Weltmärkte und Weltkriege*, eds. Akira Iriye, Jürgen Osterhammel and Emily S. Rosenberg (Munich: C.H.Beck, 2012), 33–286.

52 Matthias Middell, "Was ist ein globaler Moment? Überlegungen anhand des Jahres 1989," in *Leipziger Zugänge zur rechtlichen, politischen und kulturellen Verflechtungsgeschichte Ostmitteleuropas*, eds. Dietmar Müller and Adamantios Skordos (Leipzig: Leipziger Universitätsverlag, 2015), 103–115.

53 Theda Skocpol, *States and Social Revolutions. A Comparative Analysis of France, Russia, and China* (Cambridge: CUP, 1979).

54 Manfred Kossok, *In Tyrannos. Revolutionen der Weltgeschichte* (Leipzig: Edition Leipzig, 1989).

55 Charles Tilly, *From Mobilization to Revolution* (New York: McGraw-Hill, 1978); Charles Tilly, Die europäischen Revolutionen (Munich: C.H.Beck, 1993).

56 Jack A. Goldstone, *Revolution and Rebellion in the Early Modern World* (Berkeley, Los Angeles and London: UCP 1991); Jack A. Goldstone, "Toward a Fourth Generation of Revolutionary Theory," *Annual Review of Political Science* 4 (2001): 139–187.

will more or less linearly lead to a better world where the increase in wealth trickles down to everyone globally, more or less continuously, is disputed by a growing percentage of people who feel deep dissatisfaction with what others describe as a fortunate development. Populism, or any other name that we may give to the phenomenon, profits from the fact that global elites perceive the consensual discourse about globalisation as having no alternatives. Global history will have to react to this changing intellectual and political environment and perhaps Marx will become an interesting intellectual resource again in this respect as well.

Preben Kaarsholm

Marx, Globalisation and the Reserve Army of Labour

One thing that is definitely left of Marxism is its important place in the history of theories of history, development, and globalisation – a subject I have been teaching in recent years to students of development studies and global sociology.

In such a perspective, Karl Marx's theory of history and 'historical materialism' (as given expression, for example, in his writings on India for the *New York Herald Tribune* in the 1850s) stands out as a radical instance of uni-directional, evolutionist and Eurocentric modernisation theory. Marx presents British rule in India as the productive destruction of "Oriental despotism," Hindu superstition and "semi-barbarian" village communities "contaminated by distinctions of caste and by slavery". Though brutal and reprehensible, "the English yoke" thus paves the way for the introduction of "modern industry," "a net of railways," "the supreme rule of capital," and creates "the material conditions of a new world in the same way as geological revolutions have created the surface of the earth".[1]

Also in other respects does Marx's thinking around historical progress foreshadow that of post-Second World War modernisation theory. As explained in Marx's introduction to *Grundrisse* of 1857–1858, the emergence of 'bourgeois society' represents a *caesura* – a fundamental break – in world history, which brings about a qualitatively new dynamism that is governed solely by the social laws of the capitalist mode of production. Therefore, it sums up all earlier stages of historical development, which only give meaning as seen in retrospect as leading forward to this new epoch of capitalist history.[2] In this way, Marx introduces the idea of a break or take-off as setting the period of modern history apart from all earlier historical periods, which becomes again a fundamental ingredient and trivialised in modernisation theories of the 1950s and 1960s (most famously in

---

1 Karl Marx, "The British Rule in India," *New York Daily Tribune*, June 25, 1853, accessed November 23, 2018, https://www.marxists.org/archive/marx/works/1853/06/25.htm and Karl Marx, "The Future Results of British Rule in India," *New York Daily Tribune*, July 22, 1853, accessed November 23, 2018, https://marxists.catbull.com/archive/marx/works/1853/07/22.htm.

2 Karl Marx, *Grundrisse: Foundations of the Critique of Political Economy (Rough Draft)*, [1857–1861], trans. Martin Nicolaus (London: Penguin Books, 1973), 38. Page numbers refer to the electronic version available through https://www.marxists.org/archive/marx/works/download/pdf/grundrisse.pdf – accessed November 23, 2018.

https://doi.org/10.1515/9783110677744-014

W. W. Rostow's *Stages of Economic Growth: A Non-Communist Manifesto* from 1960).[3]

An Unfinished Theory

Marx's *Capital* and his draft manuscripts on theories of surplus value explore the basics of this purely social dynamism and logic, which *der Tendenz nach* (tendentially) are inherent in the capital-labour relationship and the bourgeois mode of production. But the whole architecture of the theoretical construct that Marx and Friedrich Engels aimed at was never completed. This means that major areas of significance were left out from what was outlined in the introduction to *Grundrisse*. This included accounts of "the three great social classes" and "exchange between them", of the "concentration of bourgeois society in the form of the state", of the "unproductive classes", of "population", "the colonies", "emigration", "international relations of production, international division of labour, and international exchange" and of "the world market and crises".[4] Therefore, the exact nature of a lawfulness which manifests itself only tendentially – for example of the inexorability of the crises and *Zusammenbruchstendenz* (tendency to collapse) that is inherent in the law of the fall in rate of profit – is not given full-scale and systematic treatment, but is left for investigation to later generations of Marxists.

Hints can be found, however, in the third volume of *Capital* (as edited and published by Engels in 1894) of some of the directions in which Marx might have taken his further analyses as well as of the challenges involved in doing so. Thus, an important set of analytical exercises apply to the obstacles, delays, extenuating and counteracting factors, which may occur or be brought into play to off-set the equalisation of profit rates between capitals and the decline of the rate of profits in an international and global perspective. One example of this is what Marx calls *koloniale Profit*e (colonial profits):

> Just as a manufacturer who employs a new invention before it becomes generally used, undersells his competitors and yet sells his commodity above its individual value, that is, realises the specifically higher productiveness of the labour he employs as surplus-labour. He thus secures a surplus-profit. As concerns capitals invested in colonies, etc., on the other hand, they may yield higher rates of profit for the simple reason that the rate of profit is

3 Walt W. Rostow, *Stages of Economic Growth: A Non-Communist Manifesto* (Cambridge: Cambridge University Press, 1960).

4 Karl Marx, *Grundrisse*, 41.

> higher there due to backward development, and likewise the exploitation of labour, because of the use of slaves, coolies, etc.[5]

What Marx refers to here, is the expansion of the world market for capitalist production in a way that involves a return from a primary focus on increased productivity through the production of relative surplus value to one that lowers prices and increases competitiveness through an increase in the production of absolute surplus value. Marx counts on 'this tendency' as being a temporary one, which will eventually be absorbed into – and will not substantially alter – the direction of decline in the rate of profit of the global *Gesamtkapital* (total or aggregate capital). It will therefore, not fundamentally change the direction or the lawfulness of the progress of history, which will continue in the direction of increasing levels of accumulation and contradictions – and eventually the collapse of the bourgeois mode of production and the opening up of the possibility for an alternative.

Globalisation Versus Modernisation Theory

At this point, however, one could argue that Marx's theory of history does not only give voice to a radical foreshadowing of *modernisation* and *development* theory, but also provides possible openings and inspiration for *globalisation* theory. In modernisation theory, 'the salient characteristics (operational values) of modernity' were understood to be:

> (1) a degree of self-sustaining growth in the economy – or at least growth sufficient to increase both production and consumption regularly; (2) a measure of public participation in the polity – or at least democratic representation in defining and choosing policy alternatives; (3) a diffusion of secular-rational norms in the culture – understood approximately in Weberian-Parsonian terms; (4) an increment of mobility in the society – understood as personal freedom of physical, social, and psychic movement; and (5) a corresponding transformation in the modal personality that equips individuals to function effectively in a social order that operates according to the foregoing characteristics.[6]

---

5 Karl Marx, *Capital: A Critique of Political Economy.* Vol. III: *The Process of Capitalist Production as a Whole, ed.* Friedrich Engels [1894], trans. Institute of Marxism-Leninism, Moscow 1959 (New York: International Publishers, n.d.), 168. The page number refers to the electronic version available through https://www.marxists.org/archive/marx/works/download/pdf/Capital-Volume-III.pdf – accessed November 23, 2018.

6 Daniel Lerner, "Modernization: Social Aspects," in *International Encyclopaedia of the Social Sciences*, vol. 9 (New York: The Free Press, 1968): 387. Cf. Daniel Lerner, *The Passing of Traditional*

What exactly is globalisation theory is in itself a disputed issue, which has also been made complicated by the way in which globalisation has been mobilised as a political and ideological agenda, linked to de-regulation and neo-liberalism. Since the 1990s, notions of globalisation have featured prominently in the discourse of Bretton Woods institutions like the World Bank and the International Monetary Fund:

> Globalization—the process through which an increasingly free flow of ideas, people, goods, services, and capital leads to the integration of economies and societies—is often viewed as an irreversible force, which is being imposed upon the world by some countries and institutions such as the IMF and the World Bank. However, that is not so: globalization represents a political choice in favor of international economic integration, which for the most part has gone hand-in-hand with the consolidation of democracy. Precisely because it is a choice, it may be challenged, and even reversed-but only at great cost to humanity. The IMF believes that globalization has great potential to contribute to the growth that is essential to achieve a sustained reduction of global poverty.[7]

Also in less directly policy-related representations of theory, globalisation has appeared as an intensified and accelerated version of modernisation, in particular as brought forward by increased technologies and flows of mobility, communication, and by networking and hybridisation.[8] These processes may involve contradictions of dis-embedding and re-embedding, and may call forth reactions of conservative and nationalist resistance, but most importantly, they bring into place a wholly new playing field of opportunities for change.[9] Globalisation

---

Society: Modernizing the Middle East (Glencoe, Ill.: The Free Press, 1958), where the development of 'empathy' – 'the transformation in the modal personality' – is discussed more substantially.

7 IMF Staff, "Globalization: A Framework for IMF Involvement," *Issues Brief*, March 2002 (Washington: International Monetary Fund), accessed November 17, 2018 https://www.imf.org/external/np/exr/ib/2002/031502.htm.

8 An interesting set of texts aiming to bridge the gap between academic and policy-oriented theorising in this field can be found in the World Bank publication *Culture and Public Action: A Cross-Disciplinary Dialogue on Development Policy*, ed. Vijayendra Rao and Michael Walton (Stanford: Stanford University Press, 2004). See in particular Amartya Sen's critique of Samuel Huntington in "How Does Culture Matter?" (37–58) and Arjun Appadurai, "The Capacity to Aspire: Culture and the Terms of Recognition" (59–84).

9 Thomas Hylland Eriksen, *Globalisation: The Key Concepts* [2007] (London: Bloomsbury, 2014); Cf. Arjun Appadurai, *Modernity at Large: Cultural Dimensions of Globalization* (Minneapolis: University of Minnesota Press, 1996); *Globalization*, ed. Arjun Appadurai (Durban, NC: Duke University Press, 2001); Jürgen Osterhammel and Niels P. Petersson, *Globalization: A Short History* (Munich: C. H. Beck, 2003).

theory is therefore not principally different from modernisation or critical modernisation theory.[10]

In other theoretical understandings, by contrast, globalisation stands out as distinct from modernisation or development, because it does not necessarily involve the same perspective of unidirectionality and progression, for instance, towards wealth, education and democracy. Unlike modernisation, processes of globalisation may also involve history moving into reverse, or leading into scenarios of post-modernity and 'time-space compression', which are not necessarily historically progressive.[11] Alternatively, in escaping national and regional boundaries for regulation, globalisation may lead to ecological destruction and political authoritarianism in ways that would make modernising development go backwards.[12]

Globalisation Versus Global History

In both sets of understandings of what globalisation implies, however, the concept involves epochal change – a break, *caesura*, the introduction into historical development of a new engine or driver of lawfulness that brings about a fundamentally different framework of trajectories from what existed before. Therefore, *globalisation history* must be seen as something different from *global history*, or global history must be periodised in a way that distinguishes carefully between the dynamics of a partial globalisation or 'proto-globalisation' that may have characterised earlier epochs and those of the era of 'globalisation proper'.[13]

Globalisation also addresses a different social and political geography of the world from that of modernisation. Development theories would distinguish between developed and underdeveloped parts of the world, centres and peripheries, first, second and third worlds, Global Norths and Global Souths.[14] By con-

---

10 For critical development theory and a critique of notions of "post-development," see James Ferguson, *Expectations of Modernity: Myths and Meanings of Urban Life on the Zambian Copperbelt* (Berkeley: University of California Press, 1999), 245–254.

11 See e.g. David Harvey, *The Condition of Post-Modernity: An Enquiry into the Origins of Cultural Change* (Oxford: Blackwell, 1989).

12 Elmar Alvater and Birgit Mahnkopf, *Grenzen der Globalisierung: Ökonomie, Ökologie und Politik in der Weltgesellschaft* (Münster: Westfälisches Dampfboot, 1996).

13 For discussions of "proto-globalisation," see *Globalization in World History*, ed. Anthony G. Hopkins (London: Pimlico, 2002); Christopher Bayly, *The Birth of the Modern World: Global Connections and Comparisons, 1780–1914* (Oxford: Blackwell, 2004); Michael Lang, "Globalization and Its History," *Journal of Modern History* 78, no. 4 (2006): 899–931.

14 See e.g. Björn Hettne, *Development Theory and the Three Worlds* (Harlow: Longman, 1990).

trast, a globalisation theory scenario is much messier, involving multipolarities, where new centres of growth in Asia and Latin America challenge the dominance of Europe–North America, labour from the Global South invades the Global North, and the poverty and subversion of peripheries migrate into the urban backyards and hidden production corners of centres.[15]

At the same time – within a globalisation scenario – frameworks and schedules of commodity production are transnationalised and disaggregated into modules situated wherever wages and production costs are at a minimum, including *maquiladoras* – the system pioneered in Latin America of setting up of factories and assemblage plants near borders to allow for tariff- and duty-free exports – and the moving back of parts of production processes from factories to domestic manufacture. Most importantly perhaps, the numbers of people and potential labourers within the reach of capitalism and the bourgeois mode of production – and without alternative means of subsistence – have increased drastically with globalisation. According to estimates by the economist Richard Freeman, the global reserve army of labour doubled in numbers from the 1980s, as China, India and the Soviet Union joined the global capitalist system, with "1.47 billion new workers [added] to the global labour supply by 2000, which effectively doubled the labor supply in the global capitalist system".[16] This means that more people have become wage labourers, but most importantly that masses of new people have been proletarianised in the sense of what Marx called 'original accumulation', have been dispossessed, expropriated, and have become 'radically dependent' for the subsistence of their livelihoods on a capitalist labour market.[17]

Such forms of dependency and of the mobility of potential workers have not only lowered the cost of labour globally, but have also established new hierarchies between forms of labour. They have extended massively the exploitation of labour through measures of the production of absolute surplus value, which is through lower wages, longer working hours, and an intensification of labour through piecework etc., rather than through technological increases of the productivity of labour. Therefore, with globalisation, what Marx saw as a temporary

15 The need for a new theoretical framework to understand such a disintegration of boundaries and distinctions between the 'first' and the 'third world' was brought to the fore by Anthony Payne in "The New Political Economy of Area Studies," *Millenium: Journal of International Studies* 27, no. 2 (1998): 265.

16 Richard Freeman, "The Challenge of the Growing Globalization of Labour Markets to Economic and Social Policy," in *Global Capitalism Unbound: Winners and Losers from Offshore Outsourcing*, ed. Eva Paus (Basingstoke: Palgrave-Macmillan, 2007), 25–26.

17 Michael Denning, "Wageless Life," *New Left Review* 66 (2010): 81.

and short-term aberration and a delay in the fall of the rate of profit through the generation of 'colonial' and extended world market surplus profits has developed into an integral and long-term ingredient of disaggregated and outsourced capitalist production on a world scale.[18]

This also means that 'free labour' – envisaged by Marx as emerging with the rule of capital in the form of wage labour (what he called in the *Grundrisse* "labour in the abstract")[19] – has receded in importance globally in comparison with varieties of bonded and unfree labour that in a modernisation theory perspective would belong to earlier historical periods, where serfdom, slavery, or other forms of coerced labour were the norm. In his 1850s writings on India, Marx was clearly influenced by abolitionist discourse ('contamination by slavery' etc.), and in this sense – as radical modernisation theory – Marxism seems to have been obviously outdated by globalisation.[20] On the other hand, Marx's sketchy and open-ended reflections on the world market, on the resurgence of methods of absolute surplus value production, and on the processes of equalisation of rates of profits within a transnationally constituted *Gesamtkapital* open up perspectives for the understanding of and coming to terms with contemporary globalisation, which stretch beyond the limitations of development theory.

Marx can, therefore, with good reason be regarded not only as a radical modernisation theorist, but also as a 'proto-theorist' of globalisation, and in this capacity he continues to be relevant and interesting to read. This is evidenced by the recent resurgence of interest in notions of 'capitalism' in publications, for example, by Jürgen Kocka, Marcel van der Linden and Karen Helveg Petersen, which demonstrate convincingly that possibilities for thinking productively with Marxism in the writing of history and economic history continue to exist.[21]

---

18 It was these reflections by Marx on the need to 'treat the whole world as one nation, and assume that capitalist production is everywhere established and has possessed itself of every branch of industry,' which Rosa Luxemburg sought to expand upon in her discussion of "The Historical Conditions of Accumulation" in *The Accumulation of Capital* from 1913. See English translation by Agnes Schwarzschild (London: Routledge and Kegan Paul, 1951), 327--467.

19 Marx, *Grundrisse*, 37.

20 On abolitionist discourse, see James Heartfield, *The British and Foreign Anti-Slavery Society, 1838–1956: A History* (London: Hurst, 2016) and Andrea Major, *Slavery, Abolitionism and Empire in India, 1772–1843* (Liverpool: Liverpool University Press, 2012).

21 Jürgen Kocka, *Capitalism: A Short History* (Princeton: Princeton University Press, 2016); *Capitalism: The Reemergence of a Historical Concept*, eds. Jürgen Kocka and Marcel van der Linden (London: Bloomsbury, 2016); Karen Helveg Petersen, *Rentekapitalismen: Økonomisk teori og global virkelighed* (Copenhagen: Frydenlund, 2017).

Theories of History

The understanding of Marx's theory of history presented above brings back to life the discussions of critical theory in the late 1960s. Critical theorists took issue with notions of Marxism as defined in writings of Engels on 'historical materialism' as a rigid succession of 'modes of production' from Asiatic, antique and feudal through to capitalist and communist. This went hand-in-hand with a critique of Marxism as 'dialectical materialism' and a philosophy of general validity, as presented as ideological dogma in writings by Stalin in the 1930s. Writings by Alfred Schmidt were particularly important in this context of a developing 'New Left', which brought into play both new readings of Marx's 1840s' Paris manuscripts, a renewed engagement through close reading with the texts of *Capital*, *Theories of Surplus Value* and *Grundrisse*, and a confrontation of Marxist theory with existentialist and structuralist thinking.[22] In these discussions, the uniqueness of capitalism as a mode of production was emphasised as against earlier modes that could be best understood as different trajectories through which the core elements and preconditions for the establishment of the rule of capital were brought together. The reason for this was that capitalist history – as configured by the structures and logic of the capitalist mode of production, by capital accumulation, and by class struggle between capital and labour – was something qualitatively new, whose global reach and dominance came to exert itself fully only from the mid-nineteenth century. Consequently, there was a fundamental difference between the ways in which pre-capitalist and capitalist histories could be theorised.

A similarly dualistic view of history can be found in post-Second World War theories of modernisation, which also argue the case for the need to differentiate between histories as they unfolded before and after the 'take-off' of development, as given expression by Rostow in his 1960 "non-communist manifesto." While *tradition* as the forerunner of *modernity* does not really have a history, the engine driving history forward in its modernisation phase is economic growth. This provides the base for a superstructure of political, cultural and psychological change from tradition through transition to modernity, with 'empathy'

---

22 See e.g. Alfred Schmidt, *Der Begriff der Natur in der Lehre von Marx* (Frankfurt am Main: Europäische Verlagsanstalt, 1962); *Existentialismus und Marxismus: Eine Kontroverse zwischen Sartre, Garaudy, Hippolyte, Vigier und Orcel. Mit einem Beitrag von Alfred Schmidt* (Frankfurt am Main: Suhrkamp, 1965); *Folgen einer Theorie*, ed. Ernst Theodor Mohl (Frankfurt am Main: Suhrkamp, 1967); *Marxismus und Geschichte*, ed. Helmut Fleischer (Frankfurt am Main: Suhrkamp, 1969); Alfred Schmidt, *Geschichte und Struktur* (Munich: Hanser, 1971).

supplying additional transformational energies.[23] What is at stake here is not really a general theory of history – the scope and context for modernisation and development are clearly seen to be national or regional rather than global. At the same time, the use of 'modernise' and 'develop' as verbs can be both transitive and intransitive. They involve political agendas (like the transformation to democracy) as well as patterns of progress with a *developed* world being contrasted with an *underdeveloped* one, and with the *first* and the *third world* offset by a *second world* of communist countries in the post-World War II geography of the United Nations and the Cold War. Therefore, the break or *caesura* between tradition and modernity – the take-off for developmental history – occurs at different times and in different settings of national or regional circumstances.

In the context of globalisation theories, by contrast, history is of course a global matter, and the discussion of whether globalisation in itself represents an epochal break that introduces a new societal logic and dynamism – and when exactly this might have occurred – is a central bone of contention among theorists of global history. To a certain extent the division here lies also between theories, which see globalisation as the highest stage of modernisation and other schools of thought that regard globalisation as something more complex, which may involve both historical progress and retrogression. In his review article, Michael Lang uses publications by David Held, Anthony McGrew, David Goldblatt, Jonathan Perraton, Paul Hirst and Grahame Thompson to illustrate the two positions within globalisation theory. These are also positions within a "globalization discussion", which "by the second half of the 1990s ... had shifted into a contest over history."[24]

Lang's own position is on the sceptical side. This does not mean that he agrees overall with the analysis of Hirst and Thompson, but in contrast to the views of Held et al. of globalisation as a new 'borderless world' and 'the retreat of the state', he does not think that post-World War II globalisation represents a historical break as much as a continuation. Rather "contemporary global integration is both exaggerated and precedented ... constraint upon the state is overestimated in the present and underestimated in the past." The "cause of the distortion in perspective is the ahistorical abstract separation of political and

---

23 As given voice in e.g. Daniel Lerner's *The Passing of Traditional Society: Modernising the Middle East* (see reference in footnote 6).

24 Lang, "Globalization and Its History," 901. Cf. Paul Hirst and Grahame Thompson, *Globalization in Question: The International Economy and the Possibilities of Governance* (Cambridge: Polity Press, 1996); David Held, Anthony McGrew, David Goldblatt and Jonathan Perraton, *Global Transformations: Politics, Economics, and Culture* (Stanford: Stanford University Press, 1999).

economic affairs."[25] Lang sees the beginning of a new era as situated rather in the 1850s than in the 1950s or the 1980s. He uses a U-shaped curve to illustrate the development in global economic integration in terms of both production, trade and finance from the late nineteenth to the late twentieth century. He argues that in both cases the economy can only unfold as it does because it relies on a political framework, be it imperialist and colonialist or so-called neo-liberal. He also argues – against "approaches to globalization [that] historicize a golden age of Westphalian sovereignty now coming to an end" – that such "Westphalian" models are largely mythological, and that the most important political frameworks for global economic development remain national or regional.[26]

Globalisation and Accumulation by Dispossession

Against Michael Lang's toning down of the epochal shift brought about by globalisation, a number of arguments can be brought to bear. Most importantly, in his analysis of production, trade and finance, Lang does not address the ways in which the capital–labour relationship has been extended globally, and how labour markets have been globalised through ongoing 'original' or 'primitive' accumulation. This is the "sogenannte ursprüngliche Akkumulation," which Marx discussed in the famous twenty-fourth chapter of the first volume of *Capital*, and for which David Harvey has suggested the best English translation would be "accumulation by dispossession".[27]

In quantitative and spatial terms – since the late twentieth century – this has meant an enormous expansion of the global territory of capitalism and of the number of people in the world dependent on capitalist wage labour, no matter whether employed or unemployed.[28] In qualitative terms, it has meant that capitalism has been revitalised through the opportunities offered by globalisation to outsource and compartmentalise production processes, and to allocate and move around globally production capacities between the environments most cost-effective in terms of the labour force and the reserve army available at any given time.

A good example of this in laboratory form are the so-called Export Processing Zones (EPZ), which have sprung up across the globe, and which offer seemingly time- and spaceless, de-regulated environments for the maximisation of ex-

25 Lang, "Globalization and Its History".

26 Lang, "Globalization and Its History," 912.

27 David Harvey, *The New Imperialism* (Oxford: Oxford University Press, 2013), 116–151.

28 Freeman, "The Challenge of the Growing Globalization" (see reference in footnote 14).

ploitation and profits.[29] Thus, for example, in the Kenyan EPZ at Athi River on the outskirts of Nairobi, authentically branded American garments like Calvin Klein boxer shorts and Speedo swimming trunks are produced by HELA, a Sri Lankan enterprise. The factory employs around 4,000 Kenyan, primarily female, machine operators, who are paid the monthly equivalent of the Kenyan minimum wage, if they are able to live up to the production targets, they have had to agree to. Though their monthly pay of around 170 USD is above what workers in competing countries like Bangladesh or Ethiopia are paid, their productivity is higher as well. One reason is that their monthly wages are really a disguise for their being paid piece rates. This is a technique for intensifying exploitation through the combination of absolute with relative surplus value production, which was tried out and refined in the nineteenth century in the context of plantation and indentured labour.[30] Together with other benefits, such as a ten-year tax holiday, and subsidised freight rates on the new Chinese-built train to Mombasa, this makes the production of textile garments profitable in Kenya, at least for a while, after which capital can then move on to different global settings.[31]

Together with the acceleration in the mobility of capital, new forms of global mobilisation and control of migrant labour have become established, which within certain sectors of production make it possible to move large numbers of labourers around globally from poor peripheries to centres of growth. Increasingly, in contrast with earlier historical frameworks for labour migration, this has involved time-limited contracts without citizenship or permanent residence rights. Recruitment of labour is effected through agents, and typically includes both a suspension of the direct contractual relationship between capitalists and labourers, and a restriction in the patterns of mobility of labourers to fixed trajectories between sites of belonging and sites of labour.[32]

---

29 See e.g. Patrick Neveling, "Export Processing Zones and Global Class Formation," in *Anthropologies of Class: Power, Practice and Inequality*, eds. James G. Carrier and Don Kalb (Cambridge: Cambridge University Press): 164–182.

30 Kris Manjapra, "Asian Plantation Histories at the Frontier of Nation and Globalization," *Modern Asian Studies* 52, no. 6 (2018): 2145.

31 Information based on visit to the Athi River Export Processing Zone on 14 September 2018. For more overview and general information including "Annual performance reports" for the years 2012–2017, see the web site of the Athi River Export Processing Zone Authority – http://www.epzakenya.com/, accessed November 23, 2018. For detailed information on minimum wages in Kenya, see https://mywage.org/kenya/salary/minimum-wage/, accessed November 23, 2018.

32 Cindy Hahamovitch, "Men Do Not Gather Grapes from Thorns: Indenture Labor, Guest Workers, and the Failure of Regulation," in *Work Out of Place: Work in Global and Historical Perspective*, ed. Mahua Sarkar (Berlin: De Gruyter, 2017): 23–53.

Through such measures, globalised capitalist exploitation has been able to combine effectively and innovatively forms of relative and absolute surplus value production – profiting from robotisation and growth without employment on one hand, and from over-exploitation through precarianisation, informalisation and fragmentation of production on the other. In global terms, this has meant that the two ends of the spectrum have come together increasingly with prosperity and marginalisation being mutually dependent, and that the spatial configuration of centres and peripheries has undergone fundamental changes. Through these changes, 'the West' has tended more to become like 'the Rest' than the other way round, as had been the assumption of development and modernisation theories.[33]

In this sense, the globalisation of capitalism has brought with it both increasing integration and increasing inequalities. It has involved new articulations between economy and politics, with different kinds of political institutions and settings coming into place and proving conducive compared to those expected to result from growth by modernisation theorists. In particular, the emergence of China as a leader of capitalist globalisation has shown that liberalism and authoritarianism can come together profitably to provide a disciplined and cost-effective environment for capitalist mass production, thus outshining and outstripping China's former more democratic BRICS (Brazil, Russia, India, China and South Africa) allies like India or Brazil. State or political party controlled market capitalism has been a particularly powerful engine for globalisation through its capacity to suspend or repress class struggle and thereby control the reproduction costs of labour and maintain rates of surplus value production that are more than globally competitive. Whether such a Chinese model represents a form of "social embedding" in Karl Polanyi's sense – which could save capital-

---

33 Jan Breman and Marcel van der Linden, "Informalizing the Economy: The Return of the Social Question at a Global Level," *Development and Change* 45, no. 5 (2014): 920–940. On informalisation, informality and precarity, besides the reference to Denning, "Wageless Life" above, see also Jan Breman, "A Bogus Concept?," *New Left Review* 84 (2013): 130–138; Fred Cooper, "From Enslavement to Precarity? The Labour Question in African History," in *The Political Economy of Everyday Life in Africa: Beyond the Margins*, ed. Wale Adebanwi (Woodbridge: James Currey, 2017), 135–156; Andreas Eckert, "Von der 'freien' Lohnarbeit zum 'informellen' Sektor: Alte und neue Fragen in der Geschichte der Arbeit," *Geschichte und Gesellschaft* 43, no. 2 (2017): 297–307. The work of Elmar Altvater – who passed away on 1 May 2018 – should also not be forgotten, see Elmar Altvater and Birgit Mahnkopf, *Globalisierung der Unsicherheit: Arbeit im Schatten, schmutziges Geld und informelle Politik* (Münster: Westfälisches Dampfboot 2002).

ism from self-destructing – remains to be seen. It is certainly not one "that is not based on profit, exploitation and inequality".[34]

It can therefore be argued convincingly, I think, that globalisation from the late twentieth century has indeed involved epochal and long-term changes in terms of fundamentally changing labour markets, sustaining ongoing 'original accumulation', and establishing new institutional frameworks for political–economic interaction that have so far been able to withstand forcefully a decline in average global rates of profit. It can be argued further that changes like these – involving historical regression as well as modernisation – have been more significant than the concurrent changes in communications, mobility and digitalisation, which have been highlighted by theorists who would rather see globalisation as the highest stage of modernisation.

Epochal Shifts and the Relevance of Marx

What is left of Marxism, then? The arguments above have tried to show that globalisation and global capitalism in the late twentieth century represent a historical break or epochal shift of comparable significance to that of the establishment of the rule of capital and the hegemony of capitalism in the late nineteenth century. At the same time, having capitalism at its core, globalisation of course also represents continuity, and maybe even the defeat of efforts and utopias to establish an alternative to the rule of capital. Globalisation could also be said to represent the triumph of a set of socially and historically created logics and determinants for development over natural boundaries, the final end to the *Naturwüchsigkeit* (embeddedness in nature) from which – according to Marx – it had been the destiny of human history to liberate itself.

There are therefore important aspects of globalisation, for the understanding of which a re-reading of the writings of Marx and Marxist theory can still be helpful and an important inspiration – most significantly perhaps the labour theory of value and surplus value production, without which the contradictions of contemporary accumulation are difficult to understand. However, there are also important respects in which a theory of globalisation – as well of advanced or late capitalism – requires Marxism to be supplemented or remedied by other theoretical approaches. Issues of regulation and social embedding as raised by Polanyi

34 I am quoting here the discussion on the relevance of Polanyi for "present day issues," in Stephen Castles, "Unfree Labour, Migration and Social Transformation in Neoliberal Capitalism," in *Work Out of Place*, ed. Mahua Sarkar, 151–153.

are one of the examples, given renewed urgency by the coming to prominence of new global liberal-authoritarian (rather than neo-liberal) political regimes for capital accumulation. To what extent can Marxism be an inspiration in creating the foundations for a global democratic strategy to break the tyranny of liberal authoritarianism?

At the same time, *Naturwüchsigkeit* – embeddedness in nature – seems to be catching up with the historical efforts of humanity to liberate themselves from it. It is not new for Marxists to point to the self-destructive tendencies of capital in eroding its own natural base and repertoire of resources. With climate change and global warming, however, globalisation and global capitalism appear to be striking at the very foundations of any possibility for economic and human life altogether.[35] This calls for historical interventions that would break with the logic of capital and the social laws of development, which Marxists have shown to be dominant in the history of the last two centuries. Will Marxism be able to provide inspiration also for the theoretical design of such interventions and of political strategies to make them possible on a global scale?

---

35 On the possible mutual acceleration of interacting consequences of environmental and climate change, see Jonathan Watts, "Domino-effect of climate change could move Earth into a 'hothouse': Leading scientists warn that passing such a point would make efforts to reduce emissions increasing futile," *The Guardian*, August 7, 2018, accessed November 24, 2018, https://www.theguardian.com/environment/2018/aug/06/domino-effect-of-climate-events-could-push-earth-into-a-hothouse-state?CMP=share_btn_link.

Biographical Notes

Amar S. Baadj is a Postdoctoral Research Fellow at the Bonn University and the Trier University. He obtained his B.A. (2004) from the University of Toronto, his M.A. (2006) from the American University in Cairo, and his Ph.D. (2012) from the University of Toronto. His main areas of research are the medieval history of North Africa and Arabic historiography. He is the recipient of a DFG (Deutsche Forschungsgemeinschaft) individual research grant for the project "Land-Tenure and Agriculture in the Medieval Maghrib from 1000 to 1500" and is a research fellow in the DFG-Leibniz Research Group "The Contemporary History of Historiography: International Perspectives". In 2014–2015 he was a research fellow at the Annemarie Schimmel Institute for Mamluk Studies at Bonn University and in 2006–2007 he was a Fulbright fellow at Damascus University. His publications include: *Saladin, the Almohads and the Banu Ghaniya: The Contest for North Africa (12th and 13th centuries)* (Leiden: Brill, 2015); "The Political Context of the Egyptian Gold Crisis during the Reign of Saladin," *International Journal of African Historical Studies*, Vol. 47, No. 1 (2014): 117–134; and "Travel by Sea and Land between the Maghrib and the Mamluk Empire" in Stefan Conermann and Bethany J. Walker (ed), *The Mamluk Sultanate from the Perspective of Regional and World History* (Bonn: V&R Unipress: 2019), 279–306.

Brigitta Bernet is Senior Research Fellow at the DFG Leibniz Research Group "The Contemporary History of Historiography: International Perspectives" at Trier University, and Visiting Fellow at the Centre d'Histoire at Sciences Po in Paris. She studied History and Philosophy at the Universities of Bielefeld and Zürich where she obtained her PhD in 2013. Her research interests include intellectual history of historiography in the twentieth century, history of work, therapeutic cultures and the human sciences. Her publications include *Schizophrenie. Entstehung und Entwicklung einer wissenschaftlichen Tatsache um 1900* (Zürich: Chronos 2013); "Arbeit in der Erweiterung", special issue of *Historische Anthropologie* 24, 2 (2016) (edited, with Juliane Schiel and Jakob Tanner); and "Die Welt eines Historikers um 1970. ‚Der Käse und die Würmer' von Carlo Ginzburg und die Microstoria," in *Geschichte der Gegenwart* (2019), https://geschichtedergegenwart.ch/die-welt-eines-historikers-um-1970-der-kaese-und-die-wuermer-von-carlo-ginzburg/

Jorge Grespan is Professor of Theory of History at the Department of History of the University of São Paulo in Brazil. He studied Economics and History at the same university and obtained his PhD in Philosophy from the University of Campinas in 1994. Between 1996 and 1997 he was a postdoctoral researcher at the Institute of Philosophy in the Free University Berlin. He is the author of books and articles in Portuguese and Spanish about Marxist Critique of Political Economy and Western Marxism. He also wrote on Latin American History and Latin American Historiography with emphasis on authors who investigated the permanence of colonial traits in contemporary Brazil and Latin America. Among his books are *Marx* (São Paulo: Publifolha, 2008); *O negativo do capital: o conceito de crise na crítica de Marx à economia política* (São Paulo: Expressão Popular, 2012); and *Marx e a crítica do modo de representação capitalista* (São Paulo: Boitempo, 2020).

Preben Kaarsholm is Professor of Global and International Development Studies at Roskilde University, and a Research Fellow at re:work at the Humboldt University in Berlin and at STIAS (the Stellenbosch Institute for Advanced Study). His research interests have moved from romantic anti-capitalism and anti-imperialist movements in Europe to settler states and post-colonial development in Southern Africa. He has published on violence and democratic struggles, and on moral debates and local politics in urban slum settlements. His recent research has focused on the Indian Ocean, on transnational Islamic movements, and on the history of slavery, abolition and indenture. Among his books are *Violence, Political Culture & Development in Africa* (Oxford: Currey, 2006); and with Iain Walker and Manuel Ramos) *Fluid Networks and Hegemonic Powers in the Western Indian Ocean* (Lisboa: Centro de Estudos Internacionais, 2017).

Mohammed Maraqten, born in Palestine and based in Germany, is a specialist of Ancient Near Eastern languages and cultures. He received his PhD degree in Semitic and ancient Near Eastern studies from the University of Marburg (1987), is affiliated with the University of Heidelberg, and is now working for the Doha Historical Dictionary of Arabic, in Qatar. He has conducted archaeological excavations and surveys in Jordan, Bahrain, Yemen, Oman, Morocco, Algeria and Tunisia, and has published extensively on cultures and epigraphy of Ancient Arabia and especially on ancient South Arabian inscriptions. Among his more recent works is the monograph *Altsüdarabische Texte auf Holzstäbchen: Epigraphische und kulturhistorische Untersuchungen* (Beiruter Texte und Studien Nr. 103), (Würzburg: Ergon, 2014).

Matthias Middell is Professor of Cultural History and Director of the Global and European Studies Institute, University of Leipzig. His research interests include the writing of global history and the development of historiography and the historical profession beyond national traditions. His recent publications include the *Handbook of Transregional Studies* (Routledge, 2019); *Kommunismus jenseits des Eurozentrismus* (= Jahrbuch für Historische Kommunismusforschung 2019) (Berlin: Metropol-Verlag, 2019); *Spatial Formats under the Global Condition* (with Steffi Marung) (Berlin: de Gruyter, 2019); and *Cultural Transfers, Encounters and Connections in the Global 18th Century* (Leipzig: Leipziger Universitätsverlag 2014).

Nasser Mohajer is an independent scholar specialising in the political and social history of modern Iran. He currently resides in Paris, is on the editorial board of *Noghteh Books*, and works with *Noghteh Resources* on Iran. He is the former editor in chief of two periodicals on Iranian politics and culture: *Aghaz-e No* (1985–1994) and *Noghteh Journal* (1995–1999). He served on the editorial board of the periodicals *Noghteh Review (*1995–1997) and *Iran Bulletin* (1992–2000), which cover Iranian history and culture. His articles have been published in numerous journals. He has taught courses and given lectures on issues of modern Iranian history. He is the author or editor of over a dozen works spanning the nineteenth and twentieth centuries, including *Khizesh Zanan dar Esfand 1357* (The Iranian Women's Uprising in March 1979) and *Baqer Momeni: Rahravi dar Rah-e Bipayan.* (Baqer Momeni: Walking in the Nonending Path). His forthcoming work, *Voices of a Massacre*, is the first monograph in English to focus on the 1988 mass killing of political prisoners in Iranian jails.

Kavita Philip is Professor of History and affiliate faculty in Informatics at UC Irvine. Her research addresses the colonial history of science, technology and the environment, as well as post-colonial technology studies and global science fiction. She is author of *Civilizing Na-*

tures: Race, Resources and Modernity in Colonial South India (New Brunswick: Rutgers University Press, 2004) and co-editor of five volumes of interdisciplinary work, engaging with the history of computing, international politics, art, activism, gender, and public policy. She has a Ph.D. in Science and Technology Studies from Cornell University, an M.S. in Physics from the University of Iowa, and a B.Sc. in Physics from the University of Madras, India.

Lutz Raphael is Professor of Contemporary History at the University of Trier. Recently he has been Visiting Fellow at the European Studies Centre of St Antony's College Oxford, and Gerda Henkel Guest Professor at the German Historical Institute London and the London School of Economics. In 2013, he received the Wilhelm-Gottfried-Leibniz-Prize of the DFG. His research focusses on the contemporary history of historiography in time of globalisations and the social history of de-industrialisation in Western Europe since the 1970s. His recent publications include *Jenseits von Kohle und Stahl. Eine Gesellschaftsgeschichte Westeuropas nach dem Boom* (Berlin: Suhrkamp 2019), *Ordnungsmuster und Deutungskämpfe. Wissenspraktiken im Europa des 20. Jahrhunderts* (Göttingen: Vandenhoek & Ruprecht 2018); (as editor and co-author): *Poverty and Welfare in Modern German history* (Oxford: Berghahn 2017); and together with Anselm Doering-Manteuffel and Thomas Schlemmer (eds), *Vorgeschichte der Gegenwart.* (Göttingen: Vandenhoek & Ruprecht, 2016).

Jakob Tanner is Professor Emeritus at the History Institute and the Research Center for Social and Economic History at Zurich University. Among his research interests are the history of science and popular forms of knowledge, especially in the fields of nutrition, drugs and psychiatry. He aims at connecting historical anthropology, history of science and history of emotions. From 1996 to 2001 he was a member of the Independent Commission of Experts Switzerland-Second World War, working on financial entanglements between the National Socialist regime in Germany and neutral countries. After a Fellowship at the Wissenschaftskolleg in Berlin (2001–02), he was from 2004 to 2009 a Fellow at the Collegium Helveticum (Swiss Federal Institute of Technology/UZH) and he is also a founding member of the Centre for the History of Knowledge (SFIT/UZH). In 2011, he was fellow at the Freiburg Institute for Advanced Studies (FRIAS). His first co-authored book was a Marx-based analysis of the economic crisis of the mid-70s (*Krise. Zufall oder Folge des Kapitalismus? Die Schweiz und die aktuelle Wirtschaftskrise. Eine Einführung aus marxistischer Sicht* (Zürich: Limmat 1976). His recent publications include *Geschichte der Schweiz im 20. Jahrhundert* (München: Beck 2015); (edited with Brigitta Bernet): *Ausser Betrieb. Metamorphosen der Arbeit in der Schweiz* (Zürich: Limmat 2015); "Wirtschaften, Wertlogik und die ‚Religion des Kapitals'," in: Karl Braun et al (eds): *Wirtschaften. Kulturwissenschaftliche Perspektiven* (Marburg: MakuFEE, Förderverein der Marburger kulturwissenschaftlichen Forschung und Europäischen Ethnologie e.V. 2019), 91–108.

Kaveh Yazdani received his PhD in social sciences from the University of Osnabrück, Germany (2014). He was granted the Prince Dr Sabbar Farman-Farmaian fellowship at the International Institute of Social History in Amsterdam (2015) and received the title of Mellon Postdoctoral Research Fellow at the Centre for Indian Studies in Africa, the University of the Witwatersrand, Johannesburg, South Africa (2015–2017), where he now holds the position of a research associate. He was a visiting residential fellow at the Warwick Institute of Advanced Study, United Kingdom (2017), and Visiting Professor in Global Economic and Social History at the University of Vienna (2020). He is currently working as a lecturer of economic history at the University of Bielefeld, Germany. His most recent publications include the monograph *India, Modernity and the Great Divergence: Mysore and Gujarat (17th to 19th Century)* (Leiden: Brill, 2017), and the co-edited volume *Capitalisms: Towards a Global History* (Delhi: Oxford University Press, 2020).

Benjamin Zachariah is Senior Research Fellow at the DFG Leibniz Research Group "The Contemporary History of Historiography: International Perspectives" ' at Trier University. He read history at Presidency College, Calcutta, and at Trinity College, Cambridge. His current research interests include historiography and historical theory, the movements of ideas in the twentieth century, international revolutionary networks, and global fascism. He is the author of *Nehru* (London: Routledge, 2004); *Developing India: an Intellectual and Social History, c. 1930–1950* (Delhi: Oxford University Press, 2005; 2nd edn 2012); *Playing the Nation Game: the Ambiguities of Nationalism in India* (Delhi: Yoda 2011; 2nd edn 2016); and *After the Last Post: the Lives of Indian Historiography in India* (Berlin: De Gruyter 2019). He is co-editor of *The Internationalist Moment: South Asia, Worlds and World Views 1917–1939* (Delhi: Sage 2015).

Index

https://doi.org/10.1515/9783110677744-016

www.ingramcontent.com/pod-product-compliance
Lightning Source LLC
Chambersburg PA
CBHW020455270326
41926CB00008B/606

* 9 7 8 3 1 1 0 9 9 2 5 9 5 *